Praise for *For Antifascist Fu*

"This extraordinary volume ranges engages historical formations and trajectories The authors, writing in a variety of genres and from many fields of study, illuminate the makings of racialized violence, the role of untruths, post-truths, and ideologies, the afterlives and ongoing effects of colonial force, and the role of capital accumulation in the making of modern varieties of fascism. Every page of *For Antifascist Futures* forces us to face and reckon with the lacerating effects of fascist power on the body politic"
—**Laleh Khalili**, author of *Sinews of War and Trade* and *Time in the Shadows*

"Globalizing and reframing fascisms on a world scale, this urgent and powerful volume analyzes fascism as the convergence of authoritarian state and extralegal racial nationalist violence responding to the historical and material crises of capitalism and imperialism. The collection constellates a stunning range of antifascist practices, from Black radical internationalism, anticolonial movements, and insurgencies in the Philippines, Palestine, and South Asia, and across Latin America and Africa, on the one hand, to a long history of antifascisms and racial justice movements in the U.S. and Indigenous demands for return of stolen land, on the other."
—**Lisa Lowe**, author of *The Intimacies of Four Continents*

"*For Antifascist Futures* is a searing and necessary collection for our times. The precise and unsparing indictment of fascism—and its enduring entanglements in imperialist and capitalist expansion—is the urgent world-making project that we all need. By deftly engaging the analytic of fascism across time and geography, this constellation of intellectually and politically fierce essays narrates a simultaneously sobering and inspiring political vision of internationalist antifascism against authoritarianism. This book is a tour de force."
—**Harsha Walia**, author of *Border and Rule* and *Undoing Border Imperialism*

For Antifascist Futures: Against the Violence of Imperial Crisis
Edited by Alyosha Goldstein and Simón Ventura Trujillo

© 2022 Alyosha Goldstein and Simón Ventura Trujillo
© Individual contributors

This edition © 2022 Common Notions

ISBN: 978-1-94217-356-4 | eBook ISBN: 978-1-94217-364-9
Library of Congress Number: 2021953451

10 9 8 7 6 5 4 3 2 1

Common Notions
c/o Interference Archive
314 7th St.
Brooklyn, NY 11215

Common Notions
c/o Making Worlds Bookstore
210 S. 45th St.
Philadelphia, PA 19104

www.commonnotions.org
info@commonnotions.org

Discounted bulk quantities of our books are available for organizing, educational, or fundraising purposes. Please contact Common Notions at the address above for more information.

Cover design by Josh MacPhee
Layout design and typesetting by Morgan Buck

Printed by union labor in Canada on acid-free

For Antifascist Futures

Against the Violence of Imperial Crisis

Edited by Alyosha Goldstein and Simón Ventura Trujillo

Brooklyn, NY
Philadelphia , PA
commonnotions.org

Acknowledgements

We would like to express our gratitude to Christine Hong, Neda Atanasoski, Trung PQ Nguyen, and Jane Komori for their labor on and support for the "Fascisms" special issue of *Critical Ethnic Studies* 7, no. 1 (Spring 2021) that was the starting point for this book and in which a number of the chapters were first published. The editors and publisher also wish to acknowledge "The Resurgent Far Right and the Black Feminist Struggle for Social Democracy in Brazil" is republished with permission of John Wiley & Sons, from *American Anthropologist*, Anthropological Society of Washington, American Ethnological Society, American Anthropological Society 122, no. 1 (2020).

We are also grateful to Malav Kanuga, Josh MacPhee, Erika Biddle-Stavrakos, Nicki Kattoura, and everyone else at Common Notions for their work to bring this book into the world. An extra thanks to Malav for the initial idea to expand the journal issue as a book and for his ideas and encouragement throughout the process. Thanks as well to Dylan Miner for permission to include his artwork "New Futures Are Possible Right Now."

Figure 1. Dylan Miner, New Futures Are Possible Right Now, 2020.

Contents

IV. PRESENT HISTORIES

V. SOLIDARITY IN STRUGGLE

APPENDIX

Fascism Now?

Inquiries for an Expanded Frame

Alyosha Goldstein and Simón Ventura Trujillo

Authoritarian political leaders and violent racist nationalism are a resurgent feature of the present historical conjuncture that will not be resolved by electoral politics or bipartisanship. The widespread support for Donald Trump in the United States, Jair Bolsonaro in Brazil, Narendra Modi in India, Rodrigo Duterte in the Philippines, Recep Tayyip Erdoğan in Turkey, and Viktor Orbán in Hungary, among others, is an expansive turn to counter-revolution and punitive governance in an era of escalating ecological crisis, political antagonism, and social uncertainty.[1] Responding to the urgency of the current moment, *For Antifascist Futures: Against the Violence of Imperial Crisis* explores what the analytic of fascism offers for understanding the twenty-first century's authoritarian convergence. The essays and interviews included in this collection build a critical conversation that centers the material and speculative labor of antifascist, antiracist, and anticolonial social movements and coalitions. These inquiries deliberately connect multiple world contexts to consider what fascism and antifascist movements might mean during the current moment or historically with relevance for the current moment.

For Antifascist Futures examines fascism as a geopolitically diverse series of entanglements with (neo)liberalism, racial capitalism, imperialism, settler colonialism, militarism, carceralism, white supremacy, racist nationalism, xenophobia, Islamophobia, antisemitism, and heteropatriarchy. The analytic of fascism situates right-wing reaction within the historical and material crises of imperialism. Racialized and colonized peoples have been at the forefront of theorizing and dismantling fascism, white supremacy, and other modes of authoritarian rule. Drawing from these histories and present-day

---

1 On the often-neglected ecological dimensions in this regard, see: The Red Nation, *The Red Deal: Indigenous Action to Save Our Earth* (Brooklyn: Common Notions, 2021); Andreas Malm and the Zetkin Collective, *White Skin, Black Fuel: On the Danger of Fossil Fascism* (London and New York: Verso, 2021).

struggles, our invocation of fascism places various iterations of authoritarianism and state and extralegal violence directly in relation to racial and gendered capitalist crisis and the expanded reproduction of imperialism.

Colonialism, imperialism, and fascism

This collection's emphasis on fascism as a global phenomenon, and on radical internationalist forms of antifascism, is intended to challenge the Eurocentrism common within studies of fascism.[2] There are multiple valences for an expanded frame of fascism. Among the most frequently referenced examples of links between European fascism and colonial policy are Germany's 1904–1908 genocide against the Herero and Nama peoples in South-West Africa (now Namibia) and US policy toward Indigenous peoples and Jim Crow laws as models emulated by the Third Reich.[3] The racial terror and genocide wrought by slavery and colonialism preceded, were co-constitutive of, and continued after Mussolini's *Fasci Italiani di Combattimento*, the National Socialist German Workers' Party, and Japan's *Shōwa* nationalism. In her 1923 address and resolution for the Enlarged

2 Our intention is for this book to be in conversation with other works that trouble the conventional parameters of the study of fascism, including: Samir Gandesha (ed.), *Spectres of Fascism: Historical, Theoretical and International Perspectives* (London: Pluto Press, 2020); Julia Adeney Thomas and Geoff Eley (eds.), *Visualizing Fascism: The Twentieth-Century Rise of the Global Right* (Durham: Duke University Press, 2020); Patrik Hermansson, David Lawrence, Joe Mulhall, and Simon Murdoch, *The International Alt-Right: Fascism for the 21st Century?* (New York: Routledge, 2020); Daniel Brückenhaus, *Policing Transnational Protest: Liberal Imperialism and the Surveillance of Anticolonialists in Europe, 1905–1945* (New York: Oxford University Press, 2020); Arnd Bauerkämper and Grzegorz Rossoliński-Liebe (eds.), *Fascism without Borders: Transnational Connections and Cooperation between Movements and Regimes in Europe from 1918 to 1945* (New York: Berghahn Books, 2017); Mark Bray, Jessica Namakkal, Giulia Riccò, and Eric Roubinek (eds.), "Fascism and Anti-Fascism since 1945," a special issue of *Radical History Review* 138 (October 2020); Kasper Braskén, Nigel Copsey, and David J. Featherstone (eds.), *Anti-Fascism in a Global Perspective: Transnational Networks, Exile Communities, and Radical Internationalism* (New York: Routledge, 2020); Hugo García, Mercedes Yusta, Xavier Tabet, and Cristina Clímaco (eds.), *Rethinking Antifascism: History, Memory and Politics, 1922 to the Present* (New York: Berghahn Books, 2016).

3 Zoé Samudzi, "Reparative Futurities: Postcolonial Materialities and the Ovaherero and Nama Genocide," in this volume; Jürgen Zimmerer and Joachim Zeller (eds.), *Genocide in German South-West Africa: The Colonial War of 1904–1908 and Its Aftermath* (London: Merlin Press, 2008); James Q. Whitman, *Hitler's American Model: The United States and the Making of Nazi Race Law* (Princeton: Princeton University Press, 2017); Edward B. Westermann, *Hitler's Ostkrieg and the Indian Wars: Comparing Genocide and Conquest* (Norman: University of Oklahoma Press, 2016); Jens-Uwe Guettel, *German Expansionism, Imperial Liberalism and the United States, 1776–1945* (Cambridge: Cambridge University Press, 2012). For a generative resituating of the Nazi Holocaust in relation to the context of decolonization see Michael Rothberg, *Multidirectional Memory: Remembering the Holocaust in the Age of Decolonization* (Stanford: Stanford University Press, 2009).

Plenum of the Communist International's Executive Committee, Clara Zetkin argued that "fascist forces are organizing internationally, and the workers' struggle against fascism must also organize on a world scale."[4] She contended that fascism emerged as a "sham revolutionary program" in response to "the imperialist war and the accelerated dislocation of the capitalist economy." In contrast to the shortcomings of the Second International, Zetkin described the Comintern as a necessary counterforce to fascism because it "is not an International for the elite of white proletarians of Europe and America. It is an International for the exploited of all races."[5]

Between the end of the First World War and the early Cold War, numerous anticolonial writers of color emphasized the direct connection between the atrocities of imperialism and fascism. They persuasively argued that fascism was fundamentally entangled with the form and practice of colonial rule, racialized organization of dispossession and death, and insatiable imperial aspiration in order to insist that defeating fascism required ending all manner of colonialism and imperialism. In 1936, Langston Hughes insisted that "fascism is a new name for that kind of terror the Negro has always faced in America."[6] George Padmore first wrote about what he called "colonial fascism" in *How Britain Rules Africa* (1936), further developing this analysis in publications over the next two decades.[7] In his 1938 address to the Conference on Peace and Empire, Jawaharlal Nehru observed that "the essence of the problem of peace is the problem of empire," declaring that fascism is simply an "intensified form of the same system which is imperialism."[8] Writing in 1949, Claudia Jones called attention to the "growth of militancy among Negro women" as having "profound meaning, both for the Negro liberation

4   Clara Zetkin, *Fighting Fascism: How to Struggle and How to Win*, ed. Mike Taber and John Riddell (Chicago: Haymarket Books, 2017), 73.

5   Zetkin, *Fighting Fascism*, 34, 67, 61.

6   Langston Hughes speaking at the American League against War and Fascism's Third Congress. Quoted in "Introduction: Anti/Fascism in the United States," in Bill V. Mullen and Christopher Vials (eds.), *The U.S. Anti-fascism Reader* (London and New York: Verso, 2020), 8.

7   George Padmore, *How Britain Rules Africa* (New York: Negro Universities Press, 1969 [1936]).

8   Quoted in Michele Louro, *Comrades against Imperialism: Nehru, India, and Interwar Internationalism* (Cambridge: Cambridge University Press, 2018), 230.

movement and for the emerging antifascist, anti-imperialist coalition."[9] In the wake of the Second World War and rising tide of anticolonial independence movements, in *Discourse on Colonialism*, Aimé Césaire described the "decivilizing" consequences of colonialism for colonizers themselves as a root cause of Nazism and other Euro-American fascisms.[10]

In the immediate aftermath of the Second World War, African American petitions to the United Nations were exemplary of a burgeoning Black antifascism. W.E.B. Du Bois and the NAACP's 1947 *An Appeal to the World: A Statement of Denial of Human Rights to Minorities in the Case of Citizens of Negro Descent in the United States of America and an Appeal to the United Nations for Redress* condemned the US as part of "the imperialist bloc which is controlling the colonies of the world."[11] The 1951 Civil Rights Congress' *We Charge Genocide: The Crime of the Government Against the Negro People* likewise connected fascism to the liberal status quo of anti-Black colonial violence.[12] In turn, similar demands for redress and liberation framed in relation to fascism extended through the 1955 Bandung Conference, the 1966 Tricontinental Conference, and the growing momentum for worldwide decolonization.[13]

---

9   Claudia Jones, "An End to the Neglect of the Problems of Negro Women" (1949), in *Claudia Jones: Beyond Containment*, ed. Carole Boyce Davies (Oxfordshire: Ayebia Clarke Publishing, 2011), 74.

10 Aimé Césaire, *Discourse on Colonialism*, trans. Joan Pinkham (New York: Monthly Review, 2000 [1950]).

11 W.E.B. Du Bois, *An Appeal to the World: A Statement of Denial of Human Rights to Minorities in the Case of Citizens of Negro Descent in the United States of America and an Appeal to the United Nations for Redress* (1947), 13.

12 Highlighting the significance of Black antifascism, Christine Hong argues that "Black radicals during World War II wielded the term *fascism* to expose the illegitimacy and counterrevolutionary nature of the racial capitalist state, including waging its domestic war" against Black people. Christine Hong, *A Violent Peace: Race, U.S. Militarism, and Cultures of Democratization in Cold War Asia and the Pacific* (Stanford: Stanford University Press, 2020), 183.

13 See Adom Getachew, *Worldmaking after Empire: The Rise and Fall of Self-Determination* (Princeton: Princeton University Press, 2019); Jini Kim Watson, *Cold War Reckonings: Authoritarianism and the Genres of Decolonization* (New York: Fordham University Press, 2021); Luis Eslava, Michael Fakhri, and Vasuki Nesiah (eds.), *Bandung, Global History, and International Law: Critical Pasts and Pending Futures* (Cambridge: Cambridge University Press, 2017); Quỳnh N. Phạm and Robbie Shilliam (eds.), *Meanings of Bandung: Postcolonial Orders and Decolonial Visions* (New York: Rowman & Littlefield, 2016); Christopher J. Lee (ed.), *Making a World after Empire: The Bandung Moment and Its Political Afterlives* (Athens: Ohio University Press, 2010); Anne Garland Mahler, *From the Tricontinental to the Global South: Race, Radicalism, and Transnational Solidarity* (Durham: Duke University Press, 2018); John Munro, *The Anticolonial Front: The African American Freedom Struggle and Global Decolonisation, 1945–1960* (Cambridge: Cambridge

During the 1960s and 1970s, the Black Panther Party likewise called out as fascist the constitutive white supremacism and imperialism of the United States—brutally enacted by the everyday actions of the police, counterinsurgency operations, and the military—and sought to build a broad coalition of activists with initiatives such as the United Front Against Fascism conference in 1969.[14] Activist groups such as the John Brown Anti-Klan Committee and Anti-Racist Action in the United States, and the Anti-Nazi League and Anti-Fascist Action in Britain, were explicitly organized against the fascism of the racist New Right, the National Front in England, and skinhead gangs of the 1970s and 1980s.[15] More recently, a heterogeneous group of antifascist organizations, initiatives, and actions sometimes collectively referred to as antifa have mobilized against rightwing and white racist terrorism.[16]

Working against the mainstream representation of antifascism as predominantly white, we aim to think with such genealogies to further question how fascism as a heuristic can be more thoroughly situated with respect to imperialism and settler colonialism. Our effort here is a provisional exploration of what such a heuristic might offer anticolonial thought and action. In each of these instances, the continuities, tensions, and disjunctions of what gets named fascism in particular times and places matter within and across national and international frames.

During the present conjuncture, when the question of fascism appears resurgent, genealogies of anticolonial and anti-imperialist critique are

University Press, 2017); Vijay Prashad, *The Darker Nations: A People's History of the Third World* (New York: The New Press, 2007); Robin D. G. Kelley, "A Poetics of Anticolonialism," in Césaire, *Discourse on Colonialism*, 7–28.

14 Robyn C. Spencer, "The Black Panther Party and Black Anti-Fascism in the United States," January 26, 2017, https://dukeupress.wordpress.com/2017/01/26/the-black-panther-party-and-black-anti-fascism-in-the-united-states/. See also: Robyn C. Spencer, *The Revolution Has Come: Black Power, Gender, and the Black Panther Party in Oakland* (Durham: Duke University Press, 2016); Joshua Bloom and Waldo E. Martin Jr., *Black against Empire: The History and Politics of the Black Panther Party* (Berkeley: University of California Press, 2016).

15 Hilary Moore and James Tracy, *No Fascist USA!: The John Brown Anti-Klan Committee and Lessons for Today's Movements* (San Francisco: City Lights Books, 2020); David Renton, *Never Again: Rock against Racism and the Anti-Nazi League 1976–1982* (New York: Routledge, 2018). For an excellent compilation of primary sources from the US context, see Mullen and Vials, *The U.S. Anti-fascism Reader*.

16 Mark Bray, *Antifa: The Anti-Fascist Handbook* (Brooklyn: Melville House, 2017); Devin Zane Shaw, *Philosophy of Antifascism: Punching Nazis and Fighting White Supremacy* (New York: Rowman & Littlefield, 2020).

indispensable for understanding and dismantling the far-reaching entanglements of right-wing authoritarianism. Fascism is a mass movement, rather than a term for all manners of dictatorship, repressive regime, or despotic aspiration. Such movements are often propelled by the so-called middle class, although, in the context of the United States today for example, mainstream analysis often blames working and impoverished people as the populist source of such movements. Fascism situated in the expanded frame of anticolonial struggle can be understood as a mode of punitive governance partially animated by a politics of fear, cruelty, racism, and heteropatriarchy that serve as screens for unsatiable demands for unobstructed access to land and labor. This reactionary appeal to the certainty of authority and order against demonized and otherized groups emerges in opposition to the promise and popularity of a radical politics of redistribution (e.g., anarchist and communist revolutionary movements and Pan-Africanist internationalism during the early and mid-twentieth century) and abolition (e.g., the Movement for Black Lives and initiatives to defund the police today). During the current moment, it is also a revanchist alignment against the momentum of trans* and queer liberation, climate justice, migrant and asylum seeker assertions of life against border imperialism, and Indigenous peoples' demands for the return of stolen land.[17] Fascism requires violence, terror, and repression, whether by formal state-sanctioned means such as the police, immigration agents, or military, or by informal vigilantism, directed against racialized or other specifically scapegoated groups.

---

17 Ewa Majewska, for instance, argues that antifascism requires an explicitly feminist politics. We agree that a feminism grounded in a broadly intersectional analysis that challenges fascism is crucial. However, from our perspective, what Majewska terms a "counterpublics of the common" can be more substantially reoriented toward a politics of difference and incommensurability by way of Jean-Luc Nancy's conception of being-with or being-in-common, the work of José Esteban Muñoz, the anti-imperialist perspectives of women of color feminism and queer critique, and the everyday organizing of anticolonial and anti-imperial movements. See: Ewa Majewska, *Feminist Antifascism: Counterpublics of the Common* (London and New York: Verso, 2021); Jean-Luc Nancy, *Being Singular Plural* (Stanford: Stanford University Press, 2000); José Esteban Muñoz, *Cruising Utopia: The Then and There of Queer Futurity*, 10th anniversary ed. (New York: NYU Press, 2019). Also see Ejeris Dixon, "In the Face of Far Right Violence, We Must Organize to Survive," *Truthout*, January 11, 2021, https://truthout.org/articles/in-the-face-of-far-right-violence-we-must-organize-to-survive/; Alyosxa Tudor, "Decolonizing Trans/Gender Studies?: Teaching Gender, Race, and Sexuality in Times of the Rise of the Global Right," *TSQ: Transgender Studies Quarterly* 8, no. 2 (May 2021): 238–256; Tiffany Florvil, "Queer Memory and Black Germans," June 8, 2021, http://newfascismsyllabus.com/opinions/queer-memory-and-black-germans/; and Roderick A. Ferguson, "Authoritarianism and the Planetary Mission of Queer of Color Critique: A Short Reflection," *Safundi* 21, no. 3 (July 2020): 282–290.

Fascism's reliance on raw power and rule by violence remains a fundamentally unstable basis of authority and control.[18] The ordained truths and relentless didacticism of authoritarian knowledge regimes are similarly fragile. As we discuss below, twenty-first century right-wing attacks on pedagogies that challenge white supremacy and empire, such as those campaigns in the United States targeting ethnic studies and critical race theory, seek to curtail this fragility by marshalling the affective power of hatred, white entitlement, and disavowal to rally support and to vilify those deemed enemies. We argue that the material and epistemological challenge to white supremacy and empire posed by ethnic studies and antiracist, anti-imperialist pedagogy offers a vital resource to counter the opportunistic spectacle and deeply racist and imperial investments of the present authoritarian convergence.

Reframing and pluralizing fascism through a cartography of anticolonial and decolonial struggle that does not take Europe as the center is a challenge that asks us to reckon with the emergence of fascism as shaped by continuities and ruptures across feudalism, industrial capitalism, imperialism, colonialism, and liberalism. Our concern in this book is with the broad resonance and rhetorical salience of fascism and how such resonance is always shaped by the dynamics of particular places and conjunctures.[19] Our analysis thus seeks at once to de-exceptionalize fascism and to comprehend its specificity in an expanded global context. The global arena of racialized violence, plunder, and exploitation was, in this sense, an arena extended through imperialism and colonialism. Fascist movements may appear antagonistic to particular fractions of capital or be assertively nationalist or isolationist in reaction to the crisis of imperialist worldmaking, while still ultimately being aligned with the social and political imperatives of capitalism and empire. Fascism is thus *symptomatic*

---

18 Kyle Burke, *Revolutionaries for the Right: Anticommunist Internationalism and Paramilitary Warfare in the Cold War* (Chapel Hill: University of North Carolina Press, 2018); Gerald Horne, *White Supremacy Confronted: U.S. Imperialism and Anti-Communism vs. the Liberation of Southern Africa from Rhodes to Mandela* (New York: International Publishers, 2019); Daniel Geary, Camilla Schofield, and Jennifer Sutton (eds.), *Global White Nationalism: From Apartheid to Trump* (Manchester: Manchester University Press, 2020).

19 For arguments that likewise challenge narrow definitional originalism while also emphasizing the importance of historical specificity and the broader significance of attributions of "fascism," see: Geoff Eley, "What is Fascism and Where does it Come From?," *History Workshop Journal* 91 (Spring 2021): 1–28; Shane Burley, *Fascism Today: What It Is and How to End It* (Chico, CA: AK Press, 2017).

of imperial and capitalist crisis rather than necessarily or only a movement weaponized on behalf of capital itself.

Without overstating continuities or equivalencies, we contend that naming fascism can serve to index the relationship among state power, imperialism and colonization, religious/racist nationalism, and white supremacist terrorism as the reactive conditions of counterrevolution and racial capitalism. We believe that insights can be gained by thinking with reference to fascism across multiple and categorically slippery sites. This entails engaging with what Nikhil Pal Singh calls the "afterlife of fascism," Alberto Toscano names "late fascism," and Enzo Traverso refers to as "neofascism."[20] These include, for instance, the United States and its colonial contexts of policing,[21] new modes of racialized surveillance and counterinsurgency,[22] white supremacist vigilantism,[23] border regimes against migrants and

---

20 Nikhil Pal Singh, *Race and America's Long War* (Berkeley: University of California Press, 2017); Alberto Toscano, "Notes on Late Fascism," *Historical Materialism*, April 2, 2017, http://www.historicalmaterialism.org/blog/notes-late-fascism; Enzo Traverso, *The New Faces of Fascism: Populism and the Far Right* (London and New York: Verso, 2019).

21 Julian Go, "The Imperial Origins of American Policing: Militarization and Imperial Feedback in the Early 20th Century," *American Journal of Sociology* 125, no. 5 (March 2020): 1193–1254; Marisol LeBrón, *Policing Life and Death: Race, Violence, and Resistance in Puerto Rico* (Berkeley: University of California Press, 2019); Stuart Schrader, *Badges without Borders: How Global Counterinsurgency Transformed American Policing* (Berkeley: University of California Press, 2019); Brendan McQuade, *Pacifying the Homeland: Intelligence Fusion and Mass Supervision* (Berkeley: University of California Press, 2019); Micol Seigel, *Violence Work: State Power and the Limits of Police* (Durham: Duke University Press, 2018); Jordan T. Camp and Christina Heatherton (eds.), *Policing the Planet: Why the Policing Crisis Led to Black Lives Matter* (London and New York: Verso, 2016); Alfred W. McCoy, *Policing America's Empire: The United States, the Philippines, and the Rise of the Surveillance State* (Madison: University of Wisconsin Press, 2009); Laurence Armand French, *Policing American Indians: A Unique Chapter in American Jurisprudence* (Boca Raton: CRC Press, 2019); Luana Ross, *Inventing the Savage: The Social Construction of Native American Criminality* (Austin: University of Texas Press, 1998).

22 Ruha Benjamin, *Race After Technology: Abolitionist Tools for the New Jim Code* (Medford, MA: Polity, 2019); Nicole Nguyen, *Suspect Communities: Anti-Muslim Racism and the Domestic War on Terror* (Minneapolis: University of Minnesota Press, 2019); Ronak K. Kapadia, *Insurgent Aesthetics: Security and the Queer Life of the Forever War* (Durham: Duke University Press, 2019); Simone Browne, *Dark Matters: On the Surveillance of Blackness* (Durham: Duke University Press, 2015); Brian Jefferson, *Digitize and Punish: Racial Criminalization in the Digital Age* (Minneapolis: University of Minnesota Press, 2020); Alex Lubin, *Never-Ending War on Terror* (Berkeley: University of California Press, 2021).

23 Kathleen Belew, *Bring the War Home: The White Power Movement and Paramilitary America* (Cambridge, MA: Harvard University Press, 2018); Monica Muñoz Martinez, *The Injustice Never Leaves You: Anti-Mexican Violence in Texas* (Cambridge, MA: Harvard University Press, 2018); Matthew N. Lyons, *Insurgent Supremacists: The U.S. Far Right's Challenge to State and Empire* (Oakland: PM Press, 2018); Alexandra Minna Stern, *Proud Boys and the White Ethnostate: How the Alt-Right Is Warping the American Imagination* (Boston: Beacon Press, 2019); Daniel Martinez HoSang and Joseph E. Lowndes, *Producers,*

refugees,[24] anti-Muslim racism;[25] and the ongoing dispossession of Native peoples.[26] The authoritarian convergence today points to not a singular tradition or trajectory of fascism, but rather unveils the multiplicity of fascism across a spectrum of imperialist time-space conjunctures. To invoke fascism as a plurality—that is, to grapple with *fascisms*—is to reckon with a range of concerted formations of brute force against those deemed enemies and the ways such acts of brutality manifest cloistered ways of knowing the world. Fascisms reference real-time spectacles and structural formations of state violence, a heuristic for intellectual and activist practice, and manifold objects of deeply contested historical knowledge. At the same time, we aim to be attentive to how centering "fascism" can itself obscure arenas of struggle. For instance, Anne Spice notes, "I deliberately refuse to differentiate between the 'colonial' and 'fascist' forces we oppose, because I think that antifascist organizing often ignores the (centuries) of experience that Indigenous peoples have in standing up to the imposition of state violence, surveillance, military occupation, and extralegal violence."[27]

Fascisms, organized violence, and regimes of knowledge

What does the analytic lens of fascisms in the plural offer to address the multivalent formations of right-wing authoritarianism in historical perspective? Among the contradictory or seemingly incommensurate ways a global authoritarian turn is currently unfolding, fascisms help us make

Parasites, Patriots: Race and the New Right-Wing Politics of Precarity (Minneapolis: University of Minnesota Press, 2019); Dylan Rodríguez, *White Reconstruction: Domestic Warfare and the Logics of Genocide* (New York: Fordham University Press, 2021).

24 Harsha Walia, *Border and Rule: Global Migration, Capitalism, and the Rise of Racist Nationalism* (Chicago: Haymarket, 2021); Alison Mountz, *The Death of Asylum: Hidden Geographies of the Enforcement Archipelago* (Minneapolis: University of Minnesota Press, 2020); Todd Miller, *Empire of Borders: The Expansion of the US Border Around the World* (London and New York: Verso, 2019); Catherine Besteman, *Militarized Global Apartheid* (Durham: Duke University Press, 2020).

25 Nguyen, *Suspect Communities*; Sohail Daulatzai and Junaid Rana (eds.), *With Stones in Our Hands: Writings on Muslims, Racism, and Empire* (Minneapolis: University of Minnesota Press, 2018); Junaid Rana et al., "Pedagogies of Resistance: Why Anti-Muslim Racism Matters," *Amerasia Journal* 46, no. 1 (2020): 57–62.

26 Joanne Barker, *Red Scare: The State's Indigenous Terrorist* (Berkeley: University of California Press, 2021); Nick Estes, Melanie K. Yazzie, Jennifer Nez Denetdale, and David Correia, *Red Nation Rising: From Bordertown Violence to Native Liberation* (Oakland: PM Press, 2021).

27 Anne Spice, "blood memory: the criminalization of Indigenous land defense," in this volume.

connections across the specificities of revanchist state and extralegal counterformation. This includes: the incoherent cohabitation of trajectories of violence that are simultaneously for and against state power; anti-intellectualism that is nonetheless deeply invested in particular traditions of thought and interpretations of history; populism that is exclusionary and narrowly defined by race or religion; ideology that is insistently illiberal yet constitutive for certain variations of neoliberalism. Across this spectrum, we find fascism's relation to organized state and extralegal violence works in tandem with efforts to impose a particular regime of knowledge and aesthetics of power.

For Antifascist Futures underscores the epistemological threat that fascism poses to critical thought, creative practice, and collective study. This is not only a threat to professionalized research cultures and pedagogies in academic institutions. Nor is it only directed at—and produced by—culture industries, social media, and news platforms. Fascisms are threats to critical thought, creative practice, and collective study enacted in quotidian activist, artistic, and community encounters. Fascisms seek to destroy non-normative and subjugated knowledges that might provide survival, solace, and futurity under conditions of imperial and colonial domination.

When viewed from the horizon of knowledge production, the racialized criminalization of enemies central to shoring up fascist domination has deep epistemological implications. Fascist regimes of knowing (and unknowing or deliberate acts of ignoring) are premised on a volatile cohabitation of silence and monumentality.[28] With such regimes, there is compulsion to impose and administer secrecy, erasure, and removal of dissent and difference. Fascist regimes of silence and compliance are fundamentally imperialist technologies whose unrelenting condition of possibility is the erasure of the presence of Indigenous people, their relation and claim to land, as well as their modes of governance because of their fundamental challenge to the imperialist mythology of fascist claims rooted in blood and soil. Fascist silencing is not merely negative, repressive power but is rather a performative force that employs destruction to calibrate capitalism's labor exploitation and the racialized nativisms central to state authority.

---

28 Manu Vimalassery, Juliana Hu Pegues, and Alyosha Goldstein, "On Colonial Unknowing,"
    Theory & Event 19, no. 4 (October 2016), https://muse.jhu.edu/article/633283; Denise
    Ferreira da Silva, "Toward a Black Feminist Poethics: The Quest(ion) of Blackness Toward
    the End of the World," *The Black Scholar* 44, no. 2 (Summer 2014): 81–97.

In its self-aggrandizement and blood and soil fantasy, fascist silencing like-wise strives to eviscerate the living knowledges of Black geographies and placemaking. It attempts to erase fugitive and migrant thought born out of displacement, diaspora, and movement.

In its drive for monumentality, fascist knowledge regimes also seize "scholarly and popular mediums," in Toni Morrison's words, to "palisade all art forms," "create sources and distributors of information who are willing to reinforce the demonizing process," and reward "mindlessness and apathy with monumentalized entertainments."[29] In this way, fascisms require regimes of knowledge that stem from epistemologies, aesthetics, and juridical structures that underpin colonial racisms. We know, for example, as noted above, that Nazi jurists and legal scholars produced an array of studies based on the racist statutes embedded in US federal and state laws as a way of building the juridical infrastructure of the Third Reich. This example points not only to a racialized fascist jurisprudence, but also connects to the ascendance of area studies and the knowledges produced out of imperial and settler state formation. Fascisms are predicated on and perpetuate the militarization of knowing. Fascisms proliferate a certain regime of study and a cross-colonial politics of knowledge whose vocation is to perpetuate imperial responses to the worldwide volatilities of cap-ital accumulation. Fascisms highlight within imperialism's expansionist response to capitalist crisis an interconnected settler logic of state-sanc-tioned migrant and refugee punishment, racialized and gendered preda-tory value regimes, and the criminalization of Indigenous governance.

Antifascist solidarities and anti-imperial study

Right-wing attacks on ethnic studies and critical race theory curricula in the United States are examples of a specific recoding of fascist epistemol-ogies of ignorance, didacticism, and control. These campaigns cast ethnic studies as a divisive, ideologically motivated curriculum in which the focus on race, imperialism, and colonization endanger civil and respectful dia-logue and impose a victimizer/victimized dichotomy on students. In the context of California's adaptation of an Ethnic Studies Model Curriculum in 2020, right-wing organizations such as the Alliance for Constructive

---

29 Toni Morrison, "Racism and Fascism," *The Journal of Negro Education* 64, no. 3 (Summer 1995): 384.

Ethnic Studies and the AMCHA Initiative condemn all criticism of Israeli settler state violence as antisemitism. The concerted reactionary attempt to excise discussion of Palestine further contends that *critical* ethnic studies "imposes a narrow political ideology, promotes a militant, anti-Western agenda, polarizes students, and views history and civics entirely through a racial lens," whereas something called "constructive ethnic studies" instead teaches "critical analysis of multiple perspectives, informed decision making, and respectful dialogue."[30] Here, such "constructive" exchange is emptied of substance, serving to silence critical examinations of empire in historical structures of power and institutional order. What is particularly insidious about such campaigns are how the liberal pieties of free speech, open dialogue, and civility sanitize modern history of the unseemly baggage of racism, colonialism, and empire.

Similarly, right-wing lawmakers and media have sought to make critical race theory (CRT) fodder for sensationalized outrage against antiracist pedagogy. Deploying the stock reactionary maneuver of casting straight cisgender white men as the true victims of bias and silencing, Fox News pundit Tucker Carlson helped launch the attack on CRT, which he and other conservatives demonized in order to undercut the ongoing labor of critically naming and dismantling racism. Donald Trump's September 2020 Executive Order 13950 on "Combating Race and Sex Stereotyping" denounced CRT as responsible for diversity training that highlighted structural racism and white privilege in an ostensibly misguided emphasis on race and gender discrimination. Although the Executive Order was revoked by President Biden, "anti-critical race theory" legislation targeting public schools and universities had nonetheless been introduced in twenty-five states by June 2021.[31] Such laws have been gleefully oblivious of the actual critical legal studies genealogy of critical race theory, which is a tradition of legal scholarship that seeks to account for the entrenchment and perpetuation of racist violence in US jurisprudence. Instead, the term is used

---

30 Alliance for Constructive Ethnic Studies, "Constructive vs. Critical Ethnic Studies," https://www.calethstudies.org/about.

31 Victor Ray, "Trump Calls Critical Race Theory 'Un-American,'" *Washington Post*, October 2, 2020, https://www.washingtonpost.com/nation/2020/10/02/critical-race-theory-101/; Cydney Hargis and Alex Walker, "Fox News' Critical Race Theory Obsession," *Media Matters*, May 7, 2021, https://www.mediamatters.org/fox-news/fox-news-critical-race-theory-obsession; Robert Kim, "'Anti-Critical Race Theory' Laws and the Assault on Pedagogy," *Phi Delta Kappan* 103, no. 1 (September 2021): 64–65.

to recycle Red Scare tropes of an anti-American menace in concert with an obstinate anti-Blackness. Tennessee's Senate Bill 0623 (TN SB0623) prohibits teachers from "promoting or advocating the violent overthrow of the United States government" or "promoting division between, or resentment of" people of different races or classes. Iowa's legislation bans educators from teaching that anyone of a particular race or sex "bears responsibility for actions committed in the past by other members of the same race or sex." Iowa's law also specifically forbids lessons that suggest "meritocracy or a hard work ethic [is] racist or sexist" or that make "any individual . . . feel discomfort [or] guilt."[32] As such, the legislation borrows as much from Arizona's 2010 legislative ban on Mexican American Studies in Tucson as the US McCarran Internal Security Act of 1950. Even as media spectacle and legislation remain performatively ignorant of the specific meaning of critical race theory, the targeting of CRT is most certainly a reaction to the everyday correlation of law, racism, and inequality highlighted by Black Lives Matter, abolitionist movements, and the widespread uprisings of 2020 in the wake of the police murder of George Floyd.

The virulence of the attack on the liberatory horizons of ethnic studies and social justice pedagogies is accompanied by the facile pretense of impartial inquiry. This mode of attack prompts us to consider how the intellectual genealogies of critical ethnic studies helps us build out a capacious understanding of fascism and the numerous struggles undertaken to dismantle its planetary ascendance. The anticolonial and anti-imperial struggles that inform critical ethnic studies are indispensable resources for antifascist intellectual production, cultural work, and movement building.[33] Eurocentric framings of fascism presume certain origins, expectations, and responses to fascism as a sociohistorical phenomenon for antifascist praxis. From this perspective, fascism emerges as a pathological historical phenomenon across a spate of European nation-states—Germany and Italy, most notably—between the First and Second World Wars of the early twentieth century. Conventional analyses of fascism search for underlying forces and structures that catalyzed the supposed break or deviation from the civil norms of liberal democracy toward an elite-induced mass will to

---

32 Quoted in Kim, "'Anti-Critical Race Theory' Laws": 64.

33 Neda Atanasoski and Christine Hong, "'No Liberation in Isolation': Collectivity, Internationalism, and Political Education," *Critical Ethnic Studies Journal* 6, no. 1 (Spring 2020), https://manifold.umn.edu/read/no-liberation-in-isolation/.

subsist in and with violence. Fascism is rendered an aberration and as thoroughly distinct from liberalism, even as such interpretations suggest that fascism stemmed from the contradictions of colonial and imperial racisms perpetuated under liberal governance.[34]

For many Black radical workers in the early twentieth century, fascism appeared as an apparatus of capitalist labor control, one that drew from the punitive cultures of colonial slavery and liberal techniques of racialized labor segmentation. "Many of the radical Black intellectuals who witnessed the rise of fascism in Europe," argues Cedric Robinson, "were convinced that whatever its origins, at some point fascism had become an instrument of capitalists with the objective of destroying working-class movements."[35] Rather than seeing fascism as a nationally bounded event, the analysis of racial capitalism animating Black radical antifascism helps us name fascism as a mode of power dispersed throughout colonial modernity's violent cross-imperial regime of spatial and racial control. Such a reading of fascism speaks to the urgency of the Black radical internationalist and transnational organizing.

Fascisms in the plural highlight the ways in which Black radical horizons of liberation exceeded incorporation and integration into the "national culture" of racially segregated liberal states and bent toward the material and speculative building of a global anticolonial and anticapitalist alliance. By deliberately framing fascisms as a heuristic to read *into* the Cold War, we can see an array of state sanctioned racialized, militaristic, and puni- tive practices—what Kelly Lytle Hernández describes as "frontlashes"— mobilized to eliminate the Black radical building of political power with

34 The most influential analysis of fascism from this perspective is Hannah Arendt's *The Origins of Totalitarianism* (New York: Harcourt, Brace and Company, 1951), which argues for situating fascism in relation to imperialism while formulating an equivalence between Nazism and Stalinism that is ultimately amenable to the propagandistic ends of Cold War liberalism. For an important critical reading of Arendt, see David Myer Temin, "'Nothing much had happened': Settler colonialism in Hannah Arendt," *European Journal of Political Theory* (December 2019), https://doi.org/10.1177/1474885119893077. For an account of fascism as interconnected with liberalism, see Ishay Landa, *The Apprentice's Sorcerer: Liberal Tradition and Fascism* (Chicago: Haymarket Books, 2012).

35 Cedric J. Robinson, "Fascism and the Response of Black Radical Theorists," in *Cedric J. Robinson: On Racial Capitalism, Black Internationalism, and Cultures of Resistance*, ed. H.L.T. Quan (London: Pluto Press, 2019), 155. Also see Robin D. G. Kelley, "Why *Black Marxism*? Why Now," in Cedric J. Robinson, *Black Marxism: The Making of the Black Radical Tradition*, Third edition (Chapel Hill: University of North Carolina Press, 2021).

classes of colonized laborers across the globe.[36] Fascisms as a heuristic calls attention to how the elevation of a Euro-American liberal antifascism continues to serve as a domesticating intellectual and cultural force, one that casts the horror of European fascism and Soviet totalitarianism as the foil against which the militarized and carceral expansion of the warfare-welfare state would be pursued as freedom.

When viewed through the register of multiple fascisms, this instance of counterrevolutionary domestication of Black radical struggle casts a different light on the many generative studies that have situated the rise of civil rights, ethnic studies, and discourses of multiculturalism within a broader Cold War strategy of US statecraft to disavow its colonial entanglements with slavery, genocide, and racial punishment. Here we see a shared horizon between genealogies of Black antifascist critique and the robust critique of racial liberalism fostered by the emergence of ethnic studies in the United States. As nodes in a global network of anticolonial struggle in the 1960s and 1970s, the Black, Indigenous, Chicanx, Latinx, Asian American, working class, feminist, and gay, lesbian, and queer and trans movements that fostered the emergence of ethnic studies and other critical pedagogies insisted on accounts of Euro-American liberal modernity as a mode of power grounded in ongoing cycles of colonialism, imperialism, racism, heteropatriarchy, and capitalism.

In this matrix, the analytic power of fascism addresses multiple directions. Building with the prescience of Black radical antifascism, the Black Panther Party invoked the term to call attention to the capitalist state's counterrevolutionary repertoire of violence and control and out of a practical urgency for multiracial coalition and alliance. Asian American activists and cultural workers excavated transpacific histories of racialized exclusion, concentration, and incarceration throughout the twentieth century in a way that pointed toward fascism as a mobile technology of racialized domination.[37] In the same period, Chicanx and Latinx movements connected what Carey McWilliams termed, and Curtis Marez subsequently reintroduced, as the

---

36 Kelly Lytle Hernández, *City of Inmates: Conquest, Rebellion, and the Rise of Human Caging in Los Angeles, 1771–1965* (Chapel Hill: University of North Carolina Press, 2017).

37 Cathy Schlund-Vials and Viet Thanh Nguyen (eds.), *Flashpoints for Asian American Studies* (New York: Fordham University Press, 2018); Jinah Kim, *Postcolonial Grief: The Afterlives of the Pacific Wars in the Americas* (Durham: Duke University Press, 2019). For an analysis of the recent conjuncture, see Simeon Man, "Anti-Asian Violence and US Imperialism," *Race & Class* 62, no. 2 (2020): 24–33.

"farm fascism" of US agribusiness[38] to both overlapping settler colonial invasions in the US Southwest as well as an apparatus of US imperialist violence in Latin America. Adjacent to the emergence of Native North American urban movements and a global Indigenous rights movement, these struggles informed the student strikes at San Francisco State University that were taken up under the banner of the Third World Liberation Front. As Gary Okihiro reminds us, the Third World Liberation Front's effort to incite a radical program of liberatory study can be seen as a particular working out of an anti-imperialist analysis of US culture that affirmed "spatial and ideological affiliation with the Third World and its peoples, not the nation-state."[39]

Our emphasis on fascisms and regimes of knowledge is therefore another way of wrestling with the epistemic potentials and paradoxes of critical ethnic studies in our current moment of danger. This is significant, for as Chandan Reddy illuminates, "critical ethnic studies points to how alternative epistemological accounts of race, or better, differing relations to our extant means of knowing, can defeat the fatal coupling of late modern US racial transformation with the growth of [the] state."[40] The analytic of fascisms thus highlights the methodological urgency of studying the dialectic of modern racisms and state formations.

In a notable example of antifascist ethnic studies methodologies reevaluating racial liberalism in the Americas, Jack D. Forbes locates the rise of fascism as appearing in "a set of mutually-supportive values which go to make up" cultures of secular and sectarian imperialist domination. In particular, he traces the rise of fascism in the relationship between imperialist domination and the emergence of the "mob" as a distinct social formation. For Forbes, the category of the mob—"as a political-religious tool"—"means more than just the masses throwing rocks or burning; it also means 'frenzied' armies of true believers."[41] Such a labor allows Forbes

---

38 Carey McWilliams uses the phrase "farm fascism" to describe the apparatus of racialized and gendered migrant labor exploitation at the heart of US agribusiness. See Carey McWilliams, *Factories in the Field: The Story of Migratory Farm Labor in California* (Boston: Little, Brown and Co., 1939) and Curtis Marez, *Farm Worker Futurism: Speculative Technologies of Resistance* (Minneapolis: University of Minnesota Press, 2016).

39 Gary Y. Okihiro, *Third World Studies: Theorizing Liberation* (Durham: Duke University Press, 2016), 7.

40 Chandan Reddy, "Critical Ethnic Studies," *Kalfou* 1, no. 1 (Spring 2014): 149.

41 Jack D. Forbes, "Fascism: A Review of Its History and Its Present Cultural Reality in the Americas," *Explorations in Ethnic Studies* 5, no. 1 (1982): 3–25. See also Simón Ventura Trujillo, "The Indigenous Materialism of Jack D. Forbes: Notes Toward a Speculative

to connect what he terms "proto-fascism" from the premodern religious empires across Europe to the "frontier fascisms" of the Spanish and British empires in the Americas, and on into the twentieth century conjuncture of Cold War geopolitics and neoliberal state evisceration in which armed white fascist mobs with slave-holding and union-busting lineages have become emboldened.[42]

At the same time, the epistemic implications embedded in the constellation of antifascism and critical ethnic studies point to radical limits on fascist violence posed by anti-imperialist and anticapitalist work on race. By not presuming fascisms as nationally or normatively bordered, anticolonial struggle affirms fascisms—and, by implication, imperialist racial capitalism—as punctuated with multiple modalities of subversion, escape, protest, and countergovernance.

The term *fascisms* gives a name to heterogeneous cycles of imperialist epistemic violence whose limits are perpetually drawn in dialectical struggle with anticolonial, anticapitalist action and potential. This analytic, practical, and theoretical maneuverability speaks to the radiant insights brought about by thinking in "Solidarities of Nonalignment," to quote the title of the *Critical Ethnic Studies* special issue edited by Michael Viola, Juliana Hu Pegues, Iyko Day, and Dean Saranillio. The editors use the phrase out of the urgency to name "new analytics that foreground Indigenous territory and Black women's fungibility and accumulation that might reveal an abolitionist and decolonial anticapitalist politics."[43] By repoliticizing, respatializing, and retemporalizing anticolonial struggle to name a practice of working with disparate legacies and logics of anticapitalist movement building, the editors situate critical ethnic studies as a place where "nonaligned theoretical frameworks and oppositional movements" can be placed "in deeper dialogue" to "make visible what has gone unnoticed or been obscured."[44]

Historiography for a Future without Europe," *Theory & Event* 23, no. 4 (October 2020): 1106–1129.

42 Forbes, "Fascism," 17, 7.

43 Michael Viola, Juliana Hu Pegues, Iyko Day, and Dean Saranillio (eds.), "Solidarities of Nonalignment: Abolition, Decolonization, and Anticapitalism," a special issue of *Critical Ethnic Studies* 5, nos. 1–2 (Spring 2019): 13.

44 Viola et al., "Solidarities of Nonalignment," 8.

If nonaligned planetary cartographies of radical antifascism and critical ethnic studies do the work of marking specific limits to our current multi-fascist moment, how, exactly, does it represent those limits? The articulation of an antifascist critical ethnic studies also brings to light a distinct set of issues for understanding fascism's coupling of aesthetics and politics, or what Walter Benjamin termed *the aestheticization of politics*. For Benjamin, the aestheticization of politics was not only a naming of how European fascism monumentalized ideal types and criminalized figures to stylize political violence and control. It was also a way of coming to terms with the political effects and possibilities that mechanized regimes of photographic and cinematic visuality opened to cognition, affect, and sensibility under capitalist modernity. His analysis points to the aesthetic as a contested category of artistic valuation, technological mediation, and social cognition that was and remains central to Euro-American colonial domination. "All efforts to aestheticize politics culminate in one point," Benjamin writes. "That point is war."[45]

Anticolonial struggle sheds a distinct light on the photographic modernity of fascisms as a modernity of total warfare waged with weaponized visual signs. Consider the legacies of anti-Black, Mexican, and Indigenous lynching photography; the photographic capture of Native children in US boarding schools; the emergence of war photography; racialized histories of surveillance, forensics, and criminal and immigrant database construction; and the hardening of the anthropological gaze for imperialist knowledge across the planet. This list is necessarily incomplete but nevertheless points to the colonial modes of racialized control of Indigenous, Black, and migrant peoples that photographic visuality amplifies under liberal statecraft. Formulated under the duress of these conditions of racialized domination, the definitions and enactments of culture articulated in genealogies of critical ethnic studies build deeper dimensions to genealogies of antifascist aesthetic experimentation. These dimensions to aesthetic analysis, according to Kandice Chuh, emphasize "sensibility as a crucial domain of knowledge and politics; it affords recognition of both the relations and practices of power that legitimate and naturalize certain ideas

---

45 Walter Benjamin, "The Work of Art in the Age of its Technical Reproducibility: Third Version" (1939), in *Walter Benjamin: Selected Writings: Volume 4, 1938–40*, ed. Howard Eiland and Michael W. Jennings, trans. Harry Zohn and Edmund Jephcott (Cambridge, MA: Belknap Press, 2003), 269.

over others, and the knowledge and ways of living subjugated or disavowed in the process."[46] Our use of *fascisms* not only gestures to what can be visually mediated as violence but also brings into focus spectral forms of domination, destruction, and performed ignorance that aren't always evident in the historiographies or popular narratives of Cold War liberalism and neoliberal revanchism. Fascisms as a heuristic calls attention to the flexible and brutal repertoires of racialized domination that are also profoundly frail in the sense that they monopolize violence and repression with a fanatical shortsightedness.

Itineraries

The essays, interviews, and syllabus gathered here attest to multiply-manifest regimes of fascist violence and horizons of antifascist possibility. They approach the question askew, working through the inflections and enjambments of the authoritarian convergence in the historical present. Some speak to the utility of fascism or fascisms as an analytic, others implicitly or overtly question the extent of its relevance for the struggles they discuss, and still others consider attributions of fascism to be an impediment to addressing the conflicts underway. As a contribution to grappling with the uncertainties of the current conjuncture, we hope this book offers resources and inspiration for collective study and struggle for antifascist futures.

For Antifascist Futures begins with the section "Openings" in order to emphasize the many points of departure through which to reframe and reorient conventional accounts of fascism and antifascism. By challenging the liberal presumption that knowledge and awareness are a sufficient ground for mobilizing resistance to fascism, and by underscoring overlapping histories and present conditions of authoritarianism and genocide, this first section establishes the global historical perspective of movement and struggle through which the volume conceives of fascism as symptomatic of the violence of imperial crisis and envisions antifascist futures.

"The Instabilities of Violence," the book's second section, builds on this expanded horizon to show how authoritarian intensifications of force and terror remain insecure and contested. Emphasizing fascism and its corollaries as responses to anticolonial revolution, abolitionist worldmaking,

---

46 Kandice Chuh, *The Difference Aesthetics Makes: On the Humanities "After Man"* (Durham: Duke University Press, 2019), 3. Also see David Lloyd, *Under Representation: The Racial Regime of Aesthetics* (New York: Fordham University Press, 2019).

and the escalating crises of capitalist accumulation, this section turns to examinations of the aesthetics of fascist devotion, the embodied internationalism of decolonial feminist queer and trans activism, and often overlooked sites of Indigenous rebellion and colonial counterinsurgency.

The arenas of organized violence and volatility examined in the second section are further evident in the specific regimes of territoriality and enforcement of the nation-state. The third section of the book looks at "Spectacles of National Security" that arise from zealously resorting to violence and terror as mechanisms of punitive governance. This section focuses on how the conjuring of enemies, modes of surveillance, and uses of states of emergency are tactics through which authoritarian and fascist states or movements seek to secure and maintain control. In the fray of such performative spectacles, however, excess investments of desire and enmity also animate ongoing instabilities, as with the siege on the US Capitol on January 6, 2021. Both the third and fourth sections of the book call attention to the anxieties and contradictions that on the one hand propel fascist mobilization, while on the other hand leave this mobilization capricious, unsettled, and unsettling.

"Present Histories," the volume's fourth section, considers the animate relation between past and present as vital for the ongoing struggle for antifascist futures and collective liberation. The historical contexts and competing imaginaries and uses of the past in evidence throughout the book return as resources for struggle. As authors in this section show, Hindu nationalism in India and white supremacist aspiration to claim the US Northwest are examples of how the right seeks to monopolize affective histories of tradition and belonging. The living histories of Indigenous coalition building, antiracist organizing, and Black radical antifascism in this section nevertheless refuse such fascist monopoly and offer crucial lessons and connections for creating a world otherwise. The final section of the book, "Solidarity in Struggle," expands the uses of such lessons and connections toward antifascist and anti-imperialist futures. The syllabus included at the end of the book is intended as a resource for readers to further engage in the collective study of antifascist futures to which the preceding chapters all contribute.

I. Openings

CHAPTER ONE

The Banality of Knowledge

Nadia Abu El-Haj

On Saturday, November 14, 2020, White House Press Secretary Kayleigh McEnany stood before reporters and declared that a million people had converged on the streets of Washington, DC to protest the electoral fraud robbing Donald J. Trump of a second term in office. Trump's presidency ended as it began: in an alternate universe in which his press secretaries proffered outright lies.[1] A presidency that cultivated and cherished brazen falsehoods culminated in an almost pitch-perfect performance of an authoritarian leader seeking to undermine an election. By January 6, 2021, there was little doubt as to the power of such lies: demonstrators stormed the US Capitol in a rally organized around the slogan "Stop the Steal." They were there to prevent Congress from certifying a "fraudulent" election.[2] Given a political climate in which outright fabrications are the name of the game, it is no wonder that so many on the left have turned to analyze and contravene the dangers of "fake news" and "post-truth" publics. Black is white, up is down. How does one undermine the coercive power of Trumpian truths?[3]

---

1 Phillip Bump, "There's No Evidence that Trump's Inauguration was the Most-Watched in History. Period," *The Washington Post*, January 23, 2017, https://www.washingtonpost.com/news/politics/wp/2017/01/23/theres-no-evidence-that-trumps-inauguration-was-the-most-watched-in-history-period/; Josh Marcus, "MAGA March: Kayleigh McEnany Falsely Claims 'One Million' Demonstrators in DC for Protest," *The Independent*, November 15, 2020, https://www.independent.co.uk/news/world/americas/us-election-2020/maga-march-dc-million-kayleigh-mcenany-b1723044.html.

2 "Inside the Capital Siege," *Embedded*, NPR, January 15, 2021, https://www.npr.org/2021/01/15/957362053/january-6-inside-the-capitol-siege; Dan Barry and Sheera Frankel, "'Be There. Will be Wild!,'" *The New York Times*, January 8, 2021, https://www.nytimes.com/2021/01/06/us/politics/capitol-mob-trump-supporters.html.

3 In Hannah Arendt's words, "All truths . . . are opposed to opinion in their *mode of asserting validity*. Truth carries within itself an element of coercion" (235, emphasis in the original). [Hannah Arendt, "Truth and Politics," in *Between Past and Present* (New York: Penguin, 2006 [1954]), 223–259.]

While I recognize the ubiquity, significance, and political power of patently false claims, I want to explore a different configuration of a post-truth world—of knowledge and power—that also operates today. What if the lie, or for that matter, the secret is not the only way to undermine the power of "facts"? How else are (significant, foundational even) "factual truths," the kinds of truths that exist in the domain of human action and are "political by nature," rendered politically inconsequential?[4] Given the now widely accepted aphorism that knowledge is power, in actual practice (how) does "knowing" inform politics?

In this essay, I address these questions in the context of two settler and self-avowedly democratic nation-states, drawing on my work on US militarism and the so-called "forever wars" on the one hand, and the struggle over history in Israel and Palestine on the other. If in the early-to-mid twentieth century, fascism operated by producing a world in which there was *nothing but* propaganda, as Hannah Arendt argued,[5] the politics of late liberalism and the (proto)fascist movements it has spawned seem to operate quite seamlessly in the face of "facts"—of war and empire or racism and economic deprivation—not because no one knows, but because they might just not care.

Writing a book about the post-9/11 wars, I have sought to give an account of a particular political common sense in the United States today that the American public (as distinct from military personnel) has been barely engaged with, interested in, or even particularly cognizant of the wars in Iraq and Afghanistan. What explains that detachment? More specifically, what are the mechanisms, political practices, and ethical horizons through which public disengagement is produced and identified, and in turn, that felicitous forms of public engagement are fashioned and demanded? There is no simple answer, although the absence of a universal draft is a crucial

---

4 Arendt, "Truth and Politics," 233. Here, Arendt draws a distinction between "rational truths" that are the domain of philosophy, and "factual truths." The latter depend on common agreement and are, thereby, decidedly precarious. Factual truth "is established by witnesses and depends on testimony; it exists only to the extent that it is spoken about, even if it occurs in the domain of privacy. It is political by nature" (233–234). Having said that, Arendt is not arguing for a subjective understanding of, or an "extreme . . . historicism" vis-à-vis factual truths (235). "Even if we admit," she writes, "that every generation has the right to write its own history, we admit no more than that it has the right to rearrange the facts in accordance with its own perspective; we don't admit the right to touch the factual matter itself" (235).

5 Hannah Arendt, *Eichmann in Jerusalem: A Report on the Banality of Evil* (New York: Penguin Random House, 2006).

element, even if in more complex ways than is often assumed: less than 1 percent of the US population serves in the military. Combine that with the geographic distribution of those "serve," and of military bases themselves, and most Americans have little contact with military personnel.[6] Why would most Americans pay attention to—let alone care about—a war fought by so few so very far away? There is also a second, oft-assumed, and sometimes articulated reason for public detachment: it is not simply a matter of apathy; there is widespread ignorance of what is *really* going on. There are too many secrets. The WikiLeaks dump on the Iraq War and Edward Snowden's revelation of the activities and reach of the National Security Agency on US soil were born of that assumption, that fear. State secrecy is a radical threat to the possibility of democratic participation. Americans *just don't know* what their own government is up to.

In *The Theater of Operations*, Joseph Masco explores the reconfiguration of the US security state in an era defined by the threat of "terror," and the impact of state secrecy is one thread of his analysis.[7] Following September 11, 2001 and the anthrax attacks carried out about a month later, as Masco documents, the federal government removed many declassified Cold War security documents from the public domain, now reclassified or more often, categorized as "sensitive but unclassified."[8] What work does secrecy do, especially in a context in which many of these very same documents remain publicly, if only unofficially available?[9] What are secrecy's "damaging domestic effects?"[10] Masco argues, "removing something from public view endows it with social power but . . . the object of secrecy—its

---

6 "By the Numbers: Today's Military," NPR, July 3, 2011, http://www.npr.org/2011/07/03/137536111/by-the-numbers-todays-military. That number includes active duty, National Guard, Air Guard, and the reserves. For a more in-depth discussion of the demographics of military service, see "Who Serves: Military Demographics in 2020," *Thank You for Your Service* (podcast), February 12, 2020, https://podcasts.apple.com/us/podcast/who-serves-military-demographics-in-2020/id1441805414?i=1000465400000.

7 Joseph Masco, *The Theater of Operations: National Security Affect from the Cold War to the War on Terror* (Durham: Duke University Press, 2014).

8 Masco, *The Theater of Operations*, 113.

9 For example, Masco recounts, in search of a photograph "concerning a dismantled nuclear device known as the B61," he discovered that the original image (of which he had a scanned, low-quality copy) "was not available for use in a scholarly project" (115). An email sent in response to his inquiry read: "'In regards to the B61 picture, after September 11, 2001, a review was conducted of our visuals library. As a result, some images are not being released due to security reasons'" (116). But the image is still out there, circulating in a book published by the Department of Energy in 1994.

10 Masco, *The Theater of Operations*, 134.

information—is often less important than the organizational approach to managing it." The "role of deception [itself is] . . . crucial to the transformation of a democratic state into a security state."[11] Drawing on Jodi Dean's work,[12] Masco explains, "recognition of state secrecy—and the accompanying conspiratorial subtext to everyday life that it engenders—functions today to block political participation and curtail the possibility of truly democratic endeavors"; "the national security state's system of compartmentalized secrecy produces a world in which knowledge is always rendered suspect."[13] What *don't I know?*

Masco's analysis offers insight into our political present, in ways he could not have foreseen in 2014. If the expert in the know, and more specifically the authority of the national security expert, renders public knowledge suspect in Masco's account,[14] by the time of Trump's rise to power a different configuration of knowledge and power had come to the fore: a deep and abiding suspicion of "intellectual elites," of "experts,"—including those very same national security experts who have access to classified information not available to the rest of us—and of the so-called deep state they are seen to represent and uphold. The relationships among expertise, secrets, suspicion, knowing, and state power endure, but there is more than one pervasive iteration of it, and each requires a different kind of critical response. Following the logic of Masco's argument, countering the antidemocratic impulses of the antiterror state demands that we call into question the authority of national security experts and the secrets they presumably "know." We must refuse to defer to their knowledge.[15] But countering the Trumpian configuration in which the *expert* is herself the object of suspicion requires a very different move. Does she know secrets or does she just lie? As the COVID-19 pandemic has made eminently clear, this critical project demands reestablishing the authority of (certain kinds of) experts and expertise: the public needs to *believe* that figures like Anthony Fauci actually *do know.*

---

11 Masco, *The Theater of Operations*, 136.

12 Jodi Dean, *Publicity's Secret: How Technoculture Capitalizes on Democracy* (Ithaca: Cornell University Press, 2002).

13 Masco, *The Theater of Operations*, 135.

14 Masco, *The Theater of Operations*, 134–136.

15 Jodi Dean has argued that the "secret" is, and has always been, constitutive of what she calls "publicity." The public on which democratic politics supposedly rests is constituted through the secret—something that some know, and others believe because of those who know.

The workings of secrecy and lies provide only partial insight into the crisis of contemporary democratic citizenship, however. What if secrecy and lies are less significant than analyses suggest? What else might be going on in the here and now? If one is concerned with the epistemologies of contemporary forms of politics, a focus on the functions of secrecy, suspicion, organized lying, and the ever-proliferating rabbit holes of patently false claims may not produce an analysis quite up to the task of accounting for the operation of far-right nationalisms, let alone the relentless militarism and racial-settler democracies sustained by a far broader swath of citizens than those who have drunk from either the national security state or the Trumpian poison chalices. To return to the question of the American public's apparent disengagement from and ignorance of the forever wars[16]—despite all the classification, the state and military secrets, and the problems posed by the practice of embedded journalism—doesn't the public *know enough*? That the American war in Iraq was launched on a lie? That the US military has unleashed enormous harm on Iraqis, Afghans, and everyone else caught in the vortex of its violence? If those are secrets, they are secrets living in plain sight. If they are secrets, they are "publicly known" and at one and the same time, excluded from "public discussion and treat[ed] . . . as though they were what they are not—namely, secrets."[17] How might we address the problem of public secrets? And what if *they are not secrets at all*? I consider those questions via a detour through a foundational historical dispute among Israeli and Palestinian publics: what happened in 1948?

The war of 1948 is known as the "War of Independence" in Israeli society. Palestinians refer to it as the *Nakba*—the catastrophe. 750,000 Palestinians were expelled from their villages and cities during the war, a reality widely dismissed in both Israeli society and the Euro-American world for decades. The forms of denial were seemingly endless: the land was empty; there is no such thing as a Palestinian; Arab regimes misled the Arab inhabitants of Palestine, telling them to flee Zionist forces which meant them no harm.

---

16 I write "apparent" because while the US public might pay very little attention to what is going on in Iraq, Afghanistan, and elsewhere given the increasingly global footprint of US military operations, the American soldier and veteran is far from absent in the public domain. On television, in movies, in novels, in long-form journalism, memoirs, and literature, the American soldier is a ubiquitous figure through which the wars appear on the home front, and in whose name, as I argue in a forthcoming book, contemporary American militarism is both fashioned and sustained.

17 Arendt, "Truth and Politics," 232.

The late 1970s witnessed the beginning of a discursive shift. In 1978, the Israeli state declassified documents pertaining to the war, Israeli historians gained access to previously unavailable "official" sources, and a few began to rewrite the history of their state. They began to challenge hegemonic narratives regarding the state's founding moment. State secrets were coming to light. Most fundamentally, historians such as Benny Morris, Simha Flapan, and Ilan Pappé rewrote the war of 1948; they documented that the vast majority of Palestinians on the land that was to become the State of Israel were expelled by Zionist brigades during the course of the war, even if their fate was sealed long before the first shots were fired.[18] There were disagreements among these so-called New Historians, and on the part of Palestinian scholars and others who challenged them: was the expulsion intentional, pre-planned, essential to the establishment of the Jewish state? Was it an "event" that unfolded during the chaos or "fog" of war? Over time the basic parameters of this "new" history, one known to Palestinians for decades, became widely accepted in the Israeli academy, even in the Israeli public domain. During its "War of Independence," Zionist military brigades expelled the vast majority of the Palestinian population so that the Jewish state could be born, its borders established, and a Jewish majority ensured.

Two decades hence: in the early years of the new millennium, teams sent by the security department of Israel's Defense Ministry began to pore through documents in Israeli state archives, removing some from the public domain. In an Israeli state veering ever closer to fascism, state secrecy was being reinstated: previously declassified documents having to do with the state's founding were resealed into vaults of state security. Quite specifically, one of the main documents—the basis for Morris' seminal 1986 essay "The Harvest of 1948 and the Creation of the Palestinians Refugee Problem"[19]—disappeared from public view. In recounting this project of reclassification, a reporter for *Haaretz*, the liberal Israeli newspaper, asked the former head of the Defense Ministry's security department about the logic of the state secrecy project: why remove a document whose content

18 See: Benny Morris, *The Birth of the Palestinian Refugee Problem, 1947–1949* (Cambridge: Cambridge University Press, 1989); Simha Flapan, *The Birth of Israel: Myths and Realities* (London: Croom Helm, 1987); Ilan Pappé, *The Making of the Arab-Israeli Conflict, 1947–1951* (New York: Taurus, 1994).

19 Benny Morris, "The Harvest of 1948 and the Creation of the Palestinians Refugee Problem," *Middle East Journal*, Vol. 40, No. 4 (Autumn 1986): 671–685.

is so widely known? The former official responded: [I]f he quoted from it and the document itself is not there [i.e., where Morris says it is], then his facts aren't strong. If he says, 'Yes, I have the document,' I can't argue with that . . . there's a difference of day and night in terms of the validity of the evidence."[20] By the early 2000s, Morris himself had shifted from a reluctant post-Zionist to a staunch defender of the Israeli state, although he still positioned himself on the liberal side of the Israeli political spectrum. In contrast to the state project, however, Morris didn't need the document to disappear in order to make that political turn: all nations are founded in violence. Israel is no exception. It had to be done, he declared. Ben-Gurion should have finished the job.[21]

Several years after Morris' defense of the war of 1948, a prominent, left-leaning Israeli columnist published a book, part history of the Israeli state and part the author's reckoning with the violence and ethnic cleansing on which his homeland was built. In the most widely cited chapter of *My Promised Land*,[22] Ari Shavit recounts the war of 1948 through events that transpired in the Palestinian town of Lydda, culminating in the expulsion of the town's inhabitants and a massacre of those who had sought refuge in the city's mosque. Shavit represents the story of Lydda as a tragedy, an inevitability not recognized by Jewish settlers until it was too late. "Lydda is our black box," he writes. "In it lies the dark secret of Zionism. The truth is that Zionism could not bear Lydda. . . . If Zionism was to be, Lydda could not be. If Lydda was to be, Zionism could not be."[23] With Lydda, Zionism lost its innocence, and not just because of the massacre. The massacre might have been avoided, but its conditions of possibility could not. "Do I turn my back on the Jewish national movement that carried out the deed of Lydda?" Shavit asks, rhetorically.

<hr>

20 Hagar Shezaf, "Burying the Nakba: How Israel Systematically Hides Evidence of 1948 Expulsion of Arabs," *Haaretz*, July 5, 2019, https://www.haaretz.com/israel-news/.premium.MAGAZINE-how-israel-systematically-hides-evidence-of-1948-expulsion-of-arabs-1.7435103.

21 See Ari Shavit, "Survival of the Fittest? An Interview with Benny Morris," *Counterpunch*, January 16, 2004, https://www.webcitation.org/5pvy2Rvfw?url=http://www.counterpunch.org/shavit01162004.html.

22 Ari Shavit, *My Promised Land: The Triumph and Tragedy of Israel* (New York: Spiegel & Grau, 2013). The article on Lydda was excerpted in *The New Yorker* in advance of the book's publication. See Ari Shavit, "Lydda, 1948: A City, A Massacre, and the Middle East Today," *The New Yorker*, October 14, 2013, https://www.newyorker.com/magazine/2013/10/21/lydda-1948.

23 Shavit, *My Promised Land*, 108–109.

Like the brigade commander, I am faced with something too immense to deal with. . . . For when one opens the black box, one understands that whereas the small mosque massacre could have been a misunderstanding brought about by a tragic chain of accidental events, the conquest of Lydda and the expulsion of Lydda were not accidents . . . the choice is stark: either reject Zionism because of Lydda or accept Zionism along with Lydda.

Shavit chooses to "stand by the damned."[24]

Shavit's "reckoning" with the *Nakba* speaks to a particular kind of struggle over historical—and political—facts and truths. There is no outright denial here, no need for patently false claims, for secrets and lies. These are not even *"public* secrets," facts widely known but "taboo" in the public domain. They are widely discussed, recognized as true, even if immediately set aside. Perhaps then this story troubles, at least a little bit, a widespread sensibility on the left, and especially among scholars, that recuperating (some sense of) the (historical) truth is not just ethically significant but also politically salutary. If this story suggests anything at all, it is that reading against or along the archival grain, or more simply, countering the outright lies on Fox News and spread on alt-right social media platforms may make little difference at all. And that may be the case *even if one can come to some general agreement about the "facts."* That is, even if one interprets, at least in large part, "what happened" or "what is happening" in a similar way.

I do not mean to dismiss the significance of efforts to recuperate histories long repressed or forgotten, or for that matter to fight against the saturation of the public domain with patently false claims. I just want to suggest that there is another configuration of a "post-truth politics" here, and it too demands analysis and political attention. To rely on a distinction made by the philosopher Stanley Cavell, *"knowing"* and *"acknowledging"* are not the same thing.[25] In deciding to reclassify documents that revealed the "secrets" of 1948, the Israeli state may have been a little too frightened of the evidence. The history that the declassified (and now partially reclassified) documents tell is widely "known." That genie isn't going back into any bottle anytime soon. And what is more, that Zionist brigades forced

---

24 Shavit, *My Promised Land*, 131.

25 Stanley Cavell, *Must We Mean What We Say?: A Book of* Essays (New York: Scribner, 1969).

the vast majority of Palestinians to flee their homes and cities and villages during the war of 1948 is known, accepted even, within the Israeli Jewish public, and among the American liberal establishment that enthusiastically embraced Shavit's book as a profound and admirable ethical self-reckoning by a liberal and deeply thoughtful Zionist.[26] Those facts, however, are not acknowledged: the Nakba has not emerged as *a matter of (urgent) public concern and action*. In its current configuration of power (as distinct from the 1940s well into the 1980s), Israeli settler-nationhood no longer depends on the suppression of the "truth" of 1948. Instead, it operates through the embrace of a far more brazen and explicit seizure of power and knowledge: yes, the Nakba. And no, we—Israelis—don't care. Rather than expressing a commitment to justice or to political and moral repair, admitting the facts—speaking that truth—emerges as a practice of late liberal self-fashioning. In recognizing the tragedy and in narrating his own guilt and pain in facing it, Shavit represents himself as the ethical (and ethically pained) liberal subject (that his enemies, for the most part, presumably are not).[27]

This particular configuration of power and knowledge is prevalent in the United States as well. There are myriad proto-authoritarian and protofascist impulses in the present moment—the desire to wall in the US Southern border and to diminish voting rights and thereby save the nation for white Republicans are but two stark examples. Such impulses are grounded in the commitment to, or at least the consent and complicity of, a significant sector of the American public to a particular order of things. And (most of) that public certainly *knows more than enough*: that migrant children, separated from their parents, are being caged and/or deported to Mexico, even if they are not Mexican; that 750,000 and counting of their fellow citizens have died of COVID-19, a death toll that has been borne disproportionately by minority, immigrant, and Indigenous communities; that Black citizens are killed, repeatedly, relentlessly and, thanks to smartphones, in

---

26 See: Leon Wiesseltier, "The State of Israel," *The New York Times*, November 21, 2013, https://www.nytimes.com/2013/11/24/books/review/my-promised-land-by-ari-shavit.html; Jonathan Freedland, "The Liberal Zionists," *The New York Review*, August, 14, 2014, https://www.nybooks.com/articles/2014/08/14/liberal-zionists/.

27 There is a thread of the pain of having to face the truth that runs through Shavit's account of Lydda and the positive reviews of the book. The very experience of guilt renders one a liberal ethical subject, it seems, regardless of whether one does anything to make amends. For an incisive account of war, guilt, and the constitution of the liberal subject-qua-soldier (as distinct from the terrorist), see Talal Asad, *On Suicide Bombing* (New York: Columbia University Press, 2007).

full view of the American public by the police. And yet, they just don't care (enough). Such "truths" do not rise to the level of public concern and action, at least not for a considerable portion of American citizens. And that may be far less about disagreements over the facts of the matter (e.g., was George Floyd's death a racist murder or merely a regrettable accident? Is the COVID-19 crisis really all that deadly?) than about who and what are considered worthy of attention, redress, and justice. While clearly ubiquitous, neither secrecy nor lies are the only mechanisms through which settler-democratic nation-states, teetering ever more rightward every day, reproduce the racial order of things on which they were founded. To focus on secrets and lies, on fake news and politics as outright fabrication, may be to let too many citizens off the ethical and political hook.

CHAPTER TWO

blood memory

the criminalization of Indigenous land defense

Anne Spice

Figure 2. The gate of entry to the Unist'ot'en encampment near Houston, British Columbia, December 17, 2018. Photograph by and courtesy of Amber Bracken.

when the colonizers imagine a criminal, do they picture cedar hats/
button blankets
that indian with her hunting rifle
that indian with his fish net
that indian with their eagle feather
that indian with their drum[1]

---

1 I switch genres to avoid capture. I shapeshift to avoid capture. I learned from Raven. Raven who knew when to walk on human feet and when to fly. Raven who knew when to escape and live to tell the story. The language of the colonizers is easily appropriated.

During the police raid on Wet'suwet'en territories in February 2020, approximately seventy tactical officers descended on a makeshift watchtower to arrest me and three other Indigenous land defenders. They brought dogs, semi-automatic weapons, snipers, helicopters, snowmobiles, heavy machinery. They pointed their guns at us. They read the civil injunction over the sound of our drums. They removed us from the tower. They removed us from the territory. They brought us to jail. My work dwells in the carceral geographies created for Indigenous people through the collusion of the state and extractive industries. The spaces of unfreedom on unceded Indigenous territories.[2] The bureaucratic criminalization of traditional activities through environmental permits, civil injunctions, industrial allowances. State activities that some experience as new expressions of fascism are, for us, timeless colonial techniques. Nothing has changed.[3] Here, I exhume the traces of fascist practice in the everyday experience of colonial occupation. Instead of illuminating the forms of authoritarianism emerging in a formal political realm, I delve into the old colonial tricks that continue to motivate settler-colonial dispossession, despite how democratic settler governments might appear.

Scholarship can be a technology of capture. When I start to sense they're onto me, I change it up. Quote this piece in your police report, I dare you. Remain unmoved.

2   Wet'suwet'en territory is unceded, meaning it has never been surrendered through treaty or war. The provincial and Canadian governments have no treaty agreements, no legal paperwork through which they can claim the territory as belonging to anyone other than the Wet'suwet'en people.

3   At the same time, everything has changed. We've lived through apocalypse and genocide. The colonizer now knocks on our doors to invite us to the table, to join in negotiations. The colonizer wants reconciliation without giving up control. The timeless colonial techniques fold in new tactics to pacify us: the politics of recognition holds up our cultures but not our law and governance. [See Glen Coulthard, *Red Skin White Masks: Rejecting the Colonial Politics of Recognition* (Minneapolis: University of Minnesota Press, 2014) and Audra Simpson, *Mohawk Interruptus: Political Life across the Borders of Settler States* (Durham: Duke University Press, 2014).] Here is the thing that is fascist about it: we never consented to be governed in this way and our old ways are not allowed. No amount of recognition will give us back our autonomy, will bring back the millions lost to war and disease, will give us back the children stolen and assimilated, will convince us that this new "democracy" cribbed from notes on the French Revolution and the Iroquois Confederacy gives us more freedom than what we had when we were exercising our own peoples' rights to govern in accordance with natural law, in accordance with our inherent title to our lands, in good relation with the land and with each other. In the meantime, the "rule of law" contains us to the reservation, incarcerates us at alarming rates, guarantees premature death, and limits the possibilities of life. The colonizers will grieve with us when we describe what we've lost, but they will not let us protect the little we have left.

i met my ancestors in jail
some blood memory awoke
to fluorescent lights and piss and
indignity
but my rage muscled out
the shame
and after 3 nights
when i emerged from the cell
we had shut down canada
and reconciliation was dead[5]

how many of my ancestors
held drums and sang,
defiant
at the barrel of a gun
this anger flows in my blood
fills my throat
rivers run
through me

we built a tower
stood on higher ground
screamed at the invaders
when we were surrounded
by the enemy
we kept singing

---

4   The Gidimt'en access point was set up 44 km along the Morice River West Forest Service Road in 2018, in order to buffer the neighboring Dark House territory and protect the land-based healing work of the Unist'ot'en Healing Center (located at 66 km along the Forest Service Road). The first raid of the checkpoint occurred on January 7, 2019. The actions of the police—including the use of "lethal overwatch"—elicited a national outcry. (For details, see https://www.theguardian.com/world/2019/dec/20/canada-indigenous-land-defenders-police-documents.)The second set of raids on Wet'suwet'en territory occurred in February 2020 and are documented in this piece.

5   After the February 2020 raids, solidarity actions across the country shut down railways, highways, ports, bridges, and offices under the hashtags #ShutDownCanada and #ReconciliationIsDead. The rail blockades, especially those on Mohawk territories, paralyzed the Canadian economy and made national headlines for weeks, and catalyzed a series of negotiations between Indigenous leaders and Canadian politicians.

i dreamt once
i ripped out a human heart
with my hands
and when i awoke
i was calm as a frozen lake
some blood memory

The night before the raid it is cold and clear. The moon is bright and casts crisp shadows on the snow. The ring around the moon glows, a message from our ancestors that we are protected, loved. Surrounded by kin. We know the police are coming in the morning. I do not sleep.

A raven warns us of their approach. We hear the drone first, and then the snowmobiles. Then we see vehicles, police pouring out. Then rustling in the bushes as they snowshoe the perimeter. Then the excavator, the chainsaws, to break down the barricades. Two black helicopters fly low, unloading tactical teams behind us. Two more. Two more. Two more. Eight in total. They have dogs. A sniper kneels behind a flipped-over van and aims his weapon at us. We are surrounded, two of us on the tower, two in the bus below. They are all armed. Semi-automatic weapons, tactical gear. We call out the ones with name badges. Others are only marked by numbers; we call out to them as well.

you are invaders
this is conquest
this is genocide
we have permission to be here
we are unarmed
we have our ancestors behind us
think of your children
think of the river
think of the land
are you proud of yourselves
your spirits will never recover from this

i tell myself to be calm. to move slowly.
i tell myself:

there are four of us
there are over 70 of them
armed.
they have come for us
their guns are for us
they have trained for this
be calm
be calm
be calm

The police move into the bus below and take my friends away. I sing the women's warrior song[6] until I am breathless. Then they begin to scale the tower. They cut our prayer ties off with a chainsaw. I cry angry tears. They ask if we will hurt them if they climb, we say that they are the violent ones. They put us in harnesses and lower us down with dead-eyed precision. They take us to jail.

We are encouraged to sign conditions of release that would disallow us from returning to Wet'suwet'en territory. These conditions are later dropped, we are released and cleared. The entire police operation was mounted to clear a blockade to allow the Coastal GasLink pipeline to access the territory without the consent of house group chiefs. The entire police operation was mounted to undermine a system of Indigenous governance that predates Canadian occupation and settler law by thousands of years. The entire operation, the weapons, the lethal force, the millions of dollars spent—all were in service of enforcing a *civil injunction*.[7]

---

6   The women's warrior song was given to Martina Pierre of the Lil'wat Nation. According to my late friend and mentor Brian Grandbois, the song first came to her in jail during the 1990 Lil'wat blockade (a four-month highway occupation begun in solidarity with the Kanehsatà:ke Mohawks in the siege at Oka).

7   Secwepemc leader Arthur Manuel referred to the injunction as a "legal billy club," noting that "the weight of this club is provided by the racist colonial doctrines of discovery claiming that we have been fully and irreversibly dispossessed of our territories. That is the underpinning behind the Canadian state's vision of Crown land, and it's the force behind the injunctions that industry and governments use to get enforcement orders that allow them to use the police, paramilitaries and even at the army to crush our efforts to inhabit the lands given to us by our Creator." [Arthur Manuel, *The Reconciliation Manifesto: Recovering the Land Rebuilding the Economy* (Toronto: James Lorimer & Company Ltd., 2017), 215.] In a policy paper released by the Yellowhead Institute, they found that "76 percent of injunctions filed against First Nations by corporations are granted, while 81 percent of injunctions filed against corporations by First Nations are denied." [Yellowhead

For months in the lead up to the raid, we were painted as criminals for living as Indigenous people. The police knocked on the doors of our remote cabins just to "check in." They recorded our movements and filmed our license plates. They followed us berry picking. They pulled us over on back roads. They strode into our encampments. They asked us for ID. They enforced nonexistent traffic control laws on remote forest service roads. They flew surveillance drones overhead and tracked our communications. They mapped our encampments with aerial surveillance. Our lives were tightly monitored and controlled. And, in the end, they did not have to press criminal charges to deploy dozens of armed and trained tactical forces, ready and able to kill.

Months after the raid, I have a dream that I am trapped in a police encampment. When I try to escape, I am stopped by a smiling, white-haired policeman who presses a gun to my temple. "I WILL shoot you," he is still smiling, "and no-one will care." I wake up, but am I free from this dream? This nightmare?

This is what criminalization feels like.[8]

The omnipresence of state violence. It's the atmosphere we live in.[9] The air we breathe. The gaze of the state, the knowledge of the growing police files on each of us, the fear of slipping up. Paranoia. Worthlessness. Depression. The police invade our dreams. Etched over the unceded lands of Wet'suwet'en *yintah* are carceral geographies. The boundaries are patrolled, our actions are monitored. Spaces of unfreedom are a shadow over us. Every time we step into the light, we are reminded that it is illegal to seek our own liberation.

Institute, *Land Back: A Yellowhead Institute Red Paper* (Toronto: Ryerson University, October 2019).] CGL's original application for injunction is analyzed by the Yellowhead Institute here: https://redpaper.yellowheadinstitute.org/wp-content/uploads/2019/11/coast-al-gaslink-injunction-analysis.pdf.

8   Heidi Kiiwetinepinesiik Stark discusses how Indigenous criminality is constructed by the US and Canadian governments throughout the nineteenth century to mask colonial illegality, impose colonial law, and reify settler sovereignty. [Heidi Kiiwetinepinesiik Stark, "Criminal Empire: The Making of the Savage in a Lawless Land," *Theory and Event* 19, no. 4 (2016): n.p.]

9   Kristen Simmons describes "settler atmospherics" as "the normative and necessary violences found in settlement—accruing, adapting, and constricting indigenous and black life in the U.S. settler state . . . . Some of us cannot breathe." [Kristen Simmons, "Settler Atmospherics," *Society for Cultural Anthropology*, November 20, 2017, https://culanth.org/fieldsights/settler-atmospherics.]

We must train ourselves in the laws of the colonizers. I spent months liaising with lawyers and preparing legal documents and advising the chiefs.[10] In the end, the best advice I can give is that the courts will not serve us, this legal system is meant to displace us and reify colonial power. In the end, Indigenous laws are swept aside and the uncertainty of Canada's title is glossed over. Never mind that British Columbia has no legal title to these lands. Never mind that the *Delgamuukw v. British Columbia* decision affirmed that the Indigenous title to these lands was never extinguished.[11] Never mind the generations of oral history proving that Wet'suwet'en house chiefs have occupied and cared for their territories for thousands of years. The colonizers have the power to violently enforce their laws, so their laws prevail.[12] Industry uses every loophole to check the boxes they need to continue. Consent doesn't matter. The project pushes on.[13]

10 This was in preparation for the court hearing that would determine whether the interim injunction would be expanded to an interlocutory injunction. The court's granting of the interlocutory injunction in December 2019 resulted in the police enforcement actions described in this piece.

11 *Delgamuukw v. British Columbia*, [1997] 3 SCR 1010 (aka the Delgamuukw-Gisday'wa court case) determined that Aboriginal title still exists on Wet'suwet'en and Gitxsan territories and has not been extinguished by the province or through settler occupation of Indigenous lands. The affidavits from the case make clear that the title holders on Wet'suwet'en territory are the hereditary chiefs whose names tie them to the house group territories for which they are responsible.

12 One of the most recurrent questions as the injunction case was heard in court was: why doesn't the *Delgamuukw* decision matter? Shouldn't the precedent be to recognize Aboriginal title, to respect Indigenous law? Justice Church dodged this by insisting that while the Wet'suwet'en may have legitimate claim to their territory (and therefore the ability to make decisions about access and any industrial projects on it), that was a question for a higher court. The work of the civil injunction is to separate the question of whether or not an injunction is necessary from the status of the land over which the injunction applies. In essence, she ruled that CGL could legitimately obtain an injunction against Wet'suwet'en people on Wet'suwet'en land, and that injunction could be enforced. The fact that the Crown has no legal claim to the land in question becomes a question for a later date and higher court, and one that would require a massive title case (and millions of dollars) to fully resolve. This is understandably infuriating for Wet'suwet'en people who spent ten years (and millions of dollars) advocating for their jurisdiction on their house group territories through the *Delgamuukw* court case already, only for the decision to be inapplicable when a territorial dispute actually occurs.

13 Resource wealth continues to be extracted from Indigenous territories in the name of national prosperity, and petro-fueled capitalist accumulation requires infrastructures of invasion to gain access to lands under Indigenous jurisdiction. [Anne Spice, "Fighting Invasive Infrastructures: Indigenous Relations against Pipelines," *Environment and Society* 9, no. 1 (2018): 40–56.]

When the daily police patrols, the jeering white supremacists, the surveillance, and threat of violence starts to wear on us, we remind each other that we have done nothing wrong. That we are not criminals. That we are defending the land. That we love the land and each other. But the feeling remains, tugging at the edges of our consciousness. They decide when we become criminals. It could happen at any time, for any reason. The police are on foot, at our smokehouses and cultural sites, patrolling with semi-automatic weapons. They stop our relatives when they come back from hunting. They respond to "gunshots" like we are on a city street and not in the bush. We hear that our relatives in Mohawk territory are being arrested, alone, pulled from their homes weeks and months after clashes with police. Picked off on trumped-up charges, out of the tenuous protection of the media spotlight.

This is what criminalization feels like.

We do not walk in two worlds. Or, the two worlds are not the old ways and the modern world, as some would have it. We exist, on our lands, within a web of relations that are as old as time itself. When we defend the land we are not creating barriers to outside forces, but deepening connections and responsibilities that have always been there. Connections and relations that have held us and shaped us and created us as peoples.

Colonial power attempts, at every turn, to redefine our worlds. To draw the old meanings out of our lives and inscribe these colonial relationships on everything. To make us think this is the way it must be, has always been. Our hunting grounds become construction sites. Our ancient trails become highways. Our rivers are technical problems. Our medicines are cleared for more profitable things. We are meant to look at the photograph of the police officer beside our smokehouse and see nothing unusual. The daily patrols fold into the rhythm of life for us. Police control is normalized. Our existence has always been criminal.

We walk in our own world, this world born of rivers spilling from Raven's beak, this world watched over by glacier women, this world where light spills from cedar boxes into the sky, this world where our ancestors walk and whisper to us from mossy corners of the forest.

And the colonizers, they walk all over us.

Here is what we must remember. When the police patrol ancient trails, they are walking in a world in which they do not and cannot belong. A world that will not claim them as it claims us. Our storytelling is powerful because it is a reminder of our belonging. A reminder that the invasion, the conquest, is not normal or natural or the way things need to be. A reminder that we are connected to this land. We need to choose to live in this reality. The one where we are free and autonomous on our lands. The one where our lives and stories matter. This other world is a smokescreen, a cheap simulation, and we can see through it.

When we speak of decolonization, or land back, or whatever the current language of resistance offers, we are talking about peeling back this layer of violence that has (literally) settled over Indigenous lands. We are talking about naming this system as oppressive, violent, foreign, and out-of-place.[14] These lands do not belong to Canada, and Canada does not belong here. We are talking about treating our Indigenous laws as if they are The Law (they are), about treating Indigenous peoples as if they are The People (we are), about treating other oppressed people here as our honored guests, about finding reciprocal relations with those who are capable and powerful and generous enough to return the gifts we have given them.

Neofascist and white supremacist movements also attempt to make a deeply hierarchical social order appear to be the natural order of things. This is an old colonial trick, and one that Indigenous people know about. We can be on the lookout for the naturalization of the carceral. Who belongs in power? Who belongs in jail? When does the "rule of law" apply?

---

14 The line between colonial capitalism and fascism is blurred. Fascist practice is evident when the state uses violence to undermine the will of the people, to consolidate control outside of community decision-making processes, and to criminalize and punish dissent. Indigenous liberation movements are anticolonial and so they are antifascist, and there is much possibility for combining Indigenous strategies against colonization with antifascist organizing. I deliberately refuse to differentiate between the "colonial" and "fascist" forces we oppose, because I think that antifascist organizing often ignores the (centuries) of experience that Indigenous peoples have in standing up to the imposition of state violence, surveillance, military occupation, and extralegal violence. We can unite against the codification of white supremacy within settler state institutions and agree that when we fight "the colonizers" and "the fascists," we are likely talking about the same systems and people.

How is our mobility limited? When are our movements surveilled? How are our actions made suspect? Whose power is threatened by our existence? Carcerality seeps into our relations. Into our dreams. But we can shake off this illusion. Colonizers have never been much good at magic.

On the top of the tower, I feel a circle around me like the ring around the moon. The matriarchs are drumming for us. The ancestors are holding us and protecting us. I am wearing my mother's parka; I gather it around me. Looking out over the snow below, drab police teeming at the base of the tower, I see the layer underneath. I peel away this illusion of control, of ownership, of colonization. They do not belong here. They do not belong to this land. We have permission to be here. Our ancestors are behind us. Our spirits will recover. We can dream something different.

CHAPTER THREE

On the Historical Roots of US Fascism

Johanna Fernández

In 2016, a fascist-leaning candidate won the US election. Had it not been for an epic uprising of Black people in spring and summer of 2020, the electorate might have voted him in for another four years. In the end, the riots that engulfed Minneapolis days after the police lynching of George Floyd inspired a national political awakening of people of all races and classes that tipped the scales in the presidential contest. The atmosphere of indignation had been primed in the preceding weeks, as Americans witnessed the state's failure to adequately respond to the biggest national health crisis in 100 years: the novel coronavirus outbreak. Only when unfathomable images of George Floyd's murder by police officer Derek Chauvin surfaced did close to 40 million people take to the streets. And when the government deployed repressive action against protesters and unsubstantiated media narratives deprecating Black Lives Matter circulated, public discourse shifted to the imperiled state of American democracy. Together, these events galvanized one of the largest voter turnouts in the country's history during the 2020 presidential election.

The presence and influence of fascist ideologues in the nation's highest office from 2017 through 2021 posed a clear threat to the country. Yet journalists, pundits, academics, and others often dismissed such assessments of Donald Trump and his cabinet as hyperbole. As the world witnessed during the January 6, 2021 storming of Congress, avoidance of critiques of an unhinged reality has dangerous consequences. This avoidance was baked into the national culture by an uninterrupted history of government-led purges, political repression, and anticommunist fear mongering, which long ago groomed Americans to restrain their speech and deny reality.

What is fascism exactly?

Many scholars agree with Marxists' interpretations of fascism as a historical phenomenon: a government of last resort erected by a wing of the capitalist class in response to three emerging dynamics: deep economic collapse; widespread dissatisfaction with the status quo; and threats to capitalism posed by organized sections of society, especially a radicalized working class, and its proposals for a socialist alternative. Fascism asserts control amid crisis by conferring absolute power to captains of one of the most autocratic and unyielding institutions in society—the corporation—through "the merger of state and corporate power," total control of labor and production, and suspension of civil society and claims to any and all individual rights.[1]

As seen in 1930s Germany, following the stock market crash of 1929, captains of capital relied on a charismatic fascist leader to win the consent and cooperation of German citizens for their project of "restoring order" to the nation. Unlike authoritarian rule or dictatorship, fascism depends on a large swath of the population to carry out the interests of the state. The fascist leader achieves this by articulating the anger of those deeply dissatisfied with the way things are, legitimizing that dissatisfaction before national audiences. Disproportionately found among the struggling and disgruntled middle classes, especially shopkeepers and middling professionals, the fascist constituency laments its lost standing in a changing world. Through manipulation of fears, the fascist leader channels social anxieties of this sector, whose members feel that their place, livelihood, and social standing have been usurped. Blame is cast on immigrants, outsiders, and undeserving "others" perceived to be destroying the social fabric of the nation and enjoying its fruits without effort or sacrifice. Acting independently of the state, yet also in concert with it, the foot soldiers of fascism come to see it as their duty to contain and repress those who are then depicted as "enemies of the country."

The economic underpinnings of global political crisis

On the eve of the coronavirus outbreak in the fall of 2019, a wave of protests swept through every corner of the globe. Protests against a subway fare

---

1 See Franz Neumann, *Behemoth: The Structure and Practice of National Socialism, 1933–1944* (New York: Oxford University Press, 1944).

hike in Santiago, Chile snowballed into large-scale national protests and occupations calling for sweeping change. Uprisings also erupted in France, Lebanon, Egypt, Bolivia, Ecuador, the United States, Algeria, Zimbabwe, Poland, Georgia, Iran, Sudan and beyond, as masses of people took to the streets to protest austerity. For example, the price of onions in India, the cost of oil in Iran, and an unpopular tax on WhatsApp usage in Lebanon.

As if on cue, the word "neoliberalism" was on people's lips around the world, and everyone seemed to have had enough of it. Introduced to rescue capitalism from its precipitous fall after the oil crisis and recession of 1973, neoliberalism's logic has enshrined market interests in culture and law above all else. Since then, governments have served business interests through corporate tax cuts and bailouts, deregulation of industry and financial markets, the dismantling of labor protections, privatization of public sector services, and cuts to social welfare spending that have eliminated subsidies for electricity, gasoline, propane, and food.[2] This war on the commons has deepened inequality across the globe. In 2018, the wealthiest 1 percent controlled more than 50 percent of the world's wealth and the bottom 80 percent owned merely 4.5 percent.[3]

The global uprisings we've seen identify the unequal distribution of resources as the source of social problems. On the opposite end of the political spectrum, growing fascist currents interpret the social malaise of this moment as a loss of national greatness and blame it on the advances of immigrants, Muslims, Jews, Marxists, and feminists. Across the globe, neofascist movements have either won elections or entered the political mainstream in Denmark, Italy, England, France, Germany, Greece, Turkey, Brazil, Ukraine, and beyond. In the United States, these political currents are mostly made up of angry white men and their elected officials. These groups posit that their culture and very existence as Euro-Americans face grave threats from those outside their white supremacist conception of the nation. To that end, they're committed to forced deportations, heavy and often militarized policing of urban areas disproportionately populated by Black Americans, Latinos, and other people of color,

---

2 See David Harvey, *A Brief History of Neoliberalism* (London and New York: Verso, 2007) and Wendy Brown, *Undoing the Demos: Neoliberalism's Stealth Revolution* (Brooklyn: Zone Books, 2017).

3 Oxfam (London), *Wealth: Having it All and Wanting More*, January 19, 2015. Cited in William I. Robinson, "A Disease Deadlier than COVID-19: Global Capitalism in Crisis," in Cynthia McKinney (ed.), *When China Sneezes: From the Wuhan Lockdown to the Global Politico-Economic Implications* (Atlanta: Clarity Press, 2020), 145–160.

and a patriarchal order in which men work and women stick to childrearing and the home.

The political polarization seen in global protests against austerity and state violence on the one hand and those calling for the closing of national borders and a return to tradition on the other is the product of a global economy that has been trapped in a longstanding, unresolved economic crisis—with no relief in sight. At the end of 2019, even before the pandemic wreaked havoc across the globe, the world economy had been unable to fully recover from the Great Recession of 2008. In the US, the picture was mixed. In 2019, the American economy registered its longest period of expansion, but the expansion was anemic. The country's economy also hit a record thirteen straight years with less than 3 percent growth of real GDP. And while the US economy created 20 million jobs, they were mostly low-wage and part-time in a world of workers looking for full-time employment.[4]

At its core, twenty-first-century capitalism suffers from what economists call a deep crisis of overaccumulation—an overconcentration of capital that cannot find outlets for reinvestment. In a system dependent on expansion to overcome cyclical crises of overproduction, the absence of new investment frontiers is one of the major sources of global economic stagnation. To circumvent crisis in the short-term, capitalists invested heavily in consumption markets with guaranteed short-run returns. Writing during the pandemic, David Harvey observed that this "instantaneous consumerism required massive infrastructural investments in airports and airlines, hotels and restaurants, theme parks and cultural events, etc. This site of capital accumulation is now dead in the water."[5]

As the ratio of capital investment to profit has declined over the last fifty years, corporations have increased their profits, in part, by relying on an army of low-paid, part-time workers and by slashing benefits like healthcare. In the early decades of the twenty-first century, US workers are more exploited, more debt-ridden, and making less money than they were in the 1970s. And while Black American workers, and other workers of color, like Puerto Ricans, have always faced low wages and Depression-era conditions, white workers have seen their livelihoods decline significantly as well. The

---

4   Pat Evans, "11 Mind Blowing Facts about the US Economy," *Business Insider*, April 10, 2019, https://markets.businessinsider.com/news/stocks/us-economy-facts-2019-4-1028101291.

5   David Harvey, "Anti-Capitalist Politics in the Time of COVID-19," *Jacobin Magazine*, March 2020, https://jacobinmag.com/2020/03/david-harvey-coronavirus-political-economy-disruptions.

wages of white males with only a high school diploma declined by 9 percent during the eighteen-year period between 1996–2014—a far cry from the experience of white workers with a high school diploma between 1945 and the early 1970s.[6]

Over the course of this fifty-year period of economic decline, white Americans have contended with another "social injury"—a perceived fall from the top of the country's racial hierarchy. For them, the advent of economic hardship coincided with the growing presence of people of color, gays and lesbians and women in the country's public, economic, and political life—a consequence of the gains of the civil rights, women's, and 1960s social movements. The perceived rising fortunes of these Others flouted their sense of white superiority. This reality, which shattered the American Dream, produced a profound existential meltdown, an identity crisis with macabre consequences. White men in America are disproportionately dying of drug overdoses, alcohol poisoning, and suicide. Princeton researchers call these "deaths of despair," which also includes, "a slowdown in progress against mortality from heart disease and cancer, the two largest killers in middle age."[7]

In the United States, the media have masterfully channeled the extraordinary social alienation and tensions produced by this level of inequality through spectacle TV—morning show "poverty porn" stereotyping the poor in the 1980s and 1990s and, in the first two decades of the twenty-first century, reality TV (Trump's *The Apprentice* and *The Real Housewives* franchise). Politicians of both parties and the nation's parroting corporate media deflected social tensions by erecting straw-man policy debates in the 1980s and 1990s against drugs, welfare, and crime that demonized and blamed Black Americans and immigrants from Mexico and Latin America for America's social problems. They also channeled Protestant work ethic propaganda—the notion that, unlike hard-working white Americans, Black people are lazy and undeserving of the franchise and their advances in

6   John Coder and Gordon Green, "Working Class Males Falling Behind," *Household Trends Statistical Brief*, Press Release, 2016, Sentier Research. See also, "Comparing Earnings of White Males by Education for Selected Age Cohorts: High School vs. College Graduates," October 2016, Sentier Research. See Tami Luhby, "Working class white men make less than they did in 1996," *CNN Money*, October 5, 2016, https://money.cnn.com/2016/10/05/news/economy/working-class-men-income/.

7   Anne Case and Sir Angus Deaton, "Rising morbidity and mortality in midlife among white non-Hispanic Americans in the 21st century," Proceedings of the National Academy of Sciences of the United States, November 2, 2015, 1–6.

the polity—a recycled Reconstruction-era trope. Late-twentieth-century Democrats added to the conversation with the "super-predator" assignation in criminology.

Psychoanalyst and social psychologist Erich Fromm offered perspective on the social infrastructure that fuels the white-supremacist perspective. He wrote, "a society that lacks the means to provide adequately for the majority of its members, or a large proportion of them, must provide these members with a narcissistic satisfaction of the malignant type if it wants to prevent dissatisfaction among them. For those who are economically and culturally poor, narcissistic pride in belonging to the group is the only and often a very effective source of satisfaction."[8]

History that should frighten us

Many American journalists, pundits, and academics have recoiled from interpretations that linked the Trump phenomenon to a creeping fascism because they lack familiarity with the period of American history that most closely resembles the dynamics of fascism that we see now: namely, the period in which the former slaveholders and their allies reacted against the social gains made by Black people during Reconstruction.[9]

What exactly was at stake? To understand this, we must grasp the magnitude of slavery as an economic system. First and foremost, American slavery was an economic system concerned with production—of cotton, tobacco, rice, and indigo—valuable as a means of exchange in the world market.[10] Life was brutal in the US South for the four million enslaved Africans. By the mid-nineteenth century, their labor produced the second wealthiest society humanity had seen, second only to the British Empire.

When the full participation of enslaved Africans in the theater of war finally defeated the South in the Civil War, the old slave-owning class, which

---

8   Erich Fromm, *The Heart of Man: It's Genius for Good and Evil* (Brooklyn: American Mental Health Foundation, 2010 [1964]), 79.

9   The US did not lack its own manifestations of 1930s fascism, see Michael Joseph Roberto, *The Coming of the American Behemoth: The Origins of Fascism in the United States, 1920–1940* (New York: Monthly Review Press, 2018). The rise of McCarthyism drew on similar forces, see Cedric Belfrage, *The American Inquisition, 1945–1960* (Indianapolis: Bobbs-Merrill, 1973). What I contend is that the underlying drive was set in motion much earlier; see also Jonathan Scott (ed.), *US Fascism Comes to the Surface*, special issue of *Socialism and Democracy*, Vol. 22, No. 2 (July 2008).

10 Barbara Jeanne Fields, "Slavery, Race and Ideology in the USA," *New Left Review* 181 (1990): 95–118.

had earlier seceded from the Union, seemed finished—trapped in an irreversible political and economic crisis. Its system was ostensibly overturned. But, because Presidential Reconstruction set lenient terms for rejoining the Union, the old planter class kept its foothold in society.[11] Ironically, the class that lost the war was invited back to help remake the new society.

This leniency had consequences which continue to the current day. The old planters immediately launched a bloodthirsty counterrevolution, with the object of regaining political power and control of Black labor to return the Southern economy to as close a replica as possible to slavery. Even though their plantations suffered destruction, they still owned most of the land. In the face of economic collapse, the old slavocracy achieved dominance through the consolidation and concentration of its plantation holdings: In Marengo County, Alabama, 10 percent of landowners came to control 63 percent of real estate.[12] To legislate in their interest, they joined both the Republican and the Democratic parties, eventually dominating both by disenfranchising the freedmen.

Still, the old slavocracy faced an increasingly confident and organized challenge from formerly enslaved people, whose consciousness had been transformed by their participation in the US Civil War. And while most of them were forced to work for the old planter class in an economy that continued to be tied to cotton production, they fought fiercely for what they believed they deserved. They refused to work daylight to dusk as they had under slavery. They demanded wages, not provisions, and went on strike for better terms of hire. The fierce strike of Atlanta laundresses in 1881 best captures what the old planters were up against. Influenced by the revolutionary consciousness of an era wherein enslaved Africans struggled for liberation in the context of the Civil War, the washerwomen struck not only for higher wages but to gain control of production—namely, to be allowed to work from their home. They sought to avoid employer supervision, to be able to tend to family and children during work hours, and to collectivize their labor alongside other washerwomen. They won.[13]

---

11 Eric Foner, *Reconstruction: America's Unfinished Revolution, 1863–1877* (New York: Harper Perennial Modern Classics, Revised Edition, 2014).

12 Jack Bloom, *Class, Race, and the Civil Rights Movement: The Changing Political Economy of Southern Racism* (Bloomington: Indiana University Press, 1987), 18–58.

13 Tera Hunter, *To 'Joy My Freedom: Southern Black Women's Lives and Labor after the Civil War* (Cambridge, MA and London: Harvard University Press, 1997).

In order to consolidate political power and regain control of the land and Black labor, the South's old ruling class would have to snuff out epic examples of autonomy by Black people like these, which modeled alternative modes of organizing production. In the face of the freedmen's confidence and growing power, the old planters crafted a multipronged campaign of white supremacy. The Ku Klux Klan (KKK) became the terrorist wing of this campaign, recruiting white people of all classes as its foot soldiers. For the next century, white Southerners carried out pogroms against Black people as a matter of communal ritual. These campaigns of terror were animated by the logic that white people were victims of Black aggression, threatened by the possible takeover of a mongrel race. Their real purpose, however, was to control Black labor by keeping the freedmen in their place tied to cotton production on rented land, away from potential alliances with poor white farmers.[14]

The KKK was the most extreme form of white supremacist repression. Control was also wielded in the courts, through the Black Codes, a series of laws passed during reconstruction whose purpose was to contain Black life and subdue Black labor. The laws denied Black people the right to vote, to serve on state militias, testify against whites, and serve on juries. They also criminalized and imprisoned the freedmen for loitering, failure to pay their debts, and for failing to hold to work contracts with the old planter class. To save the state the expense of imprisonment, the labor of the imprisoned was auctioned and the first bid given to the prisoner's former master.

As ideology, white supremacy won over poor whites to a cross-class alliance. It offered them a psychological wage, conferring onto them the sense of superiority over Black people.[15] It erected a patriarchal society where the defense and protection of white womanhood—ever threatened by the alleged predatory sexuality of Black men—became the charge of white men.[16] And with the help of the Daughters of the Confederacy, the old planter class rewrote the history of the US Civil War.

In America, the past is prologue. And in the era of Donald Trump, we hear the echo of the slavocracy's counterrevolution. His propaganda fits well with the ideology that the keepers of the Old South have fed generations of

---

14 Charles M Payne, *I've Got the Light of Freedom: The Organizing Tradition and the Mississippi Freedom Struggle* (Berkeley: University of California Press, 1995).

15 W.E.B. Du Bois, *Black Reconstruction in America* (New York: Harcourt, Brace and Company, 1935).

16 Timothy B. Tyson, *Radio Free Dixie: Robert F. Williams and the Roots of Black Power* (Chapel Hill: University of North Carolina Press, 2001).

school children: that the Confederacy fought a valiant fight for the dignity of a glorious South; that Southerners were victims of Northern tyranny, abuse, and corruption; and that the North forsook those of their own "glorious" race to give the crown jewels to an allegedly criminally minded, inept, undeserving race whose men pose a threat to white women.

The mass recruitment of citizens in the execution of Southern race terror and the legal character of US race-based citizenship and immigration policy inspired Nazis to travel to the United States in the 1930s, on official business, to study the country's race law and culture.[17]

If active buy-in from and participation of large self-deputized sectors of the civilian population is a lynchpin of fascism, the entire history of the United States has well prepared it for the advent of the protofascist currents of today. As historian Roxanne Dunbar-Ortiz shows, in the face of Native American resistance and rebellions by enslaved Africans, the colonial governments of what later became the United States made gun ownership compulsory among white men and women of all classes. Seventeenth-century Virginia, for example, advanced loans to those who could not afford to buy personal weapons and required that men carry arms with them to work and church or be fined. White citizens were also compelled by law to serve in self-organized militias and later slave patrols. In essence, the colonial governments deputized Euro-American residents to secure the borders and integrity of the nascent American state. Before long, war against Indigenous peoples gave way to "savage war"—the targeting and killing of Native American men, women, and children by self-organized militias—a practice that continued until the last of the Western territories were settled in the late nineteenth century.[18]

The country also has a profoundly conservative citizenry that's been raised on anticommunism and subjected to Americanization campaigns throughout the twentieth century. Many live in remote rural settings and after the 1950s most were suburbanized, atomized in private homes, living in fear of Black people and Black crime, raised on a strong diet of middle-class individualism, and living with high levels of indebtedness.[19]

---

17 James Q. Whitman, *Hitler's American Model: The United States and the Making of Nazi Race Law* (Princeton: Princeton University Press, 2017).

18 Roxanne Dunbar-Ortiz, *Loaded: A Disarming History of the Second Amendment* (San Francisco: City Lights Books, 2018).

19 Lisa McGirr, *Suburban Warriors: The Origins of the New American Right* (Princeton: Princeton University Press, 2001).

We recognize the 1960s for the many ways the decade's struggles civilized the country, expanded the meaning of freedom for historically oppressed people, and popularized critiques of US government and foreign policy. But the 1960s also brought dramatic government-sponsored violence in the theater of war and against dissidents at home, which set the country along the dangerous path we are on today. Under Robert McNamara, the US Secretary of Defense, the military mandated "kill ratios" in Vietnam that pressed American soldiers to kill any Vietnamese in sight. We dropped napalm and more bombs in Vietnam than were dropped by all sides combined during World War II. War policy skirted genocide. Unlike the founding days of the nation that witnessed the genesis of savage war, acts of resistance from different sectors of society including the military exposed these war crimes and challenged standards of acceptable conduct.[20]

At home, the police murders of dozens of Black Panthers rivaled the rampages of Latin American dictators. The FBI recruited citizen-agents on a mass scale to disrupt organizations fighting to expand the meaning and experience of democracy for women, racialized people, and the poor. In spring 1969, the Black Panther Party sounded the alarm: they held an anti-fascism conference in Oakland. In part, it was a response to the ruthless and homicidal character of state-sponsored violence. Features of this repression have been normalized since then in other less obvious ways, through prison and police expansion and the mass employment of Americans in the carceral industry, the third largest employer in the nation.[21]

A confluence of American exceptionalism and the suppression and rewriting of history has left the nation clueless about the extent of its barbarism. This leaves it ill-equipped to fend off the rise of a fascist leader, especially in the context of economic and social crisis. The only thing that can save us is a political movement that identifies the root cause of social antagonisms and, on that basis, radically transforms society.

---

20 On military resistance, see: Christian G. Appy, *Working Class War: American Combat Soldiers and Vietnam* (Chapel Hill: University of North Carolina Press, 1993); Jonathan Neale, *The American War: Vietnam, 1960–1975* (London: Bookmarks, 2001); Terry Wallace, *Bloods: Black Veterans of the Vietnam War, An Oral History* (New York: Ballantine Books,1985); and David Zeiger's 2005 documentary, *Sir! No Sir!* (Displaced Films, 2005).

21 See Mumia Abu-Jamal and Johanna Fernández (eds.), *The Roots of Mass Incarceration in the US: Locking Up Black Dissidents and Punishing the Poor*, special issue of *Socialism and Democracy* 28, no. 3 (November 2014).

CHAPTER FOUR

Reparative Futurities

Postcolonial Materialities and the Ovaherero and Nama Genocide[1]

Zoé Samudzi

At the end of May 2021, the German government announced it would finally recognize its early-twentieth-century genocide of the Ovaherero and Nama people in what was then German South-West Africa (present-day Namibia). After a rejected compensation offer of €10 million (USD $11.8 million) in 2020, the long-awaited recognition would be accompanied by €1.1 billion (USD $1.3 billion) paid "to existing aid programs over 30 years," which calculates to roughly the same amount of annual development funding that Germany has given Namibia since its independence in 1990. The aid—which emphatically should not be considered as reparations—would include infrastructural projects and €50 million (nearly USD $60 million) "towards setting up a foundation for reconciliation between the two states."[2] The deal was born out of bilateral negotiations between the German and Namibian governments but with the notable omission of Ovaherero and Nama traditional leaders. Representatives of the affected communities have rejected this deal, including late Ovaherero Paramount Chief Vekuii Rukoro who described it as "an insult," a fair assessment of the crafty discursive transformation of ongoing disbursements of development aid into a grand conciliatory gesture.[3]

---

1 This piece is a merging of two previously published essays: (1) "Reparative Futurities: Thinking from the Ovaherero and Nama Genocide," originally published in the July–August 2020 "Reparations" issue of *The Funambulist*; and (2) "In Absentia of Black Study," published in May 2021 as part of a series of responses to Dirk Moses' essay "The German Catechism" (referred to as "The Catechism Debate") curated by Jennifer Evans for *The New Fascism Syllabus*.

2 Philip Oltermann, "Germany Agrees to Pay Namibia €1.1bn Over Historical Herero-Nama Genocide," *The Guardian*, May 28, 2021, https://www.theguardian.com/world/2021/may/28/germany-agrees-to-pay-namibia-11bn-over-historical-herero-nama-genocide.

3 Caroline Copely, "Germany apologises for colonial-era genocide in Namibia," *Reuters*, May 28, 2021, https://www.reuters.com/world/africa/

This alleged deal, which has been celebrated by many Germans as a political and moral success, arrived during a potentially paradigm-shifting debate about German statecraft. On one side rests the insistence on a genocide exceptionalism, a singularity of Germany's genocide of German, Polish, and other European Jews; and on the other, there exist various articulations of a historical relationship between the genocidal violences of German imperialism and those committed in Europe during World War II. This continuity thesis describes not only the shared characteristics of the Ovaherero and Nama genocide and the Nazi Holocaust, but the multiply deployed racialist concepts and hierarchies of *Lebensraum* [living space/living room] and *Rassenschande* [racial defilement] as justification for antimiscegenation and racial separation; and the mechanics of genocidal harm in the use of forced labor camps, summary executions of women and children, sexual violence, and mass deaths by starvation and enslaved labor. (The continuity thesis, however, does not hold that German violence in Namibia was "practice" or a "rehearsal" for Nazi violence in Europe: anti-Black violence is an end game and politic in itself, and history—i.e., Germany's attempted annihilation of European Jews—is not inevitable.) There is a strange sentimentalism attached to insistences on genocide uniqueness: there has been some deliberate imputation of rhetorical red herrings and unmade intellectual claims (for example, the idea that structural relationality or continuity is synonymous with causation)[4] that betrays disciplinary and epistemic shortcomings and investments alike. The admission of responsibility is hardly synonymous with an apology.

Germany began its colonization of Berlin Conference-acquired South-West Africa in 1884. In its Southern African colony, Germany strove to internationalize its *Lebensraum* and create an outpost "that did not have to shy away from a comparison with the German homeland": Germanness as a national expression would be revitalized and strengthened through overseas expansion where racial separation could be more easily maintained.[5]

---

germany-officially-calls-colonial-era-killings-namibia-genocide-2021-05-28/.

4 For a conception of collectivized memory as "multidirectional" (i.e., "as subject to ongoing negotiation, cross-referencing, and borrowing; as productive and not privative") rather than competitive and zero-sum, see Michael Rothberg's *Multidirectional Memory: Remembering the Holocaust in the Age of Decolonization* (Stanford: Stanford University Press, 2009).

5 Wilke Sandler, "'Here Too Lies Our *Lebensraum*': Colonial Space as German Space," in *Heimat, Region, and Empire: Spatial Identities Under National Socialism*, ed.

A production of racial geography through genocide is inhered within *Lebensraum* and the romantic nationalist ideals that characterized imperial German (and then Nazi) settler expansionism—"living space," after all, is incomplete without a corresponding *Entfernung* [removal] in whatever manner the specific racialized national project entailed. Germany's settler expansion in Africa was marked chiefly by the desire to establish dominion over land, which necessitated deterritorialization. In classic settler form, the arrival of Germans and competition over land quickly demanded the elimination of native peoples.[6]

The German campaign of racial extermination in the 1904–1908 Herero Wars saw the devastating elimination of 80 percent of Ovaherero people and over half of the Nama. Examining the scientific afterlife of this genocide via anti-Blackness and its relationalities with other racializing frames and practices enables better understanding of the prevailing imperial structure within which both Wilhelmene and Nazi racecraft were enacted via *Lebensraum*. In looking at the work of influential anthropologist Eugen Fischer, for example, his study of the mixed-race communities in Rehoboth came to widely influence Germany's antimiscegenation policy: from the criminalization of mixed-race marriages in the German colonies and metropole,[7] to the *jus sanguinis*-based 1913 Nationality Law,[8] to the moral panics around the mixed-race children of French colonial soldiers and

---

Claus-Christian W. Szejnmann and Maiken Umbach (London: Palgrave Macmillan, 2012), 148–165.

6 The relationship between settlers and genocide is most classically explicated by Patrick Wolfe in "Settler Colonialism and the Elimination of the Native" [in the *Journal of Genocide Research*, Vol. 8, No. 4 (2006): 387–409.] He writes: "The logic of elimination not only refers to the summary liquidation of Indigenous people, though it includes that. . . . Negatively, it strives for the dissolution of native societies. Positively, it erects a new colonial society on the expropriated land base—as I put it, settler colonizers come to stay: invasion is a structure not an event" (388).

7 See Krista Molly O'Donnell, "The First *Bestazungskinder*: Afro-German Children, Colonial Childrearing Practices, and Racial Policy in German Southwest Africa, 1890–1914" (2005) and "The Talk of Genocide, the Rhetoric of Miscegenation: Notes on Debate in the German Reichstag Concerning Southwest Africa, 1904–14" (1998) by Helmut Walser Smith.

8 For more on the implications of the Nationality Law for Germanness/German citizenship as whiteness, see: Fatima El-Tayeb, "'Blood Is a Very Special Juice'*: Racialized Bodies and Citizenship in Twentieth-Century Germany" (1999); Anil Merih, "No More Foreigners? The Remaking of German Naturalization and Citizenship Law, 1990–2000" (2005); and Marc Morjé Howard, "The Causes and Consequences of Germany's New Citizenship Law" (2008).

white German women,[9] to his influence on Adolf Hitler and the creation of the 1935 Nuremberg Laws, which codified Nazism's own regime of anti-miscegenation. The transmutation of racial frames from South-West Africa to the lands and populations of Eastern Prussia[10] permits a tracking of the trajectory of Germanness' calcification as whiteness: German citizenship's preclusion of Blackness and Jewishness and other "racial impurities" necessitated hygiene science as a tool for population management, enforced segregations, and then, necessarily, genocide. Writing on antisemitism in the French empire, Dorian Bell refers to the "tendency of racializing logics to change scales in an effort to resolve contradictions internal to the logics themselves" as *racial scalarity*, which can duly be understood as the ways that "it was as possible for race to produce space as for space to mediate race."[11]

Engagements with Germany's colonial genocide bring into focus a fundamental historiographic tension between the exceptionalization of the Nazi crimes against Jews, Roma and Sinti peoples, and other communities during World War II, and some conceptualization of a political continuity or shared relational frame within which both German South-West African and European genocides can be considered. Focusing on anti-Blackness as a core of the trajectory of German statecraft (i.e., the defining and refining of what constitutes the German citizen) underscores what Michelle Wright describes as *epiphenomenal time*, a "'now,' through which the past, present, and future are always interpreted" through a rejection of "*direct*, or *linear*, causality."[12] There needn't be a claim of causality for a meaningful acknowledgment that Germany's colonial ambition folded itself into post-World War I politics in the metropole, that the genocide of the Ovaherero and Nama people brought mass extermination into the arsenal of (bio/

---

9   See: Tina M. Campt, Pascal Grosse, and Yara-Colette Lemke-Muniz de Faria, "Blacks, Germans, and the Politics of Imperial Imagination, 1920–60" (1998); Iris Wigger, "'Against the Laws of Civilization': Race, Gender and Nation in the International Racist Campaign Against the 'Black Shame'" (2002); Julia Roos, "Nationalism, Racism and Propaganda in Early Weimar Germany: Contradictions in the Campaign against the 'Black Horror on the Rhine'" (2012) and "Racist Hysteria to Pragmatic Rapprochement? The German Debate about Rhenish 'Occupation Children,' 1920–30" (2013).

10 Sandler, "'Here Too Lies Our *Lebensraum*.'"

11 Dorian Bell, *Globalizing Race: Antisemitism and Empire in French and European Culture* (Evanston, IL: Northwestern University Press, 2018), 7–9.

12 Michelle Wright, *Physics of Blackness: Beyond the Middle Passage Epistemology* (Minneapolis: University of Minnesota Press, 2015), 4.

thanato) political possibility, or that Nazi *Lebensraum* had markedly settler colonial characteristics. It is the Césaireian notion that the machinations of Hitlerism were fundamental to European coloniality: that imperialism yielded fascism, and that Hitler's crimes were the enactments of "colonialist procedures" on the European continent that had previously been reserved for racialized subjects.[13] More pressing than contestations about whether the German path from Windhoek to Auschwitz was a direct, indirect, or nonexistent one is the inconsistency with which experiences of genocide are regarded. Despite colonialism acting as the foundation for Raphael Lemkin's coining of the term—he was influenced significantly by the Ottoman Turkish genocide of the empire's Armenian, Assyrian, and Greek populations, as well as Spanish colonization in the Americas[14]—there is little space for considerations or indictments of European colonialism itself as mass violence/collective punishment or genocide-producing.[15] As we debate whether Nazi genocide is exceptional or historically connected, the victims of Germany's prior genocide are presented an insulting and undignified bare minimum: survivor communities are expected to accept this rhetorical recognition without meaningful (i.e., direct) compensation despite their long held maxim that there actually *cannot* be recognition without reparations.

Reparations discourses articulate a grammar of futurity: not simply a world that does not exist, but a world that *could* exist through attempts to repair historical harm and trauma. The imagining of hypotheticals, the meaningful address of genocidal harm, always demands an ontological shift. Because the world that accommodates a reparation—a wound remedy demanded by an aggrieved party—is not a world that presently exists, it is one that has to be created.

---

13 Aimé Césaire, *Discourses on Colonialism*, trans. Joan Pinkham (New York: Monthly Review Press, 2000), 36.

14 Daniel Marc Segesser and Myriam Gessler, "Raphael Lemkin and the international debate on the punishment of war crimes (1919–1948)," in *The Origins of Genocide: Raphael Lemkin as a Historian of Mass Violence*, ed. Dominik Schaller and Jürgen Zimmerer (London: Routledge, 2009); A. Dirk Moses, *The Problems of Genocide: Permanent Security and the Language of Transgression* (Cambridge, UK: Cambridge University Press, 2021), 136–168.

15 Dominik J. Schaller, "Raphael Lemkin's View of European Colonial Rule in Africa: Between Condemnation and Admiration," *Journal of Genocide Research* 7, no. 4 (2005): 531–538.

To understand the political character, national ethos, and development path that eventually yielded the brutalities of Nazism's genocidal violence, one ought to begin with the first materialization of *Lebensraum*. The first iteration of this settler colonial "living space" coupled territorial expansion with a biologization of Germanness as superior whiteness contra, here, to the barbarism of uncivilized Africans who held no legible land tenure or claim to this *German* land. In understanding *Lebensraum* as a land-based definition of German self and racialized other, one can conceptualize Blackness as not simply a thing being defined, but also in the "*when* and *where* it is being imagined, defined, and performed and in what locations both figurative and literal."[16] The glaring absence in this debate around continuity is that of Black people themselves: the shocking deprioritization and disinterest in both living and dead Black people, the abstracted treatments of African/Black people as subjects of historical contemplation when they comprise communities still demanding recompense for their suffering. What is the function of depoliticizing attempted extermination as simply an "ideological" matter as though there are not, per the machinations of the Westphalian system, clear political motivations for othering, demonizing, and attempting to exterminate entire peoples? What if this story were to begin with Ovaherero and Nama survivor-descendant communities rejecting the deal rather than that critical rejection being relegated to an end-of-story afterthought in Western commentary? What if postcolonial African materialities comprised a major core of the debate rather than simply our interpretations of the violence of their oppressors? What if Ovaherero and Nama people were entrusted as suitably reliable narrators and we held their worldviews, historical interpretations, ongoing traumas, and calls of reparations as *our* defining truths?

In April 2019, while en route to Yerevan, Armenia I had a 24-hour layover in New York City. I emailed the American Museum of Natural History hoping to access the archival records of Ovaherero and Nama cultural artifacts and physical remains held by the museum. The remains were originally a part of Austrian anthropologist's Felix von Luschan's personal collection, which included thousands of skulls of different Indigenous peoples from around the world. He sold his collection to the museum at the beginning of the twentieth century, which doubled the size of its physical anthropology

---

16 Wright, *Physics of Blackness*, 2–3.

collection and positioned them as leaders in the field. Contrary to art historiography, "collecting is not separate from other foundational practices, procedures, institutions, concepts, and categories operative in the field of art shaped through imperialism," writes Ariella Aïsha Azoulay.[17] These human remains are caught in the convergence of eugenic science and hegemonic curatorial practice; the collection of Ovaherero and Nama skulls from genocide-era concentration camps lays bare relationships between extractive imperial processes and the formation of the museum.

Tony Bennett writes that the museum "cannot be adequately understood unless viewed in the light of a more general set of developments through which culture, in coming to be thought of as useful for governing, was fashioned as a vehicle for the exercise of new forms of power."[18] Because of the now-dismissed class action lawsuit brought against the German government by Ovaherero and Nama descendants of genocide survivors, the museum denied my request for access as well as additional information about when the collection would once again be accessible to the public. I contacted the Nama Traditional Leaders Association (henceforth, the NTLA) who were surprised to hear the museum had restricted archival access. Their answers to my questions about that institutional denial and their visions of/for justice made me realize that two major constituent parts of their struggle for reparations are time and land. The former pertains to the timescale created by Indigenous historiographies and memory, as well as the disparity between Indigenous time and colonial time:[19] between Indigenous phenomenologies and the German preclusion of Indigenous peoples from modernity, from the genocide as an event in the relatively near past rather than an ongoing dispossession and violence with resonance in the present.

---

17 Ariella Aïsha Azoulay, *Potential History: Unlearning Imperialism* (London and New York: Verso, 2019), 75–82.

18 Tony Bennett, *The Birth of the Museum: History, Theory, Politics* (London: Routledge, 1995), 19. Bennett's analysis of the coevolution of the prison and the museum in the "Exhibitionary Complex" (1988) aids in the triangulation of an international regime of carceral geography from the camp-prison(s) in German South-West Africa to the museum archives populated with the racist spoils of genocidal plunder: "The institutions comprising 'the exhibitionary complex,' by contrast, were involved in the transfer of objects and bodies from the enclosed and private domains in which they had previously been displayed (but to a restricted public) into progressively more open and public arenas where, through the representations to which they were subjected, they formed vehicles for inscribing and broadcasting the messages of power (but of a different type) throughout society" (74).

19 Giordano Nanni, *The Colonisation of Time: Ritual, Routine and Resistance in the British Empire* (Manchester: Manchester University Press, 2012).

In response to my questions, the collective of these representatives—the now late Gaob[20] Eduardo Afrikaner, Gaob Johannes Isaack, Gaob Petrus Simon Moses Kooper (chairman of the NTLA), Gaob Daniel Luipert, and Gaob David Hanse—expressed a sense of the enduringness of the genocide through the museum's refusal to repatriate cultural materials and apparent denial of access to information:

> As part of the universal human rights and heritage principle, heritage is considered to contribute to human well-being and capabilities. Therefore heritage rights would include the rights of self-determination, rights of access and management of one's heritage products, the rights of veto and the rights to accrue benefits, whether social, economic or spiritual. Cultural materials form an essential part of the genocide charges since the initial plan in the case of Namibia involved 'cultural genocide' leading to impoverishment. Denying access is therefore tantamount to perpetuation in violation of international mechanisms, the original sin of barbarism. . . . Considering that the information and the material evidence in question is a significant part of the Nama/Ovaherero cultural heritage, denying access amounts to manipulation and or interference with the content. It censors available data and by doing so wants to weaken us in our quest for restorative justice.
>
> It is critical that reliable sources of knowledge are available in order to prove the Nama and Ovaherero genocide which is currently still denied by both the German and Namibian governments. Archives [hold] massive human rights violations records that are important for ensuring accountability and conflict transformation. The denial of access to such information can only foster new conflict, cause further resentment and deny dealing with the past. If access is denied we cannot find common understanding of what has happened in the past and therefore cannot find common solutions for what should happen in the future. Archival records are also critical for the reparation process. Reparation however needs to be seen within the context of restorative justice which involves apologies, returning of human remains and archive collections, compensation for confiscated property, as well as symbolisms of memorialisation.[21]

---

20 The word "Gaob" means "captain" and denotes a position of community leadership.

21 Nama Traditional Leaders Association (NTLA), "Denial of Archival Materials," statement, June 7, 2019, Keetmanshoop, Namibia, https://35c940da-ccee-4f32-b54e-bd2ec9f51a57. filesusr.com/ugd/4fbf94_3535d029dc234db9903630405efd7049.pdf.

A critical part of Indigenous self-determination both within and beyond processes of reparation is the right to know: the right to, returning again to Azoulay, form a "nonimperial grammar" that is "not to be heard as scattered cries in an alienated world but as truth claims about stolen shared worlds."[22] It is a way of having existed in a distant past, continuing to exist in the present, and plotting an existence in the future—a life beyond the perpetual relegation of Indigeneity to pre-modernity and to the kind of functional extinction that strikes them from historical record. These restructurings of time are also picnoleptic as historical omissions, the mythologies and half or nontruths of imperial historiography, become exculpatory: "nothing has really happened, the missing time has never existed," and so genocidal processes and the communities they target are disappeared from the epistemic record.[23] This is reparation, further, as ontological and epistemological correction:

> The Nama and Ovaherero people have a right to know, and that right can be facilitated through access to information. The Updated Set of Principles for the Protection and Promotion of Human Rights to Action to Combat Impunity (2005) of the United Nations High Commission on Human Rights declares that victims of serious crimes have a right to know the truth about the violations. The descendants have a right to keep the injustice in their cultural memory so that they can make sense of their own history and identity which is bound up with their belongings. By denying access to material, we deny descendants the right to know, the right to their identity and the right to justice. Our knowledge of our history of oppression is part of our heritage. Therefore access to evidence and archival material concerning violations ought to be the duty of the institution. It would serve no constructive purpose to sink memory into the background because it only aggravates denial of justice.[24]

The land question plagues former settler colonies in Southern Africa despite at least two decades of Black majority rule. The land question is related to ancestralization in its foregrounding of the matter of

---

22 Azoulay, *Potential History*, 195–200.

23 Paul Virilio, *The Aesthetics of Disappearance*, trans. Philip Beitchman (Los Angeles: Semiotext(e), 2009), 11–19.

24 NTLA, "Denial of Archival Materials."

incarcerated ancestral remains that will someday, hopefully, be returned. Ancestralization speaks to the performance of traditional funerary practice, the transition of Indigenous dead from this life to the next, and the failure for the lives taken to receive any semblance of proper burial. It is not simply an anthropological phenomenon or alternative way of knowing studied from afar, but a metaphysical regime taken seriously as a means of contesting colonial/Christian understandings of death and that inform material-cultural-juridical arguments against the German state from whom the Ovaherero and Nama seek recompense for genocidal destruction.

The *Deutscher Museumsbund* [German Museums Association], for example, states that while people in charge of physical anthropological collections should be mindful of genealogical connections between remains and living community members, "from an ethnological perspective, memories of a deceased person fade after approximately four to five generations"— approximately 125 years.[25] While the organization states that this should only be a guideline in individual cases and dialogue should be sought in repatriation cases outside of this, these deadlines represent a scientistic political imposition of Western mathematics on an "ontological level,"[26] from the expressions of death tolls to financial compensation to a kind of statute of limitations on restitution claims and the quantification of presumed familial memory. From collecting specimens by grave robbing to forcing Indigenous women to scrape clean the skulls of the dead in concentration camps, these bones were used as evidence of European superiority and harvested to supply demand for eugenic research and display. Their return is deeply meaningful for the peoples to whom they belong, and they bear implications for cultural-national memory projects more generally.[27] While Blackness precludes humanity in a racial regime that, in Alexander Weheliye's words, "disciplines humanity into full humans,

---

25 Deutscher Museumsbund, "Recommendations for the Care of Human Remains in Museums and Collections," 2013, https://www.museumsbund.de/wp-content/uploads/2017/04/2013-recommendations-for-the-care-of-human-remains.pdf.

26 Diane M. Nelson, *Who Counts? The Mathematics of Death and Life After Genocide* (Durham: Duke University Press, 2015), 3–4.

27 See: Vilho Amukwaya Shigwedha, "The Return of Herero and Nama Bones from Germany: The Victims' Struggle for Recognition and Recurring Genocide Memories in Namibia" (2016); Nick Sprenger, Robert G. Rodriguez, and Ngondi A. Kamatuka, "The Ovaherero/Nama Genocide: A Case for an Apology and Reparations" (2017); Elise Pape, "Human Remains of Ovaherero and Nama: Transnational Dynamics in Post-Genocidal Restitutions" (2018); and, Jeremiah Garsha, "Expanding *Vergangenheitsbewältigung*? German Repatriation of Colonial Artifacts and Human Remains" (2019).

not-quite-humans, and nonhumans,"[28] repatriation and reinterment is a cultural affirmation of the individual-collective personhoods foundational to many continental African ways of knowing:[29]

> Skulls and human remains of Nama origin must be buried in Great Namaqualand in accordance with centuries old Nama religious customs. Even before Christianity, the Nama believed in the Supreme Being known by the name *Tsui//goab*. In Nama religion, He is the Creator of the entire universe and Giver of life to all creatures through His powerful Spirit. He has the power over rain, wind and all life forces. The Nama believed the human soul returns to its Master, the Creator Tsui//goab, upon a person's death. Equally the human body is created from soil of earth and thus must be returned to the soil. The graves in which the remains will be buried are marked extra ordinary into monuments as per Nama custom. In the Nama religion, the Messenger of Goodwill of Tsui//goab was named Haitsi Aibeb. He dies under extra ordinary circumstances and rose from death many times according to Nama folklore. His graves were turned into monuments made of rocks, as people who passed by each grave said praises to Him and added another rock. Many of the graves are still found in Great Namaqualand. According to Nama culture, the spirit of the deceased remains restless until it is returned to the soil from which it is made by the Creator. Keeping human remains in museums denies us our right to practice our customs.
>
> The skulls are the remains of our people and it is only culturally appropriate to have it handed over to us for the purpose of a dignified burial. As for the archival materials they are our valuable material and we have the right to claim them. It is important to prove to the world

---

28 Alexander G. Weheliye, *Habeas Viscus: Racializing Assemblages, Biopolitics, and Black Feminist Theories of the Human* (Durham: Duke University Press, 2014), 4, 21–32.

29 In addition to fighting for political and cultural rights denied by racializing assemblages precluding them from full humanity and citizenship, Indigenous Africans duly prioritize the collective as a reflection-extension of the self, i.e., individual personhood is attained through incorporation by others in the community/society. In "Person and Community in African Traditional Thought" (1984), Ifeanyi Menkiti writes, "A crucial distinction thus exists between the African view of man and the view of man found in Western thought: in the African view it is the community which defines the person as person, not some isolated static quality of rationality, will, or memory." This is one of the ontological and affective tensions at the heart of the repatriation of Ovaherero and Nama human remains: the archive-incarcerated material objects used for Western edification represent existential wounds to Indigenous communities from which the remains are taken and withheld.

that Germany did not find us in a static state, we too were in motion in tandem with the then-prevailing historical conditions. *We are bound morally, socially and spiritually to ensure the burial of the remains of our families* and no individual, institution or government has the right to keep the remains.[30]

Intimately related to the burial of repatriated remains in familial and ancestral community lands is the matter of land reform. In the present, the land question is not only about the release and redistribution of land from the structures of racialized ownership but also the situation of Indigenous peoples in the postcolonial/independent nation-states into which they are being assimilated (or against which they are resisting assimilation) and the role of that state in mediating reparative processes of which affected communities are not a part. Because political and economic priorities of the state generally take precedence over justice for aggrieved peoples, we must constantly remind ourselves of and return to the latter's desires:

> Our watch word is 'Nothing about us without us.' Firstly, representation on the negotiating table is of paramount importance so that the content and the process for an apology and reparation are agreed upon as *a priori* matter. For the NTLA repentance and forgiveness are the starting point. Instead, we have only witnessed arrogance on the part of the German government. This would mean the current process must cease in order to restart in new mode. The NTLA subscribes to some fundamental principles of restorative [justice] which include the fact *the victim communities must be central to the process of defining the harm done and how it must be repaired....* The victim communities must be actively involved in holding the offender accountable and ensure opportunities for the offender to make amends. In line with the 2006 Resolution taken by the Parliament of Namibia, *the government must merely oversee a process driven by victim.*[31]

The land question forces a consideration of what exactly is understood by "Indigenous." All peoples were designated as a "native" foil to whiteness during colonialism, and that native identity as related to land became particularly apparent in the creation of apartheid-era Bantustans, in which

---

30 NTLA, "Denial of Archival Materials." [Emphasis mine.]

31 NTLA, "Denial of Archival Materials." [Emphasis mine.]

South-West Africa was administered as an unofficial province of South Africa. The Odendaal Commission (formally, the Commission of Enquiry into South-West Africa Affairs), whose findings were announced in 1964 and implemented in 1968, created the infrastructure for the two-tiered development of white settler society and native societies segregated to their respective homelands.[32] As with apartheid in South Africa, land was familiarly territorialized into Hereroland, Namaland, Ovamboland, and so on. Although every native group was in some way subjugated by the imperial German and then Afrikaner nationalist regimes, these universalized harms are not reflected in present ethnopolitical realities:

> For the Nama leaders, landlessness and political/economic/social marginalization is directly linked to genocide. Calls for the return of ancestral land and initial response of [the 2016] Namibian government amounted to trashing such calls, with utterances such as 'You don't eat land,' 'what ancestral land are you taking about?' and 'how do you want to hold present generations accountable for something they did not do?' These are sentiments of the same regime claiming to negotiate in the interest of victim[ized] communities. *There is deliberate refusal on the part of both governments to admit that landlessness of the Nama people is a structural issue never addressed by any regime. We shall remain resolute to regain our ancestral land, notwithstanding state tricks to render our people perpetually landless and poverty stricken for good. German genocide facilitated the structural loss of ancestral land, and therefore the two issues will not be separated.* . . To this effect, a comprehensive forensic audit of Namibia's resettlement program since independence is critical. In our book, ancestral land will remain the deal breaker to national unity and President Geingob holds the key: for his regime to resolve ancestral land honestly, or take responsibility for the looming disintegration of Namibia's first republic.
>
> As for Germany's denial of genocide, it amounts to selective morality with blatant racist undertones. What Imperial Germany did to the Nama and Ovaherero people was licensed by being white and European against Africa Nations. . . . They must own up to the deeds of their predecessors and come clear of it. The ongoing negotiations behind closed doors without acknowledged and authentic representation of victim

---

32 Robert Gordon, "How Good People Become Absurd: J. P. van S. Bruwer, the Making of Namibian Grand Apartheid and the Decline of Volkekunde," *Journal of South African Studies* 44 (2018): 103–105.

communities must stop. Exclusion violates victim centered principles of restorative justice and the resolution of parliament.[33]

Nama leadership, further, accuses the Namibian government not only of flouting a parliamentary resolution that formed the basis of the charges and reparations procedures against the German government, but of supplanting Nama and Ovaherero-specific needs but "by unilaterally appointing a 'special envoy' who by no means has any mandate from the Nama leaders and the Nama people to speak on their behalf."[34] This is what compels them to continuously state—both before and after the announced German intention to name its attempted exterminations as genocide—that the "Namibian [g]overnment is the first obstacle to genocide recognition and reparations, because *its approach allowed Germany to package the deal through increased bilateral development aid arrangements, thereby completely exonerating the German [g]overnment from the barbaric historical carnage left behind in Namibia*."[35]

Even the genocide's appeal to uniqueness—its chronological position, its firstness in the twentieth-century genocide canon—cannot negate the foundational Westphalian impulse to undermine Indigenous sovereignty and political claims. The competing political interests of German-Namibian bilateralism and the self-determining maxim of "nothing about us without us" necessitates consideration of how the Black/African deaths necessary to sustain Euromodernity could possibly "constitute [the] acute crisis of recognition"[36] demanded to recognize Ovaherero and Nama suffering as legible enough to compel the payment of reparations. Because of the transnational nature of the genocide's afterlife, and because of how imperial dispossession in Namibia was perpetuated by and ossified through apartheid governance and then the independent Namibian state, bilateral recognitions represent a collusion between complicit (to significantly varying degrees and registers) nation-states. In another statement, Lazarus Kairabeb (writing on behalf of the NTLA) described how bilateralism's preclusion of affected communities positions them as a "legal obstruction"

---

33 NTLA, "Denial of Archival Materials." [Emphasis mine.]

34 NTLA, "Denial of Archival Materials."

35 NTLA, "Denial of Archival Materials." [Emphasis mine.]

36 Zoé Samudzi, "Paradox of Recognition: Genocide and Colonialism," *Postmodern Culture* 31, no. 1 (2020), https://doi.org/10.1353/pmc.2020.0028.

and "provides room for the creation of symbiotic relations, to exonerate the Germans from the historical guilt ... which gives the Namibian government complete control over the process for apology and the managing of the resource[s] for restitution."[37]

Although financial restitution is an important part of Ovaherero and Nama reparation demands, the reparative futurity articulated by the NTLA and other Nama and Ovaherero organizations is a sovereignty-affirming restorative justice that reverses the century of enclosure and loss of ancestral land initiated by German settler colonialism. Where acknowledgment of genocide unfolds before a passive and spectatorial international community and where retrospective recognition is avoided because of its political inconvenience, inaction or incomplete acknowledgment is tantamount to a kind of genocide denial. This is an especially damning charge considering Germany's statements throughout the lawsuit's proceedings: how they described well-documented genocidal phenomena as "alleged" seizures of land and livestock, murders of tens of thousands of people, systematic rape, and uses of concentration camps.[38] It is common legal parlance to use "alleged" in describing contested acts or violations that have not been litigated and/or convicted in a court of law. However, law and historiography exist in different domains of facticity because the existing historical consensus of a phenomenon is neither legally binding nor obligating. Historians' agreement that Germany *was* responsible for the attempted extermination of Ovaherero and Nama people is not the same as the conclusion of responsibility from a legal ruling or international tribunal. Thus, Germany's use of "alleged" in describing documented and widely affirmed genocides—violences largely confirmed by the government in subsequent political gestures towards financial settlement and acknowledgment—is attempting to exploit these semantic ambiguities and slippages. It is attempting to expedite reconciliation without process, without ever having delivered an apology. Reparations for the Nama and Ovaherero, thus, demands a twofold reconciliation of these past and ongoing harms in order to meaningfully address the materialities of affected communities.

---

37 Nama Traditional Leaders Association (NTLA) statement, entitled "The Pockets of the SWAPO Government After Rewriting the Nama, Herero Genocide History of Namibia," May 18, 2021, Keetmanshoop, Namibia, https://35c940da-ccee-4f32-b54e-bd2ec9f51a57.filesusr.com/ugd/4fbf94_79b606414c8e4eadb1da416d50081bcb.pdf.

38 Brief for Defendant-Appellee. *Rukoro v. Federal Republic of Germany*, Second Circuit US Court of Appeals, Case 0:19-cv-0069, Document 69, 2019.

II. The Instabilities of Violence

CHAPTER FIVE

Left Alone with the Colony

Allan E. S. Lumba

To many in the Philippines, President Rodrigo Duterte's promise to establish peace and order through punitive justice appears a success. Since his 2016 election his popularity has steadily grown. In an October 2020 survey conducted by the polling agency *Pulse Asia*, Duterte reached an unprecedented approval rating of 91 percent. This placed him, according to one article, as the "world's most popular leader."[1] Human rights groups find this popularity shocking, especially as the unofficial estimates of extrajudicial killings have reached tens of thousands of deaths under Duterte. For some leftists, his attacks on international and domestic liberal institutions, derision of human rights organizations and other international bodies, and gleeful deployment of military, police, and vigilante violence all signal a move toward fascism.[2]

However, the supposed elusiveness of Duterte's ideological commitments has led only a handful of public intellectuals and journalists to describe his authoritarianism, and the populism that propelled him to power, as fascist. Indeed, since the beginning of his presidency, it has been solely the radical and revolutionary left—those in the streets protesting or those in the countryside waging an armed revolution—who have habitually used the term "fascist" to describe Duterte. Despite his violent attacks on civil society (particularly dissenting voices in the church and the media) and civility (he is willfully vulgar and profane), liberal critics in particular find Duterte politically slippery. Adding to his ideological ambiguity, the president has, at different times, claimed to be a socialist, a women's and Indigenous rights advocate, and an anti-imperialist.

---

1 Richard Javad Heydarian, "Why Duterte is the world's most popular leader," *Asia Times*, October 9, 2020, https://asiatimes.com/2020/10/why-duterte-is-the-worlds-most-popular-leader/.

2 Walden Bello, "Rodrigo Duterte: A Fascist Original," in *A Duterte Reader: Critical Essays on Rodrigo Duterte's Early Presidency*, ed. Nicole Curato (Ithaca: Cornell University Press, 2017), 77.

In this essay, Filipino authoritarianism is explored in its historical relation to fascism. Fascism is not a neat category of political ideology, but rather a historical reaction to the recurring threat of revolutionary decolonization and the chronic instability of a geopolitical system structured around capitalist empires. I examine the massive ideological and material investment of Filipino authoritarianism into the enforcement of punitive justice, and the unexpectedly durable popular libidinal investment in punitive justice; especially punishment deployed by "strongman" regimes upon the bodies of the vulnerable and marginalized. Tracing how US colonial authority in the Philippines was fundamentally dependent on the policing and punishment of real or imagined crimes, I then turn to how a nominally independent nation like the Philippines inherited this colonial structure of punitive justice, and why crimes against the state and crimes against moral norms are commonly blurred together. (Fascism, after all, operates through the legal and extralegal punishment of real or imagined radical threats to state order and moral norms.) Finally, I probe into how and why Duterte continues to gain support through his fascistic deployment of punitive justice.

When examining the interwar period (between WWI and WWII), there seems to be a connection between the emergence of fascism as a political assemblage and the counterdecolonization practices deployed by colonial states. Mass arrests and incarceration, brutal systemic torture, social death, and genocide were most notoriously meted out by fascist regimes in interwar Europe. However, as Aimé Césaire argues, fascist atrocities in the West were first put on spectacular display in the colonies. For the colonies, as Césaire declares, the rule of law and the moral norms of Western civilization were especially used to justify the kinds of white supremacist punishment of suspected criminals.[3] This recalls Fanon's assertion that the colonizer is fundamentally an "exhibitionist" preoccupied with the security and order of colonial society and is always already prepared to test brute force against the masses.[4] Yet this gratuitous force was not exceptional. As Angela Davis has argued, colonial systems were structured by the logics of punitive justice.[5]

---

3 Aimé Césaire, *Discourse on Colonialism* (New York: Monthly Review Press, 2000 [1950]), 36.

4 Frantz Fanon, *The Wretched of the Earth* (New York: Grove Press, 2004 [1963]), 17.

5 Angela Y. Davis, *Are Prisons Obsolete?* (New York: Seven Stories Press, 2003), 22.

This is not to say that fascism is simply the same as colonialism. Instead, I am interested in situating fascism within a world ruled by colonialisms. Fascisms that emerged during the 1920s and 1930s were a historically produced reaction to the tumultuous realignment of relations between capitalist empires and the critical mass of revolutionary decolonization movements across the planet during the interwar period.[6] Therefore, fascism was a reaction to the economic, geopolitical, and territorial imperial realignments caused by the Great War. On the other hand, fascism was a reaction to the globally shocking events of the revolutions in Mexico and Russia.[7] After these two world-shaping events, movements in the "darker nations" for decolonization would generate great stresses on capitalist empires and even greater anxieties within white colonizer societies, in particular during the 1920s and 1930s.[8]

Both fascists and liberals were correct to be nervous about possible worldwide decolonization. Indeed, throughout the colonies, a revolutionary internationalism was steadily growing from the end of the 1910s through the 1920s, one based on both communism and decolonization. In 1928, Crisanto Evangelista, one of the founders of the *Partido Komunista ng Pilipinas* (the first communist party of the Philippines, now called the PKP-1930 to distinguish it from the Communist Party of the Philippines, formed in 1969) argued: "the independence of the Filipino people is dependent on the problem and the fate of the other colonies and semi-colonies."[9] Evangelista's notion of Philippine decolonization was inextricably linked to present and pending global anticolonialisms. While organizing toward international revolution, the Filipino communist also saw the possibilities of working through a nationalist revolution within and against US empire and capital. For Evangelista, Philippine decolonization could act as a

---

6   In his introduction to *Discourse on Colonialism*, Robin D. G. Kelley writes of the critical mass of prominent Black radical thinkers during the 1940s and 1950s and how they debated fascism's relation to revolutionary forms of anticolonialism, antiracism, and anticapitalism. [Aimé Césaire, *Discourse on Colonialism*, 8.]

7   For more on how the Mexican Revolution and the Russian Revolution would reshape notions of self-determination during the interwar period, see Erez Manela, *The Wilsonian Moment: Self-Determination and the International Origins of Anticolonial Nationalism* (Oxford and New York: Oxford University Press, 2007).

8   For more on internationalisms from the colonial world, see Vijay Prashad, *The Darker Nations: A People's History of the Third World* (New York and London: The New Press, 2007).

9   Crisanto Evangelista, *Nasyonalismo Proteksiyonismo vs. Internasyonalismo Radikal* (Manila: K.A.P., 1928), 22.

vanguard for the Asian and Pacific world: "If we are freed, it would change the shape of colonialism in the world." He envisioned it leading to "an outbreak of fire that would burn and smolder inside the people of Taiwan and Korea to fight against Japan; the Indonesian against the Netherlands; in Indo-China against France and Portugal; the Indians, the Malaysians, and other English colonies against England."[10]

The possibility of revolutionary decolonization in the Philippines, however, did not first occur during the 1920s. In 1896, Filipino revolutionaries attempted to liberate the Philippines from three centuries of Spanish colonial rule. Two years later, Filipino revolutionaries would resist a US-led racial and genocidal war.[11] Policing and punishment would be fundamental to counterrevolutionary campaigns. After all, the pacification of both internal and external enemies was paramount to the paranoia characteristic of the occupying US colonial state, always concerned about potential disorders. In response to these conditions, American colonial authorities established the Philippine Constabulary (PC) in 1901.

Responsible for policing both civil and martial arenas, the PC was a crucial instrument of state punitive violence against vice and insurrection during a long and protracted colonial war. Moreover, the PC would become a powerful institution, outliving the official American colonial state, and deployed by Filipino authoritarians throughout the twentieth century. However, the PC is perhaps more powerful as a figure of the kinds of punitive logic that course through Filipino authoritarianisms and their popular support. Through the PC, policing did not differentiate between crimes against the state (such as sedition or treason) and crimes against the norms of civil society (such as drugs, gambling, and sex work).[12] Under this logic, any form of disorder—political or moral—could be subject to severe punishment, such as incarceration, torture, or death.[13]

Punitive violence was fundamentally necessary to Filipino

---

10 Evangelista, *Nasyonalismo Proteksiyonismo vs. Internasyonalismo Radikal*, 21.

11 On US colonialism in the Philippines as a "race war," see Paul A. Kramer, "Race-Making and Colonial Violence in the US Empire: The Philippine-American War as Race War," *Diplomatic History* 30, no. 2: 169. On US colonialism as anti-Filipino genocide, see Dylan Rodríguez, *Suspended Apocalypse: White Supremacy, Genocide, and the Filipino Condition* (Minneapolis: University of Minnesota Press, 2009).

12 Alfred McCoy, *Policing America's Empire: The United States, the Philippines, and the Rise of the Surveillance State* (Madison: The University of Wisconsin Press), 16.

13 Frank Golay, *Face of Empire: United States-Philippine Relations, 1898–1946* (Quezon City: Ateneo de Manila University Press, 1997), 125.

authoritarianism as the Philippines transitioned from US colonial possession to US Commonwealth in 1935, and finally to an independent Republic of the Philippines in 1946. The first strongman Filipino leader, Commonwealth president Manuel Quezon, would exploit the deep anxieties over social and moral disorders in civil society. Quezon regularly deployed anti-imperial rhetoric throughout his leadership. Outside of public vision, however, Quezon would actively collaborate with US colonial authorities to maintain political hegemony and power throughout the archipelago until his death in 1944.[14] To maintain political power and achieve national sovereignty, Quezon projected a sense of order and security throughout the 1930s, mainly by the intense policing of revolutionaries. It is telling that these anxieties about revolution were expressed during the Great Depression and the increasing rise of European and Asian fascisms. Indeed, during this moment of global economic and political crisis, Filipino politicians and the US War Department obsessed more over the spread of communism than fascism in the Philippines.[15] This is reflected · in the US Department of War's 1932 counterdecolonizaiton warning that Philippine independence "would merely invite chaos and revolution."[16]

Throughout the 1930s, American authorities, and later, the Quezon administration, would intensify punitive measures against potential "chaos and revolution." For instance, the years leading to the Commonwealth witnessed mass arrests of members of socialist, labor, and peasant organizations, and the outlawing of the Partido Komunista ng Pilipinas.[17] Punishment was meted out most spectacularly during a peasant rebellion in 1935. The *Sakdalistas*, an organization and social movement demanding immediate liberation and radical land redistribution, were violently suppressed by the PC. Dozens were killed, hundreds incarcerated, and

---

14 Alfred McCoy, "Global Populism: A Lineage of Filipino Strongmen from Quezon to Marcos and Duterte," *Kasarinlan: Philippine Journal of Third World Studies* 32, nos. 1–2 (2017): 13.

15 There are substantial files dedicated to monitoring communism in the records of the US Bureau of Insular Affairs. See especially Box 1295, Folder 28342, Records of the Bureau of Insular Affairs, Record Group 350, National Archives and Records Administration (from here on BIA RG350, NARA).

16 *Independence for the Philippine Islands: Hearings before the Committee on Territories and Insular Affairs* (Washington, DC: US Government Printing Office, 1932), 108.

17 See Luis Taruc, *Born of the People* (New York: International Publishers, 1953) and Jim Richardson, *Komunista: The Genesis of the Philippine Communist Party, 1902–1935* (Quezon City: Ateneo de Manila University Press, 2011).

thousands detained, harassed, and intimidated by the PC and local police forces.[18] The suppression of the Sakdalistas provided a model for the Commonwealth government. Quezon would continue to use the PC to violently suppress dissenting voices, particularly those of the poor and the peasantry. Moreover, through the deputizing of plantation owners, vigilante militias, and Christian settlers, the Commonwealth government would imprison leftist revolutionaries in Luzon and Muslim autonomists in Mindanao.[19]

From the 1940s to the 1950s, the PC was again crucial in deploying punitive violence against perceived disorders. Under Japanese colonial occupation during World War II, the PC arrested and tortured suspected dissidents, focusing especially on communist and anti-Japanese peasant guerillas, known as the *Hukbalahap* (and later the *Huks*) in the countryside. After the 1946 US imperial recognition of Philippine sovereignty, the Huks would transform their political platform from anticolonial defense into a revolutionary movement. In response to the so-called Huk rebellion, the nascent postcolonial state would revive the PC.[20] Immediately, the PC would adopt brutal methods of mass torture and detention of any supposed rebel or those suspected of abetting rebels. PC methods were spectacular; in some instances, dead bodies were stacked along roads as warnings to Huk members and sympathizers.[21]

In terms of the history of punitive violence in the postcolonial Philippines, perhaps no other state regime is more infamous than the dictatorship of Ferdinand Marcos. From 1965 until his "People Power" propelled ouster in 1986, the Marcos regime relied on the brutal punishment of those deemed domestic enemies of the state. Suspected dissidents and critics were targeted by the police and military. An astounding number of estimated human rights violations were carried out under Marcos' martial law: 70,000 were arrested, 35,000 were tortured, and 3,257 were extrajudiciously killed. Many of those murdered were first tortured, and

---

18 "Sakdal Uprising Report," Box 13, Folder 11, Joseph Ralston Hayden Papers, Bentley Historical Library, University of Michigan.

19 "Text of President Quezon's Message to the National Assembly," *Manila Bulletin*, February 1, 1941, Box 24, Folder 1, Joseph Ralston Hayden Papers, Bentley Historical Library, University of Michigan.

20 Ben J. Kerkvliet, *The Huk Rebellion: A Study of Peasant Revolt in the Philippines* (Quezon City: New Day Publishers, 1979).

21 McCoy, *Policing America's Empire*, 375.

their mutilated corpses were left out for public display in a cruel practice known as "salvaging."[22]

Under Marcos, the PC was a hybrid military and civilian institution, thus it operated with civil immunity. During an era when the Third World was a world-shaping force for Cold War geopolitics, Marcos justified his crackdown on criminality through anticommunist, counterrevolutionary, and antisedition discourse. For US allies and the local Philippine elite and middle classes, the desire to securitize capitalist society enabled the Marcos regime to pursue legal and extralegal punishment on a mass scale. It is fitting, therefore, that the end of the Marcos regime also marked the beginning of the end of the PC as an autonomous institution. In 1991, PC personnel were absorbed into the Philippine National Police, designated as a nonmilitary force, and stripped of civil immunity.[23]

What is most striking about the PC's style of punishment was its spectacular display of violence. The public exhibition of dismembered and mutilated bodies was certainly intended to serve as warnings to those considered potential rebels or insurgents. At the same time, the debasement of body parts to the point of abjection seemed to serve another purpose.[24] For instance, the kinds of "salvaging" that occurred under Marcos never seemed to fundamentally unsettle the broader population. Marcos remained—and remains—immensely popular.[25] It is as if those who witnessed these public displays of gratuitous violence chose not to identify with the punished or even the potentially punishable. Rather, they chose to identify with those meting out punishment: Marcos and the PC. As Neferti X. M. Tadiar has argued about the Marcos regime, the popularity (and nostalgia) for the strongman was fueled by a popular desire for authoritarian leadership and the possible access to the spoils of capital accumulation.[26]

---

22 McCoy, *Policing America's Empire*, 403.

23 McCoy, *Policing America's Empire*, 403.

24 Nerissa Balce, *Body Parts of Empire: Visual Abjection, Filipino Images, and the American Archive* (Ann Arbor: University of Michigan Press, 2016), 22.

25 Floyd Whaley, "30 Years After Revolution, Some Filipinos Yearn for 'Golden Age' of Marcos," *The New York Times*, February 23, 2016, https://www.nytimes.com/2016/02/24/world/asia/30-years-after-revolution-some-filipinos-yearn-for-golden-age-of-marcos.html.

26 Neferti X. M. Tadiar, *Fantasy Production: Sexual Economies and Other Philippine Consequences for the New World Order* (Quezon City: Ateneo de Manila University Press, 2004), 52.

I wonder, therefore, if this popular identification with the masculine figures of violence—the strongmen of the PC and the patriarchal authoritarian leader—expresses what Tadiar calls a fascistic desire to be part of the "People-as-One."[27] As Tadiar clarifies, various desires for mass unity that have emerged over time are not inherently fascistic. It is when these desires for mass unity are *represented* by a singular figure—in this case the strongman—that it can be deployed for fascist power. To identify as the one who punishes rather than as the one punished means that one desires to inflict punishment upon the abject, those excluded from the "People-as-One." Moreover, this identification with the strongman is perhaps not necessarily grounded in what punishment is supposed to prevent (crimes and disorder) or even uphold (the law or the nation), but rather in the spectacle of punishment itself.

Duterte's tenure is especially defined by the spectacle of punishment. He has threatened to revive the PC,[28] frequently expresses his admiration for the order and security under the Marcos regime,[29] and instituted martial law in parts of Muslim Mindanao.[30] Although he at first committed to peace talks with communists, he has, for most of his tenure, been vehemently anticommunist. Indeed, although many critics have argued that he is ideologically nebulous, his sole consistency is his commitment to punitive justice. Duterte's obsession with punishing all those who disturb authority and security has earned him the nickname "The Punisher," a reference to a fictional vigilante antihero who hunts and kills suspected criminals.[31] Duterte's desire to punish extends to all those who appear as instigators of "political and moral disorder," and has led to the aggressive targeting of a multitude of media groups, activists and organizers, and even celebrities.

Take for example, the July 2020 Anti-Terrorism Act, which expanded the definition of terrorism to include any activities or speech that may threaten

---

27 Tadiar here refers to Claude Lefort's concept of "People-as-One." [Tadiar, *Fantasy Production*, 253.]

28 Pia Randa, "Duterte to revive Philippine Constabulary," *Rappler*, September 20, 2016, https://www.rappler.com/nation/duterte-revive-philippine-constabulary.

29 Pia Randa, "Duterte: If I won't be a dictator, nothing will happen to PH," *Rappler*, February 9, 2018, https://www.rappler.com/nation/duterte-dictator-change-philippines.

30 JC Gotinga, "After 2 and a half years, martial law ends in Mindanao," *Rappler*, December 31, 2019, https://www.rappler.com/nation/martial-law-mindanao-ends-december-31-2019.

31 Erik De Castro, "The Punisher," *Reuters*, June 30, 2016, https://www.reuters.com/investigates/special-report/philippines-duterte-photos/.

harm or destruction to people, property, or infrastructure. Additionally, the act granted the government with far more punitive powers, including surveillance, detainment, and incarceration without basic protections or legal recourse. In the lead up to its passage, the vagueness of the law was widely denounced by both domestic and foreign critics. Leftists, liberals, and human rights groups in the Philippines argued that the act allowed government agents to consider any criticism as a threat to state security. Indeed, one definition of a terrorist included anyone who would "propose, incite, conspire, and participate" in seriously destroying or destabilizing "the fundamental political, economic, or social structures in the country."[32] Sedition, the desire for liberation, and challenges to government authority were now under the umbrella of terrorism.

A prominent target of Duterte's regime has been communism. Anticommunist punishment commonly operates through "red-tagging," whereby Duterte government agents and supporters accuse public figures or organizations of being communists or communist sympathizers. Working primarily through social media, red-tagging has mainly targeted human rights advocates and leftist critics of the Duterte government. In a country with the longest, ongoing armed communist rebellion in Asia (the New People's Army, or NPA), any sort of demands for social justice or forms of political dissent can be "red-tagged" by authorities and portrayed as sedition or terrorism against the government.

Red-tagging does not merely operate as a mode of suppressing dissent, but also creates the grounds for capture, detention, or even death.[33] In 2020, under the direction of the National Task Force to End Local Communist Armed Conflict (NTF-ELCAC), there was a deluge of arrests, detentions, and killings of university students, as well as Indigenous, peasant, and labor activists and organizers.[34] The Duterte regime rationalized this state campaign against communists in strongman language. In a March 2021 press

---

32 "Philippines: Dangerous anti-terror law yet another setback for human rights," *Amnesty International*, July 3, 2020, https://www.amnesty.org/en/latest/news/2020/07/philippines-dangerous-antiterror-law-yet-another-setback-for-human-rights/.

33 During 2020 there was rampant red-tagging. For some of the most highly public examples, see: Rambo Talabong, "Parlade warns Liza Soberano on supporting Gabriela: 'You will suffer the same fate' of those killed," *Rappler*, October 22, 2020, https://www.rappler.com/nation/parlade-warns-liza-soberano-supporting-gabriela-youth; and Distraught Angel Locsin on being red-tagged—People I help could be accused, too," *ABS-CBN News*, October 31, 2020, https://news.abs-cbn.com/news/10/31/20/distraught-angel-locsin-on-being-red-tagged-people-i-help-could-be-accused-too.

34 Alan Robles, "Philippines: 'Bloody Sunday' killings show Rodrigo Duterte's brutal presidency isn't letting up in his last full year," *This Week in Asia*,

conference, he claimed to have ordered the military to "shoot and kill right away" any supposedly armed communist.[35] A Duterte spokesperson supported the president's right to "kill, kill, kill," declaring it legal "because the rebels really are armed [*dahil . . . ay iyong mga rebelde na meron talagang hawak na armas*]."[36] For Duterte, communists simply embodied disorder; they were roving and violent "bandits" with no recognizable or legitimate political ideology. From his perspective, in contradistinction to the law and order forcefully instituted by communist governments, what Duterte offered under his regime was "the kind of discipline where one truly believes and follows the rules in order to live peacefully."[37]

Finally, the Duterte regime has most notoriously pursued the punishment of moral crimes, particularly the use and sale of illegal drugs. His regime has made explicit the fundamental connection between political and moral disorders, and their threat on Filipino life. As Duterte has maintained, "[W]hen you save your country from the perdition of the people like the NPAs and drugs, you are doing a sacred duty."[38] Through waging what he calls a "Drug War," Duterte promised to bring "peace and order" to the Philippine public. The punishment of accused drug smugglers, dealers, and addicts has been most spectacularly covered by major corporate and grassroots media outlets. Since 2016, murders from police and vigilantes have been estimated to be between 6,000 and 20,000 or more. Additionally, there are almost 200,000 officially imprisoned or detained in a carceral system that was built for a tenth of that number.[39]

Despite worries from liberal critics, the Drug War has not been bad for business. Its stockpiling of corpses sheds light on racial capitalism's capacity

---

March 10, 2021, https://www.scmp.com/week-asia/politics/article/3124907/philippines-bloody-sunday-killings-show-dutertes-brutal.

35 Catherine Valente, "Duterte orders military to 'shoot and kill' armed communist rebels," *The Manila Times*, March 6, 2021, https://www.manilatimes.net/2021/03/06/news/duterte-orders-military-to-shoot-and-kill-armed-communist-rebels/847906/.

36 Jamaine Punzalan, "Duterte 'kill, kill, kill' order vs rebels is 'legal,' says spokesman," *ABS-CBN News*, March 8, 2021, https://news.abs-cbn.com/news/03/08/21/duterte-kill-kill-kill-order-vs-rebels-is-legal-says-spokesman.

37 Valente, "Duterte orders military to 'shoot and kill.'"

38 Jim Gomez, "Duterte: Hold me responsible for killings in drug crackdown," *ABC News*, October 20, 2020, https://abcnews.go.com/International/wireStory/duterte-held-responsible-drug-killings-73707854.

39 "Bachelet renews call for accountability in Philippines' war on illegal drugs," *UN News*, June 30, 2020, https://news.un.org/en/story/2020/06/1067462.

to profit from gratuitous violence.[40] Racial capitalism devalues a body's life, but at the same time can valorize the body through dispossession. For instance, in the microeconomic register, police quotas and funerals monetize the accumulation of corpses to reap profit.[41] The seized narcotics publicly appraised by police illuminate the fungibility of dead bodies to the street price of drugs.[42] At the same time, Duterte's war on drugs is bundled along with the budgeting of infrastructure and development, illustrating its macroeconomic implications. The proposed 2021 national budget has allocated a combined P450 billion pesos (approximately USD $9.4 billion) to military and police,[43] with a substantial "chunk" dedicated to the increase in military and police salaries, pensions, and life insurance.[44] To pay for this increased budget, over P3 trillion pesos will be added to the national debt, with a sixth of the debt coming directly from foreign lenders.[45] In addition, since 2016, the United States has provided $554 million in military assistance to the Duterte regime.[46] All in all, both US empire and international finance have established ways to profit from Duterte's punitive regime.

Intertwined with capital investment in the Drug War is the popular libidinal investment in the figure of the strongman. In April 2021, Duterte publicly stated: "[Y]ou can hold me responsible for anything, any death that has occurred in the execution of the drug war." He argues that "if there's killing

---

40 In some ways, this resonates with Sayak Valencia's assertion that "there is a hyper-corporealization and a hyper-valorization applied to the body" within the organized crime markets of border territories. See Sayak Valencia, *Gore Capitalism* (South Pasadena: Semiotext(e), 2018), 131.

41 Vicente Rafael, "The Sovereign Trickster," *The Journal of Asian Studies*, Vol. 78, No. 1 (2019): 149.

42 For more on how fungibility and accumulation remain essential logics in the production of racial capitalism, see Saidiya Hartman, "The Belly of the World: A Note on Black Women's Labors," *Souls*, Vol. 18, No. 1 (2016): 166–173.

43 "By the Numbers: The Philippines' proposed 2021 budget," *Rappler*, October 22, 2020, https://www.rappler.com/business/by-the-numbers-show-episode-one-2021-philippine-national-budget.

44 Chistopher Lloyd Caliwan, "Big chunk of PNP 2021 budget mostly for personnel services," *Republic of the Philippines Philippine News Agency*, September 15, 2020, https://www.pna.gov.ph/articles/1115431.

45 Ben O. de Vera, "PH debt to breach P10 trillion in 2020, nearly P12 trillion in 2021," *Inquirer*, August 26, 2020, https://business.inquirer.net/305953/ph-debt-to-breach-p10-trillion-in-2020-nearly-p12-trillion-in-2021.

46 Renato de Castro, "Duterte admin (finally) acknowledges value of Philippine-US alliance," *Stratbase ADR Institute*, September 19, 2020, https://adrinstitute.org/2020/09/19/duterte-admin-finally-acknowledges-value-of-philippine-us-alliance/.

there, I'm saying I'm the one."[47] With this claim of responsibility, it is as if his finger ultimately pulls all the triggers of police firearms. By claiming, "I'm the one," Duterte sets off a chain of identifications. As the one who punishes, he is the source of all the extrajudicial killings, the one who animates the spectacle of gratuitous violence. This claim of responsibility is not meant to distance himself from the police or the people. Instead it is meant to collapse that distance. According to this logic, if one identifies with the Filipino people, this one is not meant to identify with the dead criminal, but rather with the figure who takes pleasure in killing for the "People-as-One." Indeed, Duterte posits his form of punitive justice as being driven by a higher calling, the natural and national law of the "People-as-One" when he asserts, "bring me to court to be imprisoned . . . if I serve my country by going to jail, gladly."[48] With this statement, Duterte expresses his pleasure in his martyrdom, not just willing, but "gladly" willing, to be prosecuted for the "People-as-One."[49]

Despite the international condemnation of Duterte's government as authoritarian and excessively punitive, the Philippines is nevertheless considered by its inhabitants as one of the fifty safest countries in the world. According to a Gallup Report released in November 2020, seven out of ten residents of the Philippines self-reported that they felt more secure, mainly because of the high visibility of law enforcement and the official reports of decreased crime rates.[50] For Filipino revolutionaries, the most unnerving aspect of life under Duterte is not simply that the majoritarian opinion accepts the state's punitive violence. Perhaps equally disturbing about Duterte's continued popularity—despite his botched response to the COVID-19 pandemic and typhoon disasters during 2020 and the

---

47 Associated Press, "'I'm the one': Philippines president takes responsibility for drug killings," *The Guardian*, October 20, 2020, https://www.theguardian.com/world/2020/oct/20/im-the-one-philippines-president-takes-responsibility-for-drug-killings.

48 Associated Press, "'I'm the one': Philippines president takes responsibility for drug killings," *The Guardian*, October 20, 2020, https://www.theguardian.com/world/2020/oct/20/im-the-one-philippines-president-takes-responsibility-for-drug-killings.

49 Duterte remains unrepentant in his policy of extrajudicial killing, as evident in his recent, and final, State of the Nation address in which he reinforces his "shoot them dead" policy. See Genalyn Kabiling, "Duterte vows to end armed communist struggle 'once and for all,'" *Manila Bulletin*, July 27, 2021, https://mb.com.ph/2021/07/27/duterte-vows-to-end-armed-communist-struggle-once-and-for-all/.

50 Krixia Subingsubing, "Gallup: PH among the safest countries in the world," *Inquirer*, November 5, 2020, https://globalnation.inquirer.net/191954/gallup-ph-12th-safest-country.

beginning of 2021—is the seeming continued desire by the majority of the electorate to witness others be punished.[51] As several interviews conducted during Duterte's lame-duck period of rule suggest, those perceived to be excluded from the realm of the people—communities regularly targeted by authorities—are actually "relieved" about the extrajudicial killings of communists and drug addicts. This relief is a consequence of identifying communists and drug addicts as "being against the law."[52] Thus, if fascism is the counterrevolutionary and authoritarian desire to punish those considered threats to law and order, then it can also be said that fascism is the pleasure one gains from seeing authoritarian rule succeed.

To combat fascistic forms of pleasure, antifascists in the Philippines must go beyond the logic of ethical condemnation or intellectual criticism. They must also go beyond the desire to find a different, more palatable (preferably liberal) populist leader, to substitute in place of the fascistic strongman.[53] It may be more generative for antifascists to recall the desires of past revolutionaries, and in particular, strategies of organizing around an identification with the people and rejecting identification with the "People-as-One." To follow revolutionaries that rejected representations of the masses and instead drew from, and were a part of, the pleasures of mass movements toward collective liberation.

---

51 Neil Arwin Mercardo, "Duterte casts out 'lame duck' spell, retains popularity unseen before," *Inquirer*, July 22, 2021, https://newsinfo.inquirer.net/1462537/ duterte-casts-out-lame-duck-spell-retains-popularity-unseen-before.

52 Pia Renada, "Duterte may cap term as most popular president. So what?," *Rappler*, June 30, 2021, https://www.rappler.com/newsbreak/in-depth/ so-what-if-duterte-may-cap-term-as-philippines-most-popular-president.

53 This was of course the case that occurred with the liberal authoritarian figure of Corazon Aquino, as Tadiar argues, and the recent nostalgia for the recently deceased Benigno Aquino III. See Tadiar, *Fantasy Production*, 253.

CHAPTER SIX

Race, Cinema, and the Disorganized Crime of Fascist Devotion

Simón Ventura Trujillo

This essay explores the persistence of what Leslie Marmon Silko has termed the "border patrol state" to discern the contours of fascist devotion in the contemporary conjuncture of US settler colonialism. I approach fascism as a formation of structural violence and political affect embedded in the interrelated practices of indefinite detention, torture, border territoriality, and anti-Indigenous cruelty. This essay in particular turns to the terrain of popular culture to trace the entanglements of fascism with the colonial and imperial violences that established and persist in US social life. In particular, I analyze the subversive aesthetics of Alfonso Cuarón's *Children of Men* (2006) and Alex Rivera's and Cristina Ibarra's The Infiltrators (2019) to examine cinematic production as offering distinct valences of antifascist critical practice.

The relationship between cinema, aesthetics, fascism, and other modes of technologically reproducible imagery has been a topic of concern for many filmmakers, photographers, cultural workers, intellectuals, and scholars. In the early twentieth century, cinematic representation became an emergent yet constitutive element of state propaganda for Nazism and the fascist regimes in Italy and Japan. In the same period, a culture industry organized around film and mechanized photography also mediated the quotidian fascisms that disciplined the racial hierarchies of US and European settler empires. For certain critics, the aesthetics of fascist cinema animate visual fields that drive toward unification, simplification, idealization, and the glorification of violence, cruelty, and brutality. According to Lutz P. Koepnick, Nazism "reshaped common ideas of beauty in order to render aesthetic pleasure a direct extension of political terror, a form of violence in the service of future warfare."[1] At the same

---

1   Lutz P. Koepnick, "Fascist Aesthetics Revisited," *Modernism/modernity* 6, no.1 (1999): 51.

time, Koepnick also usefully points out the ways that the state aesthetics of fascism are more dispersed into seemingly "apolitical leisure activities in the niches of private life," and include both promises for "career opportunities" but also "new tactics of diversion and commodity consumption."[2] Aesthetics therefore enable fascist formations to appropriate "certain properties of social and cultural modernity in order to reconstruct the modern state as a phantasmagoria of power and community." The state as a result morphs into "a shifting series of deceptive appearances that change the very parameters according to which people perceive the real. By doing so in effect it changes reality itself."[3]

The critical and creative response to the aesthetics of fascist statecraft has been myriad and evolving. One key effect of antifascism on intellectual practice remains the production of frameworks that stress the materiality of history and understandings of culture that are contextualized in political economic structures. Likewise, the influence of antifascism for cultural workers is evident in work that emphasizes disjuncture and dissonance, directing concentration to the ways the nature and experience of "reality" proceed from the paradoxes and constraints of representation itself. Building with these repertoires of antifascist intellectual work, my approach to the critical possibility embedded in cinematic production draws from Eva Cherniavsky's work on the stakes of critical practice under the neoliberal erosion of liberal political culture. Cherniavsky takes the moment of neoliberal state evisceration to interrogate the function of critical intellectual practice when the state is "no longer invested in (or dependent on) the production of conviction or consent." Naming the crisis in neoliberal state formation as also a crisis in the "abiding value and the limits of critical defamiliarization," Cherniavsky asks us to resituate the work of critique when it is no longer fastened to the presumption that state power is guised and available for unmasking through critical discernment. Resituating intellectual work beyond the critical defamiliarization of liberal ideology critique requires that we come to terms with the ways the shift in the political economy of liberal statecraft has radically altered the discursive and mediated terrain of civil society that underlies critical intellectual practice. Notably, what Cherniavsky names as filling the vacuum of

---

2 Koepnick, "Fascist Aesthetics Revisited," 52.

3 Koepnick, "Fascist Aesthetics Revisited," 53.

liberal state hegemony uncannily resonates with the polarities of fascist statecraft. Critical intellectual practice navigates a reckless cohabitation of "overtly particularistic ethnonationalisms emancipated from the (always fraught) universalism of modern nation-state formations" and relentless "noise, a kind of media static whose main purpose, far from commanding hearts and minds, is simply to drown out anything of critical moment that might otherwise aspire to its mass dissemination."[4]

The interrelation of antifascist critical practice, aesthetics, and epistemologies of state violence illuminates a particular riddle at the heart of fascism's terrible threat: if fascism reveals the breakdown of a liberal code of rationality and perception by which to govern a civil society, it also discloses the intensity of mob devotion as a volatile laboratory of social order achieved through racialized political violence. Fascism underscores how derealization—that is, the deliberate breakdown of a shared principle of reality and governance—can also operate as a key component to the formation of mob devotion to racialized state control.

Devotion, in this way, provides useful framings of the logic and affect of mob formation under the derealizing effects of fascist political culture. Devotion straddles the secular and sectarian polarities of mob formations central to fascist reason. In its religious usages, according to the *Oxford English Dictionary*, devotion defines a "solemn dedication," a consecration, or the "setting apart to a sacred use or purpose." In secular contexts, it names an "earnest addiction or application" to a person, cause, or pursuit. It also denotes an "attached service" and a state of being at another's command and disposal.[5] Devotion in this sense is neither fully antithetical to liberal reason even as it manifests most virulently in mob attempts to dismantle the democratic procedures of civil society. Devotion rather draws our attention to how "much of what influences and unites people in a political cause is aesthetic in nature and involves the desire to worship something, even if it is only an image."[6]

In the United States, Donald Trump's presidency stoked a resurgence in the established field of devotion to white dominance in a number of ways.

---

4 Eva Cherniavsky, *Neocitizenship: Political Culture After Democracy* (New York: NYU Press, 2017), 17.

5 "devotion, n." *OED Online*, Oxford University Press, September 2021, www.oed.com/view/Entry/51579.

6 Jennifer Lynn Barker, *The Aesthetics of Antifascist Film* (New York and Milton Park, Abingdon, Oxon: Routledge, 2012), 1.

One notable and devastating example remains his regime's aestheticization of Mexican and Latin American migrants into a criminal threat to US sovereignty—as figures who require the violence of indefinite detention, child separation, and deportation. Before and throughout the time the Trump regime occupied the White House, the promises of building a wall along the US-Mexico border aestheticized the more brutal and mundane practice of migrant detention and child separation that occurred in established and makeshift centers across the United States. As Cristina Beltrán argues, immigrant incarceration is but one component of the broad complex of participatory practices devoted to fashioning white dominance out of migrant punishment under US nationalism. For Beltrán, the upsurge of border militia groups, the insidious expansion of police power for ICE and state border enforcement, and an entrenched anti-immigrant multimedia public sphere is evidence of the ways in which migrant suffering enables nativists to "feel stronger, freer, and more agentic, transforming acts of racialized violence—whether people are committing, witnessing, or merely describing such acts—into feats of heroism, democratic redemption, civic engagement, and virtuous sovereignty."[7]

In what follows, I discuss how *Children of Men* and *The Infiltrators* reveal the ways a media complex and mob sociality of migrant punishment fosters fascist devotion to the border violence of US white supremacy. By routing my critique of fascism through cinematic production, I explore how what is termed "popular culture" also bears the conditions for an antifascist field of representation that may more readily interconnect and subvert the seemingly incomprehensible set of fascist phenomena besieging the current conjuncture. I examine how their representational politics of migrant punishment "fuse," in the words of Jennifer Ponce de León, "artistic production with practices considered extraneous to disciplinary understandings of fine art and literature, such as direct action tactics, public history, gaming, cartography, and solidarity economies."[8] By tracing the distinct politics of representation in each film, I show how *Children of Men* and *The Infiltrators* build out a multiplicity of antifascist actions and labors possible under aesthetic practice.

---

7   Cristina Beltrán, *Cruelty as Citizenship: How Migrant Suffering Sustains White Democracy* (Minneapolis: University of Minnesota Press, 2020).

8   Jennifer Ponce de León, *Another Aesthetics Is Possible: Arts of Rebellion in the Fourth World War* (Durham: Duke University Press, 2021).

Children of Men and the tragedy of fascist state formation

Set in England during the year 2027, premised on a future freighted with uncontainable and widespread global violence that itself is punctuated by an equally devastating eighteen-year worldwide human infertility pandemic, *Children of Men* presents a world for its viewer uncannily containing the precariousness of our own historical multifascist moment.

Part science fiction, part dystopia, part tragedy, the film offers a vision of the world in which the stability of the nation-state as the preferred mode of social collectivity has utterly collapsed due to mass migratory movements resulting from either devastating natural disasters, nuclear fallout, or a combination of the two. Only England, as a propaganda video announces through a montage of global carnage, "soldiers on." It is a hypermediatized society trudging through an immense despair wrought equally by the infertility pandemic if not, more intensely, a state indistinguishable from a permanent war zone. As such, the film spectacularizes a militarized state form completely unbounded from the task of generating hegemonic consent for the application of its intensified coercive functions. Bereft of the ability to reproduce humanity, the state can only, to paraphrase Toni Morrison, reproduce the environment that supports the health of fascist dominance: "fear, denial, and an atmosphere in which its victims have lost the will to fight."[9] Immigrants of all nationalities, races, and ethnicities are criminalized, publicly incarcerated, and aggressively deported.

Territorially, England is structured as a condensed hypercapitalist geography. Radical class difference (assuming that the mode of social dominance within the film could even be labeled as "class") exists within intensified spatial intimacy and militarized stratification. It is at this level, then, that the film offers a panorama of the contradictions of the fascist response to US imperial crises taken to radical, and radically plausible, extremes. Or rather, the film contains the contradictions and interwoven incoherencies of the contemporary neoliberal world order precisely to the extent that it speculates a future where its logical premises—state deregulation of capitalist industry and finance, privatization of public goods and services, and the obliteration of a social safety net[10]—are taken to their fascist and vio-

---

9   Toni Morrison, "Racism and Fascism," *The Journal of Negro Education*, Vol. 64, No. 3 (Summer 1995): 385.

10 David Harvey, *Spaces of Global Capitalism: Towards a Theory of Uneven Geographical Development* (London and New York: Verso, 2006), 25–29.

lently terminal postulates. These postulates are connected to "a provocative system of consumption," according to Eduardo Subirats, "which, regardless of whether it is dedicated to sexual trafficking, the corporate production of ecologically devastating seeds, or trafficking in arms, generates progressive degrees of violence, the exponential growth of hunger, epidemics, death, and the indefinite expansion of war."[11]

Formally, *Children of Men* is edited into a series of long, uninterrupted takes in which the camera mostly assumes the perspective of an invisible spectator following the characters, operating in the same partiality of their own field of vision. The film mobilizes partial vision and extended takes to render a fascinating tension between the foreground and background of each scene, one in which the plot and characters themselves become the rather arbitrary vehicle for the telling of the film's worldly context. In many scenes, the camera patiently lingers and hovers over the characters with a distance that is neither too intrusive nor remote. This has the particular effect of both effacing and reinstating consciousness of the camera's presence for the viewer. It is in this sense that the camera assumes the perspective of an invisible spectator from today, moving through and circling about the characters with an unflinching, partial, and voyeuristic energy only to periodically rest on, say, a defaced mural or a mourning woman holding her dead son.

The fascism saturating the film's narrative sphere, in other words, is itself thrust as a protagonist through which we as viewers identify the political and social horizons of possibility furnished through the spectacles of imperial violence and settler elimination that organize the US state. Treating the background of *Children of Men* as we treat a protagonist requires our focus to sit with the ways fascist devotion and belief manifest from the objects and products that circulate in the movie. The film's aesthetic flow of fascist objects and practices include a celebrity-driven media culture and a political economy proliferating industrial pharmaceuticals, guns, bombs, and a range of militarized weaponry. Under these conditions, denizens of England 2027 pessimistically slouch around disrepaired infrastructures controlled by a police force operating what appears to be state-of-the-art communication and forensic science.

---

11 Eduardo Subirats, "Totalitarian Lust: From Saló to Abu Ghraib," *South Central Review*, Vol. 24, No. 1 (Spring 2007): 180.

In the contradiction of cultivated disrepair, social collapse, and hypermediated police violence, a peculiar and specific set of objects emerge repeatedly: cages. Specifically, cages for migrants—or those who the characters in the film refer to as "fugees" in a diminution of the term "refugee." Cages are displayed publicly in train stations and outside dilapidated housing projects confining a multicultural and multinational population of fugees. Their multicultural and multinational character doesn't signify the evaporation of racialized subjection. Rather, it signals the production of a public for whom subjection to the coercive, terrifying, and violent tactics that have historically preceded and materially animate fascist subjection—slavery, imprisonment, segregation, torture, indefinite detention—are now pervasive, intractable components of social existence. In their caged visibility, incarcerated migrants are simultaneously specter and spectacle—that which must be removed *yet also* displayed as an emblem of hypermilitarized, coercive power. Theirs is the spectacle achieving the violent reincorporation of national coherency through the expansion of terror and fear. It is the form of terror the state has historically reserved for the procurement and perpetuation of colonial dominance, only now, as an object of fascist devotion, it has co-opted the universalism of modern liberalism.

Fascist devotion to cages lends insight into what is arguably the most horrifying scene within the film: the violent, hypermilitarized setting of Bexhill Refugee Camp. The rampant violence executed by the guards as the bus carrying Theo, Kee, and Miriam initially enters the camp is rendered as a spectacle of simultaneous order and chaos. Alongside scenes of heavily armed guards relentlessly beating newly arrived inmates we see ordered rows of hooded individuals, forced to kneel with their hands behind their head. The camera, whose angle again assumes a spectator locked within the confines of the bus, pans through the scene. We see a row of medium-sized cages in which two to three individuals rest on their knees as their arms are bound to the walls, confined in semi-prostration, with chains and bright orange belts. The bus stops and light floods the cabin as more guards with dogs enter to perform random searches. Miriam is both beaten and removed from the bus while fervently distracting the guards from Kee, who has just gone into labor. The camera tracks her removal by setting it against the background of a cage containing a lone figure standing on a small stool in what appears to be a burlap sack, whose outstretched arms are attached to nothing. Hence, as the bus continues moving, the camera tracks a rapid sequence of orchestrated brutality rendered visible through a political aesthetic furnished by the Abu Ghraib torture photographs. It is a succession of events in which we see more guards force a black hood over Miriam's head and shove her to the ground. Her prominence within the camera's field of vision is replaced by the lone caged prisoner, who is then passed and replaced by a line of half-naked individuals being inspected by dog-wielding guards alongside an armored truck.

Even while this scene's reference to the Abu Ghraib photographs is relatively explicit, its formal delivery is worth pausing over for a moment. The scene's use of a long unedited take successively renders each instance of torture visible and contained tensely against the foreground of Kee's crying and shocked face. The tortures enter and pass the camera's line of vision in a type of uninterrupted montage of horror and brutality. In mobilizing Abu Ghraib's political aesthetic as the *modus operandi* of state power within the film's own narrative sphere, *Children of Men* confronts the profoundly virtual and performed character of that aesthetic. It is in this sense that the film engages with the hypermediation of the war on terror *and* the centrality of torture and incarceration as a fundament of migrant life under US state power.

On one level, the scene is a cinematic representation of torture referring to an actual practice of torture that itself found public legibility as a photographed spectacular scandal. The scene, in this sense, portrays performances of torture whose utility operates equally as an emblem of the film's "objective" world as it does for the current US visual field, furnished by spectacles of state-sanctioned migrant punishment. The result calls attention to the ways state power fetishizes visual mediation as the simultaneous representation and fictionalization of social truth. The tortured and incarcerated within the film are rendered as both violently malleable and observable objects, individuals whose splaying figures equally as a spectacle and a disciplinary tactic—if not the profound confusion of the two. By enfolding a regime of torture within a regime of immigrant detention, Cuarón's use of the long uninterrupted take to render the tortures visible has two principal effects. On one hand, it forces the viewer into a mode of self-reflexivity (a spectacle of a spectacle within a spectacle) that radically rearranges our sense of the relationship between the past, present, and future. By virtue of this self-reflexive aesthetic, the scene compresses the actual history of Abu Ghraib into a virtual future dystopia of migrant punishment, figuring the present conditions of US state power into, according to Subirats, a "somber spectacle that simultaneously incorporates a totalitarian political and military machinery and a genocidal principle of annihilation."[12]

This compression in temporality prompts our recognition of state power in profoundly tragic terms. "Tragedy," according to David Scott, "may offer us some guidance in reconceiving the moral-political predicament of a postcolonial present ... confronted by the seemingly intractable dilemmas of modernity."[13] The film's spectacularly tragic performance of torture reconfigures our sense of possibility, reorganizes our cognition of temporal continuity, and renders visible the fascist "mix of the violence founding law with the violence maintaining law."[14] Instead of rendering the Abu Ghraib tortures as an aberration of state power to be overcome though the imperialist occupation of Iraq, the film posits these acts as state power as such, *par excellence*, and in total impunity. The spectacular sense of tragedy occasioned by the film prompts us to conceive of an expanding and intensifying fascist apparatus as the fetid underbelly of liberal values that is now outliving the shell of its ideal benevolent aspirations. Through tragedy, *Children of Men* indicts US border patrol's current incarcerational regime by figuring it as the expression of a US imperial state whose substructure of racialized violence increasingly exists as its preferred mode of power. The scene is a tragic spectacle that reveals our contemporary neoliberal moment as one producing, through the specter of incarceration, the simultaneous intensification of imperial sovereignty and mass rightlessness.

In this sense, *Children of Men* depicts a world, much like ours, existing in a formation of global, racial violence unfolding without the conditions of hegemonic dominance. Yet its use of tragedy also summons the realization that if the current regime of US fascist violence both produces and exists in a social sphere constituted by an increasingly incoherent system of racialized subjection and coercion, it is also a social sphere marked by a profound crisis. In other words, if *Children of Men* outlines a festering crisis in the legitimacy of the US neoliberal state, then it also makes visible a power without a coherent hegemonic structure and therefore signifies an opportunity for this crisis to host subversive aesthetic responses and modes of social and political collectivity that nullify fascist authority.

---

12 Subirats, "Totalitarian Lust," 177.

13 David Scott, *Conscripts of Modernity: The Tragedy of Colonial Enlightenment* (Durham: Duke University Press, 2005), 172.

14 Michael Taussig, *The Magic of the State* (New York: Routledge, 1997), 121.

"Everyone needs a plan"

While powerful and urgent, the limits of *Children of Men*'s critique of fascist devotion are bound to a politics of visuality whose vocation is making crisis visible for critical appraisal. For these reasons, *The Infiltrators* stands as an unsettling cinematic counterpart, one whose antifascist horizons represent crisis as a possibility for collective, youth-led mobilizations toward dismantling the infrastructure of US border fascism. Set in the United States in 2012, *The Infiltrators* is a film that combines documentary footage and dramatic recreations of Dreamer activists organizing against the US state deportation regime. Directed by Alex Rivera and Cristina Ibarra, the film tracks the work of the National Immigrant Youth Alliance (NIYA) to free Claudio Rojas and other detainees at Broward Transitional Center, a private immigrant detention facility in Florida. A mobile and savvy network of undocumented youth, NIYA's main protagonists in the film are Marco Saavedra, Viridiana Martinez, and Mohammad Abdollahi. Their liberation work takes them into directions and places that appear initially counterintuitive. Rather than running or hiding from the carceral machine, the group willingly strategizes the detention of certain members as a way of opening paths to escape. The film in this way opens for viewers a vision of critical labor as always embedded in the collective struggle for migrant dignity under fascist violence—a vision that also importantly opens participatory pathways for viewers to connect with movements.

The formal politics of *The Infiltrators* is bound within the urgencies of direct action against state deportation and the courage, innovation, and intergenerational wisdom of multiple genealogies of immigrant rights activism in the United States. In 2010, the film was conceptualized by Rivera and Ibarra as a traditional documentary of Dreamer mobilizations against the shadow deportation regime of the Obama administration. Dreamers are also known as recipients of the Deferred Action for Childhood Arrivals (DACA) policy that deferred the deportation of children of undocumented parents and provided pathways for work authorization, college admission, and military service. Struck by the Dreamer insistence on defiantly refusing the silence, secrecy, and fear that characterize the conditions of undocumented life and struggle, Rivera and Ibarra began to follow NIYA activists for two years. During this period, the proliferation of actions, mobilizations, and protests undertaken by the Dreamers confounded the filmmakers' attempts to bind the story into a clear narrative arc. While frustrating the desire to represent in documentary form the Dreamer struggle for justice, this period also enabled Rivera and Ibarra to become embedded in the everyday machinations of the movement, and to thus be positioned to witness and document one of the group's most audacious actions: the infiltration of Broward County detention center to free Claudio Rojas.

"How can stateless people build political power?" Rivera asks this question in an accompanying documentary to *The Infiltrators* that details the conditions of the film's emergence and its formal employments.[15] The confrontation between those stripped of state protection and the apparatus of incarceration here grants insight into the border-crossing work that accompanies antifascist practice. As an action for migrant justice that called into question the solidity of carceral borders, the infiltration of Broward County detention center also confronted the machinery of fascist silence that controls the movement of undocumented people and conceals the scope and scale of detention. In a voiceover early in the film, Saavedra relays the scale of the industry, authority, and infrastructure of immigrant control in the United States. Immigrant and Customs Enforcement (ICE) is the world's largest law enforcement agency. Twice the size of the FBI, ICE manifests fascist violence through a peculiar confluence of corporate, private, informal, and governmental power. At the time when the film's footage was taken, nearly forty thousand undocumented people were being held in over 200 for-profit detention centers operating across the US.

For Rivera and Ibarra, assembling a narrative form to depict the organizing work within detention centers opened a different question, one posed by Ibarra: "How do you document something that is being hidden?" The film employs a hybrid structure that integrates interviews, real-time footage of NIYA's mobilizations, and dramatic recreations of events inside the Broward County detention facility. In turning to dramatic recreation—or the space of fiction and speculation—Rivera and Ibarra also began a dialogic process of scripting and set design with Rojas, Saavedra, and Martinez, among others. Yet in turning to a hybrid film genre, *The Infiltrators* also defies the genre's temporal expectations. Typically, hybrid documentary/dramatic recreation genres—"true crime" television programming, for example—employ fictive recreations to narrate a set of events that the documentary interviews are supposedly discussing in retrospect. Yet *The*

---

15 See *Making of the Infiltrators* (dir. Alex Rivera and Cristina Ibarra), 2020, https://vimeo.com/412724394/31527fef8a.

Infiltrators employs fictional recreation to amplify the urgency of the spatial constraints of the story rather than attempting to capture a single character's experience as a flashback. The result is a weaving of discrete cinematic techniques to both counter the reality principle of US regimes of migrant punishment and build a public sphere predicated upon pathways to direct action mobilization for migrant dignity.

While pointedly focused on the deportation machine sustained during the Obama administration, *The Infiltrators'* debut would occur nearly seven years later, at the Sundance Film Festival in 2019, in a particularly dispiriting stretch of the Trump regime's depraved intensification of anti-immigrant cruelty. While its irruption into the mediated field of state sanctioned anti-immigrant violence would mark a decisive intervention, it would also coincide with the deliberate retargeting of Claudio Rojas for deportation. On April 5, 2019, ICE would deport Rojas to his birthplace of Argentina, although he and his family had been living in and building their home in the United States for over twenty years. The deportation of Rojas, as obvious retaliation for his role in movements for immigrant rights, fit within a broader strategy of targeting leadership of immigrant rights movements across the United States.[16]

While seemingly also concluding in tragedy, there is another temporality at play in the field of action galvanized by *The Infiltrators.* In the dissonance between Rojas' initial release from detention, its cinematic recreation, and the ongoing real-time devastation of his deportation, a different horizon of antifascist activity is presented. Viewers of the film are asked to confront its generic hybridity as a provisional binding of a longer, more dispersed dialectic of state violence and migrant justice. Rather than accepting the anti-immigrant spectacles of fascist devotion as objects for mere viewing, the audience of *The Infiltrators* are now asked to participate in an even more audacious and improvised action: to bring Claudio Rojas home. And with his homecoming, we are invited to dream of an even more expansive and capacious network of care, representation, shelter, and dignity by which collective senses of home overtake the current fascist epoch of curated destruction and aestheticized violence.

---

16 See Nick Pinto, "Across the U.S., Trump Used ICE to Crack Down on Immigration Activists," *The Intercept*, November 1, 2020, https://theintercept.com/2020/11/01/ice-immigration-activists-map/.

Toward antifascist origination

As an issue laced with racialized divisions and anxieties, immigration reveals not only the theoretical and material tensions of the settler nation form, but it also sets in relief the contradictory aspirations of US imperial sovereignty. Through a contradictory ideological regime of national identity and sovereignty, US settler colonialism forwards arguments for both boundless imperial expansion and bounded national space. Part and parcel of this contradiction and its sustained disavowal is the production of racialized identities that both provide the United States its purchase of national identity and a way of managing the differential forces of global capital.

Animating my analysis is not only the various ways in which US national identity perpetually mobilizes shifting racialized discourses to constrict and regulate access to its borders, but how race remains that symbolic and material institution through which the fascism of US immigration control is translated into a global harbinger of democratic freedom. On one hand, immigration regulation attempts to constitute US national identity by articulating the necessity of "safe" borders not only between domestic and foreign territories, but also between "citizen" and "immigrant." On the other hand, historically reinflected imperial warfare and expansion, such as the wars in Iraq and Afghanistan, sought to codify national integrity through the extension of US territorial sovereignty at the expense of foreign territorial sovereignties and the sovereignties of Indigenous nations across North America.

Rather than spectacularizing idolized strongmen as pinnacles of fascist devotion, *The Infiltrators* and *Children of Men* bring the technologies of domination, epistemologies of time, and infrastructures of control to the fore as formations for an antifascist reckoning. If the current forms of political violence, commodity exchange, and rights-based discourse remain bound up in the persistent codification and dissolution of fascist boundaries and devotions, then both films urge us to reconceptualize modes of seeing, time, and history in a way that counters the predation of life, both physical and symbolic, which have marked this cycle in tragic terms and in terms whose articulation is still pending.

CHAPTER SEVEN

At the Razor's Edge of Democracy

Authoritarian Capitalism and Decolonial International Feminisms

Macarena Gómez-Barris

> In opposition to state-centric perspectives, ours does not continue to prioritize the state as a privileged site of transformation. At the same time, it does not ignore the state in its limited political capacity. —Verónica Gago, *Feminist International* (2020)

> There was always another truth, behind the truth.—Gabriel García Marquez, *The Autumn of the Patriarch* (1975)

On October 18, 2019, during the continued rise of white nationalism in the United States and fascist racial autocracy in Brazil, Chilean President Sebastián Piñera ordered a 4 percent hike in subway fares. By putting the squeeze on workers, Piñera's new draconian policies ignited massive protests in Santiago, attracting more than 1.2 million participants. In a society where 33 percent of the nation's wealth resides with the top 1 percent, and where ex-military officials and a tiny elite control the majority of the country's remaining precious natural resources, Piñera's fare hike led to what became a key slogan of the ensuing movement: "*Chile se despertó*," or "Chile woke up."

In the immediate aftermath of the fare hike, dozens of Santiago's subway stations were burnt down. Following a well-choreographed media campaign, Piñera blamed protestors for the arson and declared a state of emergency. Reminiscent of Augusto Pinochet's authoritarian period (1973–1990), Piñera also used heightened rhetoric, referring to protestors in his national speeches as "the enemy of the state."

During the last few months of 2019 and in the early months of 2020, prior to the global COVID-19 pandemic, tens of thousands of police and military units were mobilized by the state to put down the rebellion. In addition to committing a wide range of human rights abuses, police used antiriot shotguns to shoot activists, more than 346 of whom lost their eyes. Further, rape and torture were used to "quell" the popular uprising.[1] Militarization in the streets created fierce opposition by a frontline movement that took over Plaza Italia and other parts of the downtown corridor as spaces of popular reoccupation. These movements staged solidarity with the long practices of frontline resistance by Mapuche communities in Wallmapu, the Indigenous territories that cross the Andes between Chile and Argentina. Yet, amidst the power of such mass and heterogeneous protests sparked by the fare hike, it was the transversal and feminist performances of Colectivo Las Tesis, founded by Daffne Valdés, Paula Cometa, Lea Cáceres, and Sibila Sotomayor, that reverberated around the globe.

"*Un violador en tu camino*" [A Rapist in Your Path], commonly translated into English as "The Rapist is You," are lyrics written and choreographed by the Chilean feminist group and then enacted by tens of thousands of Chilean feminist, nonbinary, trans, and queer [*cuir*] activists. Performing the choreography in front of La Moneda Palace as well as pointing to the state, Las Tesis enlivens an anti-authoritarian critique at the core of the international trans*feminist movement.[2] Performed hundreds of times in Chile and then creatively appropriated around the world, its aims have been to denounce femicide, sexual assault, patriarchal authority, gender inequality, and the sovereignty of state power. These aims are carefully articulated within broader abolitionist efforts against the state's repression and brutality. Indeed, the sheer public display of hundreds of thousands of unwavering female activists using their bodies as a collective denouncement of authoritarian capitalism makes visible the immense intersectional strength of a movement that foregrounds liberation by declaring a counterwar on the state.

To their credit, new feminist and anticapitalist movements in the hemisphere—like the one in Chile and the transversal feminist struggle in Argentina—have often been leaderless, making it difficult to co-opt or corrupt individual interests over collective ones. Further, movements for gender, sex, and reproductive rights have not been articulated through single-issue concerns, but instead through an expansive and transformative

---

1   See Human Rights Watch Report, "Chile: Events of 2019," https://www.hrw.org/world-report/2020/country-chapters/chile#.

2   See https://www.youtube.com/watch?v=tB1cWh27rmI.

agenda aimed at changing the elite colonial, economic, political, and legal model of the nation-state, as well as raising environmental, Indigenous, immigrant, health, education, living wage, and multispecies justice, as well as anti-extractive land and water protection.[3] The widely circulating phrase "Chile was the birthplace of neoliberalism, and Chile is where neoliberalism will die" encapsulates the sentiment that global capitalism failed the majority. It is this broader decolonial feminist resistance that points to the state as well as the political economy of extractive neoliberal capitalism at the heart of resuscitating, invigorating, and deepening radical democracy in the hemisphere.

In this essay, I use the term "authoritarian capitalism" to consider features of new/old fascism that are rooted in colonial and patriarchal structures and that have been reconfigured within this latest stage of the global capitalist political economy. Ruth Wilson Gilmore refers to the "antistate state" as a system of governance that does the work of continually dismantling the social and economic gains and liberal protections within the state.[4] Authoritarian capitalism, I contend, is the structure that underpins the antistate state (or the neoliberal state) that consolidates precisely when capitalism has reached its maximum growth point under democracy. To put this directly, the fact of radical wealth inequality is that ten white men, eight of whom are from the United States, own as much wealth as half of the population on the planet. This is a model that cannot be sustained under the pretense of democracy. Instead, such skewed injustice and disparity, like in earlier historical periods, must be continually sustained with strong-arm apparatuses of police and military governance.

In the essay's second part, I address how rupturing, dismantling, and conclusively undoing authoritarian capitalism and white patriarchal supremacy is a complex task and requires many approaches—including the powerful organizing work of Black Lives Matter, Critical Resistance, Indigenous

---

3   For a detailed analysis of Indigenous resurgence and alliances, see: Nick Estes and Jaskiran Dhillon (eds.), *Standing with Standing Rock: Voices from the #NoDAPL Movement* (Minneapolis: University of Minnesota Press, 2019); The Red Nation, *The Red Deal: Indigenous Action to Save Our Earth* (Brooklyn: Common Notions, 2021). On decolonization in the broader Americas, see Silvia Rivera Cusicanqui, "Chi'ixinakax utxiwa: A Reflection on the Practices and Discourses of Decolonization," *The South Atlantic Quarterly* 111, no. 1 (Winter 2012): 95–109.

4   The formulation of the antistate state appears in Ruth Wilson Gilmore's "In the Shadow of the Shadow State," in *The Revolution Will Not Be Funded: Beyond the Non-Profit Industrial Complex*, ed. Incite! Women of Color Against Violence (Boston: South End Press, 2009).

land and water defenders, and multiple horizontal efforts aimed at abolition and decolonization. International feminist mass movements in the Global South make central the degree to which the state under patriarchal rule is not the arbiter of gender/sexual and transphobic violence, but its key perpetrator, and must be addressed as such.

Many of these mobilizations have learned from Black, Indigenous, and immigrant struggles that make feminist and gender/sex analysis central, and therefore have produced broad-based efforts that work to delegitimize the normative functions of patriarchal state authority. These efforts include articulating zero tolerance for femicide and the routinized forms of sex/gender violence under authoritarian capitalism; working to dismantle carceral logics; creating visibility for gender parity in political processes; putting queer and trans* rights first; and raising forms of coalitional politics that consider Afro-Indigenous struggles and territories. Together these efforts counter the paradigm of war unleashed by the colonial-modern state.[5] By drawing upon examples in the Américas, I address the need for transversal and decolonial, cuir-trans*feminist approaches to imagine a future beyond the fascist shadow of our time-space present.

Colonial authoritarian origins

Aimé Césaire's *Discourse on Colonialism* draws a direct line between colonial systems and modern fascism:

> [W]e must show that each time a head is cut off or an eye put out in Vietnam and in France they accept the fact ... each time a Madagascan is tortured and in France and they accept the fact, civilization acquires another dead weight, a universal regression takes place, a gangrene sets in, a center of infection begins to spread; and that at the end of all these treaties that have been violated, all these lies that have been propagated, all these punitive expeditions that have been tolerated, all these prisoners who have been tied up and interrogated, all these patriots who have been tortured, at the end of all the racial pride that has been encouraged, all the boastfulness that has been displayed, a poison has been instilled into the veins of Europe and, slowly but surely, the continent proceeds toward *savagery*.[6]

---

5   On the paradigm of war, see Nelson Maldonado-Torres, *Against War: Views from the Underside of Modernity* (Durham: Duke University Press, 2008).

6   Aimé Césaire, *Discourse on Colonialism* (New York: Monthly Review Press, 2000). For a critical Indigenous studies perspective on colonialism, see Jodi Byrd, *The Transit of*

In this powerful inversion that moves the object of scrutiny from the colonized other to the savaging subject of Empire, Césaire articulates—in Stuart Hall's sense of the word—the concentration camps and the plantation systems of European colonialism to its twentieth-century incarnation as modern fascism. The infection that spreads, and the poison that Césaire refers to in the quote above then, is the rise of state and populist collusion with mass and targeted racialized death in the twentieth century that currently continues unabated.

Attempts to define recent forms of fascisms by theorists on the political left, whether Marxists, Trotskyists, autonomists, or anarchists, often miss what decolonial theory reveals, which is how colonial systems of global power are continuous in modernity; though racial capitalism mutates and proliferates, its underlying system is based in colonial extractive relations that originate within racialized structures of punishment and death so aptly described above by Césaire.

As we know from abolition scholars, the history of the police and the military emerged from within plantation and settler colonialism whose objective was to rule over and repress organized rebellion.[7] As Victor E. Kappeler describes in the US colonial context:

> New England settlers appointed Indian Constables to police Native Americans (National Constable Association, 1995), the St. Louis police were founded to protect residents from Native Americans in that frontier city, and many southern police departments began as slave patrols. In 1704, the colony of Carolina developed the nation's first slave patrol. Slave patrols helped to maintain the economic order and to assist the wealthy landowners in recovering and punishing slaves who essentially were considered property.[8]

Colonial slave patrols underpin the system of modern policing that manufactured Indigenous and African-descended people as criminals, displacing the organization of an economic and affective economy founded upon

---

Empire: Indigenous Critiques of Colonialism (Minneapolis: University of Minnesota Press, 2011), 13.

7   There are many scholars and theorists to cite here, but an essential classic reference is Cedric Robinson, *Black Marxism: The Making of the Black Radical Tradition* (Chapel Hill: University of North Carolina Press, 1983).

8   Victor E. Kappeler, "A Brief History of Slavery and the Origins of American Policing," November 18, 2020, https://plsonline.eku.edu/insidelook/brief-history-slavery-and-origins-american-policing.

massive violence and dispossession. As Sarah Haley shows in relation to the imprisonment of Black female labor, policing evolved upon the structure of racialized domestic labor. "The sight of black women on the streets in black neighborhoods," Haley writes, "perhaps with their voices raised, was an assault on the model of a docile black woman in the white domestic sphere, and therefore subject to punishment."[9] The Jim Crow system of punishment that protected white women's domestic spheres of influence was key to the broader logics of white supremacy as an authoritarian structure that punished non-white subjects through a trans-temporal penal system, that we now refer to as the "US prison industrial complex" and more broadly to "carceral capitalism," to name how we are all imprisoned by the digital surveillance apparatus of a corporate state.

In the Global North and the Global South, authoritarian systems depend upon structures of punishment and criminality that instantiate a gender, class, and color order that continually criminalizes and widens the net on dissent. As I have written elsewhere, authoritarian states like this are usually associated with Latin America, Asia, Africa, and the Middle East (or what we might refer to as the Global South), and target poor, female, queer, trans, Indigenous, and Black populations, converting those already expelled from the logics of primitive accumulation and dispossession into objectified subjects of the colonial rule of law.[10]

Authoritarianism and liberal democracy often share a symbiotic relationship, especially given that the racial state deploys differential systems of brutality to secure private property, extracting surplus from Black and Indigenous bodies and biodiverse territories (in rural peripheries or urban centers). Capitalism produces high consumer debt ratios and ratifies impossibly unequal concentrations of wealth, while it continually represses potential opposition. More recently, this has been rhetorically and politically accomplished through a series of authoritarian tactics that include popular appeals to a mythic white past of law and order, anxiety about race and sexuality, anti-intellectualism, and misinformation campaigns and policy maneuvers that perpetuate a series of fabricated histories without addressing the fungible origins of property theft.

---

9   Sarah Haley, *No Mercy Here: Gender, Punishment, and The Making of Jim Crow Modernity* (Chapel Hill: University of North Carolina Press, 2016).

10 See chapter 5 of Macarena Gómez-Barris, *The Extractive Zone: Social Ecologies and Decolonial Perspectives* (Durham: Duke University Press, 2017).

A key marker of fascist and authoritarian rule is not only its rhetorical strategies, but the symbolic and material targeting of enemies. As Pratap Mehta writes:

> The targeting of enemies—minorities, liberals, secularists, leftists, urban *naxals*, intellectuals, assorted protestors—is not driven by a calculus of ordinary politics. . . . When you legitimize yourself entirely by inventing enemies the truth ceases to matter, normal restraint of civilization and decency cease to matter, the checks and balances of normal politics cease to matter.[11]

Though Mehta describes the fascist directions of Narendra Modhi and the BJP in India, similar authoritarian tactics have been utilized in Trump's America, Duterte's security regime in the Philippines, Bolsonaro's racist imaginary of Brazil, and Piñero's criminalization of protestors in Chile. These autocratic figures work to center their patriarchal authority, challenging the liberal notion of multiracial democratic societies by first attacking racialized and sexualized others.[12] Indeed, new forms of global fascism continue to be rendered through patriarchal figures and their monocultural representations. The authoritarian antistate state casts an ever-widening net over those it criminalizes and capitalism expels. What the current political moment crystalizes is that liberal democracy has never been the end game. Astra Taylor reminds us of this with her recent book *Democracy May Not Exist, but We'll Miss It When It's Gone* (2020).

White and ethnic nationalist sentiments run through nostalgic representations of the past that imbue strong men with virulent capacities. For instance, Trump's 2017 "Make America Great Again" campaign, Jair Bolsonaro's recursion to the traditional Brazilian Christian family in

---

11 Pratap Bhanu Mehta, "JNU Violence Reflects an Apocalyptic Politics Driven by a Constant Need to Find New Enemies," *The Indian Express*, January 7, 2020, cited in Jason Stanley, *How Fascism Works: The Politics of Us and Them* (New York: Random House, 2018), 10.

12 For instance, Jair Bolsonaro has used a war of words to criminalize queer and trans* peoples and as well as same-sex sexual relations, and even though new protections have narrowly been granted by the Brazilian Supreme Court, hate speech and anti-LGBTQ* violence has increased. Of course, this keeps changing as Bolsonaro continuously attacks the Supreme Court for rights projections, as well as stacks the vociferous conservative as-of-now court minority. See Fabio Teixeira and Oscar Lopez, "With Brazil's Bolsonaro Attacking the Supreme Court, Are Gay Rights at Risk," July 20, 2021, https://www.reuters.com/article/brazil-lgbt-politics-idINL8N2EE6CH.

2018, and Duterte's "Fearless Solutions, Fast Actions" slogan in 2016 interpolate an electorate that gives primacy to militarized security, heteronormative exclusivity, and an anti-Indigenous, anti-Black, and antiminoritarian understandings of white phantasmatic national coherence. These strategies also function through ongoing violent expulsions of foreign others. As Jason Stanley described in relation to Trump's xenophobia, protecting the nation from Foreign Terrorist Entry into the United States was an executive order that not only halted refugees from the war in Syria, placing a travel ban on citizens of seven Muslim Countries, but its specific focus on religious identity contradicted the Establishment Clause of the US Constitution. As Stanley notes, this makes evident the fact that the Constitution can be manipulated for fascist political ends.[13] I will return to the issue of the Constitution, since it is a document that births the nation-state and structurally organizes illiberal and unequal societies, yet it has also become a site of revisioning and imagining toward a deepening of radical democracy. Yet, I would like to emphasize Stanley's point because it shows that liberal democratic institutions are not a fait accompli but are constantly unmasked, reworked, deliberated upon, and manipulated in directions that either produce positive rights or that contribute to their undoing.

In this period of a highly visible global resurgence of far-right ideology, we must also consider how antifeminist and antigay discourses have become central to the dangerous rhetoric used by political leaders, movements, and parties to advance political agendas with fascist underpinnings. The historical connections with targeting queer populations in relation to European fascism is clear, such as the burning down of Institut für Sexualwissenschaft (a foundation that campaigned for what today would be called LGBTQ+ rights) during the German Third Reich, and other forms of terror, deportation, and persecution against those Hitler's regime coded as subversive. Bolsonaro's outlandish statements about rather having his son be dead or a drug addict than gay, and his effort to ban homosexual references from textbooks are just two of the many examples that could be noted in the current homophobic and transphobic strains of autocratic demagoguery.

---

13 See Stanley "Preface," *How Fascism Works.*

Authoritarian capitalism

Whether a state is truly "fascist" is almost beyond the point, given that authoritarian practices run amok within liberal democracies in order to feed the beast of capitalist extraction. For instance, "nature" in capitalism is conceived as an input; soil, water, timber, minerals, ore, and oil are represented as commodities, converting biophysical resources into primitive accumulation. Given that racialized, poor, Indigenous, and Black communities are more likely to live and exist in spaces where extractive industries operate, they become targeted by the state as that which must be either removed or eradicated. When Indigenous and Afro-Indigenous land and water defenders protect spaces of high biodiversity they become targets of the military security apparatus, precisely because such anti-extractive organizing impedes the accumulative progress of the corporate state.

India, Brazil, Canada, Guatemala, and Honduras all experience high degrees of targeted violence against anti-extractive activists. Where policing and military actively secure new territorial frontiers, Black and Indigenous female bodies literally become the block to extractive capitalism. The Honduran state-sponsored militia death of the Lenca Indigenous activist Berta Cáceres in 2014 is an example of the overlapping structures of ecocide, feminicide, and genocide that are core practices of global capitalism under authoritarian governance.

Those experiencing the imperial and colonial imprint of racialized governance both "at home and abroad" understand the demagogic intolerance at the root of the 400-year-old US experiment with liberal democracy. Let me state the obvious: the rise of fascism in the globalized world today may surprise many, but least of all Black, Indigenous, and other colonized peoples who have observed state governance as one long and continuous abuse of power with recent fascisms as its apex expression. Authoritarianism looms large as a planetary condition, hovering as the polluted fodder that continually erodes democratic gains and capacities. It's the toxins poured into US communities of color and the Global South, the increased forms of Indigenous land dispossession, the dearth of quality unionized jobs, increased surveillance practices, dispossessions created by gentrification, lack of access to quality housing, healthcare, clean water, and public education, ongoing attacks on non-normative bodies, and the precarious structures of Black and Brown female labor. This violence against the people that capitalism leaves out must be quelled.

In the words of Jamil Khader, Professor of English at Bethlehem University in Palestine:

> Trump's objection to outsourcing, rejection of free-trade treaties, and his call for more government economic intervention are all symptoms of the fact that neoliberal economic policies and the democratic values associated with them can no longer drive capitalist growth. As a result, the crisis of global capitalism today is driving nations worldwide toward new forms of politico-economic organization—namely *authoritarian capitalism*.[14]

Thinking with this quote we might conjecture that the ghostly trace of neoliberalism may have had its last gasp. In its place, we might refer to a "new" old system: authoritarian capitalism. As Khader synthetically outlines about democracy's tipping point and the drive capitalist growth, new consolidations of racialized global capital rely on the rule of law. We can only conclude that authoritarian and fascism are embedded within institutions of liberal democracy, rather than outside of them, precisely because of their entanglement with racial capitalism.

If neoliberalism has ended and we are moving closer to what we might call authoritarian capitalism, then what are the ways that this new/old formation begs for a decolonial, queer of color,[15] and trans*feminist critique? *After neoliberalism* what must be burned to the ground in order to build anew?

The film *At the Edge of Democracy* by Petra Costa (2019) describes the precarity of a system based on electoral democracy that is built upon unsolid foundations. Its haunting opening scene describes the origin name for the country in which Costa was born, the Brazil tree, which is now extinct. "Only the name remains," she says, in voiceover, as if speaking to the phantasms of the colonial Anthropocene.[16] She also references the transatlantic slave trade and the inheritances of a nation steeped in the colonial military structures that first put down the rebellions of Afrodescendant peoples

---

14 Jamil Khader, Trump's Popularity and the Rise of Authoritarian Capitalism, *The Palestine Chronicle*, March 25, 2016, https://www.palestinechronicle.com/trumps-popularity-and-the-rise-of-authoritarian-capitalism/.

15 See Roderick A. Ferguson, "Authoritarianism and the Planetary Mission of Queer of Color Critique: A Short Reflection," *Safundi* 21, no. 3 (July 2020): 282–290.

16 See Macarena Gómez-Barris, "The Colonial Anthropocene: Damage, Remapping, and Resurgent Resources," *Antipode Online*, March 2019, https://antipodeonline.org/2019/03/19/the-colonial-anthropocene/.

and then became the root of modern authoritarian regimes. As Costa narrates about the present period in describing the military regime that lasted between 1964–1985: "In Bolsonaro's cosmology, militants like my parents should have been killed. It was the face of a country that had never punished the crimes committed under military rule. A country that had been shaped by slavery, privilege, and coups."

After its military dictatorship, one of the longest in the region, Brazil did little to formally address the atrocities of modern authoritarianism, just as it had not confronted its colonial legacies and brutality. There is an important scene in *At the Edge of Democracy* when the military police activate against the protestors, violently beating a Black man on camera while the filmmaker says in voiceover, "Our democracy was founded on forgetting." This is a profound statement of how racialized brutality and its erasure underlies the making of the nation-state. The occluded horrors that are buried but persist within democratic institutions, even during transition to democracy periods.[17] In this way, Brazil is not exceptional, since the settler nation-state indeed is amnesiac and relies upon the continual recurrence of anti-Black, anti-Indigenous, and misogynistic strategies as its operational foundation.

Writing in the 1940s at the height of Hitler's power, Walter Benjamin observed that "fascism tends to an aestheticization of politics,"[18] by which he meant fascism produces spectatorship that allows popular classes to feel recognized within the structure without upending the relations of power and ownership that produced that structure in the first place. In *Surviving Autocracy* (2020), Masha Gessen writes of the difficulty and toll of living under Trumpian news cycles, a way of being that is both fragmented and scattered. We may indeed be living and differentially dying within authoritarian capitalism, a structure of feeling so fragmented and disorienting that it confuses us into not being able to name its deciduous and hidden, but not yet extinct, colonial root.

---

17 The dynamics of burial, resurgence, and symbolic and material incorporation of the afterlives of colonialism and nation-building in many ways define the nation, as I wrote about in *Where Memory Dwells: Culture and State Violence in Chile* (Berkeley: University of California Press, 2009).

18 Walter Benjamin, "The Work of Art in the Age of its Technical Reproducibility: Third Version" (1939), in *Walter Benjamin: Selected Writings: Volume 4, 1938–40*, ed. Howard Eiland and Michael W. Jennings, trans. Harry Zohn and Edmund Jephcott (Cambridge, MA: Belknap Press, 2003).

The autumn of authoritarianism

How can we theorize new forms of authoritarian governance that operate from within the structures of illiberal democracy? How can we cut at the root of authoritarian capitalism to reimagine power as non-extractive? These are questions that cannot be resolved by the Biden administration or the taken-for-granted gains of liberal democracy. As the pandemic has made evident, antidemocratic forces like social media, the spread of fiction not facts, and disinformation campaigns are embers that ignite the populist wildfires of global fascism. The fact of more than seven million voters for Donald Trump in the presidential election, with white women increasing their support this election, is more evidence of the US electorate's ongoing investment in racial supremacy as well as authoritarian rule. Yet, the movement of Black Lives Matter, Indigenous proposals like the Red Deal, as well as UPROSE's Just Transitions efforts all show the propulsive and urgent force of anti-extractive organizing against racial capitalism.[19]

If the gains made under liberal democracy were only partial and have continued to sustain white heteropatriarchal supremacy, then it is through transversal struggle that radical democracy can be deepened. Learning from US Native feminisms, Black feminisms, queer and women of color feminist theories and activisms in the Global North, as well as anarcho-Indigenous feminisms, ecological socialisms, and decolonial praxis from the Américas allows us to address long-standing issues of how to historicize gendered violence within the matrix of coloniality that is the modern nation-state.[20] Antiracist, trans*feminist, and queer and trans people of color movements directly counter the patriarchal heterosexism of the state, and their on-the-ground struggles nurture radical democracy as a living practice.[21] It is the collaborative and cutting-edge work of abolition and decolonization activists that continues to unravel white patriarchal authority, revealing the many horizons of planetary futures.

---

19 The Red Nation, *The Red Deal: Indigenous Action to Save Our Earth* (Brooklyn: Common Notions, 2021).

20 On Native and Indigenous feminisms, see especially: Mishuana R. Goeman and Jennifer Nez Denetdale, "Introduction: Native Feminisms: Legacies, Interventions and Indigenous Sovereignties," *Wacazo Sa Review* 24, no. 2 (Fall 2009): 9–13; and Joanne Barker (ed.), *Critically Sovereign: Indigenous Gender, Sexuality and Feminist Studies* (Durham: Duke University Press, 2017). For intersections with queer theory, see Jodi Byrd, "Loving Unbecoming: The Queer Politics of the Transitive Native," in *Critically Sovereign*, and Leanne Betasamosake Simpson, *As We Have Always Done: Indigenous Freedom through Radical Resistance* (Minnesota: University of Minnesota Press, 2021).

21 See Macarena Gómez-Barris, Beyond the Pink Tide: Art and Political Undercurrents in the Américas (Berkeley: University of California Press, 2018).

In *Feminist International*, Verónica Gago describes how the female body is a site of war for the patriarchal state, and how it is only through counterweaponization and embodiment that the body will bring a new world into being. In the daily work of bodily living, new forms of power, or *potencia*, generate decolonial alternatives.[22] Through the nexus of the collective actions of sex workers, contingent labor, migrants, and reproductive rights activism, Gago describes another possible world: one of wide and interlinked global coalition.

Throughout Argentina and Chile, prior to the pandemic and even during, feminist movements have taken over the streets by the hundreds of thousands. Feminist struggle considers longer histories of social movements that counter state-sanctioned violence, repression, and fiscal austerity.[23] The massified use of repressive tactics by the state against these movements for radical change reveals the weakness of current models of democracy that use the weapons of war, military tanks, bullets, torture, rape, and the dispersion of chemicals to disarticulate the heterogeneity of such uprising.

Despite war as statecraft, profound democratic processes and a deepening of horizontal power takes place through hundreds of mobilizations that traverse all sectors, genders, social strata, and generations of Chilean society. Since 2006, mass mobilizations have effectively built upon student and worker movements that demanded less austerity, better wages, and free public education. More recently, constituent assemblies have fortified a sense of localized community and invigorated participation, fending off the social fragmentation that characterized the period during and following authoritarian rule. Popular assemblies that have taken place throughout Ecuador, Bolivia, and other parts of the Américas deepen the reach of democracy into local and communal spaces. They offer a potent form of popular power, such as the recent plebiscite vote for constitutional change in Chile (in 2020), an effort to rewrite the 1980 Constitution left in place by Pinochet. That 80 percent of the electorate voted for the drafting of a new constitution is the result of months of work in popular assemblies, with rich discussions on the character of the problems within the

---

22 Verónica Gago, *Feminist International: How to Change Everything* (London and New York: Verso, 2020).

23 For a powerful instance of this, see Maria Galindo and Mujeres Creando Comunidad, "Feminist Constitution," in "Decolonial Gesture," ed. Macarena Gómez-Barris, Marcial Godoy-Anativia, and Jill Lane, special issue, *e-misférica* 11, no.1 (2014): http://archive.hemisphericinstitute.org/hemi/en/ emisferica-111-decolonial-gesture.

neoliberal capitalist model that has privatized social security, healthcare and education, and left many Chileans in consumer debt.

Embers and ashes

Can we imagine a way out of such uneven and differentiated systems of economic and racialized state power? In a depressing political climate of illiberal democracy and rising neofascism, we must look beyond individual personality traits to focus instead on the contemporary authoritarian character of governance, and at the same time, name and dismantle new forms of capital accumulation and the militarized police state. Mariame Kaba describes the necessity of abolition for horizontal redress and restorative justice. The dismantling of police and military occupation is necessary to move towards fundamentally addressing and imagining beyond the violence of a vertical world.[24] We might also return to the Indigenous Mapuche women's call for Indigenous sovereignty,[25] and the specific proposal demanding plurinational shared governance, *Escucha Huinka* [Listen White Man], written by community historians.[26]

The collective dance of Mapuche Indigenous women who reworked the choreography of Colectivo Las Tesis to powerfully incorporate the sacred Kultrum drum was aimed directly at the colonial state, to address its terracide. As the trans*feminist and Indigenous expressions of Colectivo Las Tesis demand, we must seek accountability from those in power and from those who perpetuate the structures of authoritarian violence. The feminist, decolonial queer and trans life worth living demands an anti-authoritarian future, one born from the ashes of colonial and authoritarian capitalism.

---

24 On restorative justice and the profound work of abolition and transformative political struggle as well as forms of seeking justice, contending with harm, and addressing accountability beyond the punishment system, see Mariame Kaba's recently published brilliant book, based on decades of abolitionist struggle: Mariame Kaba, *We Do This 'til We Free Us: Abolitionist Organizing and Transforming Justice* (Chicago: Haymarket Books, 2021).

25 See Moira Millán, "Stop the Terricide: Manifesto for Buen Vivir," *Kedistan*, April 28, 2021, https://www.kedistan.net/2021/04/28/buen-vivir-manifesto/. For an important discussion on Indigenous sovereignty, see Aileen Moreton-Robinson's Introduction to her edited volume on Indigenous sovereignty in *Sovereign Subjects: Indigenous Sovereignty Matters* (Sydney: Allen and Unwin Publishers, 2009).

26 See Pablo Marimán, Serqio Caniuqueo, José Millalén, and Rodrigo Levil, ¡*Escucha Winka!* (Santiago: Lom Ediciones, 2006). For Mapuche scholar Luis Cárcamo Huechante's introduction to the epilogue, https://hemisphericinstitute.org/en/emisferica-11-1-decolonial-gesture/11-1-essays/epilogue-to-listen-huinka.html.

CHAPTER EIGHT

Colonization Calls My Home a Disturbed Area

A Conversation

Elspeth Iralu and Dolly Kikon

In the following interview, two Naga scholars discuss Naga experiences of colonialism and counterinsurgency in Nagaland, India—an Indigenous territory at the junction of India, Myanmar, and China. Internationally recognized scholar Dr. Dolly Kikon (Lotha Naga) of the University of Melbourne is interviewed by Elspeth Iralu (Angami Naga), a doctoral candidate in American Studies and visiting assistant professor of Indigenous Planning at the University of New Mexico. Recent Naga scholarship examines questions of self-determination, sovereignty, territory, and human rights of Naga people in a South Asian context. Naga scholarship remains marginalized within South Asian studies because of its focus on Indigeneity, self-determination, and sovereignty, as well as within Indigenous studies, perhaps because many scholars of Indigeneity are not familiar with the contexts of India and South/Southeast Asia.

Nagas first encountered the British in the early nineteenth century, as Britain sought to determine the eastern boundary of British India. British administration was installed in what is now Northeast India and American missionaries followed in the late-nineteenth century. In 1928, representatives of Naga tribes wrote a letter to the British Simon Commission expressing Naga intent to remain separate from the "scheme" for the nation-state of India. Nineteen years later in 1947, Naga people declared their independence from Britain one day before India and Pakistan's declarations of independence. In a Naga national plebiscite in 1951, Nagas voted to remain independent from India. In the following decades, the Indian state launched a low-intensity civil war and a series of counterinsurgency operations across the Naga homelands. The Naga-inhabited areas across Northeast India were declared a "disturbed area" under the extra-constitutional regulation of the Armed Forces Special Powers Act (AFSPA 1958). This act provides extraordinary power to Indian security forces and grants them impunity for actions carried out in the Naga areas. Over a period, India extended the AFSPA to the neighboring states of Assam, Manipur, Arunachal Pradesh (Tirap, Changlang, and Longding) and Mizoram, as well as Kashmir in 1990, despite outcry within India that the act is unconstitutional and critique by the United Nations that the act is a violation of human rights.

While Naga people have been the subject of scholarly research throughout the twentieth century, particularly by European and American historians and anthropologists, the voices of Naga writers and thinkers within the academy have emerged more recently. Much of the early and current anthropological and historical research conducted in the Naga areas focused on aspects of Naga culture, religious and spiritual practices, ecological and agricultural practices, history of early Naga contact with British colonists, the significance of Nagaland in World War II, or India-China-Myanmar international relations. Dolly Kikon's work marks a shift towards Naga research that centers contemporary Naga political lives. Her work has inspired a generation of scholars to address issues of structural violence, militarization, and gender justice. She has focused on extractive resource regimes in the backdrop of armed conflict and analyzed how the normalization of violence and military presence has deeply shaped contemporary political, cultural, and environmental processes. She draws from Indigenous epistemology that centers orality, storytelling, and dialogue to explore new practices and connections to generate conversations about relationship to land and community.

Kikon is a senior lecturer in Anthropology and Development Studies in the School of Social and Political Sciences at the University of Melbourne. Prior to earning her doctorate in Anthropology at Stanford University, Kikon briefly worked as a human rights lawyer at the Supreme Court of India (New Delhi) and the Gauhati High Court (Assam), before devoting her time fully to human rights activism in Northeast India. Her early legal work focused on land rights and gender disparities among Indigenous communities in Northeast India, themes that have continued in her scholarly research and writing.

Kikon's latest book, written with Duncan McDuie-Ra, is Ceasefire City: Militarism, Capitalism and Urbanism in Dimapur, *published in 2021 by Oxford University Press. In 2019, Kikon published two monographs:* Living with Oil and Coal: Resource Politics and Militarization in Northeast India, *published by University of Washington Press, and, with Bengt G. Karlsson,* Leaving the Land: Indigenous Migration and Affective Labour in India *with Cambridge University Press. In 2015, she published* Life and Dignity:

Women's Testimonies of Sexual Violence in Dimapur (Nagaland) *with the Northeast Social Research Centre Publication, Guwahati, Assam. In 2019, Kikon also directed and produced the documentary* Seasons of Life: Foraging and Fermenting Bambooshoot during Ceasefire (2019). *Her ongoing writing projects includes an anthropological monograph on fermentation and Indigenous food cultures.*

Her prolific scholarship and community engagement has made Kikon a role model and mentor for a younger generation of Naga scholars. Kikon's work unapologetically centers Naga experiences of colonialism and militarization—not as a side note of modern Indian history but as Indigenous histories and narratives of global import. What sets Dolly Kikon apart from her peers is the global reach of her scholarship. Kikon insists not only that her research is motivated by the goal of ultimately repealing laws that suppress Nagas and other Indigenous peoples in Northeast India and Kashmir, but she maintains that local Indigenous experiences of land dispossession, resource extraction, and militarization are events of global significance.

Elspeth Iralu: I'd love to begin with the politics of Indigeneity in India. How would you differentiate between categories such as Scheduled Tribes, Adivasi, Aboriginal, Indigenous, and tribal? Would you differentiate at all? How has the differentiation of these categories shaped Naga political identity formation or political identities?

Dolly Kikon: The debate about Indigeneity in India is grounded on struggles for the right to self-determination. In India, the term "Indigenous people" encompasses communities who are categorized as Scheduled Tribes (STs) and Adivasis. In that context, the term Indigenous in India operates as a bridge to bring together communities who recognize themselves as "tribal people" or "Adivasi" but use the term Indigenous interchangeably to refer to themselves as a political community.

Of course, the government of India has rejected the concept of Indigenous people and noted that the category is irrelevant in the case of India, but this position of the Indian government has not stopped the proliferation of the term Indigenous. For the Naga people, it is a political identity that establishes them as members of a regional, national, and global alliance.

As a member of the Naga Peoples Movement for Human Rights in the mid-1990s, I remember how we became conscious of the Indigenous rights movements across the world through different Indigenous assertions and resistance. It was also under the term Indigenous that Adivasi and Naga groups, including many other tribal groups in India, gathered as political communities to speak about land and justice in international forums across the world.

The term Indigenous allows us as tribal people and Adivasi communities in India to embody our knowledge and past as practices to be cherished and celebrated. To learn and connect with a Naga tribal pedagogy includes the possibility of calling our future generations wise and intellectual. Tools such as storytelling, fellowship, or eating together are not simply everyday affairs; these are both personal and collective processes that enable us to reflect and explore our lives, language, and land.

I am using broad examples here, but the value and significance of embracing the term Indigenous has allowed us as a collective to participate in generating dialogues and engaging in future visions about our communities. This did not take place overnight though. I remember that we were active and participated in various meetings in 1995. If you remember, 1995–2004 was declared "the international decade of the world's Indigenous people." I was an undergraduate student at the University of Delhi, extremely awkward and struggling to adjust to a new city and my place in the world. As a young student from Nagaland, Delhi was a difficult city, but I was also learning about the world through my tribal context.

India is soaked in caste privileges. It was extremely oppressive, but what liberated me was the grammar of feminism, justice, and Indigeneity. It enabled me to create a sense of belonging and political purpose. Underlining the demands for the right to self-determination, Indigenous struggles across Asia and around the world were like an education of the soul. They were asking important questions and standing up against powerful forces. These were extremely powerful stories for me. In my immediate world, the conversations and initiatives to make Delhi University a safe campus for women taught me how to mobilize, protest gender violence, and question patriarchy.

In my sense, the process of becoming politically conscious is to recognize the political violence and sacrifice of the past—be it colonization, genocide, or apartheid—and seek ways to collaborate and forge a path of justice for the future. However, being political is also a term that states use to profile people and communities. This splits our world into political and nonpolitical units. Some of us begin to believe in this division so much so that we position ourselves as apolitical/nonpartitional/objective people to accomplish certain tasks and projects. Mastering language and being articulate to reject movements and realities on the ground not only reduces the space of solidarity and alliance—it also enables authoritarian states to accomplish their mission to subjugate, divide us, and spread terror.

For the Naga people, the movement for the right to self-determination was a people's movement. There were community exchanges about a Naga future and what followed was several decades of armed conflict and counterinsurgency operations. Coming to Delhi and enrolling in a History Honors degree made me curious about my own people and the stories of my community. Ever since I entered college in 1994, and until the time I graduated with a doctoral degree from Stanford University in 2013, I never came across any readings on the Naga people or even on Northeast India. Every single text I read about my people, the region I came from, and about the history of my community was my own initiative; I had to go, as they say, "out of my way" to seek authors, activists, poets, and writers from the region and devote time to read and connect with them. The production of knowledge, I realized, is a violent form of subjugation and conditioning. These lessons in my life did not come to me overnight. The political identity I embrace and connect with—I can only speak for myself—took place as my worldview and practice as a tribal student were relegated to irrelevance and emptiness. Voices of tribal students continue to be heavily edited because they fail to generate or connect to significant or "central" themes in many class discussions.

As a student in Delhi University, the world outside the classroom was also a learning experience. We were speaking out about racism and sexual harassment but very few people believed us. Our breasts were being squeezed, our butts were pinched, male passengers on the public buses in Delhi masturbated in front of us. The landlords and their sons routinely harassed us and called us "tribal prostitutes." But these stories, contrary to establishing safety measures for us as tribal women, led to a culture of chauvinism and sexism.

The most blatant practices were established by the different tribal student unions from Northeast India. Tribal male students behaved like bullies and chiefs to control female students and penalize them randomly. Female students from Nagaland were often put under moral scrutiny and put on trial for "spoiling" the name of the community. One could say that the formation of the Naga political consciousness in the 1990s was a response triggered by the things we were seeing around us. To hold ourselves responsible meant drawing from our lived experiences and finding a way to respond to structural gendered violence as a collective political project. Looking back at the last twenty-five years of dialogues and solidarities, I value the experiences. In the chaos and violence, tribal students like myself found the ground to reflect on the meaning and action about community, feminism, and justice.

EI: "Sovereignty" has been a popular rallying cry among Nagas since at least the 1940s. In recent years, India has been in negotiations with a Naga nationalist political group, leading to discussion of "shared sovereignty." The details of the framework of this agreement are not public knowledge, but there is a stalemate between the government of India and the Naga nationalist political group with regards to a Naga demand that India recognize a Naga constitution and flag. These discussions draw on a Westphalian notion of sovereignty, but recent discussions in forums such as the Naga People's Movement for Human Rights and the Naga Scholars Association articulate a Naga sovereignty that is not limited by Westphalian understandings.

At the Naga People's Movement for Human Rights (NPMHR) 19th Morung Dialogue Naga in November 2020, Niketu Iralu called for Nagas to reexamine "the concept of sovereignty that Nagas have inherited from the colonial era."[1] Iralu articulated a Naga sovereignty that is not bound to a politics of recognition, either from the government of India or the United Nations, to whom many Naga political appeals have been directed. Two weeks later, in a keynote address to the international conference of the Naga Scholars Association, Dr. Paul Pimomo built on Iralu's articulation of an Indigenous Naga sovereignty, envisioning Naga nation-building as a process of sovereignty and self-determination beyond a nationalism that seeks recognition from a nation-state.[2] What do you think Naga sovereignty looks like today? How are Nagas generating an understanding of sovereignty that empowers rather than appealing to a politics of recognition?

---

1   Niketu Iralu, "Nation Build: The Challenge of Fragility," Nineteenth Morung Dialogue of the Naga People's Movement for Human Rights, November 20, 2020.

2   Paul Pimomo, "Living in the Present: Nagas in the 21st Century," keynote address, Naga Scholars Association International Webinar, November 25, 2020, http://www.thenagarepublic.com/news/nagaland-news/living-in-the-present-nagas-in-the-21st-century/.

DK: Perhaps applying the English term "sovereignty," particularly the Westphalian model of sovereignty based on legality and territoriality, might be unable to capture our Naga world. There is a Naga story about sovereignty which goes like this. One day a Naga insurgent leader came to a village somewhere in the hills and started to demand a feast. He said he was fighting for a Naga sovereign nation, and he demanded that the fattened duck be slaughtered for him and the best rice be served to him. An old man who was observing the drama chuckled. Feeling disrespected, the enraged insurgent leader kicked the old man's ass and sent him flying to the ground. The old man picked himself up saying, "Sovereignty is not stuck to my ass. You cannot kick me and take it out."

This story captures the tragedy and the absurdity of certain terms and political negotiations that Naga people have been trapped in. The possibility of generating anything that is meaningful and valuable for the Naga people must emerge from *within* and *from* the communities themselves. First, we must recognize that the ceasefire is a cessation of militaristic hostility between the Naga armed groups and the government of India forces. Second, there is a political negotiation since 1997 that involves interlocuters from the Naga armed forces, the government of India, and politicians. And finally, the negotiations must recognize the existing reality of Naga people on the ground who are experiencing increasing levels of inequality, gender violence, and poverty.

Any conversation for a sovereign Naga homeland means recognizing the authority to govern ourselves and the traditional power and jurisdiction we possess as tribal associations. One must reflect the common values and experiences we share as Naga people. For instance, we cannot function as Naga society without the traditional structures of governance and communitarian life. But we cannot ignore how Indian electoral politics have instrumentalized traditional bodies as vote banks. In addition, there is a culture of impunity where gender violence is on the rise. Therefore, to generate a conversation about Naga sovereignty today is to reflect on the existing tribal communitarian values we still hold dear to us.

Next, we have to call upon our politicians and ask how traditional councils, tribal elders, and clan/kin group heads have been made into managers of the Indian electoral system in Naga society. Our Naga values and connections to land and relationship is dictated by the Indian ballot and business contracts. Since the Indo-Naga ceasefire agreement in 1997, we have witnessed how the Indian electoral system has shaped the Naga political negotiation. If we accept this truth, it might allow us to see the condition of Naga sovereignty.

Voting on Indian parliamentary politics deeply influences the politics of Naga traditional councils and the composition of power across Naga cultural and tribal associations. Recognizing this is key to continuing our conversations about the future of Naga people, in two respects. First, it will allow us to reflect on the meaning and relevance of governance and how it has been reduced to national schemes and development policies on the ground. Second, the organs of state power—legislative, executive, and judiciary—which are pillars of the Indian state, have become the employment lifeline for many Naga households. We are aware of the heartaches and disappointments that Naga-elected members face as they turn down requests to provide "government jobs" to their supporters. On one side of the coin, there is deep devotion and love for our Naga elected leaders, but on the other side there is resentment and distrust. It is critical to reflect and make traditional councils and other Indigenous structures autonomous. But that is not the case on the ground. For that reason, traditional councils and tribal associations become fertile sites for Naga political leaders to sow their ambition and a hunger for infinite power. Once elected to any office, Naga leaders will do anything to control and instrumentalize the Indigenous institutions, even to the extent of splitting them.

However, not everything is dead. We continue to see strong community associations and kin connections when it comes to social and tribal obligations. Today, issues of justice and reconciliation are core components of Naga aspirations. These are topics Naga politicians currently cannot handle. This means recognizing how tribal communities and groups can adopt frameworks of care, dialogue, and engagement to reflect on a just Naga future. Unless Naga decision-making bodies and elected Naga leaders take into consideration that connections to land and customs also includes respecting women and children, we cannot talk about Naga people's aspiration for sovereignty. For me, the right to self-determination allows us to reflect and generate conversations about our Naga future, and take into consideration the reality unfolding in our society. This also means being inclusive in decision-making processes for our collective future.

EI: Your work makes clear a rejection of the racialized assumptions that underlie India's Armed Forces Special Powers Act (AFSPA), 1958. It is an act which institutes martial law in "disturbed areas" and ensures that no armed member of the military will be held accountable for violent actions against armed or civilian Nagas.

What is the significance of labeling an Indigenous territory a "disturbed area?" What is the global significance of AFSPA for Indigenous nations? Another theme I'd love to discuss is to think about AFSPA and the idea of Naga/Indigenous/Northeast territories as "disturbed."

DK: In 2009, I wrote "The Predicament of Justice," an essay where I conceptualized the logic of the "disturbed area" and being disturbed—as a region, as a citizen—a vicious cycle.[3] There is no end to this cycle and the logic of AFSPA. The notion of "disturbed area" operates on that logic. These oppressive regulations, categories, and geographies are labeled as disturbed because of the disorderly and recalcitrant citizens who inhabit these geographical spaces. The significance of these regulations is the exceptional ways state violence and impunity are legalized.

For me, the meaningful conversations about justice and human rights to repeal these extra-constitutional regulations emerged from my engagement with gender violence and the disempowerment of women and the marginalized in Naga society. How is it that we bear the trauma of being subjected to the longest insurgency in India's independence in 1947, and also witness the horrible gender violence within our societies? How is it that inclusive forums of governance and decision-making bodies continue to be elusive for Naga women? For the international Indigenous community, the significance of the AFSPA lies in the cultures of impunity that neocolonial states propagate in militarized societies. This is a reality for militarized societies, like the Naga people.

Contemporary Indigenous movements led by young thinkers, activists, and scholars stress the need to reclaim tradition and connect with politics and dialogues to decolonize pedagogy. These terrains are fraught with trauma, violence, and anger. To operate and mobilize under these existing Indigenous realities requires wisdom, patience, and a politics of care that is intergenerational and inclusive.

---

3   Dolly Kikon, "The Predicament of Justice: Fifty Years of Armed Forces Special Powers Act in India," *Contemporary South Asia* 17, no. 3 (2009): 271–282.

EI: Can we talk about how far this idea of a "disturbed area" extends into aspects of social, cultural, and political life? I'm thinking of your 2015 papers: "Fermenting Modernity: Putting Akhuni on the Nation's Table in India" and "Making Pickles During a Ceasefire: Livelihood, Sustainability, and Development," and how Naga eating is policed outside of Nagaland. In this case, it seems like the "disturbance" of/by Nagas is not confined to territorial boundaries on a map but travels with Nagas themselves.[4]

DK: My book *Living with Oil and Coal*[5] also engages with this point of disturbance. For me, this kind of disturbance is embedded in the history of the right to self-determination, and the state violence that followed—as a consequence of—the Naga movement. Therefore, the policing of Naga bodies as a "disturbing presence" is tied to the politics of identity. The notion of home/homeland is first tied to our bodies and then to the land, eventually.

In this sense, the Indigenous body is the ultimate marker of what constitutes a "boundary"; we can see this in the violence that Indigenous, Black, and queer bodies experience every day. Feminist literature, and thinkers like Gloria Anzaldua and V. Geetha, and Indigenous scholars such as Cutcha Risling Baldy, Zoe Todd, and Dalit writers like Meena Kandasamy, inform us how certain bodies can disturb the peace, stability, and status quo in society. In South Asia, Urvashi Butalia and Ritu Menon's work presents us with a feminist perspective on the partition.

If we situate our Naga Indigenous politics of belonging and the history of violence and militarization within a broader context of colonization and neo-colonization, the connecting threads are the experiences of violence and atrocities that communities have suffered.

Just like the trauma and the accounts of being hunted down by Indian soldiers during counterinsurgency operations in the Naga areas, these accounts show us what is at the core of terms like "disturbed area," and what actually goes on in these places. The impunity with which Indian security forces have operated in Northeast India, and the trauma this organ

---

4   Dolly Kikon, "Fermenting Modernity: Putting Akhuni on the Nation's Table in India," *South Asia: Journal of South Asian Studies* 38, no. 2 (2015): 320–335; Dolly Kikon, "Making Pickles during a Ceasefire: Livelihood, Sustainability, and Development in Nagaland," *Economic and Political Weekly* (2015): 74–78.

5   Dolly Kikon, *Living with Oil and Coal: Resource Politics and Militarization in Northeast India* (Seattle: University of Washington Press, 2019).

of the Indian state has caused, underlies the nature of the Indian state as a neocolonial extractive and militaristic entity in the region.

EI: AFSPA has been used to justify violence against women in "disturbed areas." Specific instances of violence against women by military forces have also served as a flash point for community political activism against AFPSA. Where do you think we can trace an emergence of Naga feminism in Naga cultural, political, and scholarly production? How is Naga feminism in conversation with other Indigenous feminisms? How does Naga feminism respond to AFSPA and politics in India-administered Nagaland?

DK: I wrote about Naga feminism in "What Kind of Nagaland Are We Moving Towards? A Naga Feminist Reflects on the Row Over the Women's Quota."[6] With this essay I was trying to conceptualize a Naga feminism.

I hope the future generation can tease out a conversation about the future of Naga feminism. Until recently, the word feminist was frowned upon in Naga society, I guess it still is. And for that reason, some Naga female researchers and writers have stayed away from it. We can have many explanations and positions on this, but for Naga society the definition of a good woman is grounded in a patriarchal framework like many traditional societies. All my works are theoretically and politically grounded on themes of gender justice. This is something that resonates with Indigenous feminist movements around the world. From raising our voices in Naga society to calling for the participation of women in decision-making tribal bodies, to including them as interlocuters in the Indo-Naga ceasefire negotiations, the theme of gender rights and decolonization are equally important.

Finally, as Indigenous feminists we recognize how Indigenous societies adopt patriarchal practices, so much so that customary laws and traditional councils interpret the Indigenous world through a patriarchal lens. For me, these are realities and not simply about shaming Naga society and our culture in the public realm. Unless we can hold ourselves accountable and use our voice to talk about difficult cultural and political issues, we will continue to live inside amphitheaters and television studios, wearing

---

6   Dolly Kikon, "What Kind of Nagaland Are We Moving Towards? A Naga Feminist Reflects on the Row Over the Women's Quota," *Scroll.in*, March 2, 2017, https://scroll.in/article/830065/what-kind-of-nagaland-are-we-moving-towards-a-naga-feminist-reflects-on-the-row-over-womens-quota.

our beads and hornbill feathers, dancing and singing for an indifferent audience.

EI: One tension I come across in my work is how we talk about time in relation to Indigenous experiences of colonization. Because of the Naga history of colonization being tied to British India, Naga scholarship is often expected to conform to the epistemic community of postcolonial theory, despite contemporary Naga lived experiences of militarization and ongoing violent erasure of Naga culture, language, and polities.

In November 2020, you gave a talk at UCLA titled "Are You Still Studying?" Anthropology, Decolonization, and Practice,"[7] in which you described decolonization in India not as a specific moment of time in the 1940s–1960s, but as a current movement and desire of Indigenous peoples in India.

DK: Let me confess. I have neither written nor presented anything that has the word "decolonization" in its title. Instead, I have devoted a lot of my adult life to human rights work in India—writing about militarization, sexual violence, armed conflicts, and resource extraction.

While protesting in rallies and conducting fact-finding trips, I learned about the contemporary political history of India: the transfer of power, accounts of partition in the Indian subcontinent, and the wars that ravaged lives. Growing up in Nagaland, a hill-state in Northeast India located at the trijunction of Myanmar, China, and Bangladesh, we grew up with stories about the Indo-China war of 1962 and the Bangladesh Liberation War of 1971. It is not because we lacked any war stories in our lives. The Indo-Naga armed conflict is listed as one of the world's longest insurgencies and played out right before our eyes.

For many thinkers, writers, and poets, independence from British colonization remained a broken dream in the subcontinent. As an undergraduate student in Delhi in the 1990s, I heard my activist friends recite the Urdu poet Faiz Ahmed Faiz's poem "Subh-e-Azadi" ["Dawn of Independence"], in which the last lines went like this:

---

7   Dolly Kikon, "'Are You Still Studying?' Anthropology, Decolonization, and Practice" (webinar), Center for India and South Asia, UCLA, Los Angeles, California, November 24, 2020, https://www.youtube.com/watch?v=vRD4yQu2Heo&t=3s.

Did the morning breeze ever come? Where has it gone?
Night weighs us down, it still weighs us down.
Friends, come away from this false light. Come, we must
search for that promised Dawn.[8]

Somehow these lines were both familiar and alienating. Familiar because our elders told us how some of the brightest thinkers and students from the Naga Hills joined the Naga national movement. They believed in calling out this false light; that the transfer of power did not end colonization. As thinkers, writers, and teachers, we too search for the promised dawn—that decolonizing light—because the night and darkness continues to weigh us down.

It is this weight I felt, as the remnants of colonization and a poison that spread across the villages and mountains, seeping into bodies, minds, and our collective soul. These deaths, the conflict and violence were not related to anything about *decolonization*, not even remotely.

The conversations that emerged from the violence centered on what was "wrong" with my Indigenous Naga world. Next, it was about how we "did not get it" that tribal communities in India were beneficiaries of affirmative actions like Scheduled Tribes.

"What do tribal people want?" "What is the solution to the Indo-Naga conflict?" "What do Naga people *really* want?"

These questions emerged from a preoccupation with postcolonial questions about citizenship and fundamental rights as enshrined in the Constitution of India. Rohit De's work highlights the role of citizens in shaping rights, debates, and practice.[9] He notes that the Constitution was "produced and reproduced in everyday encounters." Gautam Bhatia also tells us the story about the transformative journey of the Indian constitution:[10]

---

8 Faiz Ahmed Faiz, "The Dawn of Freedom (August 1947)," trans. Agha Shahid, *Annual of Urdu Studies* 11 (1996), https://minds.wisconsin.edu/handle/1793/11923.

9 Rohit De, *The People's Constitution: The Everyday Life of Law in the Indian Republic* (Princeton: Princeton University Press, 2018), 3.

10 Gautam Bhatia, *The Transformative Constitution: A Radical Biography in Nine Acts* (New York: Harper Collins, 2019). Excerpted in *Scroll.in* as "The Constitution of India was not just a founding document. It had a radically transformative vision," March 4, 2019, https://scroll.in/article/914555/the-constitution-of-india-was-not-just-a-founding-document-it-had-a-radically-transformative-vision.

For more than a hundred years, in their struggle against alien colonial role and against Indigenous social and economic domination, Indians imagined, conceptualised, and articulated a vocabulary of rights, of equality and freedom, and of dignity, a vocabulary rooted in the life-world of India.

The Constitution, according to Bhatia, was committed to ease social and economic hierarchies. He quotes Gandhi's speech in defense of civil rights, where Gandhi proclaimed how citizens shall have the freedom of speech and expression.[11] Given the prevailing political reality in India, the Constitution has become like a revolutionary charter to fight against people in power who are abusing authority, imprisoning academics, activists, practitioners, lawyers, and poets. Despite being the world's largest democracy, violence—caste-based/gender-based/on the basis of religion—persists. These realities tell us a story about what happens when ideals are compromised and a nation's citizens are stripped of their basic fundamental rights.

EI: Yes, this is what I was taught by our elders, too; that, as you say, "the transfer of power" from Britain to India "did not end colonization" for Nagas. This understanding is what animates so much of Naga political organizing, armed resistance, scholarly research, community movements, and narrations of our history. So what does colonization mean in Nagaland historically and today? If the formation of the nation-state of India was part of the decolonization of British India, how do we make sense of Naga experiences of ongoing colonialism and counterinsurgency? How do Nagas experience colonialism today?

DK: Colonization means many things. For our people in the Naga Hills, it meant being prohibited from making salt, being taxed for the cotton they sold in the markets along the foothills, being fenced out and blocked from their trading paths by British planters, disallowing them from growing tea in the Brahmaputra Valley. Colonization also meant the development of railway tracks, built along the foothills to carry Assam tea and oil out of the northeast frontier region.

When I was doing my doctoral fieldwork in 2009, I saw colonization was alive and thriving in this part of the world. Naga traders who come down

---

11 Bhatia, *The Transformative Constitution.*

to sell their produce do not cross the railway tracks even today for fear of being punished by authorities.

After India's independence, there was no desire to decolonize, but to recolonize. The colonized becoming a colonizer. There was no desire to tear down the fences along the foothills, but to transfer power to new owners who harbored the same contempt and violence towards the tea plantation workers and the tribes who lived in the hills. Colonization labels us as trouble, thieves, and suspicious people. Colonization calls my home a "disturbed area."

For decades, the violence in Northeast India, Kashmir, and the Adivasi homelands were often relegated as "marginal stories." There is no margin when it comes to violence; it is a poison that creates monsters, and for India, these "marginal" and "disturbed areas" were fertile experimental sites. Colonization stuck to these places like a stubborn stain.

For tribal students like me, getting an education was learning to kill our soul. Let me tell you why: because we are perceived as ignorant. People like me are unable to think, unable to analyze, unable to dream and aspire for a future. There is a constant correction that takes place; "but you don't get the larger picture." Who has the larger picture of India? Who has the larger picture of decolonization? Or colonization? Who?

Our understanding of the world is never good enough; our worldview is weak and childlike, we are forever frozen in innocence that is timeless. Colonization is conditioning minds to be frozen. Colonization is being ashamed of our tribal history, abandoning and rejecting our spirit world and relations that are tied to the land, other beings, and the forest. You see, before it became fashionable in anthropology to talk about "human and nonhuman relations," let me tell you, these kinds of accounts were called primitive, irrational, and practices grounded in ignorance. I was ashamed of these stories I had inherited for a long time.

EI: What Nagas have experienced, then, is colonization by multiple colonial administrative units and governments and which continues in the present. "Postcolonial" does not describe our experiences as a people, nation, or collective. Some scholarship about Nagaland and other Indigenous peoples in India poses Nagaland as a failed nation or an area which has yet to experience the full benefits of the decolonization of British India. But these approaches seem to be another iteration of the primitivity argument that you are describing. How might we conceive of Naga decolonization otherwise?

DK: If the term "postcolonial" is not an ideal place to start conversations about decolonization, where is a good place? For me, it is the urgency to consider decolonization as a collective work; to understand, heal, and create relationships. To see it as a process that will outlive us, to not be intimidated by terms such as ontological and epistemological.

How can we talk about ontologies and epistemologies if it erases the entangled intellectual histories of colonialism and hierarchies? Of validating one form of being over others, of weaponizing one form of knowledge to oppress others? Searching for a decolonizing journey means dwelling in politics, responsibilities, and a way of writing philosophy (a living ecosystem of knowledge/life/reality/practice) that is rescued from the classroom/discipline and connected to land, spirits, and meaning. For Naga people, it means taking part in healing and reconciliation between clans and kin groups to find a language of community; a language of coexistence and healing from the trauma of colonization, war, and violence.

III. Spectacles of National Security

CHAPTER NINE

"Make fascism great again!"

Mapping the Conceptual Work of "Fascism" in the War on Terror

Nicole Nguyen and Yazan Zahzah

The political charge of the fascism label

Since the 2017 presidential inauguration in the United States, political scientists and popular media alike have debated if President Donald J. Trump qualifies as a "fascist" or "terrorist" president. Social scientist and *Anatomy of Fascism* author Robert Paxton classified Trump as a fascist, calling attention to his "America First" message, "Make America Great Again" emblems, violent threats, and nationalist militias like the Proud Boys that "have stood in convincingly for Hitler's Storm Troopers and Mussolini's *squadristi*."[1] For Paxton, these acts, symbols, and armed militants make up the "anatomy" of fascism, which he defines as:

> political behavior marked by obsessive preoccupation with community decline, humiliation, or victimhood and by compensatory cults of unity, energy, and purity, in which a mass-based party of committed nationalist militants, working in uneasy but effective collaboration with traditional elites, abandons democratic liberties and pursues with redemptive violence and without ethical or legal restraints goals of internal cleansing and external expansion.[2]

Roger Griffin, political theorist and author of *The Nature of Fascism*, contends that labeling Trump a fascist is irresponsible; he notes, "You can be a total xenophobic racist male chauvinist bastard and still not be a fascist."[3] For the average person residing in the US, the fascist label has served as an

---

1 Robert Paxton, "I've Hesitated to Call Donald Trump a Fascist. Until Now," *Newsweek*, January 2021, https://www.newsweek.com/robert-paxton-trump-fascist-1560652.

2 Robert Paxton, *The Anatomy of Fascism* (New York: Penguin Random House, 2005), 218.

3 As quoted in Eliah Bures, "Don't Call Donald Trump a Fascist," *Foreign Policy*, November 2019, https://foreignpolicy.com/2019/11/02/donald-trump-fascist-nazi-right-wing/.

indictment of Trump's harmful rhetoric and policies, a rallying cry to challenge the Trump administration, and a desperate effort to define a political moment that seemed to defy all historical conventions. Political activists even transformed Trump's "Make America Great Again" slogan into a political allegation: "Make fascism great again!"

In this context, supporting Senator Joe Biden's 2020 presidential bid was framed as a "vote against fascism."[4] Accordingly, a Biden presidency would mark a return to democratic politics and values as well as the professional performances expected of a sitting president. If President Trump was an aberration from 'business as usual' in US governance, President Biden could return the country to its rightful political state, regardless of his troubling record on immigration, war, policing, and civil rights. In fact, Biden himself promised he would "be an ally of the light, not of the darkness" and help the United States "overcome this season of darkness."[5]

Reflecting on Biden's interventionist record and current administration, Center for International Policy fellow Danny Sjursen writes that "[Biden's] filled his foreign policy squad with Obama-Clinton retreads, a number of whom were architects of—if not the initial Iraq and Afghan debacles then—disasters in Libya, Syria, West Africa, Yemen, and the Afghan surge of 2009. In other words, Biden is putting the former arsonists in charge of the forever-war fire brigade."[6] While some viewed a Biden administration as a "vote against fascism," others saw it as a continuation of US governance and therefore refused to see the Trump administration as a mere "season."

These debates reflect the tension in naming political formations and the conceptual work such labels do by shaping public understandings of presidential administrations and informing subsequent political action such as voting. Rather than engage in an arguably objective assessment if either administration conforms to academic definitions of para-, semi-, generic-, or pseudo-fascism,[7] this chapter examines the conceptual work

---

4   Kelly M. Hayes, "In the 2020 Election, I'm Casting a Ballot against Full-Blown Fascism," *Teen Vogue*, August 2020, https://www.teenvogue.com/story/2020-election-voting-joe-biden-fascism-donald-trump.

5   Joe Biden, "2020 Democratic National Convention Speech," Milwaukee, WI, 2020, https://www.rev.com/blog/transcripts/joe-biden-2020-dnc-speech-transcript.

6   Danny Sjursen, "What Our Forever Wars Will Look like under Biden," *The Nation*, January 2021, https://www.thenation.com/article/politics/biden-endless-war/.

7   Roger Griffin, "Il Ventennio Parafascista? The Past and Future of a Neologism in Comparative Fascist Studies," in *Rethinking Fascism and Dictatorship in Europe*, ed. António Costa Pinto and Aristotle Kallis (London: Palgrave Macmillan, 2014), viii–xix.

the fascism label is called on to undertake. More specifically, we argue that the term fascism has been mobilized to delegitimize certain forms of US empire, war, and security—like Trump's proposed *Build the Wall, Enforce the Law Act*—while authorizing the outwardly liberal manifestations of hegemonic regimes of power, such as President Barack Obama's "deportation machine" that "turbocharged" immigration enforcement and the use of "precision" drone strikes that ostensibly targeted terrorist leaders and reduced US military casualties.

The political, polemical, and affective desires to define Trump as a fascist ruler exceptionalize his administration and its nationalist brutality. These charged desires also erase the forms of violence and death-dealing the United States uses irrespective of its presidential administration and therefore undermine a robust political analysis.

Although many political commentators worried about Trump's access to nuclear weapons, presidential administrations have long used brutal warfare to pursue its foreign policy interests. In January 2009, for example, Obama ordered his first drone strike, hitting a civilian home in North Waziristan, Pakistan. Obama justified these "surgical strikes" as a way to assassinate suspected terrorists on the Central Intelligence Agency's (CIA) Disposition Matrix. Obama insisted that these drone strikes constituted a "just war—a war waged proportionally, in last resort, and in self-defense" and therefore conformed to international and domestic law.[8] Later, he defended his use of drone strikes after the killing of two US hostages in Pakistan, stating, "one of the things that sets America apart from many other nations, one of the things that makes us exceptional, is our willingness to confront squarely our imperfections and to learn from our mistakes."[9]

To justify these illiberal practices, Obama invoked just war theory, legal conventions, and American exceptionalism. Such overtures echo Clinton-era Secretary of State, Madeline Albright's defense of US airstrikes against Saddam Hussein's regime in Iraq: "If we have to use force, it is because we

---

8   Barack Obama, "Remarks by the President at the National Defense University," Washington, DC, 2013, https://obamawhitehouse.archives.gov/the-press-office/2013/05/23/remarks-president-national-defense-university.

9   As quoted in Peter Baker, "Obama Apologizes after Drone Kills American and Italian Held by Al Qaeda," *The New York Times*, April 23, 2015, https://www.nytimes.com/2015/04/24/world/asia/2-qaeda-hostages-were-accidentally-killed-in-us-raid-white-house-says.html.

are America. We are an indispensable nation."[10] Such rhetoric forecasted Trump's invocation of "the defense of our nation and its citizens" to justify his drone assassination of Qasem Soleimani, for allegedly "plotting imminent and sinister attacks on American diplomats and military personnel."[11] Emblematic of his "America First" mantra, Trump concluded, "If Americans anywhere are threatened, we have all of those targets already fully identified, and I am ready and prepared to take whatever action necessary."[12]

Across presidential administrations, the United States has justified the use of lethal force by evoking the twin specters of national security and American exceptionalism. Even as Trump operated in a different register— distinctly refusing to disguise illiberal practices like extrajudicial killings in liberal discourses that invoke the law and humanitarian intent—his forms of death-dealing extended previous generations of US empire.

Historicizing Trump's assassination of Qasem Soleimani refuses to exceptionalize his administration as an aberration in US politics and demonstrates the nationalist political ideology—inflected by professed ideals like American exceptionalism, humanitarian intervention, and just war—that has historically organized US-led violence. Labeling Trump as a fascist ruler—an exceptional "season of darkness" in US governance— denies the ideological and material underpinnings that have shaped US violence since its very inception.

President George W. Bush, for example, mobilized nationalist rhetoric to describe the United States as a defender of liberty and justice, primed to "bring the hope of democracy, development, free markets, and free trade to every corner of the world."[13] In this political calculus, American exceptionalism justified Bush declaring war without congressional approval.

Furthermore, classifying Trump as a fascist means that what incites outrage are illiberal practices *without* liberal discourses. In other words, the fascism label has delegitimized clearly illiberal forms of US empire

---

10 As quoted in Micah Zenko, "The Myth of the Indispensable Nation," *Foreign Policy*, November 2014, https://foreignpolicy.com/2014/11/06/the-myth-of-the-indispensable-nation/.

11 Donald J. Trump, "President Trump's Statement on Death of Iranian Commander," Mar-a-Lago, FL, 2020, https://www.c-span.org/video/?467859-1/president-trump-speaks-air-strike-killed-iranian-commander.

12 Trump, "President Trump's Statement on Death of Iranian Commander."

13 George W. Bush, "The National Security Strategy of the United States," Washington, DC, 2002, https://2009-2017.state.gov/documents/organization/63562.pdf.

like Trump's border wall, while simultaneously affirming similar practices draped in a liberal veneer, such as Obama's deportation machine, which he deployed alongside his Deferred Action for Childhood Arrivals (DACA) program.

January 20, 2021: democracy prevailing?

After the 2020 presidential election, the United States faced a particularly pressured political moment. Given both intensive political repression and COVID-19 spikes, the Movement for Black Lives protests of the summer after the police killing of George Floyd began to wane. Trump warned that he would refuse to leave office, regardless of the electoral outcome. The looming threat of vigilante violence to protect Trump's declaration sent waves of instability through communities across the United States. The ensuing attempted armed takeover of the US Capitol on January 6, 2021 created a sense of imminent national crisis. As Trump deployed the National Guard to protect the Capitol from his own armed militia, people reached for terms like "coup" and "civil war" to make sense of the spectacle. Biden even called for the restoration of "just, simple decency" following the January 6 events.

Given the attempted armed takeover, the intensity of the election process, and Trump's willful delay of Biden's transition into office, by January 20, 2021, several media outlets described the inauguration as a triumph.[14] With headlines and news coverage emphasizing Biden's kindness, calm nature, and sympathetic approach, many in the United States believed that democracy had prevailed. With Trump's legacy and "season of darkness" in the country's rearview mirror, the United States could return to "simple decency" under a new administration.

Even as Biden identified the need to "repair," "restore," "heal," and "build" in his inaugural address, he almost immediately initiated military interventions, anti-Muslim national security policies, and coercive policing tactics to repress political dissidence. For example, within the first month of his presidency, Biden launched airstrikes against Iran-backed militias in Syria

---

14 With headlines such as "Biden: 'Democracy has Prevailed," "Biden Inaugural: Abrupt Pivot to Civility in Post-Trump Era," "Kamala Harris Makes History: Her Swearing in as Vice President Shows 'Strength of Our Democracy,'" "Joe Biden Consoles Country as US tops 400,000 COVID-19 Deaths," and "Vice President Harris: A New Chapter Opens in US Politics," the media reiterated that Biden marked a turning point for the country.

by bypassing congressional approval.[15] After alleging that these militias attacked US forces in Iraq, Biden warned that Iran could not "act with impunity" and described the strike as both lawful and necessary.[16] Biden's decision to suspend the second wave of airstrikes because "a woman and children were spotted in the area" became an act of emotional reprieve and military restraint, ultimately erasing the weight of his first strike—the casualties, the political unclarity around its relevance, the lack of congressional consultation. The fact that Biden bypassed Congress to enact the airstrike made fleeting waves despite its familiar connotations: acting with "impetuousness."[17]

This "firm but fair" logic, and its accompanying paternalistic approach, echoes Obama's framing of the global war on terror as both lawful and in the interests of human security. Artfully condemning war as he praised it, Obama stated the following about Afghanistan and the war at large:

> The United States of America has helped underwrite global security for more than six decades with the blood of our citizens and the strength of our arms. . . . We have borne this burden not because we seek to impose our will. We have done so out of enlightened self-interest—because we seek a better future for our children and grandchildren, and we believe that their lives will be better if others' children and grandchildren can live in freedom and prosperity.[18]

Here, Obama strategically wove a commitment to war into the poignant mourning of its inevitably and the ultimate universal responsibility of the nation to seek "a better future for our children and grandchildren and

---

15 Christian Nunley, "Democrats Criticize Biden's Decision to Launch Airstrikes in Syria without Consulting Congress," *CNBC*, February 26, 2021, https://www.cnbc.com/2021/02/26/lawmakers-react-to-biden-in-syria.html.

16 "Iran 'Can't Act With Impunity,' Biden Says after U.S. Air Strikes," *Reuters*, February 26, 2021, https://www.reuters.com/article/uk-iran-iraq/iran-condemns-u-s-strikes-in-syria-denies-attacks-in-iraq-idUSKBN2AR0BU.

17 Sarah Ferris, John Bresnahan, and Connor O'Brien, "Frustrated Dems Plan War Powers Vote over Iran," *Politico*, January 8, 2020, https://www.politico.com/news/2020/01/08/democrats-trump-iran-war-power-096193; George Packer, "The President Is Winning His War on American Institutions," *The Atlantic*, April 2020, https://www.theatlantic.com/magazine/archive/2020/04/how-to-destroy-a-government/606793/.

18 Barack Obama, "Remarks by the President at the Acceptance of the Nobel Peace Prize," Oslo, Norway, December 10, 2009, https://obamawhitehouse.archives.gov/the-press-office/remarks-president-acceptance-nobel-peace-prize.

others' children and grandchildren."

This paternalistic approach serves as the perfect embodiment of liberal masking of illiberal practices. In this case, Obama intentionally overstated the tragedy of war, at least for US soldiers, while blaming its necessity on the United States and its exceptional status. Similarly, Biden strategically blamed Iran for his attack on Syria, presenting the United States as a reluctant enforcer of what is right, rather than as a nation with political and economic interests in the dismantling of Iran, its anti-imperialist allies, and the subsequent threat they pose to US economic and political influence.

Under the Obama and Biden administrations, these multilayered interpretations of military interventions ultimately absolve the United States of its aggression by redirecting focus to Western anxieties surrounding the Axis of Resistance (the political alliance between Iran, Assad-led Syria, and Hezbollah). Yet, after the Trump administration's assassination of Qasem Soleimani, the House proposed legislation that would curtail presidential war powers.[19] For actions like this, Trump became known as a president waging "war on American institutions."[20]

In other words, while both presidential administrations used airstrikes to "send a message" to Iran, only Trump's military interventions received popular criticism that resulted in material "punishment" as a deviation from American values and as an ineffective or unnecessary strategy to effect political change. The public outcry over Trump's "fascist" leadership, evident in his "war on American institutions," set the stage for Biden to continue a long legacy of anti-Muslim and anti-Arab warfare and policing while appearing as a more liberal and less repressive political leader than his predecessor.

A new season of darkness?: anti-Muslim racism and the domestic war on terror

During his presidential campaign, Biden consulted multiple Muslim civil rights organizations to assess his platform. These organizations

---

19 Ferris, Bresnahan, and O'Brien, "Frustrated Dems Plan War Powers Vote over Iran"; "Slotkin's Bipartisan War Powers Resolution Heads to the President's Desk for Signature," Washington, DC, 2020, https://slotkin.house.gov/media/press-releases/slotkin-s-bipartisan-war-powers-resolution-heads-president-s-desk-signature.

20 Packer, "The President Is Winning His War on American Institutions."

identified serious concerns with the federal Targeted Violence and Terrorism Prevention program (TVTP) and its Obama-era predecessor Countering Violent Extremism (CVE).

The Targeted Violence and Terrorism Prevention program and other similar antiterrorism initiatives combine community policing methods and counterinsurgent social welfare by mobilizing community members, religious leaders, and social service providers like teachers to identify, report, and work with individuals perceived to be uniquely susceptible to terrorist radicalization and recruitment. Although Obama and subsequent presidential administrations framed these antiterrorism programs as an alternative to more coercive counterterrorism methods like FBI stings and blanket surveillance, national security agencies designed these programs to target refugees and racialized Muslim communities.[21]

Much like the community policing programs that came before them, these antiterrorism initiatives intend to resolve the crisis of police legitimacy while expanding police power by creating better relationships between communities and police officers, and by improving information sharing (and therefore intelligence gathering) between the two groups. In this way, TVTP and CVE alike can be understood as a liberal counterpart to blatantly "hard" surveillance programs like Suspicious Activity Reporting (SAR), the National Security Entry-Exit Registration System (NSEERS), and the Uniting and Strengthening America by Providing Appropriate Tools to Restrict, Intercept and Obstruct Terrorism (USA PATRIOT Act), which had all received extensive backlash from Muslim communities due to their numerous civil rights violations.[22]

Despite popular framings of TVTP and CVE as less coercive and more liberal antiterrorism approaches, Muslim civil rights and grassroots organizations demonstrated how these initiatives have intensified racial and religious profiling. More specifically, critics have shown how these programs use flawed indicators or warning signs of terrorist radicalization to identify

---

21 Nicole Nguyen, *Suspect Communities: Anti-Muslim Racism and the Domestic War on Terror* (Minneapolis: University of Minnesota Press, 2019); Yazan Zahzah, "Warcare Economies: Countering Violent Extremism in San Diego," Masters Thesis, Department of Women's Studies, San Diego State University, San Diego, CA, 2021.

22 Sabrina Alimahomed-Wilson, "When the FBI Knocks: Racialized State Surveillance of Muslims," *Critical Sociology* 45, no. 6 (2019): 871–887, https://doi. org/10.1177/0896920517750742; Nguyen, *Suspect Communities: Anti-Muslim Racism and the Domestic War on Terror*; Zahzah, "Warcare Economies."

vulnerable individuals. By naming religiosity, country of origin, certain political values, mental health, socioeconomic class, and citizenship status as signs of terrorist radicalization, these programs have targeted and criminalized poor and working-class Arab, Somali, Muslim, and immigrant communities.[23]

Given these concerns, Biden promised to defund the TVTP program while on the campaign trail.[24] Within his first month of presidency, Biden announced plans to expand the TVTP program and additional domestic terrorism legislation targeting Muslim, Arab, Black, and other communities of color.[25] For Muslim and Arab communities, the Biden administration did not mark a return to "simple decency" but the continuation of institutionalized anti-Muslim racism and, more recently, the domestic war on terror.

Refusing the exceptionalization of Trump: the case of anti-Muslim racism and the domestic war on terror

Using the January 6 attempted armed takeover as a platform, the Biden administration has sought to increase governmental resources to combat white supremacy as a domestic terrorist threat, including requesting an additional $84 million for the Department of Homeland Security to investigate internal workforce complaints about white supremacy.[26] Capitalizing on fears of a resurgent attack on the nation, the Office of the Director of National Intelligence released a report outlining the intelligence community's assessment that "domestic violent extremists (DVEs) who are

23 Majdal Community Center and Partnership for the Advancement of New Americans, "Countering Violent Extremism: Surveillance of San Diego's Muslim Refugee Communities," San Diego, CA, 2020, https://www.panasd.org/cve-brief; Nguyen, *Suspect Communities*; Zahzah, "Warcare Economies."

24 Joe Biden and Kamala Harris, "Joe Biden and the Arab American Community: A Plan for Partnership," Washington, DC, 2020, https://joebiden.com/wp-content/uploads/2020/08/Arab-American-Agenda.pdf; Faiza Patel, "Biden's Plan to Roll Back Discriminatory Counterterrorism Policies," New York City, 2020, https://www.brennancenter.org/our-work/analysis-opinion/bidens-plan-roll-back-discriminatory-counterterrorism-policies.

25 Julia Ainsley, "Biden DHS Plans to Expand Grants for Studying, Preventing Domestic Violent Extremism," *NBC News*, February 12, 2021, https://www.nbcnews.com/politics/national-security/biden-dhs-plans-expand-grants-studying-preventing-domestic-violent-extremism-n1257550.

26 Executive Office of the President, "Request for Fiscal Year (FY) 2022 Discretionary Funding," Washington, DC, 2021, https://www.whitehouse.gov/wp-content/uploads/2021/04/FY2022-Discretionary-Request.pdf.DC","title":"Request for fiscal year (FY

motivated by a range of ideologies and galvanized by recent political and societal events in the United States pose an elevated threat to the Homeland in 2021."[27] To guide the government's new initiatives, the report identified "DVEs with ideological agendas derived from bias, often related to race or ethnicity" and "DVEs who oppose all forms of capitalism, corporate globalization, and governing institutions" as two of the nation's most pressing terrorist threats.[28]

Although justified as a response to the white supremacist attack on the US Capitol, this framing criminalizes political ideologies well beyond white supremacy, reduces white supremacy to the violence of individual actors, and, in doing so, absolves the federal government of its role in producing, enacting, and benefiting from structural white supremacy.[29] Furthermore, the Biden administration has already weaponized these terrorism categories to crack down on anticapitalist, anti-imperialist, antipolice, and antiracist protests across the United States.[30]

These terrorism assessments and funding priorities reflect the continuation of the exact anti-Muslim and anti-Arab programs Biden previously promised to eliminate. These investments also speak to the longer legacy of racialized surveillance and political repression, as evidenced in the post-9/11 civil rights violations through national security policies, like the unconstitutional "No Fly List"[31] and the Counterintelligence Program (COINTELPRO) used to "expose, disrupt, misdirect, discredit, or otherwise neutralize the activities of the Black nationalists"[32] during the 1960s, both of which were in effect across Democratic and Republican presidential administrations.

---

27 Office of the Director of National Intelligence, "Domestic Violent Extremism Poses Heightened Threat in 2021," Washington, DC, 2021, https://www.dni.gov/files/ODNI/documents/assessments/UnclassSummaryofDVEAssessment-17MAR21.pdf.

28 Office of the Director of National Intelligence, "Domestic Violent Extremism Poses Heightened Threat in 2021."

29 Nicole Nguyen and Yazan Zahzah, "Why Treating Domestic Terrorism as Domestic Terrorism Won't Work and How Not to Fall for It," Los Angeles, California, 2020, http://www.stopcve.com/uploads/1/1/2/4/112447985/white_supremacy_toolkit__4_.pdf.

30 Michael Levenson, "As Protests against Police Violence Surge, Florida Passes a Bill to Combat 'Public Disorder,'" *The New York Times*, April 15, 2021, https://www.nytimes.com/2021/04/15/us/politics/florida-public-disorder-bill-police.html.

31 American Civil Liberties Union, "Court Rules No Fly List Process Unconstitutional and Must Be Reformed," 2014, https://aclu-or.org/en/cases/court-rules-no-fly-list-process-unconstitutional-and-must-be-reformed-0.

32 J. Edgar Hoover, "Counterintelligence Program," Washington, DC, 1967.

This utilization of progressive ideals to enact repressive policies is reminiscent of the passage of the *Mulford Act* in 1967, which repealed a law permitting the open carry of loaded firearms. Introduced by Republican State Assembly Member Don Mulford, the *Mulford Act* was crafted with the explicit intent to disarm and undermine the Black Panther Party's (BPP) cop-watch patrols in Northern California. With bipartisan support, Mulford defended the timing and targeting, arguing: "Let me assure you . . . that there are no racial overtones in this measure. There are many groups that have been active in California with loaded weapons in public places and this bill is directed against all of them."[33] Despite this denial, concerns that the Black Panther Party and other Black political groups might "overthrow" the government encouraged politicians like then-governor Ronald Reagan to support this and other gun control legislation. For example, a 1968 federal report determined that "the sharp and substantial increase in sales of firearms in US cities and nationwide is directly related to the actuality and prospect of civil disorders" and therefore concluded that "effective firearms controls are an essential contribution to domestic peace and tranquility."[34] In this case, Mulford and others drew on national security and "domestic peace" discourses to frame this gun control legislation as an ideologically ecumenical approach, targeting all forms of "civil disorder" equally.

Even though supporters of the *Mulford Act* specifically sought to disarm the Black Panther Party, conservative political leaders and gun rights organizations like the National Rifle Association (NRA) described these legislative efforts as racial neutral. The NRA specifically stated that it "does not approve or support any group that by force, violence, or subversion seeks to overthrow the Government and take the law into its hands, or that endorses or espouses doctrines of operation in an extralegal manner."[35] These framings of the *Mulford Act* echo through the Director of National Intelligence's condemnation of all forms of "violent extremism"[36] while directly targeting

33 Don Mulford, "Mulford Letter to Arthur E. de La Barra," 1967, https://sites.law.duke.edu/secondthoughts/wp-content/uploads/sites/13/2020/04/Mulford-Letter-1.pdf.

34 Stanford Research Institute, "Firearms, Violence, and Civil Disorders," Washington, DC, 1968, https://www.ojp.gov/pdffiles1/Photocopy/11802NCJRS.pdf.

35 Ashley Halsey Jr., "Rifleman Fire Back," *The Miami News*, May 20, 1967, https://sites.law.duke.edu/secondthoughts/wp-content/uploads/sites/13/2020/04/NRA-Press-Release.pdf.

36 Office of the Director of National Intelligence, "Domestic Violent Extremism Poses Heightened Threat in 2021."

communities of color. The Federal Bureau of Investigation, for example, has policed the Movement for Black Lives as terrorist threats under the national security category of "Black Identity Extremist."[37] The private mercenary TigerSwan similarly treated Indigenous water protectors protesting the Dakota Access Pipeline (DAPL) as "jihadists."[38]

Across presidential administrations, communities challenging racial profiling, coercive policing, and governmental overreaching have been treated as terrorist threats. While the Obama and Biden administrations have sought to frame their national security initiatives as alternatives to previous counterterrorism tactics such as Bush's use of torture and Trump's Muslim ban, these liberal policies still monitor, surveil, and brutalize communities perceived to threaten the homeland. Classifying Trump as a fascist leader whose Muslim ban reflects his racist authoritarianism merely erases the other ways anti-Muslim racism has been institutionalized and perpetuated in and through US governance despite its resulting in increased arrests, deportations, and torture of Muslim community members.[39] Fueled by the "fascist" label, such historical amnesia ultimately treats Trump's anti-Muslim policies and corresponding retrenchment of (white) nationalism as an aberration, rather than a continuation of anti-Muslim policing and security regimes that stretch worldwide. In this way, the term fascism has been mobilized to delegitimize certain manifestations of US empire, war, and security—like the Muslim ban—while legitimizing more liberal expressions of these hegemonic regimes of power like the Targeted Violence and Terrorism Prevention program.

The dangers of the fascist label

If the US public has used the fascist label to exceptionalize Trump, its

---

37 Federal Bureau of Investigation, "Black Identity Extremists Likely Motivated to Target Law Enforcement Officers," Washington, DC, 2017, https://www.documentcloud.org/documents/4067711-BIE-Redacted.html.

38 John Porter, "DAPL SITREP 168," 2017, https://theintercept.com/document/2017/06/21/internal-tigerswan-situation-report-2017-02-27/.

39 Department of Justice, "Brother of San Diego Man Killed Fighting for ISIS Sentenced to 10 Years for Terrorism Related Charges and Illegal Firearms Possession," Washington, DC, 2018, https://www.justice.gov/opa/pr/brother-san-diego-man-killed-fighting-isis-sentenced-10-years-terrorism-related-charges-and; Maryam Saleh, "Excessive Force: ICE Shackled 92 Somalis for 40 Hours on a Failed Deportation Flight. That Was Just the Start of the Abuse," *The Intercept*, March 4, 2018, https://theintercept.com/2018/03/04/somali-deportation-flight-ice-detention-center/.

political leaders have used a similar charge against other world leaders to justify military interventions, regime change, and economic sanctions. As the United States historically and presently has framed itself as an exceptional nation responsible for enforcing world order and protecting democracy, it interdependently defines other nations as repressive and oppressive.

For example, the Obama, Trump, and Biden administrations all have attacked Syria to punish although not entirely depose "protofascist" President Bashar al-Assad.[40] Across administrations, political leaders and military strategists have labeled certain world leaders as "fascist," "terrorist," "tyrannical," or "despotic" to legitimize military campaigns against Afghanistan, Egypt, Hezbollah, Iran, Iraq, Libya, and Somalia, and prior to that are many examples from Eastern Europe and Central America. Given the conceptual work the "fascism" label is called on to undertake, and the subsequent authorization of ensuing violence in both domestic and global contexts, we argue against using the term to understand political formations and their ideological foundations.

Ultimately, the utilization of the term "fascism" in the context of the United States is an ineffective and inaccurate portrayal that serves the very interests of the United States itself. While there are a handful of individual activists, scholars, and organizers who have used the term to describe Trump or the United States at large, the majority of the fixation comes from news outlets and political figures who position Trump as the epitome of fascism. This rhetorical work intentionally sidesteps more substantial critiques of the structures that undergird the United States, such as the myth of American exceptionalism, US empire, and white supremacy. By describing presidents like Trump as mere blips or fleeting "seasons" in the trajectory of democracy, the United States can maintain its position as a world leader in democratic politics, multiculturalism, and law and order.

As Angela Davis and many others argue, moments of progressive reform by the US government typically emerge in response to popular protest geared toward dismantling institutions of oppression.[41] Understanding the rhetorical strategies, such as the mobilization of the "fascist" label,

---

40 Fahad Nazer, "Syria: Why Fascism Is 'Never Lesser of Two Evils,'" *CNN*, February 19, 2014, https://www.cnn.com/2014/02/19/opinion/syria-assad-fascism-fahad-nazer.

41 Lanre Bakare and Angela Davis, "Angela Davis: 'We Knew That the Role of the Police Was to Protect White Supremacy,'" *The Guardian*, June 15, 2020, https://www.theguardian.com/us-news/2020/jun/15/angela-davis-on-george-floyd-as-long-as-the-violence-of-racism-remains-no-one-is-safe.

is central to challenging ostensibly liberal manifestations of US war and empire, from explicitly anti-Muslim antiterrorism programs to global military interventions. Occluding more than it clarifies, the term fascism has absolved the United States of its oppressive forms of governance by defining Trump as an aberration rather than a continuation of political practices and ideals that have justified state-sponsored violence across presidential administrations.

CHAPTER TEN

The Colonial History of the French State of Emergency

An Interview with Léopold Lambert

Léopold Lambert and Alyosha Goldstein

This interview with Léopold Lambert about his book États d'urgence: Une histoire spatiale du continuum colonial français [States of Emergency: A Spatial History of the French Colonial Continuum] *(Premiers Matins de Novembre, 2021) took place on February 24, 2021. Lambert is an architect, writer, and editor-in-chief of* The Funambulist *magazine. The purpose of discussing France's state of emergency legislation in the context of this edited volume is not to suggest a necessary equivalence between the state of emergency and fascism or fascist legal regimes. Rather, it is to further examine the various ways colonial legal regimes are historically entangled in authoritarian and militarized modes of governance—again, to de-exceptionalize fascism and situate fascist formations as responses to multiple crises of imperialism. As Nasser Hussain observes in his book* The Jurisprudence of Emergency: Colonialism and the Rule of Law, *the pretext of colonial emergency supposedly provoked by unruly and unreasonable colonized and racialized peoples has been foundational for modern conceptions and practices of the rule of law and the artifice of rational government.*[1] *Lambert's analysis of the French legislation offers a generative account of the particular legal and spatial means through which French officials and colonial administrators declare a state of emergency in order to both extend and consolidate colonial power. Furthermore, as Lambert makes clear, such measures have historically also served as precursors for establishing and generalizing intensified modes of surveillance, policing, and legal control more broadly.*

---

1   Nasser Hussain, *The Jurisprudence of Emergency: Colonialism and the Rule of Law* (Ann Arbor: University of Michigan Press, 2019 [2003]).

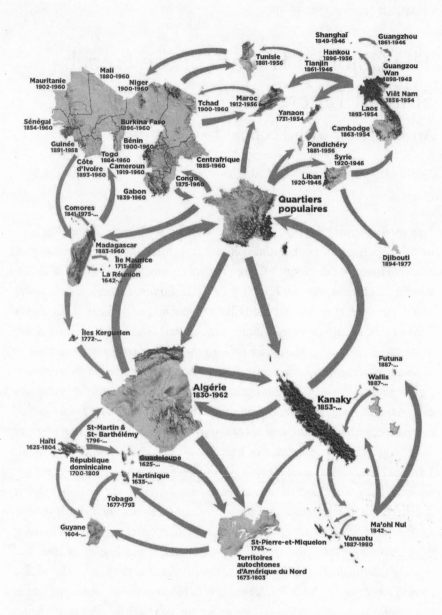

Figure 3. Diagram from the cover of États d'urgence: Une histoire spatiale du continuum colonial français. Courtesy of Léopold Lambert.

Alyosha Goldstein: Your book *States of Emergency: A Spatial History of the French Colonial Continuum* looks at the state of emergency as it was developed and deployed by the French government during the Algerian revolution, in Kanaky (New Caledonia), and in France itself. I wanted to begin by asking you to elaborate on the three primary terms of the title. In other words, what is the state of emergency legislation and how is it part of a specifically spatial history of ongoing French colonialism?

Léopold Lambert: The French state of emergency legislation was created around the same time that the British state of emergency was used in Malaya (now Malaysia) in 1949 and in Kenya against the Mau Mau insurrection in 1952. But it's not the same legislation. What the French state of emergency essentially allows is the possibility of implementing curfews and what they call "security zones," which are areas of whatever size where access can be restrained or controlled by military or police authorities. The authorities can expel people from certain territories, they can assign people to house arrest, and they can shut down gathering spaces. In more recent occurrences, the legislation has been more specifically applied to religious spaces, and in particular, to mosques. And, importantly, they can order house searches or, the search of any sort of private space, at any given moment of the day or the night without the prior authorization of a judge, which is usually required. They can also ask private individuals to give back their weapons.

The French state of emergency has been declared eight times. The first three were implemented during the Algerian revolution between 1955 to 1962, with the last of these continuing even after the end of the war until 1963. The state of emergency legislation itself was drafted in order to be immediately implemented. It essentially provided a retroactive legalization of the French counterinsurgency measures against Algerians that were already under way. Only the first one was declared in Algeria itself, while the two following ones were declared in France, where the revolution was also taking place. Those were originally taken in reaction to two coups by colonial officers in Algeria. The first one brought Charles de Gaulle back to power in 1958, who made France move to the Fifth Republic, which we are still living under now in France—a very highly presidential, highly executive power regime. Then, from 1961 to 1963, the state of emergency was implemented against Algerians in France, where the National Liberation Front had taken the revolution.

But also, quite importantly, I think the reason why this state of emergency was declared in France rather than in Algeria is because there was no longer a need for state of emergency legislation in Algeria itself. In Algeria it was very clearly a war by then. There were many military practices that could not be legal anyway, like torture, or kidnapping, or putting two million Algerians in camps.

The fourth, fifth, and sixth implementations of the state of emergency all happened in Oceania, in places colonized by France. The first one was probably the most important, during the Indigenous Kanak insurrection that lasted between 1984 to 1988. It was declared only a few hours after one of the main figures of the insurrection, Éloi Machoro, was assassinated by French military police snipers on January 12, 1985. The state of emergency was also instituted in a much more restrained way, for only one day in October 1986, in Wallis and Futuna, which are Polynesian kingdoms. Then, in October 1987, there was a massive strike by the dockworkers of Papeete, which is a port city in Ma'ohi Nui, which is the Indigenous name for what France called, without any sort of shame, "French Polynesia." The dockworkers were very much involved in a labor dispute, but, because they were Tahitians, their action was met with so much violence, including the official declaration of the state of emergency. It's because they were affecting the colonial infrastructure of supplies and food to Mururoa—which is also part of so-called French Polynesia—where French nuclear testing had been happening since 1966, after the nuclear testing was displaced from the colonized Algerian Sahara to the middle of Oceania.

The most recent declarations of the state of emergency were in France. In 2005, again, as a sort of counterrevolutionary measure against the youth of the *banlieue* [the peripheral suburban neighborhoods where many impoverished and working-class people of color live], and after the attacks in Paris in Saint-Denis on November 13, 2015 that killed 131 people. The 2015 declaration of the state of emergency lasted for two years. It resulted in the search of over 5,000 Muslim homes and the house arrest of about 10 to 15 percent of those whose homes were searched. House arrest, in this case, meant having to go to the closest police station to sign in about three times each day and being confined to one's home at night.

To be clear, I am not saying that the situation or context is the same under each of the eight declarations of the state of emergency. What is consistent is the state of emergency itself. The French state deploys the exact

Figure 4. Félix Poacoudou at his home in Nakéty, Kanaky, holding a photo of Éloi Machoro, his former comrade in arms. Photograph by Léopold Lambert, 2019.

same measures against, if not the same people, at least people who are the descendants of those people. And it's important to note that Kanaky remains a settler colony today, even though the insurrection resulted in certain accords that increased the political autonomy of the country to a certain degree.

So then, the colonial continuum that is central in the book? My very rough understanding of what a continuum is, from the point of view of physics, is that it is a topological surface of space-time, which I found very generative to describe European colonialism. We should be considering time and space as part of the same entity and, when it comes to time, we should think of it radically differently than many of us are used to. It's not about whether time is linear, or cyclical, but more in terms of stretchability of compressibility, as well as something contained within people themselves. I'm interested in thinking of history as also being something contained within people. In the beginning of the book, I write that when you kill someone, you kill history, and when you exploit people, you also destroy history. And then, there's also the spatial dimension. Each situation described in the book is unique in its specific space and time but is also connected by the conditions of French colonialism and the French state of emergency.

For instance, I start the book with the history of how communards of the Paris Commune and the anticolonial rebels from Algeria would meet after being imprisoned and deported to the furthest point of the globe in Kanaky, which was made a penal colony by the French. Many of these deported insurgents, ironically, then fought on the side of the French against the Kanak Indigenous revolt of 1878. This, to me, is also an example of the French colonial continuum.

AG: I'm interested to hear more about the circumstances under which the insurgents from the Paris Commune and Algeria ended up in Kanaky. Can you say more about that?

LL: Sure. On March 17, 1871, which is exactly two days before the Paris Commune started, in Algeria there was a massive revolt led by Sheikh Mokrani and a Sufi brotherhood against the French, who were already engaged in war against Prussia at the same time. And, so you have these two revolts [the Paris Commune in France and the anticolonial uprising in Algeria], one which is widely known by white leftists around the world and the other which is less known but is just as important if not more. They were both suppressed with the same ferocity by the French Army. There's the Paris Commune that lasts for two months and ten days, and whoever does not end up being massacred is sentenced and deported to the penal colonies of Kanaky and Guiana. Similarly in Algeria, although it takes a little more time, people are massacred, tribes are punished, and people are deported at the exact same time and with the exact same sort of charges each time to Kanaky.

After those who were deported from both France and Algeria have been held in the settler colony for about six years, there is a massive Kanak insurrection in Kanaky. Importantly, Kanaky is not a homogeneous space with one Indigenous people. Even today there are still twenty-eight languages spoken there. (And to give you an idea of the size of Kanaky, it is the exact same "length" as Palestine.) But nonetheless, in 1878, there is a massive coalition of Kanak peoples who revolt against the French colonial administration. To save itself, the colonial administration asks the people in the penal colony to fight against the uprising in exchange for becoming settlers on Kanaky land, which most of those imprisoned in the penal colony accept. Of course, we may want beautiful stories of solidarity, and there were some at that moment, but I think that it would be a very simplistic way to think of the conditions of colonialism if we only allowed ourselves to see moments of solidarity.

AG: It seems that the state of emergency legislation puts into place a number of very spatialized modes of control. Can you speak more about the multiplicity of spatial strategies involved with the state of emergency? In what way is the colonial continuum in your analysis a matter of both space and time?

LL: I try to show throughout the book the spatial strategies of resistance to the state of emergency as well. But, you have to ask, where is the state of emergency enabled? In the case of the great revolt of the banlieue in 2005, it was remarkable that youth were directly targeted. Nicolas Sarkozy, who was then Minister of the Interior and really the key person against whom the revolts were aimed, said in front of the Parliament when trying to get an extension of the state of emergency, something like, "Don't worry, we'll use it only where and when we need it." And, of course, the state of emergency is going to be used only where and when it's "needed." It's very clear against whom it is needed from the perspective of France as a colonial nation.

The implementation of the state of emergency happens at various scales. It happens at the scale of entire territories. It happens at the scale of neighborhoods. It happens at the scale of apartments and homes, which I find quite interesting, because I tend to see the walls that surround us as being the crystallization of various political regimes. Private property, and of, depending on where we are, capitalism or capitalist settler colonialism. Private property in the context of settler colonies is even more pronounced. But in the case of the state of emergency, the walls that we are used to understanding critically [as the demarcations of private property] become completely insufficient against the forces of police, who knock down the door at 3:00 a.m. and scream racist insults at parents in front of traumatized children. . . .

There's really a variety of spatial scales in which the state of emergency is enacted. When it comes to spatial typologies themselves, we can talk about camps and prisons. The first camps were built in Algeria, before the second state of emergency, and then in France. These were camps for people evicted from massive zones of security in rural Algeria, in the mountains.

Figure 5. Mobile wall used by police officers during recent implementations of the "state of emergency" in the cities of France. Photograph by Léopold Lambert, 2016.

During the entire Algerian revolution, about two million people were relocated to those camps. Even though these were not exactly concentration camps, many people imprisoned there died— particularly children—from malnutrition and a lack of medical care. Prisons themselves, of course, remain now and forever a space of the perpetual state of emergency. More recently, there are the various ways the police implement zones of security. For example, now, whenever we have a protest here in Paris, mobile walls are deployed by the police. So, there is an entire architecture of emergency that is very much at work.

I'm not saying there are some architectures that oppress and some architectures that liberate. I don't believe in liberatory architecture, I don't believe in a mindset of emancipatory architecture. However, I do believe that some spaces provide spatial conditions that are easier to organize from than others. The sort of paradigmatic example of this is the Casbah of Algiers or of other Algerian cities like Constantine. The French colonial administration and then the French Army have been unable to subdue the old city. It's too complicated for them. They perceive it as a labyrinth, which of course, it is not. It's just that it's not rationalized in the French

Haussmannian kind of way. The streets are narrow, and the roofs are used by insurgents to communicate with each other. During the revolution, Algerian people would leave their doors unlocked in order to allow insurgents to hide anywhere. When the French first invaded Algeria in 1830, one of the first things they did was to destroy half of Algiers' Casbah, and then they put numbers on buildings so as to be able to recognize and administer them. Laws such as the state of emergency also served to militarize the entire space, but even here, to a certain degree, some aspects of these circumstances can be or have been appropriated to use architecture's power against such measures.

AG: What you're speaking about brings together two of the other questions I wanted to ask you. One had to do with the ongoing or overriding interests in your work about the inherent violence of architecture and its weaponization in particular contexts. And the other is the question of how the state of emergency is not an exceptional moment; it merely intensifies already operationalized colonial or militarized forms, but it also becomes a battleground that people try to use to push back against the rationalized kind of imposition of those mechanisms of control.

LL: In terms of the inherent violence of architecture, what I primarily mean is that architecture is inherently violent at a physical level. Bodies are organized in spatial schemes that we call walls. So, that's the first way I look at walls. And then I look at how most walls crystallize and enforce private property, or settler colonial private property. Other walls might enforce carceralism within this realm of private property. Also, from a very so-called, middle-class understanding, walls manifest a social contract where I am not physically able to freely access any homes in my city except mine, but I'm okay with that, because I have my own. How a camp or prison is mobilized or, even the architecture of police stations, and the border, for example, show how architects are complicit with those regimes.

The second part of your question about the state of emergency not being an exceptional moment brings to mind the following example. In 1985, at the time when the French Parliament had to vote on whether or not to extend the state of emergency, Jean-Marie Tjibaou, the president of the provisional Kanaky government and leader of the insurrection, noted that such an extension did not matter that much given the Kanak peoples had been living under something akin to the state of emergency for 130 years anyway. And I think that was exactly right. The state of emergency is nothing other than an exacerbation of colonial logics that are at work on a permanent basis. What happens when the state of emergency is officially declared is that it makes these conditions legible. So much so that it tends to remain legible and is applied not only against colonized bodies but other bodies as well, which is exactly what's happening in France right now. Indeed, the last occurrence of the state of emergency ended on October 31, 2017, but ever since then, we've been under a law that took the bulk of what the state of emergency is about and transferred it into common law. So now we're living under the so-called "permanent state of emergency."

AG: Perhaps this transposition of the state of emergency—which had already been ongoing for people who are colonized or racialized as exploitable or disposable—into a mode of governance more broadly, suddenly becomes legible for white people or those who might somehow see themselves aligned with the colonial administration. I think in the United States, we see at moments like this the white left, or even white liberals, use the term "fascism" to describe what they perceive as a kind of overstepping of the proper terms of governance. But in fact, as with what you're describing, it's more a matter of white people being subjected to forms of policing and coercive governance that people who are racialized as nonwhite experience as part of their everyday lives. I'm wondering if there are ways that the question of fascism or authoritarian rule in this sense might be connected to how you are thinking about the state of emergency?

LL: Yes, I really think so. Just as the edited volume in which this interview will be published assumes a nonorthodox definition of fascism, I think part of what you just said has to do with the generalization of state violence and of arbitrariness, which, of course, is not arbitrariness. This is what we might want to call the "police state" in the context of France. Quite simply, the police are the last thing that holds the government in place. But the police hate this government as well. During the last presidential election there was a survey among police officers about who they would vote for, and two-thirds of them said they would vote for the National Front candidate Marine Le Pen.

I think what we're seeing now, in addition of the strengthening of the French police state, is the refinement, exacerbation, and deepening of structural

Islamophobia that is truly fascistic. I'm not sure I want to say fascist just now but at least fascistic. I might describe it also as the construction of a fascist legal infrastructure. France tends to over-legalize. I think that's what we're seeing here in France, a level of sophistication in fascist Islamophobia that is just stunning. And this has a definite connection with the history of French colonialism. We see this in France with who is identified or targeted as Muslim to begin with. I think this has to do with the history of the Algerian revolution, and in particular, with Algeria being omnipresent in wounded colonial French unconscious and state unconscious.

AG: It seems that there are different modes of racism and histories of Islamophobia that get inscribed or further perpetuated in these moments, and the ways in which that is especially prevalent in the French context seems to be very much at stake in terms of what you were just saying.

LL: And there's a reason for this, which again has to do with Algeria, with colonialism and the way secularism has been slowly weaponized by whiteness in France. This is the most disastrous political force now. Islamophobia in relation to weaponized secularism is coming from the left, actually from the center left, something called the *"Printemps Républicain* [the Republican Spring]." It has to do with whiteness, it has to do with colonialism, and it has much less to do with party politics. On the left, you find a partial-to-full embrace of this sort of weaponized notion of secularism appears as a sort of barely disguised Islamophobia.

AG: It seems like this is one of the interventions that your book makes, by foregrounding the colonial continuum and specifically how the state of emergency brings to light the organization of spatial relations as a response. It's an intervention into the white left's disavowal of that history and makes clear that this history is very much at stake in the present. That disavowal enables a kind of repurposed and weaponized secularism as a justification of Islamophobia from a left perspective.

LL: I don't talk that much about this sort of Islamophobia in the book. But I think it's fair to say that a lot of the book is about colonial strategies and colonial structures in all this. In the book's conclusion, I raise questions of space with regard to solidarities, reparations, and possible futures. These solidarities were very much Third World initiatives. For instance, when the Kanak insurrection was going on there was a conference in Guadeloupe called the "1st Conference of the Last Colonies of France," or something like that, where you had all the independence movements, and the FLNKS case, the Kanak and Socialist National Liberation Front, which, interestingly, goes back to the Algerian FLN. It's also a national liberation front, because in this case it's a Kanak and socialist national liberation front. It was very much seen as the hero of the moment, because they were managing to fight the colonial power. In the book's conclusion, I talk about Palestine as well, as being a constant object of solidarities and revolutionary imaginaries.

In the section of the book's conclusion on reparation, I discuss a few additional examples. I finish the book with an example of reconciliation. It is not, however, an example of reconciliation between the colonizers and colonized, but among the colonized themselves. This example returns to the 1878 Kanak insurrection, and the Algerians and communards fighting against the insurrection. In 2004, the tribe of the Kanak activist Djubelly Wéa undertook a customary process of reconciliation with the tribes of Jean-Marie Tjibaou and Yeiwéné Yeiwéné. In 1988, Wéa had assassinated Jean-Marie Tjibaou and number two of the FLNKS, Yeiwéné Yeiwéné, after the signing of the Matignon Accord because he believed it was a betrayal of the Kanak independence movement and an insult to the nineteen activists who had been murdered a few weeks earlier by the French army. But by doing so, he marginalized his tribe, which had just been the target of French torture and what is known as the Ouvéa massacre [after the name of the island where it took place] in May 1988.

The Kanak reconciliation process in 2004 culminated in a formal request for forgiveness and the receiving of forgiveness for the entire tribe. I think one way to understand the power of this ceremony is to understand it as an aspect of what decolonization looks like. What's interesting is that it totally decenters the colonizers. It's not about making peace with the colonizer. It's not even about obtaining things from the colonizer. It is just about repairing what has been broken. And in that case, among Kanak people, a very colonial problem, of course, because the assassination itself was based on the conditions of colonialism. Even the weapon that was used for the assassination was one of the weapons from the French police officers captured in the occupation of the police station that led to the massacre in 1988. So, this process is not so much about undoing, because it's not about forgetting what happened. It's just about being able to think of it as something that happened and then to build from there. To me, it's truly remarkable. And the best example with which I could possibly conclude the book.

AG: Decentering the colonizer is a great place to end. Thanks so much for taking the time to speak with me about your book.

CHAPTER ELEVEN

Claudia Jones, the Longue Durée of McCarthyism, and the Threat of US Fascism

Charisse Burden-Stelly

Fascism from Hitlerism to McCarthyism

On December 5, 1955, the United States government ordered the deportation of Claudia Jones, a prolific leader and theorist in the Communist Party of the United States of America (CPUSA), who, though Trinidadian by birth, had spent most of her life stateside.[1] Her expulsion was the culmination of years of harassment, surveillance, and state repression, primarily under the auspices of the Alien Registration Act of 1940 (Smith Act) and the Internal Security Act of 1950 (McCarran Act). This anticommunist violence experienced by Jones and her fellow party members was one aspect of what she feared was the rise of fascism in the United States. After World War II, Jones theorized, the threat of US fascism was manifested in the rise in white supremacist terrorism, especially against Black people; the entrenchment of "Wall Street imperialism," which included the subjugation of labor domestically and economic domination internationally; warmongering and militarism; and, of course, the government's utilization of anticommunism to crush the CPUSA and to cripple all progressive thought and activism. As the National Committee to Defend Negro Leadership argued in 1955, Jones was being persecuted because she fought against the "fascist-like abuses of the Negro people in the South," because she fought for world peace, and for her political views in general. Jones' "forcible

---

1 See, for example: "Chronology," in *Claudia Jones: Beyond Containment*, ed. Carole. Boyce Davies (Boulder: Lynne Reiner Publishers, 2011), xv; Davies, *Left of Karl Marx: The Political Life of Black Communist Claudia Jones* (Durham: Duke University Press, 2008), 131–166; Elizabeth Gurley Flynn, *The Alderson Story: My Life as a Political Prisoner* (New York: International Publishers, 1972), 115–121; Buzz Johnson, *"I Think of My Mother": Notes on the Life and Times of Claudia Jones* (London: Karia Press, 1985), 49–53; and, Marika Sherwood (ed.), *Claudia Jones: A Life in Exile* (London: Lawrence & Wishart, 1999), 20–34.

ejection," the Committee reprimanded, exemplified "the continuing abuse of the rights of colored people by the use of anti-Communist hysteria"—a practice that had been a cornerstone of Adolf Hitler's Germany in the not-too-distant past.[2]

Jones' postwar antifascism is not surprising given that it was the spread of fascism in the 1930s that drew her to the CPUSA. In particular, she was impressed by how the Party spoke about the linked fates of Africans who were menaced by fascist Italy and African Americans who were terrorized by white supremacy. "I was impressed by the Communist speakers," she wrote to her comrade William Z. Foster in 1955, "who explained the reasons for this brutal crime against young Negro boys [the Scottsboro Nine]; and who related the Scottsboro case to the struggle of the Ethiopian people against fascism and Mussolini's invasion."[3]

When the Italian fascist Benito Mussolini ordered the invasion of Abyssinia on October 3, 1935, anticapitalist activists, organizers, and intellectuals throughout the African diaspora immediately connected this aggression against one of the only African countries that had evaded colonial rule to European colonialism, white supremacy in the United States, Euro-American imperialism, and world war.[4] As long as Africans continued to be treated as inferior "others" to be ruled by Europeans, the Pan-African Marxist George Padmore contended, the threat of fascist tyranny would always be present.[5]

As early as 1934, the International Trade Union Committee of Negro Workers (ITUCNW), founded in July 1928 during the Sixth Congress of the Communist International, appealed to the global proletariat to rally against Italy's war provocations. Every subsequent issue of the ITUCNW's newspaper, *The Negro Worker*, defended Abyssinian sovereignty, condemned

---

2 Johnson, *I Think of My Mother,* 55–57.

3 Claudia Jones, "Autobiographical History," in *Claudia Jones: Beyond Containment*, ed. Carole. Boyce Davies (Boulder: Lynne Reiner Publishers, 2011), 13–14.

4 Here, the use of "anticapitalist" can be understood as e.g., socialist, communist, Marxist, anarchist, radical Pan-Africanist, and revolutionary nationalist thought and activism that, despite significant ideological differences, understand capitalism as an economic, political, and social system of exploitation, expropriation, dispossession, domination, and class antagonism. Anticapitalists of African descent in particular analyze this system to be inextricable from racist oppression, which intensifies its deleterious effects on those on the darker side of the color-line, and especially those racialized as Black.

5 John Munro, *The Anticolonial Front: The African American Freedom Struggle and Global Decolonization, 1945–1960* (Cambridge: Cambridge University Press, 2017), 48–49.

the imperialist encroachment upon the country's territory, and warned that fascist Italy's actions represented a step toward another world war.[6] "The struggle against fascism and war," the paper enjoined, was part of a larger freedom struggle that included "[the] fight for the release of class war prisoners, [the] fight for the release of the Scottsboro boys and Angelo Herndon, [and] the fight for self-determination and independence of the colonial toilers."[7] Though he was no friend to the Communist International, the anticapitalist and one-time Trotskyite C.L.R. James likewise encouraged support for the anti-imperialist movements that were cropping up among the Black masses as a result of the invasion of Abyssinia. African liberation and the eradication of racism, he maintained, were instrumental to the defeat of fascism.[8] After the invasion, labor strikes broke out across the African diaspora, from St. Kitts to British Guiana and South Africa, influenced by protests against Italian aggression and the concomitant "united front of white Europe against black Africa."[9]

For Jones and other anticapitalists, Abyssinia's fight for democracy against Italy's fascist violence and brutality paralleled the Black struggle against white terrorism in the United States. All the elements of fascism—suppression of freedom, appeal to tradition, and rigid legal-economic imposition along racial lines—could already be found in the Jim Crow system throughout the US South. In the North, too, Black people were subjected to "anti-Negro violence," including race riots, lynching, and "trumped-up" charges that resulted in unjust imprisonment.[10] Likewise, the super-exploitation of both Abyssinians and African Americans was being funded by US industrial capitalists like Henry Ford, who provided aid to fascist Italy not unlike the way they financed the subjection of Black people throughout the Southern "Black Belt" and in Northern ghettoes.

Moreover, the failure of the United States and the League of Nations to defend Ethiopia's sovereignty, despite the 1928 Kellogg Briand Pact, mirrored the US government's unwillingness to protect Black people from

---

6   Hakim Adi, *Pan-Africanism and Communism: The Communist International, Africa, and the Diaspora, 1919–1939* (Trenton: African World Press, 2013) 175–176.

7   See *Negro Worker* (July–August 1935): 3–5.

8   Anthony Bogues, *Caliban's Freedom: The Early Political Thought of C.L.R. James* (London: Pluto Press, 1997), 39.

9   George Padmore, "Ethiopia and World Politics," *The Crisis*, May 1935, 138–139.

10   Claudia Jones, "Jim Crow in Uniform," in *Claudia Jones: Beyond Containment* ed. Carole. Boyce Davies (Boulder: Lynne Reiner Publishers, 2011), 37–38.

white violence under the veneer of state's rights.[11] Italy's Assistant-Secretary of the Colonies urged the League of Nations to maintain the "solidarity of the European colonial powers in maintaining Africa as the national reserve of the white race,"[12] just as Mississippi Representative John E. Rankin sought to keep "*nigger* communists" from "infesting" Congress with the Anti-Lynching Bill of 1939.[13] Thus Italian fascism and US white supremacy were close cousins, not least because the transnational commitment to Black oppression flowed both ways.

As World War II gave way to the Cold War, the threat of fascism rose once again—this time in the United States—as the new superpower consolidated its global hegemony. Collaboration with the Soviet Union against the Axis powers quickly descended into confrontation, and as a result, radicalism generally, and communism particularly, became the main target of US foreign and domestic policy. Such antiradicalism—the disciplining of communists, socialists, and other anticapitalists whose ideas, politics, and activism are deemed subversive or threatening to the US government—presaged a US brand of fascism insofar as it all but criminalized left-wing militancy as foreign-inspired, un-American, and threatening to the stability and security of the United States. As such, those who defended the gains made by labor, African Americans and other minoritized groups, were accused of domestic subversion to rationalize the curtailment of civil rights and liberties, circumscription of freedom, and corrosion of citizenship.

The threat of US fascism was undergirded by an antiradical state apparatus that comprised a network of government organizations, including the State Department and the Federal Bureau of Investigation (FBI); congressional committees including the House Un-American Activities Committee (HUAC), and the Subversive Activities Control Board (SACB); and instrumentalities including the Attorney General's List of Subversive Organizations and the 1951 FBI Responsibilities Program. Integral to this architecture was a litany of legislation, including the 1938 Foreign Agents Registration Act, the 1939 Hatch Act, the 1940 Voorhis Act, the 1940 Alien Registration Act, the 1947 Labor Management Relations Act, Executive

---

11 For an illuminating discussion of Ethiopia's partial, burdened, and racially specified membership in the League of Nations, see Adom Getachew, *Worldmaking after Empire: The Rise and Fall of Self-Determination* (Princeton: Princeton University Press, 2019), 14–36.

12 Adi, *Pan-Africanism and Communism*, 177.

13 Jones, "Jim Crow," 31.

Order 9835 of 1947 (the "Loyalty Order") and its supersession in 1953 by Executive Order 10450, the Internal Security Act of 1950, and the 1954 Communist Control Act.[14] Reminiscent of the rise of fascism in the interwar period, these entities, among others, aimed to abject, eject, and neutralize communists and their "fellow-travelers" and "sympathizers"—a broad designation that included anyone who disagreed with or criticized the US government's fascist-like politics, including "peace activists, civil rights leaders, dissident artists, and progressive labor organizers of all types."[15]

Those like Claudia Jones, who were Black, foreign-born or "second-class" citizens, and/or communist or sympathetic to that cause, tended to interpret attacks on their freedoms of speech, press, and association as the first step toward the rise of fascism on their own shores. As the Black radical poet Langston Hughes noted about the 1948 Smith Act trial, "first [Hitler] locked up the Communists. The Jews were No. 2." Noting the United States' specific historical and material conditions, Hughes continued: "In America the Negroes are No. 2 on history's list. . . . If the twelve Communists are sent to jail in a little while they will send Negroes to jail simply for being Negroes and to concentration camps just for being colored."[16] Like Hughes, Jones analyzed the conjuncture of "peace time" upsurge in anti-Black violence in the United States, emboldened Wall Street imperialism encircling the globe, and the prospect of yet another world war, as a harbinger of fascism.

This article examines Jones' theorization of the fascist threat in the United States in the early years of the Cold War. Jones consistently described these years as protofascist, fascist-like, and outright fascist, and frequently argued that the US government specifically targeted antifascists—especially those of African descent. Drawing on her political thought and that of her comrades, including Claude Lightfoot, Benjamin J. Davis, Jr., Dorothy Hunton, and W.E.B. Du Bois, the essay begins by defining the peculiar brand of US fascism that loomed large in the minds of anticapitalists.

---

14 See Charisse Burden-Stelly, "Constructing Deportable Subjectivity: Antiforeignness, Antiradicalism, and Anti-Blackness during the McCarthyist Structure of Feeling," *Souls* 19, no. 3 (July–September 2017): 342–358.

15 Barbara Ransby, *Eslanda: The Large and Unconventional Life of Mrs. Paul Robeson* (New Haven: Yale University Press, 2013), 224.

16 Gerald Horne, *Black Liberation/Red Scare: Ben Davis and the Communist Party* (Newark, DE: University of Delaware Press, 1994), 218.

Then, it employs "the longue durée of McCarthyism" as an analytical framework to explicate the post-WWII fascist-like political formation that both preceded and exceeded Senator Joseph McCarthy's reign of repression. The next section highlights Jones' analysis of the Smith Act, the first peace-time sedition act in US history. She, along with other Black communists and anticapitalists, argued that the Smith Act's sweeping criminalization of individuals, organizations, protests, and demands aimed at fundamentally transforming society was a form of "thought control" that put the United States squarely on the path to fascism.

The essay concludes with Jones' critique of, and subjection to, the McCarran Act, which President Harry S. Truman unsuccessfully vetoed because he found it to be "the greatest danger to freedom of speech, press, and assembly since the Alien and Sedition Laws of 1798."[17] Bringing Truman's fears to fruition, the McCarran Act wreaked havoc on the lives of citizens and noncitizens alike. As Jones' early biographer Buzz Johnson notes, taken together, the Smith Act and the McCarran Act created the conditions for the persecution of thousands of progressives, launched an all-out attack on their civil rights, and laid the foundation for immigration checks, deportation, and harassment particularly aimed at Black people. Anticapitalists like Paul Robeson, C.L.R. James, and Ferdinand Smith had their lives fundamentally disrupted by this "strong anti-Black and anti-communist hysteria."[18]

Defining US fascism

In his study of fascist regimes in Germany, Indonesia, Italy, Spain, and several Latin American countries, Lawrence W. Britt identified fourteen characteristics of fascism: powerful and continuing nationalism, disdain for human rights, the construction of enemies/scapegoats as a source of unification, military supremacy, rampant sexism, controlled mass media, obsession with national security, lack of separation between government and religion, the aggressive protection of corporate power, the suppression of labor, disdain for intellectuals and artists, obsession with crime

---

17 Ellen Schrecker, *The Age of McCarthyism: A Brief History with Documents* (New York: Palgrave, 2002), 194.

18 Johnson, *I Think of My Mother*, 21.

and punishment, ubiquitous cronyism and corruption, and fraudulent elections.[19]

Jones identified a number of these factors in her Smith Act trial, and by extension, in United States society during the early Cold War. In a statement before her sentencing in 1953, she began by arguing that the US government had doubled down on its peculiar brand of nationalism, which was predicated on denying democratic rights to Black second-class citizens.[20] Endemic in the disenfranchisement of the Black population was support for fraudulent elections since the votes of those on the darker side of the color-line were excluded. The government's disdain for human rights was manifested in "the obscenity of this trial of ideas," built on the "concocted lies" of "stool pigeons and informers." She excoriated, "for me to accept the verdict of guilty would only mean that I considered myself less than worthy of the dignity of truth, which I cherish as a communist and as a human being. . . ."

In other words, the railroading of communists—who had become the enemies and scapegoats to rationalize what was fast becoming a police state—was an assault on human rights.[21] Jones further argued that she was being found guilty of struggling against military supremacy, specifically to "end the bestial Korean War, to stop 'operation killer,' to bring our boys home, to reject the militarist threat to embroil us in war with China."[22] Such a position was anathema to "the desperate drive by the men of Wall Street to war and fascism," and highlighted the government's callous protection of corporate power over and against the interests of the masses of the world.[23] Moreover, Jones' persecution was tinged with sexism insofar as her original indictment was based on her article "Women in the Struggle for Peace and Security," in which she urged Negro and white mothers and women to join their antifascist sisters throughout the world to put pressure on the US government in the cause of peace. This flew in the face of the

---

19 Lawrence W. Britt, "Fascism Anyone? The 14 Defining Characteristics of Fascism," in *Not Our President: New Directions from the Pushed Out, the Others, and the Clear Majority in Trump's Stolen America*, ed. Haki R. Madhubuti and Lasana D. Kazembe (Chicago: Third World Press Foundation, 2017), 423–425.

20 Claudia Jones, "[Black] women can think and speak and write!," in *Claudia Jones: Beyond Containment*, 9.

21 Jones, "[Black] women can think," 7.

22 Jones, "[Black] women can think," 8.

23 Jones, "[Black] women can think," 8.

Truman administration's "fascist triple-K (*Kinder-Küche-Kirche*)" ideology. This emphasis on "Children, Kitchen, Church" was deeply antiwoman and aimed to hamper women's social participation and progressive politics. As such, it penalized "especially negro women [and] the working women," and that worsened their economic status.[24] In the same article, Jones argued:

> Not always discerned by the labour progressive forces, however, is the nature of this ideological attack, which increasingly is masked as attacks on woman's femininity, her womanliness, her pursuit of personal and family happiness. Big capital accelerates its reactionary ideological offensive against [laboring and working] people with forcible opposition to women's social participation for peace and for her pressing economic and social demands.[25]

Here, she theorized the interrelationship between anticommunist persecution, the denigration of women, and the suppression of labor and the working class. Moreover, Jones' prosecution conveyed the government's desire to control the press, since she was indicted on the basis of published articles; the government's emphasis on crime and punishment, insofar as communist and progressive ideas were being criminalized and those who espoused them were being incarcerated, deported, and otherwise harassed; and the government's obsession with national security in that ideas, not actions, were construed as anti-American insurrection.

While sharing the above features with European fascist regimes, Jones and other anticapitalists theorized four distinctive characteristics of US fascism. Perhaps the most important was anti-Blackness, the systematic violence against, and devaluation, distortion, and criminalization of, persons racialized as Black to rationalize their abjection, exclusion, exploitation, domination, and oppression. Indeed, "A peculiarity of the United States is that fascist-like measures are often dispensed against African Americans . . . and not accorded to the same degree to others."[26] During the early Cold War, the most visceral articulation of anti-Blackness was white supremacist revanchism in the form of lynching, race riots, and generalized racial terrorism against veterans and civilians alike. As Jones articulated in the 1953

---

24 Claudia Jones, "International Women's Day and the Struggle for Peace," in *Claudia Jones: Beyond Containment*, 92–93.

25 Jones, "International Women's Day," 93.

26 Horne, *Black Liberation/Red Scare*, 12.

speech mentioned above, the US government continued to aid and abet "Ku Kluxers" who lynched "Negro men, women, and children."[27] Likewise, Jones held up the Rosa Lee Ingram case as the archetype of anti-Blackness; for fending off the sexual advances of a white racist, Ingram had been unjustly sentenced to life in prison in 1951. Jones explained: "The Ingram case illustrates the landless, Jim Crow, oppressed status of the Negro family in America. It illumines particularly the degradation of Negro women today under American bourgeois democracy moving to fascism and war."[28]

The second feature of US fascism was capitalist imperialism—often dubbed "Wall Street imperialism" by communists and anticapitalists—understood as the control of all aspect of economic life in the United States and economic policy abroad by Wall Street pressure, influence, or direct governance. This wealthy financial community created and controlled the prevailing political climate and equated the nation's welfare with their ability to freely accumulate wealth. Such control was imperial because it drained profit from all parts of the world, and was constitutively anti-Black because "the original base of Wall Street superprofits, and still a larger source than any single foreign country, is the oppression of the Negro people within the United States."[29] Likewise, "The Wall Street cohorts [had] unfurled the banner of Anglo-Saxon fascism,"[30] Jones and her comrades argued, in their drive to establish "world domination by Wall Street."[31] The eminent communist historian Herbert Aptheker analyzed that US imperialism was "organically connected, from its origins," to the fascist logics of "white chauvinism" and anti-Blackness. "Imperialism refurbished the racism of slavery and used this white chauvinism," he explained, "to help it succeed in the conquest of the South and the subjugation of the Negro people." Anti-Blackness was thus "integrally related to the jingoism of imperialism which appeared most virulently" in the "conquest of the

---

27 Jones, "[Black] women can think," 9.

28 Claudia Jones, "An End to the Neglect of the Problems of Negro Women," in *Claudia Jones: Beyond Containment*, 83.

29 William Patterson (ed.), *We Charge Genocide: The Historic Petition to the United States Government for Relief from a Crime of the United States Government against the Negro People* (New York: Civil Rights Congress, 1951), 134–135; 167–168.

30 "Part of discussion on concepts + 'white chauvinism' written by unknown person," n.d., Box 1, Folder 7, Pettis Perry Papers (MG 354), Schomburg Center for Research in Black Culture, New York Public Library.

31 Schrecker, *The Age of McCarthyism*, 108.

Cuban, Puerto Rican, Hawaiian and Filipino nationalities," which occurred simultaneously with and "for the same reason as the conquest of the budding Negro nation."[32] In other words, US imperialism had historically been informed by racist logics, and US fascism was inextricable from the Wall Street imperialist drive after World War II.

US fascism's third characteristic was militarism and warmongering, which included nuclear buildup, the waging of "hot" wars in Asia and Africa, and the looming drive toward World War III. The perpetual march toward war was one of the ways that the US government rationalized discrimination and repression. In 1940, Jones argued that the "demagogic slogan" of "national unity" imposed during wartime was a way of uniting the ruling class against the people "to make profits, by starvation, by clamping down on the civil rights of the people, on the basis of war."[33] Ten years later, she similarly warned that the "Truman-bipartisan war policy," the "monstrous Truman-Acheson doctrine that the war is inevitable," the "repressive and death-dealing measures carried through . . . by Wall Street's puppets in Marshallized Italy, in fascist Greece and Spain," and the "Marshall-Plan-financed war . . . against the heroic Vietnamese," paved the road to "monopoly oppression" and fascism.[34] In effect, militarism aimed to entrench monopoly capitalist US imperialism by using the "sons of American mothers as 'blue chips' in [the] vicious plot of world conquest, fascism, war, and death." Likewise, war led to the "militarization of youth," the disruption of families, labor shortages, land dispossession, shrinking incomes, and the undermining of workers who already occupied precarious economic positions—namely women and African Americans.[35] As well, militarism and warmongering were shot through with anti-Blackness and anticommunism: as the Black communist and New York City Councilman Benjamin J. Davis, Jr. fumed, Truman could "cook up a red-baiting pretext to send Negroes 10,000 miles away to die, but he can't find a single way to get the anti-lynch, anti-poll tax or FEPC bills passed."[36]

The final aspect of US fascism was anticommunism, which construed as

---

32 Herbert Aptheker, "American Imperialism and White Chauvinism," *Jewish Life*, July 1950.

33 Jones, "Jim Crow," 30.

34 Jones, "International Women's Day," 90–92.

35 Claudia Jones, "For the Unity of Women in the Cause of Piece," in *Claudia Jones: Beyond Containment*, 104–105.

36 Horne, *Black Liberation/Red Scare*, 247.

un-American not only communism, but also any support for domestic and international policies that dovetailed with those of the Soviet Union and the CPUSA. "I was a victim of McCarthyite hysteria against independent political ideas in the U.S.A.," Jones charged, "a hysteria which penalizes anyone who holds ideas contrary to the official pro-war, pro-reactionary line of the white ruling class of that country." Likewise, as a "Negro woman communist," she was targeted by the United States government for opposing Jim Crow and for urging the prosecution of white supremacists instead of communists.[37] As her comrade and codefendant Pettis Perry explained, the prosecution of communists solely on the basis of their ideas sought "to bring into being fascism in the United States in its American variety."[38] In a similar fashion, Jones noted that these trials represented the tyrannical— read fascist—violation of the American dream.[39] In effect, the "Hitler-like anti-communist hysteria" brought together the "fascist, anti-Semitic, and anti-Negro forces in the country," and threatened democracy, freedom, and standards of living in the United States.[40]

US fascism and the "longue durée of McCarthyism"

The term McCarthyism is commonly used to denote the years 1950–1954 in which the eponymous Wisconsin senator wielded considerable influence and power in Congress and was instrumental in fomenting national anti-communist hysteria. However, the broad reach of anticommunism, and its particular criminalization of Black communists and anticapitalists, both preceded and exceeded that very short era. Thus, the "longue durée of McCarthyism" describes the variety of institutions, agencies, actors, and interests invested with state power to entrench this fascist-like repression at the federal, state, and local level.

A key event in the longue durée of McCarthyism was FBI Director J. Edgar Hoover's speech before the HUAC on March 26, 1947, which played a fundamental role in establishing the threat of communism, broadened the dragnet to include all militants and radicals whose liberation struggles were consonant with that of the CPUSA or the Soviet Union, and implicitly

---

37 Johnson, *I Dream of My Mother*, 129.

38 Pettis Perry, "On a motion for acquittal" n.d. [1953], Box 4, Folder 12, Pettis Perry Papers.

39 Jones, "[Black] women can think," 8–9.

40 "We are Seven," *Jewish Life: A Progressive Monthly* (November 1953): 3.

imbued anticommunism with anti-Blackness.

In the speech, Hoover likened communism, which for him was not a merely a political party but rather a "malignant way of life," to a "disease that spread like an epidemic" and threatened to infect the entire nation.[41] As such, the primary responsibility of the HUAC and committees like it, he instructed, was to publicly disclose, expose, and spotlight communists so that they could be "quarantined" and "do no harm."[42] Even more pressing was the neutralization of "fellow travelers"—those who held ideas sympathetic or similar to communists—who, to extend Hoover's metaphor, carried the disease but concealed their symptoms. On this logic, their clandestine nature essentially made them an even greater menace than card-carrying Reds. This move to construct fellow travelers as a threat to the health and thus the security of the nation was imbued with anti-Blackness insofar as demands for Black liberation were consonant with, and supported by, the CPUSA. Likewise, an essential aspect of Soviet propaganda was to highlight the poor treatment of African Americans to undermine the United States' claim to be the world leader of democracy and freedom. Given this reality, Black challenges to racial and socioeconomic hierarchies were disproportionately Red-baited.

Hoover's speech also distorted radical discourse by implying that it was little more than doublespeak meant to conceal communist aims. For instance, he stated that when radicals used the term "democracy," what they actually meant was communism and totalitarianism; and when they critiqued United States imperialism and warned against impending fascism, they were really attempting to undermine US democracy.[43] Based on Hoover's position, demands for democracy by communists and fellow travelers—who included activists for racial equality and justice, the transformative redistribution of wealth and resources, and world peace—were little more than "Red fascism" and attempts to subvert the US order. Likewise, critiques of US imperialism and claims that fascism was looming should be ignored as assaults on democracy and freedom. In this way, Hoover implied that any critique of or mobilization against the extant social order, domestically and globally, abetted the communist "menace to freedom, to democratic ideals, [and] to the worship of God" and threatened the "American

---

41 Schrecker, *The Age of McCarthyism*, 120.

42 Schrecker, *The Age of McCarthyism*, 119.

43 Schrecker, *The Age of McCarthyism*, 116.

way of life."[44] On this logic, the best defense against communist subversion was "vigorous, intelligent, old-fashioned Americanism" and unrelenting vigilance.[45] In other words, conformity, surveillance, and uncritical support for the status quo—key elements of fascism—were essential to national security.

As such, organizations committed to social change, "hundreds" of which, Hoover claimed, had "either been infiltrated or organized primarily to accomplish the purposes of promoting the interests of the Soviet Union in the United States," had to be particularly vigilant in identifying and exposing anyone supportive of communism, and in avoiding any political aims that aligned with same. Moreover, Hoover found groups that focused on the "exploitation of Negroes in the United States" to be especially suspect;[46] consequently, "there grew steadily a pattern of linking the advocacy of full equality for Blacks and minorities with un-Americanism."[47] Hoover's speech was essential to codifying loyalty/disloyalty, American/un-American, and conformity/subversion—dichotomies that provided the scaffolding for McCarthy's brief but unfettered tyranny. Concomitantly, the heightened risk incurred by those fighting racial discrimination underscores the close connection between the long arm of McCarthyism, the threat of fascism, and anti-Blackness.[48]

A number of Black anticapitalists traced the longue durée of McCarthyism as far back as the Great Depression. The Black militant Dorothy Hunton, for example, reminisced that in the 1930s, the National Negro Congress (NNC), a Popular Front organization that specifically agitated for the rights of Black workers, was targeted by the Special Committee on Un-American Activities, the precursor to HUAC.

The Dies Committee, as it was commonly known because it was chaired by the conservative Democrat Martin Dies, labeled the NNC's campaign for Black jobs at Glen Martin Aircraft Factory subversive, claimed that Black communists in the organization aimed to sabotage defense production, and branded the leader of the campaign, W. Alphaeus Hunton, Jr., a

---

44 Schrecker, *The Age of McCarthyism*, 119.

45 Schrecker, *The Age of McCarthyism*, 119.

46 Schrecker, *The Age of McCarthyism*, 119.

47 Dorothy Hunton, *Alphaeus Hunton: The Unsung Valiant* (Richmond Hill: D.K. Hunton, 1986), 81.

48 Schrecker, *The Age of McCarthyism*, 38.

communist.[49] The government's denigration of Hunton in the 1930s proved to be a precursor to what would befall him two decades later when he was a leader in the radical Council on African Affairs (CAA). Mrs. Hunton further explained that, throughout the long durée of McCarthyism, "communism was seen as so uniquely threatening to America's survival that measures that might otherwise have been considered a serious violation of individual rights were justified on the grounds of national security."[50] Likewise, Blackness exacerbated the communist threat; given the repression of the NNC, she found it to be "no accident" that progressive Black organizations like the CAA and popular Black leaders like Ben Davis were "made the first target of the proposed police legislation"[51] during McCarthy's short rule.

Another example of the long shadow of McCarthyism, according to "professional revolutionary" Doxey Wilkerson, who joined the Communist Party in 1943, was the conjuncture of pro-fascism, imperialism, and colonialism during the Second World War. A "powerful clique of American pro-fascists and imperialists," Wilkerson argued, wanted to preserve the fascist governments in Germany and throughout Europe in order to forestall "the democratic upsurge of liberated peoples throughout the world which the destruction of fascism would surely bring." The support for fascism by segments of the US ruling class during the war, Wilkerson claimed, aimed to curb anticolonialism and self-determination in the Third World in much the same way that anticommunism worked in a fascist-like manner to undermine struggles for racial justice and decolonization after the war.

Such wartime commitment to imperialism and colonialism abroad was complemented by opposition to the progressive policies of the Roosevelt administration domestically. This "powerful clique," warned Wilkerson, would "try to establish an oppressive fascist regime here in America" to overturn the gains made by labor, African Americans, and other minoritized groups, and to crush progressive dissent.[52] Worse still, given the reality of anti-Blackness in the United States, it was Black people who would suffer most if the "real threat of a fascist America" came to fruition; they would

---

49 Hunton, *Alphaeus Hunton*, 51.

50 Schrecker, *The Age of McCarthyism*, 2.

51 Hunton, *Alphaeus Hunton*, 82.

52 Doxey Wilkerson, *The Negro People and the Communists* (New York: Workers Library Publishers, 1944), 11.

be "forced back into a slavery far worse than their forefathers ever knew."[53] Because of the ways that US fascism particularly threatened Black people, Wilkerson held that the extension of democratic rights and equality to Black people was essential to the protection of the nation as a whole.[54]

By July 1946, four years before the rise of McCarthy, Claudia Jones had become increasingly fearful that increased terrorism against Black people, like the recent lynching of two war veterans in Monroe, Georgia—among forty others that had occurred by the end of the summer—meant that fascism was imminent. This was not least because, in the United States, "fascist-like terror was aimed at blacks generally, at breaking the black-Left tie, and at breaking black Reds."[55] This analysis of the relationship between fascism, anti-Blackness, and anticommunism was shared by the CPUSA and non-communists alike.

In 1949, for example, the militant Black author, journalist, and historian Joel Augustus Rogers maintained that, because the "American spirit" was more prone to fascism, it was the latter, not communism, that posed an immediate threat to the United States. The US South, he added, was "already largely fascistic."[56] This astute analysis revealed that, given extant realities of anti-Blackness, the rise of fascism in the United States was not farfetched and anticommunism was a means of criminalizing radical thought while evading the fascist-like treatment of African Americans. As Jones lamented, "Instead of prosecuting the Ku Klux Klan, the anti-Semites, and the reactionaries, the government is arresting antifascists."[57]

The "escalation of a fascist danger at home" was one part of a "negative" trifecta that arose in the early Cold War, which also included the threat of perpetual war and, more tellingly, the violent return of the lynch mob.[58] From a prison cell in Terre Haute, Indiana, Ben Davis elaborated that impending fascism in the United States was most manifest in the oppression of Black people: "Toward the end of World War II, the pro-fascist, Negro-hating forces which had been held in check during the war,

---

53 Wilkerson, *The Negro People and the Communists*, 14.

54 Wilkerson, *The Negro People and the Communists*, 17.

55 Horne, *Black Liberation/Red Scare*, 218.

56 J.A. Rogers, *Pittsburg Courier*, September 29, 1949.

57 Johnson, *I Think of My Mother*, 26.

58 Claude Lightfoot, *Chicago Slums to World Politics: Autobiography of Claude Lightfoot* (New York: New Outlook Publishers and Distributors, 1985), 97.

began to break loose," he argued. "The first section of the population to feel the rigors of reaction was, of course, the Negro people. They were forcibly reminded that . . . the Negro was still the victim of a system of national oppression and segregation. American imperialism had not changed its spots."[59]

Davis was convinced that entrenched US imperialism and bold anti-Blackness paved the way for the rise of fascism in the United States. Relatedly, in her article "On the Right to Self-Determination for the Negro People in the Black Belt," Jones signaled the longue durée of McCarthyism, contending that anti-Black attacks—facilitated by the interests of "Big Business"—were "reminiscent of post-World War I" and were especially concerning because "the main danger of fascism to the world comes from the most colossal imperialist forces which are concentrated within the United States." Fascism was a real possibility because it was all but supported by "the most reactionary section of monopoly capital and of the semi-feudal economy of the Black Belt," which derived its power from "the oppression of the Negro people and the working class."[60] Not only was the exploitation of Black people and the working class a key element in the rise of US fascism, but war in the service of imperialism also fanned its flames. The United States, Jones opined, planned to use "the sons of American mothers"—especially Black sons—to commit "barbarous atrocities" in places like Korea to facilitate its imperial plans for "world conquest, fascism, war, and death."[61] The drive toward US fascism during the early Cold War was not only the latest stage in the longue durée of McCarthyism, but was also an extension of the nation's history of capitalist exploitation, imperialism, war, and unremitting violence against Black people and workers.

In 1956, Jones' close friend, the internationalist freedom fighter Paul Robeson, maintained that the threat of fascism was manifested not only in the United States' commitment to imperialism, but also in its aversion to peace and its empowerment of anticommunist committees. In his testimony before HUAC, he exhorted, "Fascist-minded people will not drive me from [the United States]. . . . I am for peace with the Soviet Union and

---

59 Benjamin J. Davis, Jr., *Communist Councilman from Harlem: Autobiographical Notes Written in a Federal Penitentiary* (New York: International Publishers, 1991), 161.

60 Claudia Jones, "On the Right to Self-Determination for the Negro People in the Black Belt," in *Claudia Jones: Beyond Containment*, 60.

61 Jones, "For the Unity of Women," 104.

I am for peace with China, and I am not for peace or friendship with the Fascist Franco, and I am not for peace with Fascist Nazi Germans, and I am for peace with decent people in the world." Specifically linking his repression to the fascist threat, he continued, "I am here because I am opposing the neo-Fascist cause which I see arising in these committees." Like Jones, Robeson acknowledged the long history of antiradical and anti-Black oppression that undergirded the longue durée of McCarthyism, adding, "You are like the Alien Sedition Act, and Jefferson could be sitting here, and Frederick Douglass could be sitting here and Eugene Debs could be here." [62] Robeson was arguing that, like the Alien and Sedition Acts, anticommunism trampled civil liberties and rendered dangerous those who spoke out against the government; in naming Douglass and Debs, he conveyed that Black people and anticapitalists tended to be the prime targets of such repression.

The "thought control" Smith Act and creeping fascism

The Smith Act was one of the most notorious pieces of legislation used during the longue durée of McCarthyism to criminalize radical thought and thinkers. Jones and other anticapitalists referred to it as a form of thought control because its central aim was to punish radical *ideas* and to construe them as *acts* of force and violence.

The Act was designed to "prohibit certain subversive activities" and, among other things, "to amend certain provisions of the law with respect to the admission and deportation of aliens." It criminalized those who "knowingly and willingly advocate[d], abet[ted], advise[d] or [taught] the duty, necessity, desirability, or propriety of overthrowing or destroying any Government of the United States by force or violence"; the drafting, publishing, circulation, editing, distributing, and selling of such ideas; and organizations, groups, and societies that encouraged them. Those found guilty of the latter offenses would be imprisoned, fined, and deported. [63] While the earliest victim of the Smith Act was the Socialist Workers Party, by the end of World War II, the CPUSA was its unequivocal target. In the Smith

---

62 Committee on Un-American Activities, *Hearings Before the Committee on Un-American Activities, June 12 and 13, 1956* (Washington, DC: United States Government Printing Office, 1956), 4504–4509.

63 Carole Boyce Davies, *Left of Karl Marx: The Political Life of Black Communist Claudia Jones* (Durham: Duke University Press, 2008), 149.

Act trials throughout the late 1940s and 1950s, this group was charged with conspiracy of insurrection based on books, writings, and belonging to the CPUSA generally. These "frame-ups," according to Pettis Perry, were an assault on the American people as a whole because if convicted, "the liberties of all the American people would be in grave danger." "You cannot deprive Communists of their right to speak and write," he warned in an address to the court during his 1951 trial, "without endangering the right to speak, the right to assemble, the right to freedom of the press for the entire people." Perry held that outlawing ideas, which was the primary goal of the Smith Act, was the first step on the path to fascism. He lamented, "The very fact that this trial, a trial of ideas and books, can take place in our country shows how far the Wall Street rulers have taken our country down the disastrous path of fascism." He urged the court "to help prevent this growing trend toward fascism."[64]

The 1948 trial of eleven CPUSA leaders—Eugene Dennis, Gus Hall, Henry Winston, Ben Davis, John Williamson, Robert Thomas, Gil Green, John Gates, Jack Satchel, Carl Winter, and Irving Potash—was an acute harbinger of US fascism in the longue durée of McCarthyism.[65] The defendants were charged with teaching and advocating the overthrow of the US government by force or violence. In 1951, Jones, Elizabeth Gurley Flynn, and sixteen other "working-class communists" were arrested on the same trumped-up charges. Jones' specific "crime" was "writing an article which described the forward movement of Negro and white women in opposition to the fascist bent world domination of US foreign policy."[66] Over the next ten years, more than 100 top leaders of the CPUSA across the nation were indicted based on what Jones described as a "reactionary statute under which progressive fighters are convicted and jailed not for committing any overt act, but merely for their ideas."[67] The indictment and trial of top party leadership was a "classic frame-up based on a statute ultimately viewed as unconstitutional."[68] According to Jones, it was easy to see why anticapitalists, especially those of African descent, "discerned an aroma of fascism."

To realize "McCarthyism [was] American fascism," they needed only to

---

64 Pettis Perry, "Your Honor, in addressing myself," n.d. [1953], Pettis Perry Papers.

65 Lightfoot, *Chicago Slums to World Politics*, 111–112.

66 Jones, "Autobiographical History," 14.

67 Lightfoot, *Chicago Slums*, 112; Johnson, *I Think of My Mother*, 131.

68 Horne, *Black Liberation/Red Scare*, 210.

compare the railroading of Ben Davis, Henry Winston, and their comrades in 1948 and the racist cases of the Scottsboro Nine, Angelo Herndon, the Martinsville Seven, Rosa Lee Ingram, Willie McGee, and the Trenton Six, to fascist Germany's murdering, jailing, and outlawing of communists and antifascists.[69] Jones' 1951 arrest attests to the US government's use of the Smith Act to criminalize radical ideas in an effort to regulate and discipline opposition.

The Smith Act prosecutions were especially repressive in their conflation of counterhegemonic ideas with dangerous and subversive acts to circumscribe freedom of speech and freedom of the press. As the case of the Chicago Black Communist Claude Lightfoot conveyed, the Smith Act also criminalized freedom of association. Unlike previous cases, when Lightfoot was captured by the FBI and put on trial in 1954, he was charged under a membership clause of the Smith Act that declared membership in the CPUSA was evidence enough to confirm that communists might attempt to overthrow the government by force and violence at some later date. Stated differently, membership in the CPUSA automatically meant conspiracy of insurrection.

Such disregard for the Bill of Rights and due process threatened fascism in the United States insofar as those who rejected US racial, imperial, militaristic, and exploitative policies were susceptible to the charge of subversion and punishment following therefrom. For Lightfoot, the judge and jury in his case were called upon, for the first time in US history, "to examine the contents of people's minds" to determine guilt or innocence. This was a powerful reason why Claudia Jones and others referred to the Smith Act as the "Thought Control Act," and as a "fascist drive on free speech and thought in this country."[70] This "thought control law," Dorothy Hunton charged, placed unconstitutional constraints on "the right to freedom of speech and political association" and "aimed to punish people for their ideas, and the right to advocate ideas distasteful to the rules of our government." Additionally, because it aimed to punish those who acted together to combat war, economic hardship, and white supremacy, among other things, "[t]he first victims to be tried and convicted were the top

---

69 Claudia Jones, *Ben Davis: Fighter for Freedom* (New York: National Committee to Defend Negro Leadership, 1954), 12–13.

70 Lightfoot, *Chicago Slums to World Politics*, 114; Jones, "[Black] women can think," 8.

Communist leaders, among whom were two Blacks."[71]

Since the threat of US fascism particularly menaced "all genuine fighters for Negro rights,"[72] the Smith Act was further understood as a form of thought control specifically targeting Black radicals. The Smith Act prosecutions, it was argued, were used to intimidate Black people who had any affiliation with communists, or who took a militant approach to racial justice. As Ben Davis contended, "Actually it was the purpose of the court in giving me the maximum sentence to intimidate and terrorize all militant Negroes, to serve notice that a fight for free and equal citizenship would be met with severe reprisal."[73] This was true for others, like Jones, whose thoughts, speeches, and associations were criminalized because they fought for Black freedom and rallied against anti-Black violence. As well, it was no accident that the first prosecutions under the Smith Act membership clause involved those who fought for racial justice; this was a form of browbeating meant to "halt the advances being made by Negro people as a result of their efforts . . . in the struggle for freedom and democracy."[74]

In a 1953 article in the *Daily Worker*, the radical Pan-Africanist Eslanda Goode Robeson, a close confidante of Claudia Jones, further asserted that the anticommunist crusades in the United States undermined the struggle for racial justice, since citizens were "no longer free nor brave" because they were plagued by "fear of losing one's job, home, education" and "fear of non-conforming, or of even being accused of non-conforming."[75] In other words, the Smith Act's thought control had serious anti-Black effects insofar as it forced African Americans to genuflect to the racial status quo—which at the time meant disenfranchisement, lynching, and other forms of racial violence—lest they become victims of the longue durée of McCarthyism. Likewise, an article in the *California Eagle*, a progressive Black publication, claimed that the persecution of communists and their right to free speech had particular consequences for Black people, for whom the right to dissent and disagree was essential to challenging racism and white supremacy.[76]

---

71 Hunton, *Alphaeus Hunton*, 84.

72 Jones, *Ben Davis*, 12.

73 Davis, *Communist Councilman*, 182.

74 Civil Rights Congress, *The 'Crimes' of Claude Lightfoot and Junius Scales* (New York: Civil Rights Congress, 1955), 4–10.

75 Eslanda Robeson, "A Citizen's State of the Union," *Daily Worker* (March 19, 1953).

76 Civil Rights Congress, *The Crimes*, 15.

Jones expansively argued that the fascist-like roundup of communists was not only a form of anti-Black intimidation, but also an attempt to crush those who rejected capitalist exploitation and war. After she was convicted in 1953 under the Smith Act, she queried in her speech to the court, "Is all this [the trial and conviction] no further proof that what we were also tried for was our opposition to racist ideas, an integral part of the desperate drive by men of Wall Street to war and fascism?"[77] This provocative question dovetailed with Dorothy Hunton's contention that, in the longue durée of McCarthyism, anticommunism converged with warmongering to conceal the real threat to world peace: "the oppression of the darker races."[78] This deceit transformed the Smith Act into a tool of not only mind control, but also white supremacy and creeping fascism.

The McCarran Act, precarious citizenship, and imminent fascism

"Deadlier than the Smith Act," writes Carole Boyce Davies, was the Internal Security Act of 1950, or the McCarran Act. "[R]eferred to commonly as 'the anticommunist law,' . . . the Walter McCarran Act lay the foundation for immigration checks, deportation, harassment of African Americans, and even authorized concentration camps for emergency situations. In section 22 of this far-reaching act . . . a variety of aliens are identified as inadmissible or deportable for offenses such as teaching revolutionary information." Expanding and revising the Immigration Act of 1917, the McCarran Act, in tandem with the Smith Act, provided the basis for "state surveillance and the well-known activities of the House Un-American Activities Committee (HUAC) throughout the 1950s and after."[79]

As if these stipulations weren't proof enough that fascism was imminent in the United States, the McCarran Act also authorized the loss of American citizenship for naturalized citizens based solely on their political beliefs or activities; annual registration for noncitizens; arrest without a warrant and denial of bail for noncitizens; and the deportation of noncitizens, no matter how long they had resided in the country, for any political opinion deemed threatening to the government. This "gestapo pass system for noncitizens" deprived them of all rights and

---

77 Jones, "[Black] women can think," 7.

78 Hunton, *Alphaeus Hunton*, 79.

79 Davies, "Deportable Subjects," 957–958.

liberties at the same time that it severely circumscribed the rights and liberties of citizens.[80]

The McCarran Act also required all communists to register with the Subversive Activities Control Board, and the specific penalties for not registering outright communist organizations or those that were purported to be communist fronts, communist infiltrated, communist dominated, communist supported, or communist inspired included five years imprisonment and a $10,000 fine for every day one failed to register.[81] This effectively meant that "if one decided to stand up for a principle that person could be jailed for life" or expelled from the country.[82]

Moreover, a particularly frightening aspect of the statute that portended fascist dictatorship, was the provision that the US President could take control of all government institutions and put people in jail without trial during a national emergency. This threat was made all the more realistic given evidence that concentration camps were being constructed within US borders.[83]

Thus, the McCarran Act, coupled with the Smith Act and the Taft-Hartley Act, which stripped workers of gains made during the New Deal and precluded communists from holding office in the labor movement, targeted the foreign-born, workers, and citizens whose radical ideas alone rendered them dangerous and subversive. These "terroristic forms of propaganda" were often compared to the Alien and Sedition Laws: "The Walter McCarran Act—this foul and unconstitutional statute under which I and other non-citizens are deported under," Jones seethed, "will in this process go the way of the Alien and Sedition laws of Jefferson's day."[84] Such attacks on the most vulnerable populations—"the Negroes, the Jewish people, and the foreign born citizens"—was not unlike "Hitlerism," insofar as these populations were being deprived of their civil rights and liberties and were being driven from their homes by the

---

80 American Committee for Protection of the Foreign Born, *Repeal the Walter McCarran Law*, 1950, W.E.B. Du Bois Papers (MS 312), Special Collections and University Archives, W.E.B. Du Bois Library, University of Massachusetts, Amherst, MA, http://credo.library. umass.edu/view/full/mums312-b157-i322.

81 Benjamin J. Davis, Jr., *Ben Davis on the McCarran Act at the Harvard Law Forum* (New York: The Gus Hall-Benjamin J. Davis Defense Committee, n.d.), 12.

82 Lightfoot, *Chicago Slums to World Politics*, 112.

83 Lightfoot, *Chicago Slums to World Politics*, 112.

84 Johnson, *I Think of My Mother*, 52.

"McCarthys, the McCarr[a]ns, and the authors of the Smith Act."[85]

"Repressive labor legislation" like the Taft-Hartley Act destroyed freedom, harmony, and equality in the labor movement; the Smith Act killed freedom of speech; the "McCarran Law" destroyed the peace and happiness of the foreign-born; and loyalty oaths—which often included anti-Black questions about beliefs in racial equality and whether a white person had entertained a Black person in their home—demanded fealty from the very populations the US government failed to protect. These frightening conditions compelled the radical journalist Charlotta Bass, one of Jones' sisters in struggle, to admonish: "18,000,000 American Negroes . . . went out on the battlefront in World War II and helped to defeat Hitler and German Fascism. We want no local Hitlers, and we want no American Fascism."[86]

Jones, the communist sailor and union leader Ferdinand Smith, and four others imprisoned on Ellis Island under the McCarran Act, sent a letter to the United Nations Social, Humanitarian, and Cultural Committee in November 1950 to protest their pending deportations. They warned that the dragnet of the Smith and McCarran Acts effectively criminalized any progressive ideas and activism, so everyone committed to justice or equality was a potential target—a possibility that presaged the rise of fascism in the United States. They argued, "If we can be denied all rights and incarcerated in concertation camps, then trade unionists are next; then the Negro people, the Jewish people, all foreign-born, and all progressives who love peace and cherish freedom will face the bestiality and torment of fascism. Our fate is the fate of all opponents of fascist barbarism, of all who abhor war and desire peace."[87] Here, the McCarran Act was understood as an instrument of US fascism insofar as the human rights of Jones and her comrades were denied not because they posed a physical threat, but because their fight on behalf of labor, Black rights, and true democracy threatened to subvert the status quo. Likewise, the all-encompassing nature of the longue durée of McCarthyism meant that repression of one group of "others" could quickly spread to all groups of "undesirables." Finally, the state of perpetual siege and war in which fascism flourished was becoming normalized in the United States, and values like peace and freedom were

---

85 Charlotta Bass, *Forty Years: Memoirs from the Pages of a Newspaper* (Los Angeles: Charlotta A. Bass, 1960), 189.

86 Bass, *Forty Years*, 193–194; Hunton, *Alphaeus Hunton*, 81.

87 Johnson, *I Think of My Mother*, 29.

being distorted into threats to national security to legitimate racialized carcerality and expulsion.

Describing her personal experience of harassment, incarceration, and deportation, Claudia Jones offered some of the most insightful analysis of the fascist, antiradical, and racist aspects of the McCarran Act and the longue durée of McCarthyism. In a 1956 interview with George Bowrin, she explained that she was a "victim of McCarthyite hysteria" that targeted those who challenged the "official pro-war, pro-reactionary, pro-fascist line of the white ruling class of that country."[88] Further, in a system moving quickly toward fascism, to be radical was anathema, and to be Black and radical was even worse, since the government tended to believe that "the Negro population of the United States was communistically inclined"— meaning prone to subversion—and "this attitude meant that Reds were persecuted and Black Reds were virtually flagellated."[89] Worse still was to be a "Negro woman Communist of West Indian descent," whose rights and liberties were forfeited, according to the government, if one struggled to end Jim Crow, to unite white and Black workers, to empower women, and to push US domestic and foreign policy to the side of durable peace.[90]

Additionally, Jones believed her application for American citizenship was rejected because she urged spending for social welfare instead of arms; prosecution of lynchers instead of communists and anticapitalists; and because she continually noted that it was "financiers and war mongers" who were the "real advocates of force and violence in the USA."[91] Thus, the threat of US fascism was fundamentally constituted by warmongering, the reversal of progressive gains made by workers and African Americans, the repression of communists and like-minded individuals and groups, and the violent elevation of capitalist interests.

Jones further analyzed the endemic white supremacy and anti-Blackness in a related piece of legislation, the Immigration and Nationality Act of 1952, commonly known as the McCarran-Walter Act, and how it represented the unique character of US fascism: "The very law under which I was deported, the reactionary Walter-McCarran [sic] law, [is] widely known for its special racist bias towards West Indians and peoples of Asian descent," she noted.

88 Claudia Jones, "I Was Deported Because," in *Claudia Jones: Beyond Containment*, 16.

89 Horne, *Black Liberation/Red Scare*, 207.

90 Jones, "I Was Deported Because," 16.

91 Jones, "I Was Deported Because," 17.

Jones intimated that these groups were targeted because their progressive ideas were the most threatening to the conservative foundations of the US state. "This law which came into being as a result of the whole reactionary drive against progressive ideas in the United States," she continued, "encourages immigration of fascist scum from Europe but restricts West Indian immigration once in their thousands annually to the United States, to 100 persons per year, from all Caribbean islands."[92] In perceptively pinpointing not only the restriction on the immigration of racialized people, but also the welcoming of white "fascist scum," Jones conveyed that fascism was more compatible with US policy and practice than was racial equality and justice, which gave the longue durée of McCarthyism its racist character.

Elsewhere, she made the similar argument that the "racially-based McCarran-Walter Immigration Act" aimed to protect the "white 'races' purity'" and to promote Anglo-Saxo supremacy.[93] As Jones described, the McCarran Act, the McCarran-Walter Act, and the longue durée of McCarthyism more broadly, imperiled the citizenship of, stripped citizenship from, or denied citizenship to all who struggled against anti-Blackness, white supremacy, warmongering, imperialism, and capitalist exploitation—structures that came together to augur the rise of US fascism during the early Cold War.

The continued threat of fascism in the United States

For Claudia Jones, the threat of fascism in the United States was constituted by the rise in anti-Black violence; the spread of imperialism; the increased exploitation of workers by the ruling class; perpetual war; and the repression and persecution of communists, anticapitalists, and progressives who challenged these forms of domination. The longue durée of this conjuncture extended far beyond the brief reign of Joseph McCarthy and derived much of its fascist character from its particular targeting of Black people. Such victimization included neutralization of radical Black leaders, intimidation to curb struggles for racial justice and civil rights, misrecognition of such struggles as subversion, and punishing and prosecuting communists and antifascists instead of lynchers and racial terrorists.

---

92 Johnson, *I Think of My Mother*, 129.
93 Johnson, *I Think of My Mother*, 13.

Jones and her comrades identified the Smith and McCarran Acts as particularly emblematic of the turn to fascism in the United States. They excoriated the Smith Act as a form of "thought control" that imperiled freedom of speech, freedom of the press, and freedom of assembly. They railed against the McCarran Act and its fundamental disruption of the lives of citizens and noncitizens alike through incarceration, deportation, and the threat of concentration camps. During the longue durée of McCarthyism, these Acts, among others, targeted those who envisioned and struggled mightily for a world irreconcilable with US fascism—that is, a world devoid of dehumanizing exploitation.

In our contemporary moment, talk of impending and protofascism has reappeared with the presidency and looming presence of Donald Trump, the rise of white nationalism as an increasingly acceptable form of politics, and the strengthening of the police state and its targeting of poor and working-class Black people. The latter has resulted in longstanding domestic rebellions and uprisings throughout the United States and concomitant demands for an end to police murder and occupation, justice for those slain at the hands of the state, defunding or abolishing the police and investment in social policies, and the curtailment of cultural domination manifested in settler colonial and confederate statues.

Likewise, as COVID-19 infections and deaths engulf the world, those residing in the US are being ravaged not only by the virus, but also by the economic fallout and its exacerbation by the government's refusal to offer a robust social safety net to protect the health and well-being of its population. Beyond US borders, tensions are increasing with China and Iran; talk of war and retaliation are ubiquitous; and the Trump regime continues to retreat from international cooperation, manifested most recently in the withdrawal of the United States from the World Health Organization. Given this context, the theories and analyses, warnings and fears, of Jones and her comrades take on new urgency as the elements of US fascism—prioritizing of property and profit over people, aggressive imperialism, threat of war, acute violence against Black people with relative impunity—are once again on the rise.

CHAPTER TWELVE

Right Riot

A Conversation after the January 2021 Siege on the US Capitol

Joe Lowndes and Nikhil Pal Singh, interviewed by Daniel Denvir

This exchange on The Dig *podcast was originally conceived, in the waning days of the Trump administration, as a friendly debate about whether right-wing authoritarianism posed a real political crisis in the United States. As it happened, the scheduled recording ended up taking place just two days after the January 6th takeover of the US Capitol. Many facts were yet unknown in the immediate aftermath of the event, as is clear from the conversation. Yet it nevertheless provided an extremely concrete example through which to discuss the relationship of the Republican Party to the emergent far right, the comparative threat of this right to already existing forms of neoliberal domination, and what an emancipatory movement can or should do in this moment.*

The Dig host Daniel Denvir: The ongoing debate on the left over how to characterize Trumpism continued as a mob of his followers stormed the US Capitol on January 6, 2021. On the one hand, what we saw was pretty unreal, unlike anything I've seen in my lifetime. On the other hand, instead of trying to execute Mike Pence and Nancy Pelosi, we saw these MAGA protesters aimlessly roaming around the building, live-streaming themselves on social media, taking selfies, as though they had wandered off from a guided tour. What just happened and what does it reveal about Trumpism?

Joe Lowndes: The fact that it had a kind of a buffoonish quality to it, kind of comical. There are parts of it that feel really like this was inconsequential—that it was kind of a goofy prank as much as anything else. On the other hand, they easily and quickly breached the halls of the US Capitol and made their way into the Senate and House Chambers while an Electoral College Certification was going on. So, in that sense, there's no avoiding that it was actually a grave event.

DD: Nikhil, Mike Davis wrote, "Yesterday's 'sacrileges' in our temple of democracy––oh, poor defiled city on the hill, etc.––constituted an insurrection only in the sense of dark comedy. What was essentially a big biker gang dressed as circus performers and war-surplus barbarians––including the guy with a painted face posing as horned bison in a fur coat––stormed the ultimate country club, squatted on Pence's throne, chased Senators into the sewers, casually picked their noses and rifled files, and, above all, shot endless selfies to send to the dudes back home. Otherwise, they didn't have a clue." What's your take?

Nikhil Singh: Thanks, Dan. And thanks, Joe. I would say that was pretty much my sense when I first saw it and I've been trying to sort it out in my head ever since. This has obviously opened up all the questions that we've been debating about Trump and fascism, whether the language of a coup makes sense to describe his several week effort to overturn the election. And it's kind of restrengthened the argument that people have made on the other side to me generally. Where they say, "Well, yes, look. You see, this really *is* fascism. This really was an attempt at a coup, et cetera." And I think that my sense of it when I first saw it was similar to what Mike Davis just described, but also similar to you Dan, I sort of laughed when I first saw that photograph. I was like, these guys are like, "Let's take one for the grandkids. Look where we were. Look where we are."

And I think now my position has sort of shifted a little bit as I've begun to read more and sort of look at this. I think we really are caught between two different kinds of interpretations, which we're going to have to figure out how to get right. On the one hand, and I think Joe put it well, but I think the way Joe put it also sort of illustrated the divide. On the one hand, cartoonish, ineffective, carnivalesque, uncoordinated, illustrating weakness, not strength. I mean, all of those are what came out of this in some sense. The right was probably damaged by this. At least the institutional right was damaged by this. The GOP right, I think, was damaged by this. And you saw that in the way in which all the sort of institutions of power have lined up in condemnation and opprobrium.

And, so, you have to look at that and sort of say, "Well, to what extent do we do we really judge this as a serious attempt to overthrow the American government? And should we be using that kind of language to describe it?" On the other hand, we have seen something here that is clearly unprecedented in different ways. And I've usually avoided the language of unprecedented when talking about Trump. Seeing him within the terrain of right-wing politics over many, many decades, right?

But here you have a moment in which the extra-parliamentary forces, the street forces, in some ways, are being incited by the leader to do something that has not been done before. And so, one of the questions I have, and I think it's a question that, again, we have to get right, we have to answer correctly and it might take some time to do so, is how to really assess these forces. How to really assess the so-called mob or the mass base of Trumpism in this moment.

Thus far, I think, what we've seen in far-right militancy of the most dangerous kind in this period has been the stochastic kind of terror, kind of lone wolf attacks that are spectacular and violent and truly horrifying. I think we tend to look at what happened . . . I tend to look at what happened a couple of days ago as being very different from that. But then I sometimes wonder. I do have a doubt in my mind as I sit here talking to you right now, whether we're seeing an evolution of this into something else. I'm really averse to that kind of alarmism. And I want to talk about that. It kind of inflates the sort of dangers we're facing from the far right. But I do wonder whether we're also seeing a kind of evolution of some of these groups into something more significant.

DD: Obviously when it came down to it, Mitch McConnell certainly did not want to cross this Rubicon. And more importantly, the US military certainly didn't want to. But should we be worried about conditions conceivably deteriorating enough that it could happen?

JL: Part of what's at issue here in the kind of divide that Nikhil mentioned is the use of the word fascism itself, which has become something that people get stuck on in terms of how to define this moment, or how to relate this moment to past moments. Whether or not this is fascism, there's a movement that's kind of lurching forward, finding opportunities, falling back, then finding new opportunities. In some ways, the last four years have looked like that. The Unite the Right rally in August 2017, with the alt-right coming out into the streets for the first time in a real way, turned out to be a big mistake for them. For the most part, white nationalism itself was discredited, and a number of the organizations that were involved with that kind of fell into disrepair. The Traditional Workers Party imploded, Identity Evropa changed its name and rebranded itself, and various other neo-Nazi groups fell apart. Andrew Anglin (founder and editor of the neo-Nazi *Daily Stormer* website) even came out and said something like, "Well, this was a mistake. We were not ready for this yet."

But then what happened over the next couple of years was kind of a reconsolidation of forces, partly through previously unconnected groups, like paramilitary organizations around Ammon Bundy, along with the Proud Boys and other local and regional formations, like Patriot Prayer here in Portland. They reconsolidated around an authoritarian nationalism, and embraced Trumpism, as opposed to a white nationalism that's dreaming of a utopian ethnostate.

And they were able to put thousands of people on the streets all summer in opposition to Black Lives Matter protests. And then coming into the fall, they began to begin attacking state houses. The Bundys themselves first kind of smash their way into the Idaho state house when it was discussing measures and legislation around COVID. So, I think that there are different kinds of . . . it's a very elastic and quickly changing far right, which is being expressed in different ways and which has connections to the Executive Branch but also other elements of the US national security apparatus.

So, I think there is something there we have to look at. Whether it's impending fascism, I'm not sure I would use that term. But I think we are on an altered political landscape of both left and right. And we have to, I think, be attentive to what that means, both in terms of the threats and opportunities that it poses.

DD: One big problem for Trump, though, seems to be that he courted the wrong armed agents of the state. What do you make of right-wing politics under Trump finding itself in such close alliance with cops? At least until [January 6th] when some of these Trumpists were fighting cops at the Capitol while being in such intense conflict with the FBI, the national security state, the military?

NS: I think that the police are really the outer line of what I call "decentralized despotism" in the United States. And in some ways, they end up representing more localized iterations, sometimes, of white supremacy as well. Whereas I think the national security apparatus—since the integration of the military in 1948—has been very strongly reconditioned by liberal reformists and civil rights doxa. I think that it's a very different kind of formation in that sense. It's professionalized. It has a sense of itself as integrative in a kind of a nationalist way. But a nationalist way that orients towards a kind of dominant liberal sensibility, rather than to this more revanchist edge.

One of the things that I was thinking about yesterday, or the last couple of days, was when Rudy Giuliani led a police riot against the Dinkins administration on City Hall in the 1990s, right before becoming mayor. And when he became mayor, of course, he was quite autocratic and really led the sort of law-and-order surge that has dominated New York City for the last couple of decades. And his partner there, his main advisor, Peter Powers, was quoted as saying, "Finally, we've got white guys back in charge of New York City." And there's a real sense of outer-borough, male/macho kind of white energy there that Giuliani tapped into. That's still a super part of life in New York City. And Trump tapped into it. And that's Trump's formation as well.

So, Trump goes way, way back with the cops. And his first foray into politics was calling for the execution of the Central Park Five, which was, of course, the group of wrongly accused boys who went to jail for a long time for a crime they didn't commit. And who Trump, at the time, again, called for their execution. And it really was a kind of moment in which he kind of cast himself in that sort of law-and-order mold.

So, there's an arc of politics that comes out of New York here that I think is really, really interesting. And the NYPD have been big supporters of Trump. All these sergeants, benevolent associations are pro-Trumpist in this way. And . . .

DD: The head of the SBA (Sergeant's Benevolent Association) was on TV, I believe, with a Q-Anon mug behind him.

NS: Yeah, exactly. So, I think that's always been a part of the kind of ethos and the version of populism Trump taps into. But the national security state has always been highly skeptical. From the very beginning. And obviously, they've been a big part of the opposition to Trump internally. They've never really come around, I think. And, so, he didn't master those forces and he tried to. But he really failed. And one of the questions I certainly have is whether the dispensations of the national security state would shift if there was the perception that there was a much stronger left opposition in the country.

I sort of remain in the camp that the right is a weak force and not a strong force in the United States. And that includes the institutional right. And it includes the far-right kind of street fighting groups. I don't think they have scale and coordination on the street of the kind that the scariest scenarios depict. And I don't think that their institutional ties are very stable. I mean, clearly they're making inroads at the House of Representatives, but it does remain to be seen how much the institutional Republican Party now tries to reconsolidate itself against some of these forces.

It could well be that we'll see more right-wing violence of the stochastic kind. I hate that word, but it is very, very possible that we'll see a lot of this kind of more random and aleatory expressions of violence in the coming period. But I also think what's even more likely is that we're going to see intensified repression that is embraced by all parts of the ruling order. Biden himself said today, I think, that he wants to pass a major piece of domestic antiterrorism legislation, identifying the events the other day as terrorism. And really, that's in the trajectory of exactly the kind of movements we've seen over the last twenty years within the national security state.

DD: Which, speaking of Ammon Bundy, which you mentioned earlier, Joe, reminds me of a lot of the liberal and even left reaction to the occupation of the Oregon Wildlife Refuge, which was sort of calling for a police crackdown as somehow in the interest of racial equality and proportionality.

JL: Yeah. And we'll see that again. And of course, what happens when you ramp up security legislation and policy, it always redounds on the left. (And that brings us to another conversation about what then is the best direction for the left in this moment.) But this question of how weak the right is and how large its numbers are, is complicated, because I'm not sure it's just a question of numbers, right? You can actually achieve a lot with not a lot of people. You can take over a lot of state houses with not a lot of people, which is what's been happening the last few weeks, and you can have a movement that gets a lot of media attention, and which sparks the imagination of broader elements of the public.

But if we're talking about the relative strength of the right, the question does come back in part to, as Nikhil mentioned, the Republican Party and what the relationship of this right is to the GOP. Whether there will be another charismatic leader to step into the breach and take the torch from Trump, I think is not necessarily what's going to decide it.

One thing about right-wing populism in the United States is that it's not always organized around a leader. You could say Sarah Palin, was maybe, kind of, a nominal leader of the Tea Party. But the movement itself was decentralized and partly funded from above, from donors like the Koch brothers. But also, a lot of the action was grassroots and happened at the state and local level. And so, I think the staying power of the right over the next couple of years partly depends on what happens within right-wing organizations, and their connections to state and local Republican parties.

It's slightly more exaggerated here, but for the last four years, the Oregon Republican Party has been closely tied to paramilitary organizations. The GOP in Multnomah County, which is one of the counties that Portland is in, has used militia members as private security. Militia members vowed to protect state legislators from the state police when Republicans refused to come back into session to vote on a climate change bill. There are things like that. If we have a diminishing Republican Party in terms of numbers, in terms of electoral strength, it may become more of an authoritarian party that relies more on its connections to armed and radicalized elements.

Here in Salem over the last couple of weeks, there was a standoff when far-right protesters—Proud Boys, Three Percenters, and Oath Keepers—busted into the state house here and sprayed bear repellent into the face of state troopers. It turned out that it was a Republican legislator who propped open the door to let them in. And so now, there's this question of what the relationship is between the *sitting* legislators and these movements. I think if it is the case that the institutional right is weakening in this moment, it may need to depend on elements further out.

For that matter, it's not nothing that tens of millions of people thought it [2020] was a stolen election. And that most Republicans thought the takeover at the Capitol was a good idea. So, there's a lot of, these aren't people who necessarily go put on Kevlar and strap on side arms and get out there, but this is a changed set of circumstances from anything we've seen on the right in a very long time. I think the Citizens' Councils in Southern states during the 1950s and '60s would be the most recent example. In the 1930s, there was a proliferation of fascist organizations—Silver Shirts, Brown Shirts, Black Shirts, German American Bund, whatever—but they were significantly confronted by, and had to compete with, a radical labor movement for members. And so, another thing probably worth talking about is not just how to conceive of the threat of actual members of far-right organizations, but what it means to compete for the sympathies and political allegiance of people in this country towards a different kind of vision, given the relative weakness of the left.

DD: Joe, a follow-up question on the kind of far right—the militia-right—that keeps coming up. I recently heard a recording of Ammon Bundy saying something that kind of shocked me. He said, "If you think that somehow Black Lives Matter is more dangerous than the police, you must have a problem. If you think antifa is the one that's going to take away your freedom, you must have a problem in your mind." What do you make of Bundy's surprising solidarity with Black Lives Matter (BLM) and antifa? And what does that say about where certain infractions of the militia movement are right now compared to the right-wing formations that have ended up being much more prominent under Trump, like the Proud Boys, whose whole modus operandi is fighting BLM and antifa in the streets. And then relatedly, where are Richard Spencer and the self-declared white supremacists and nazis who seem to be such a powerful force on the right until Charlottesville? It seems like there's a number of divides that aren't so visible to people outside of the far right.

JL: Charlottesville was an interesting moment because immediately the dominant interpretation was that these were a bunch of odious nazis that no one wanted anything to do with (except Trump himself). Even Steve Bannon at the time was calling them losers and people that should be shunned. And as I said before, the alt-right kind of collapsed in the wake of that. James Fields, the killer of Heather Heyer, was in no sense a sympathetic character for anyone on the right outside of white supremacists. But fast forward a couple of years, you have Kyle Rittenhouse, the seventeen-year-old kid who murdered two people and wounded a third at an anti-Black Lives Matter counterprotest in Kenosha, Wisconsin.

This egregious murder happens on the streets, and Rittenhouse is immediately depicted as an almost Norman Rockwell-esque figure of civic nationalism. There are pictures of him cherub-faced, scrubbing graffiti off walls, like, here he is just trying to take care of his community. And it's not just Tucker Carlson who was singing his praises, but members of the local GOP, the state GOP, and national Republican senators. And it's interesting because he was seen as not a white supremacist in the ghoulish sense we might think of someone like Dylann Roof, but as someone who's just trying to preserve law and order against the thuggery of Black Lives Matter and antifa activists.

DD: And he executed white people.

JL: Well, Heather Heyer (who was killed by James Fields in Charlottesville) was white too, but Rittenhouse actually, he's in a militia movement that sees itself as Trumpist—which the white nationalists did not. I was at an American Renaissance meeting—a eugenicist organization—two weeks before Unite the Right, and Richard Spencer, and Nathan Damigo from Identity Evropa, and all these other folks were there. And they all were quite critical of Trump. This militia movement on the other hand, which has emerged in the last year or so were ardent nationalists, Trump support-ers, and avidly antiracist in their literature.

If you go to the Three Percenters website, the first thing you'll see is they say they're not—in all caps—white supremacist or white nationalist. If you go to the Oath Keepers website, first thing you see is "we come in all colors," with a YouTube video about a Black Oath Keepers member. They want to make sure they are seen as civic nationalists, not racial national-ists, even though their movement over the summer was really animated against Black Lives Matter. But in terms of the other part of that, Ammon Bundy was actually going to speak at a Black Lives Matter protest earlier in the summer. And then the more ardent white supremacist elements in his milieu were like, "No, you can't do that. You're going to discredit all of us and yourself." And then he backed out of doing it.

But even prior to that, back during the Malheur takeover, after [Robert] LaVoy Finicum was shot and killed by the FBI, there were members of this kind of group doing the "hands up don't shoot protests" that Black Lives Matter had popularized. And there was even cooperation between Black Lives Matter and these militia adherents over a bill in the Oregon state legislature around whether cops accused of illegal shootings would have to have their names published. This is what Dan HoSang and I talked about in our book [*Producers, Parasites, Patriots: Race and the New Right-Wing Politics of Precarity*, University of Minnesota, 2019]. And there are other elements of the far right or fascism which don't just turn on race, of course, but glorified violence, masculinity, authoritarianism, anticommunism, and a bunch of other things. So, I think this question of race gets complicated in those ways.

NS: I think the search for an enemy is always central to [right-wing] politics. The right has a very difficult time getting traction without [an enemy]. And now I think they're fighting on a lot of different fronts and they're very, very confused and there isn't a coherent project there. They're going to need to find one, if they're going to move forward as a right-wing party, or they're going to have to kind of moderate in certain ways. And that moderation, I think, will involve trying to recompose a very different kind of relationship internally to their base. The possibilities of that were presented to them by Trump and in some ways by George Bush before them. Trump has broadened the base of the Republican Party. He brought in more voters of color in the last election.

So, Trump is a bit of a paradoxical figure for them because on the one hand, the institutional Republican Party is terrified that they cannot win national elections. They needed somebody to be able to bring in more votes, right? And on the other hand, they've pursued a strategy of voter suppression in different places. And they can't quite decide, because voter suppression—committing full-throatily to voter suppression—obviously puts them in a kind of antidemocratic, illiberal sort of a framework that risks fundamentally discrediting them. Since Americans still seem to care about elections in large numbers, and we can see that's actually growing, right? So, they have to really decide: do they want to go the illiberal route or do they want to try to compete for votes? Then, they're kind of in a bind because when they compete for votes, sort of seriously, I think they're finding now that they're being outvoted, right?

JL: The question is about the right's ability to mobilize. I actually wonder what happens under conditions of more economic instability and therefore political instability? What happens if the neoliberal center can't hold in the same way? What happens if those forces are discredited by all the conditions we're describing of empire, of the carceral state, of greater impoverishment? What happens to the center then? I mean, these are also figures that can list rightward under these conditions. I'm not sure Biden-ism is necessarily so durable itself.

NS: I think that's right about Biden-ism being a kind of a holding action, but what you just said, Joe, is exactly what they say to us all the time. They basically say, "it's only us, or it's the far right," right? They say, we're all that stands between you and the deluge. And in some ways, I think the strategic choice of Biden really reflected that it was kind of like it's Biden or fascism. And I think that's not the right way to think about what's going on. It's not that it's 100 percent wrong or that it was ineffective because I think a second Trump term would have been horrifying and disastrous in so many ways, but very few presidents were presented with the kind of opportunities for authoritarianism that Trump was presented with. And he really didn't take them. I mean, he had a major pandemic and major street protests. He kind of gestured at authoritarianism at various moments, but he could never really pull the levers, either because he didn't know how to operate them or he didn't really want to, in certain ways, and this doesn't even get into the realm of foreign policy where he pulled back many, many times from the things people were pushing him to do.

So, again this is not an apology for Trump. This is just to say let's look very clearly at everything that's going on here. I think the governing order is absolutely in crisis. It's not just the Democrats or the Republicans. And no one has a sense of a clear direction or a way of imagining how to kind of pull all the forces together at this moment.

DD: Joe, you touched on this a bit earlier, but one of the most consequential things that happened last year was that Trump not only overperformed what most anyone imagined, but that he was in particular able to win over of substantial new number of nonwhite voters, including in various places to various degrees, Latinos, Asians, Black people, some groups like Mexican Americans in the Rio Grande Valley, Latinos in South Florida, and Vietnamese Americans in Metro Los Angeles took huge lurches to the right. So, it's rather obvious that racism is core to Trumpism, but if that's a premise that we can all accept, it then leads to some big questions. Specifically, what sort of racist politics can be this racially inclusive? You and Daniel

HoSang explored just this sort of question in your book, *Producers, Parasites, Patriots*, which I discussed with you two on this podcast. What is going on?

JL: Yeah, probably a lot of things are going on at once, but what is clear is that racism is not just one thing or one discourse or one set of policies. And more than that, it's a set of interpretive frameworks that are open to various kinds of mobilization. Even in terms of events this week: Enrique Tarrio, the current putative head of the Proud Boys was arrested on Monday with high-powered magazines leading up to the events on Wednesday. He's Cuban American, which would logically put him in a right-wing camp in Florida. He describes himself as Afro-Cuban and draws on that to make his appeals about the capaciousness of the Proud Boys as a political formation. As you explored in your own book, Dan, part of how nativism can work is that you can have different generations—grandchildren of immigrants against current immigrants—or, for instance, you can have different Latinx people for whom nativism isn't necessarily a question, like Puerto Rican voters.

Trump did extraordinarily well among Puerto Ricans and not just in South Florida but in Central Florida. Part of this then is the ways in which race is attached to other either affective elements, or economic elements, or other things. So, there is a gender gap. And Trump does much better among Latinx men than women. He does better among African-American men than women. There's a way in which masculinity plays an important role in Trump's vote. Class obviously plays a role in how people perceive not just their own racial position United States, but their racial position vis-à-vis others. There are also cultural elements like evangelical Christianity that obviously play a big role, and then just kind of American nationalism generally—a broad an identity that is always simultaneously inclusive and excluding.

So, there's a lot there that I think that liberal antiracism misses in terms of who is going to be open to what appeals. Part of the question is how did Trump do so well? But the other question is why did the Democrats do as poorly as they did? Like what kind of appeals were not being made to Vietnamese American small business owners, for instance, or other groups? It was always a presumption that all people of color are going to be on the side of Black Lives Matter, all have the same position on George Floyd's murder, all have the same position on Trump's crude forms of racialized language. And that's just not always true.

DD: Something that organizers in Arizona and Georgia [during the 2020 election] never had the luxury to presume.

JL: Yes, exactly. They had to work it out on the ground as organizers and figure out how to make appeals for solidarity. And I think that this is then a question for the left as well, of what we want to build. We're going to have to be much more careful and thoughtful in terms of how we suture together alliances, how we generate shared interests and identities.

IV. Present Histories

CHAPTER THIRTEEN

Be like the wind—or better, like water

Resisting racial capitalism's fascist forever wars

Dian Million

Figure 6. Red Spirit Creations interior (detail), 1989. Photograph by Dian Million.

Is the cry familiar

we hear about the death in the south
about its rate of progress
our deaths are always linked with the death of the land
and we know this.

neither is it a secret
we have our own mass graves to remind us
that this is the principle no matter what

indigenism
is loyalty to the land
not the flags
not the corporations

if we are loyal to the land
we will live and prosper and find peace
and not live forever with the flickering image
of the pinstripe man
who takes his weapons and rapes us
again and again.

we are telling you about the wind
we are telling you that we have always shared
but some always want more
we are telling you that the earth will devour you
we are telling you that our deaths will be for naught

tell us you hear
tell us you will resist
tell us you comprehend what is happening

let the wind blow

I wrote these words some time ago; in 1988 in Portland, Oregon. At the time, I was a member of United Indian Women, a group of Native women organizers operating out of a storefront that housed a co-op childcare center, an arts and crafts gallery named Red Spirit Creations, and shared workspace. The building was located on 30th and Stark Street in Southeast Portland.[1]

Some of us lived in the back, using it as a workspace to print the Tyghe artist Susana Santos' intricate silkscreen creations along with posters for the rallies and events we organized. Susana, who organized the Sacred Earth Coalition, a Native and non-Native alliance, shared the space with us before establishing her own gallery. She provided us with salmon "hogs" that gave us steaks the size of dinner plates in return for the printing work we did for her. Other Columbia River peoples generously gave us food as well. Earlier, we had worked as a support group for David Sohappy Sr., his son, and codefendants during the years they were imprisoned for fishing in their own ancestral sites. We also provided women power for the Big Mountain Diné resistance and the Leonard Peltier Defense Committee. We were part of a larger, very vibrant American Indian activist movement in Portland from the 1970s into the 1980s. In fact, the entire Pacific Northwest and in particular the I-5 corridor from California to Seattle and Vancouver, BC connected us as various Native resistance families.

It is in those years I met Gord Hill, a young Kwakwaka'wakw organizer in Vancouver on my way to meet with Ethel Pearson and her husband Fred in Comox. Ethel, a dynamic Kwakwa̱ka̱'wakw elder, had successfully lobbied all fifty-two chiefs of her nation to formally adopt Leonard Peltier to fight his extradition from Canada on the United States' trumped-up charges.[2]

---

1   Red Spirit Creations existed twice. First as an economic development project initiated and funded by the Portland Urban Indian Council (UIC) in 1984. That arts and crafts store, located in downtown Portland in the Burnside area, eventually became a site of community organizing. When the Council was disbanded after a long decline, the Red Spirit Creations co-op on Stark was raised to try to keep its energy in the community. Red Spirit Creations closed forever in 1990. The photo I took contains the art and craft in our community gallery at that time. The large oil painting (I do not have its name) is by Susana Santos. The original is the property of the Santos family. For more information on Santos' artwork, see http://www.apoloniasusanasantos.com/index.html.

2   Leonard Peltier is a member of the American Indian Movement (AIM) who has been imprisoned for almost forty-five years. Leonard Peltier's case resulting from a shootout with FBI agents has been chronicled by several international human rights organizations, including Amnesty International. A brief synopsis of Leonard's case exists at https://freeleonard.org/case/. A more detailed chronical of Leonard's case and the larger movement exists archived in *Akwesasne Notes*, an incredibly important Mohawk-produced newspaper

She, along with many elder tribal women, were mentors to all of us in their activism and undying support for Indigenous resistance. Ethel modeled an excellent caring kinship towards Leonard that exemplified our contempt for the US-Canadian border or any claim to the right to prosecute him on the charges he faced. Gord Hill, a prolific antifascist Native artist and activist, relates that time, linking our decolonization work to the building antifascist work that engaged us all. While there were few self-identified Indigenous antifa voices doing that work then—a point Hill makes recently in his excellent interview with Allan Antliff[3]—he calls attention to the wide coalitional content the work existed in. Today, Melanie Yazzie, Leanne Betasamosake Simpson, Nick Estes, and Glen Coulthard have made it part of their work to recover and regain an understanding of the range of the national and international relations we made in that moment.[4]

The context of our Portland activism had been formed in a struggle for treaty and human rights for Indigenous peoples. It was formed in the knowledge that this was a global struggle, one that acknowledges our ties with both Indigenous and other liberation movements across continents. In reflection and solidarity with the International Treaty Council's work at

---

that was published from around 1970 until the 1980s. See *Akwesasne Notes* Collection, American Indian Digital History Project, University of Kansas, University of Nebraska at Omaha, https://aidhp.com/items/browse?collection=1.

3   Gordon Hill and Allan Antliff, "Indigeneity, Sovereignty, Anarchy: A Dialog with Many Voices," in "The Politics of Indigeneity, Anarchist Praxis, and Decolonization," Special Issue of *Anarchist Developments in Cultural Studies*, no. 1 (2021), https://journals.uvic.ca/index.php/adcs/issue/view/1506?fbclid=IwAR3sq1qAYA478GcPn_32kpCk5g3kELOKsEw-bRF3svPn0ofQSAnfWXWmjM_U. Gord Hill is a prolific artist and writer who produces zine art and illustrated social histories that are stunning testimonies to the continuity of Indigenous and radical struggle. See Gord Hill and Mark Bray, *The Antifa Comic Book: 100 Years of Fascism and Antifa Movements, The Anti-Capitalist Resistance Comic Book, The 500 Years of Resistance Comic Book*. Taiaiake Alfred and Glen Coulthard introduce Wasáse as "an intellectual and political movement whose ideology is rooted in sacred wisdom" that provided tenets of Anarch@Indigenism. See Taiaiake Alfred and Glen Coulthard, "Wasáse Movement: Indigenous Radicalism Today," *New Socialist*, no. 58 (September–October 2006): 2. Also see Jacqueline Laskey, "Indigenism, Anarchism, Feminism: An Emerging Framework for Exploring Post-Imperial Futures," *Affinities: A Journal of Radical Theory, Culture and Action* 5, no. 1 (2011) who introduces the importance of Indigenous feminisms to antifascist movements, a framework that Melanie K. Yazzie has more fully articulated.

4   Glen Coulthard, Leanne Betasamosake Simpson, and Rinaldo Walcott, "Situating Indigenous and Black Resistance in the Global Movement Assemblage (Video Presentation)," *Studies in Social Justice* 12, no. 1 (2018). Also see: Nick Estes, *Our History Is the Future: Standing Rock Versus the Dakota Access Pipeline, and the Long Tradition of Indigenous Resistance*; and Melanie K. Yazzie, "US Imperialism and the Problem of 'Culture' in Indigenous Politics: Towards Indigenous Internationalist Feminism," *American Indian Culture and Research Journal* 43, no. 3 (2019): 95–118.

that time, I opened Red Spirit on some evenings to teach a class I called *"pejuta sapa"* (in Lakota "coffee," or black medicine, something to wake you up) outlining our international struggles with murderous nation-states across hemispheres and continents. We were specific about our nations' differences from nation-states and specifically our reverence for a living Earth whose spirit could not be owned or reduced to capitalist property. A great deal of our work followed our ardent desires for honoring the treaties of our nations, for the protection of our lands and for our other-than-human relatives. We understood that our existing nations had been fought for. Our ancestors as well as our present members have given their lives over many generations to preserve ways of life in specific places. As activists we worked often in urban settings, sometimes displaced from specific lands—but also recognizing that there was no place in the continent that was not stolen land. At that juncture, I think we believed in education; that if the genocidal actions that nation-states perpetrated against us as Indigenous peoples were more widely known that we might force colonial states to admit to their violations and establish more just relations. The list of atrocities we understood and fought to make apparent was very long, beginning with the theft of a continent, of continents, of homelands, of children, of livelihoods, of life itself, since death and brutality were like atmospheres to us—so thick—that in many ways it was just what we knew. Thus, I recognized early on, like Indigenous peoples in every generation we were and are engaged in a struggle that does not end, but only morphs.

The American Indian Movement was founded in Minneapolis, Minnesota in the 1960s. It seems fitting that it was first an urban-based coalition of protectors and that it quickly developed many of the same defensive tactics that the Black Panthers used in defending their communities against police brutality—work that included both education and mutual-aid work. It is also fitting to recognize the support work that we did in those days that was allied with other movements were always attempts to protect American Indian and Alaska Native peoples from racist assault and police brutality. It was common, parcel and part of our everyday experiences in any city or rural area where we tried to make our lives. Our work always included organizing support for prisoners and protests over the ongoing murder and untimely deaths that our communities suffered. Our support groups were like families because we understood that we needed to take care of each other as a very deep part of the fabric of our activism. Our ideas, our philosophies from those times, are well woven into our present activism. Such generational knowledge sharing is a mark of Indigenous caring for our past, our present, and our future generations.

Our vocabulary did not differentiate colonization from fascism. I think that considering what we now characterize as "racial capitalism" and "settler colonialism," we must recognize that colonization and fascism are deeply entwined projects. The colonization of these lands is a racialized, murderous, and ongoing pursuit, a pogrom that has displaced and enslaved many peoples, seeking to ensure death, destitution, and exclusion. This deserves our resistance.

Returning to Red Spirit Creations and 1988, there is one more story I want to recall here. We saw anti-Indian hate up close in the years we organized on behalf of the fishing communities in Oregon and Washington—a hate that intensified as US Judge Boldt decided for these peoples' treaty rights. Red Spirit occupied the downstairs of a building we renovated with the help of many relatives. The owner rented the upstairs to various characters. That summer we had it out with one particularly loud and obnoxious nest of skinheads. Their music kept us awake all night. The back parking lot where one of our members had built a smokehouse for salmon was filled with their beer bottles. We confronted these people many times finally convincing the landlord to evict them. I wasn't really scared of these scrawny, often drunk white boys, but I didn't completely understand why some people thought what we did was big deal until that fall. In November of 1988, Mulugeta Seraw was beaten to death with a baseball bat on Southeast 31st and Pine—just blocks from us—by members of a Portland skinhead group called East Side White Pride. We were shocked; this murder was basically next door. And instantly, we were more aware of what these white supremacist "skinheads" were capable of.

Mulugeta was an Ethiopian man who came to the US seeking an education. He didn't know his attackers. He was targeted because he was Black and an immigrant. Was this a rare incident? No. Portland, Oregon—and Oregon in general, and the entire Pacific Northwest where I live now—has ongoing experience of deeply racist actions like Mulugeta's murder. With organized militias all over the region, it is a history that has been well detailed. Native families in our neighborhood experienced very pointed anti-Indian statements tacked to their doors. We quickly organized ways of checking in on each other, particularly for women who lived alone with their children. Many of us documented the rise of these myriad, prolific anti-Indian organizations, many who remain active to this day, who are strangely not seen as terrorists while Indigenous activists increasingly are. Yet, any recounting of the litany of these atrocities would only divert us from considering the nature of the struggle that we have conducted, it seems, mostly in self-defense in a never-ending war, one that appears to deepen now.

Of that generation of activists that I worked with in Portland, many left after the 1980s to go home to their own communities. Some passed away, such as Susana Santos in 2006. Ethel Pearson passed in 1999. Organizing here ebbs and flows, as we become part of exceedingly changed and charged political landscapes. Yet, there is a great deal of continuity between those times and these. Despite the victories that returned fishing rights to the federally recognized Native peoples of the Puget Sound and Columbia River, the ardent hate that permeates this country is still the air we breathe, for air that we can breathe, and for the water that is life itself. We face the possibility that the salmon will disappear threatening our ways of life in ways we did not think were possible.

I have written about how the United States and Canada have perpetrated ongoing violence to Indigenous lives for the better part of thirty years now. The continuity of this violence is a knowledge that threads pasts and futures. I also began to call attention to the specific racial context of the violence embedded in any "policing" of Indigenous lives in the United States. I wasn't "discovering" anything not known. I sought then as now a deeper critical understanding of how colonization works inside us. In graduate school I wrote an article called "Policing the Rez: Keeping No Peace in Indian Country."[5] I detailed the close connection between the colonial erasure of Indigenous sovereignty and the creation of mass jurisdictional spaces where local Indigenous governance became nearly impossible. This left Indigenous communities open to waves of violence that are known to this day, such as the ways women became vulnerable to not only death and disappearance in their homelands but to chronic illness and environmental assault. While the appearance of multiple militia groups seemingly sanctioned by the US mainstream may appear shocking to some, at this point—to many of us—it is the surfacing of the real nature of how racialized

5   Dian Million, "'Policing the Rez': Keeping No Peace in Indian Country," *Social Justice* 27, no. 3 (2000): 101–119.

orders are kept stable in many places. I wrote in "Policing the Rez" how the maintenance of a racialized state relies on grassroots racist acts to police Native lives. These "neighbors," sometimes just "the skinheads upstairs," are most certainly well integrated with the policing and military institutions of this country. I was extremely happy when my colleague and friend Jennifer Denetdale wrote a related assessment of this local "policing" or lack thereof in "'No Explanation, No Resolution, and No Answers': Border Town Violence and Navajo Resistance to Settler Colonialism."[6] Denetdale argues that the impoverishment, policing, and murder of Diné relatives is accomplished with the cooperation of white settler citizens, such as the vigilantes and militias in border towns, and in tandem with the colonization of their lands and homeplaces. The establishment of the reservation and the "border town" creates a jurisdictional black hole where the Diné Nation cannot properly protect their peoples who live in the limbo of such a "border." The creation of reservations with their impossibly complex policing jurisdictions go hand in hand with what Ruth Gilmore, after David Harvey, calls "organized abandonment" in reservation border towns and in Black and Brown communities.[7]

In the summer of 2020, one of my own young relatives fought police brutality in the streets of Portland with Black Lives Matter (BLM)-led affinity groups. He grew up in Oregon and our lives in this region circled around again. He told me about the kinds of weapons that police launched against them and the medical care he learned to give to other BLM protesters. Eye and face injuries were common from smoke bombs and gas. He also told me that many of the fascist and white supremacist groups present were ignored by the police while their Black and Brown contingent bore the brunt of the police violence. How did he understand the struggle he was part of? Joining a mixed group of Black Lives Matter activists and others from many backgrounds, including American Indian and Alaska Native, they were united in their common purpose. They often fought next

---

6   Jennifer Nez Denetdale, "'No Explanation, No Resolution, and No Answers': Border Town Violence and Navajo Resistance to Settler Colonialism," *Wicazo Sa Review* 31, no. 1 (2016). An illustrated version of this article appears in *The Funambulist* 20, a special issue coedited by Melanie Yazzie and Nick Estes.

7   Ruth Wilson Gilmore and Léopold Lambert, "Making Abolition Geography in California's Central Valley," *The Funambulist* 21, December 20, 2018, https://thefunambulist.net/magazine/21-space-activism/interview-making-abolition-geography-california-central-valley-ruth-wilson-gilmore.

to antifascists, "antifa," sometimes with singular purpose and sometimes not, frustrated by differences they could not articulate at times. He calls the organizing work that he continues to do "antiracist." I do not think he ever doubted that their collective work was antifascist.

It may be good to debate the tactical and strategic differences in the work we do, but it is time to understand fascism as this country's ongoing past and present. And, I think, we call it by its name rather than ever believing it as any misguided "patriotism." Patriotism upholds a murderous racially capitalized patriarchal order that has been continuously maintained and perpetrated.[8] These "patriots" are not an aberration but the glue that allows the fully capitalized to thrive and continue to oppress.

The poem fragment I began this essay with reminds us that we engage in forever wars, and that while we call our lived experiences with fascist regimes by other names, we need to continue to recognize our shared struggles; here we might also take responsibility to enter conversations that take us forward.

Is the cry familiar

we hear about the death in the south
about its rate of progress
our deaths are always linked with the death of the land
and we know this.

neither is it a secret
we have our own mass graves to remind us
that this is the principle no matter what

"Is the cry familiar, we hear about the death in the South, about its rate of progress, our deaths are always linked with the death of the land, and we know this." Yes, if anything, the fires in the Amazon and the cries of Indigenous land defenders in the Global South as they die under the orders of fascist regimes like in Bolsonaro's Brazil right now are an unrelenting pain that no amount of human rights recognition has stopped in any way. The deaths and invasions remain as common now as then. The old paths northward fill with refugees, many who are Indigenous fleeing from the

---

8   Roxanne Dunbar-Ortiz, *Loaded: A Disarming History of the Second Amendment* (San Francisco: City Lights Books, 2018).

Global South, always linked with the taking of land, the starvation and destitution of livelihoods while capitalism thrives even in a time of pandemic.

In June 2021, a Canadian First Nations community located 215 unmarked graves of Indigenous children at an old boarding school site. After that, the numbers of children's bones found began to climb into the thousands and Canada admits there are probably more, while we are reminded that new mass graves are in process and that this is the principle, no matter what.

> indigenism
> is loyalty to the land
> not the flags
> not the corporations
>
> if we are loyal to the land
> we will live and prosper and find peace
> and not live forever with the flickering image
> of the pinstripe man
> who takes his weapons and rapes us
> again and again.

"Indigenism is loyalty to the land, not the flags, not the corporations." Our liberation can never be in fealty to racial capitalism. I do not believe that capitalist nation-states can create the democracies that many are pining for at the same time these states' natal fascism gains ground here. How is that we do not understand that since the time when I wrote this poem in 1988, the capitalist system has forced us all into accepting whole cities of peoples and families that have been stripped of their land and livelihoods, living in tents on the streets, where mental health care is often a bullet administered by a cop, where Indigenous women top the charts in those who are brutalized and disappeared. Any often-touted "wealth" here is the result of a richly documented ongoing racial hierarchy that is enforced each generation—it is built into the structures of the states we live in, policed officially and informally by those who benefit from this order and those who don't but just believe that they do.[9]

Corporations are not returning land to peoples so that they can make their lives on them—nor are they stopping the mass desertification of land,

---

9   Jackie Wang, *Carceral Capitalism* (South Pasadena: Semiotext(e), 2018).

or the ongoing last mad rush for the oil that lies under Indigenous and poor peoples' lands. They are the pinstriped men who return to raping us again and again, and who propagate wars against our ways of life. "If we are loyal to the land, we will live and prosper and find peace," is my ardent desire for people to understand Indigeneity as lifeways that create conditions for abundance rather than seeking more efficient death or to produce more profit. Indigeneity as practice holds knowledges of how we might live in places, where we can choose not to strip them, refuse to participate in capitalist ways of life, and seek ways that honor the relations that we are. We should define exactly what we are as nations rather than being mini nation-states, always seeking new ways to be recognized by the murderers of our children's bodies and futures.

We seek to learn among others who want freedom from this system. How might Indigeneity uphold the call for abolition, for instance? Ruth Gilmore tells us: "Abolition requires that we change one thing: everything," and to think "freedom as a place" inviting our collaboration on crucial questions for those of us whose lives are entwined in "places."[10] Our entering into abolitionist practice confronts and demands a deep conversation on the actual underpinning of our dreamed and practiced ways of making "freedom places," now. This is a conversation I hope will become an ardent one among American Indian, Alaska Native, First Nations, Black and myriad peoples whose experiences are deemed diasporic as we dream and practice the making of "freedom" in "places." I first read Ruth Wilson's words above as an invitation to muse on the actual and practical ways in which we might create an order that secures safety and peace; an order that is not carceral or results in our production for capitalist exploitation. *Place* has specific meaning in an Indigenous sense. Glen Coulthard describes *place* as "a way of knowing, experiencing, and relating with the world—and these ways of knowing often guide forms of resistance to power relations that threaten to erase or destroy our senses of place."[11]

I suggest that Indigeneity is foremost a practice of governance, ontologically and epistemologically lived within *places* that are not imagined as static. Indigeneity is a global practice in living that liberal humanism/

---

10 Ruth Gilmore and Léopold Lambert, 19.

11 Glen Coulthard, "Place against Empire: Understanding Indigenous Anti-Colonialism," *Affinities: A Journal of Radical Theory, Culture and Action* 4, no. 2 (2010), https://ojs.library. queensu.ca/index.php/affinities/article/view/6141.

racial capitalism has tried to eradicate from the Earth for over 500 years. Indigeneity posits ways of living that create governances that are never the same across places or times. Indigenous practices emerge specifically within a set of relations that are material, spiritual, and dynamic. Indigenous practices form governances not nation-states. Our peoples have variously expressed their ontology, their premise for being as a set of relations where all are sentient and possessing agency.[12] Indigeneity strives to create relations of care and reciprocity, understanding the interdependence of all in a "place," with a shared goal of thriving in a place without destruction. This is governance that seeks to continue the conditions for all life. This is the core of what became understood as Indigeneity globally: the oft-expressed caretaker relations of peoples with "land," denying a singular understanding of land as property. Land is not property. It is part of a relation—and "land" is not the entirety of any relations as they are understood in any place. In North America, this living dynamic became reduced and severed by the racialization of myriad peoples into a managerial identity of "Indian" or "Aboriginal." Some of us have argued that when Indigenous peoples' governing epistemologies are reduced to capitalist schemes of recognition, this forecloses what our larger legacy as peoples point to.

I read an invitation to a conversation on what Indigeneity means to the abolitionist call for practices of "freedom" in places. It is to speak to the sometimes fraught and sometimes generous questions that are posed between Black and Indigenous feminisms, about land and about the after lives of enslavement, and what we might dream of just futures together if we think relationally, in "constellations" rather than from silos.[13] Some see Indigenous practices of sovereignty as practices of liberal property ownership, carceral-like, and dependent on seeing others who have come—including the Indigenous peoples from the South—as settlers, as unwelcoming to other communities and collectivities and their place-making or their mobility.[14] How might we enact Indigeneity as a practice of life-making in *places* in this moment rather than consume the whisper of capitalism, the

---

12 Vanessa Watts, "Indigenous Place-Thought & Agency Amongst Humans and Non-Humans (First Woman and Sky Woman Go on a European World Tour," *Decolonization: Indigeneity, Education and Society* 2, no. 1 (2013): 20–34.

13 Leanne Betasamosake Simpson, *As We Have Always Done: Indigenous Freedom through Radical Resistance* (Minneapolis: University of Minnesota Press, 2017).

14 Harsha Walia, *Border & Rule: Global Migration, Capitalism, and the Rise of Racist Nationalism* (Chicago: Haymarket Books, 2021).

lure of turning Indigenous *places* into corporate mini-economies, where the "implacable logic of debt takes over for the implacable logic of the white man's burden . . . of the need for people cut off from circuits of capital accumulation to develop their capacities, to adjust to the standards of the more advanced world, to reform their backward ways."[15] The reward for full immersion into neoliberal capitalist economy is also to accept the order of neoliberal policing and surveillance—where carceral capitalism is a way of life and death.

We now return to the work that Ruth Wilson Gilmore proposes above to "change one thing: everything" from our difference and our similarities. How do our different place-making knowledges share in making abolition work now? How might we make a multiplicity of places that answer our desires and demand to remake systems of US and Canadian settler colonialism and racial capitalist carceral systems of "unfreedom," to stop the violence against our peoples, the ways we are gendered, sexualized, and individualized that make impossible collective forms of care, that make impossible our ways of life? It seems essential to be aware of the fragility of any dream we might have for obtaining justice in reparations and reconciliations, promises made by capitalist orders now so bent on normalizing the right-wing fantasies and basest desires of their citizenry. No, we really do have to dream larger—"to change one thing: everything." It seems imperative that we think beyond silos, to rather be like the wind—or better, like water.

> we are telling you about the wind
> we are telling you that we have always shared
> but some always want more
> we are telling you that the earth will devour you
> we are telling you that our deaths will be for naught
>
> tell us you hear
> tell us you will resist
> tell us you comprehend what is happening
>
> let the wind blow

---

15 Jodi A. Byrd, Alyosha Goldstein, Jodi Melamed, and Chandan Reddy, "Predatory Value: Economies of Dispossession and Disturbed Relationalities," *Social Text* 36, no. 2 (June 2018): 10.

CHAPTER FOURTEEN

Fighting Hate by Fighting for Dignity
An Interview with Subin Dennis

Manu Karuka and Subin Dennis

This interview with Subin Dennis, a researcher with Tricontinental Research, New Delhi was conducted remotely in September 2020. That month, the Indian Parliament passed three laws to increase corporate control over Indian agriculture. Beginning on November 26, hundreds of thousands of farmers occupied the outskirts of Delhi, "in explicit recognition that the fight is against corporate rule."[1] November 26 also saw a nationwide general strike by the workers' unions in India, drawing the participation of 250 million people. In March 2021, India saw a devastating second wave of COVID-19, contributing to the world's second-highest number of confirmed cases (after the United States). As Subin argued, the BJP government "has displayed an astounding level of incompetence in handling the COVID-19 crisis," even as it used the pandemic as an opportunity to ram through antiworker laws and continued its assault on science, while seeking to deliver super-profits to the corporate-financial oligarchy.[2] In the elections held in April 2021 to several state legislative assemblies, the BJP suffered a series of reversals. It suffered defeats in West Bengal and Tamil Nadu, while voters in Kerala kept the Left Democratic Front in power, with a mandate to end absolute poverty.[3] While the BJP government remains in power, and the RSS

---

1   See: Subin Dennis, "India's Farmers Revolt," *Tribune*, December 14, 2020, https://tribunemag.co.uk/2020/12/indias-popular-revolt; Subin Dennis, "Elite Despair About 'Farmers Lack of Discipline' Is Comical, Though Not Innocent," *Newsclick*, January 27, 2021, https://www.newsclick.in/Elite-Despair-About-percentE2 percent80 percent9C-Farmers percentE2 percent80 percent99-Lack-of-Discipline percentE2 percent80 percent9D-is-Comical-Though-Not-Innocent.

2   Subin Dennis, "How Modi's Failures Led to India's COVID Catastrophe," *Tribune*, May 5, 2021, https://tribunemag.co.uk/2021/05/how-modis-failures-led-to-indias-covid-catastrophe/. The failures of the BJP government can be counterposed to the successes of Kerala's Left Democratic Front government. See also, Subin Dennis and Vijay Prashad, "Kerala Is a Model State in the COVID-19 Fight," *MR Online*, April 15, 2020, https://mronline.org/2020/04/16/kerala-is-a-model-state-in-the-covid-19-fight/.

3   Subin Dennis, "The Kerala Model at the Crossroads," *The Hindu*, April 5, 2021, https://www.thehindu.com/opinion/lead/the-kerala-model-at-the-crossroads/article34239506.ece.

project to remake Indian society proceeds, progressive forces in India continue the long struggle for freedom.

An economist by training, Subin was active with the left student movement in India during his university days. He is currently based in Thiruvananthapuram (also known as Trivandrum), Kerala.

Manu Karuka: What is the BJP (*Bharatiya Janata* Party, or Indian Peoples Party)? Is it a fascist party? What is the BJP's relationship to the RSS (*Rashtriya Swayamsevak Sangh*)?

Subin Dennis: The BJP is India's current ruling party. It was founded in 1980 and came to power for the first time in 1996, for only thirteen days. It returned to power in 1998 and ruled until 2004. The BJP was out of office for ten years after that, and then won the elections again in 2014. In 2019, they were reelected with a much bigger majority than earlier. Narendra Modi of the BJP has been the Prime Minister since 2014.

When we talk about the situation in India, we need to clarify two concepts. The first is *communalism*. In South Asia, communalism refers to the idea that religious communities are political communities with secular interests that are opposed to each other.[4] So Hindus would be a political community whose secular interests are opposed to the secular interests of Muslims. Organizations or political parties organized around this principle are called communal organizations or communal parties. The BJP is a Hindu communal party. We also have Muslim communal organizations, like the *Jamaat-e-Islami*. Communal organizations are quite common in India.

But the BJP is not just a communal party and it is not an independent political party. It is the political wing, the main electoral instrument, of another organization. That organization is RSS, the *Rashtriya Swayamsevak Sangh* [National Volunteer Organization]. The RSS was formed in 1925, many decades before the BJP was formed, and it is possibly the world's largest fascist organization. So, to ask whether BJP is a fascist organization is somewhat less relevant. The RSS is the driving force of the BJP. Narendra

---

See also Vijay Prashad and Subin Dennis, "Why One State in India Is Showing Promising Signs of Democracy as the World Goes More Authoritarian," *Peoples Dispatch*, May 14, 2021, https://peoplesdispatch.org/2021/05/14/why-one-state-in-india-is-showing-promising-signs-of-democracy-as-the-world-goes-more-authoritarian/.

4   Bipan Chandra, *Communalism: A Primer* (New Delhi: National Book Trust, 2008).

Modi is an RSS man. He was sent to the BJP by the RSS to eventually lead it in Gujarat. As the chief minister of Gujarat, Narendra Modi presided over a communal pogrom in 2002 in which about 2,000 Muslims were massacred. After that, he was reelected as chief minister in Gujarat. In a long-term sense, his popularity did not decrease after the pogrom.

What does the RSS want? What is the ideology of the RSS? That is where we get to the second term: *Hindutva*. Hindutva literally means Hindu-ness. It is right-wing political Hinduism or, you could say, it is *Hindu supremacism*.[5] It is often said that fascism doesn't have a coherent strategy for economic and social reconstruction and so on. That is applicable to Hindutva as well. Basically, they want to create what is called a *Hindu Rashtra*, that is, a Hindu state. That is their objective.

RSS has 8 million members in nearly 60,000 branches, which they call "*shakhas*." RSS has only male members. It has a mind-boggling array of affiliated organizations. These include organizations working among students, lawyers, workers, and farmers. They have set up organizations to provide social services and charity. There is an organization to rewrite history to suit the RSS' worldview, for example, to say that India had a glorious Hindu past, that Muslims invaded India and thus led to India's degeneration. There is a children's cultural organization. There is one for cow protection, because many Hindus consider the cow to be a sacred animal. There is an organization to promote "family values." There is an organization to promote small industries. There is one for doctors and one for veterans. There is one for writers. There are organizations to work among Indigenous communities. They have organizations that run schools. They have a religious wing: the *Vishwa Hindu Parishad* (VHP) or Universal Hindu Council.

Aijaz Ahmad has a formulation that RSS wants to be both the church and the state.[6] That prospect is truly terrifying. The RSS is indeed moving in that direction—it is trying to control Hindu monks; it is taking control of Hindu temples. There are countries where religion and state are deeply enmeshed, deeply intertwined, but if the RSS manages this in India, the scale of it will be unprecedented.

---

5   A.G. Noorani, *Savarkar and Hindutva: The Godse Connection* (New Delhi: LeftWord Books, 2002).

6   Aijaz Ahmad, "India: Liberal Democracy and the Extreme Right," *Indian Cultural Forum*, September 7, 2016, https://indianculturalforum.in/2016/09/07/india-liberal-democracy-and-the-extreme-right/.

The VHP, the religious wing of the RSS, has a paramilitary wing called the *Bajrang Dal*. They are among the most important sections of storm troopers in Indian fascism. They are young, excitable people, often unemployed. In classical fascism, storm troopers were often drawn from the ranks of the lumpenproletariat, a large section of which would be unemployed young people. There is a clear parallel here.

Communal violence polarizes people based on religious lines. That is beneficial for parties like BJP which seek to create a "Hindu vote bank." Once people are polarized on religious lines, and more Hindus consolidate behind the idea that Hindus should unite against Muslims and Christians, it creates a very conducive atmosphere for a party like BJP, which presents itself as the savior of the Hindus. Communal violence is something that the RSS has systematically used from the time of its birth. That is how the RSS-BJP increased its mass support in many parts of India. The RSS also provides physical and arms training to its cadre, and regularly uses violence to try and subdue its political opponents.

In the 1980s, the RSS, the VHP, and the BJP embarked on a campaign to build a new temple for the Hindu god Rama at a place called Ayodhya in the state of Uttar Pradesh. They wanted to build this temple on the site of a sixteenth-century mosque, the Babri Masjid. RSS and VHP claimed that the mosque had been built at the place where Rama, the Hindu god, was born. They claimed that Muslim rulers had destroyed a temple that stood at that spot and then built a mosque over it. So, they wanted to demolish that mosque and build a new temple for the Lord Rama.

They were helped along by decisions of the Congress government, led by Rajiv Gandhi, which facilitated the entry of Hindus into the Babri Masjid to offer prayers there. In 1992, a massive mob of activists of the RSS, VHP, BJP, and Bajrang Dal demolished the Babri Masjid, while the state machinery passively stood by. That was a major event, the destruction of a major monument which was important for the Muslim community. Communal violence raged across India. This campaign to build a temple, the demolition of the mosque, and the communal clashes afterwards all led to a strengthening of the communal camp and mass support for the BJP and the RSS.

MK: With this backdrop of communal violence and communal polarization, what kinds of economic policies has the BJP pursued in power?

SD: After Modi took power, there were a series of blunders in economic policy. The worst of these was demonetization—announced in November 2016—in which the government withdrew currency notes of denominations Rs. 500 and Rs. 1000, thus sucking 86 percent of the Indian currency in circulation out of the economy. There was also the introduction of the goods and services tax which had a deeply adverse impact on the informal sector and on the finances of state governments. And of course, the thoroughly incompetent manner in which the Modi government has handled the pandemic. All of these have contributed to the Indian economy now facing among the worst recessions in the major economies of the world. There is a deep crisis of livelihood as far as the Indian people are concerned.

Like classical fascism, the BJP also came to power amid worsening economic conditions, although there was no prospect of the Left coming to power. There is no political party strong enough to take power on behalf of the workers and peasants of India.

Nevertheless, India's monopoly capitalists all lined up behind Narendra Modi, even before he was elected. They saw him as a leader who could serve their interests, even more than the Congress Party. The Congress had introduced neoliberal economic reforms in India and did the bidding of finance capital. Their rule led to an agrarian crisis in India. About 400,000 farmers took their own lives as a result of this crisis. That was very much part of the economic situation that paved the way for the rise of the BJP.

Ever since coming to power, the BJP has faithfully carried out their duty on behalf of the corporate-financial oligarchy. It is neoliberalism on steroids. They have been selling our public sector industries. They have been trying to dilute labor laws to the detriment of workers, reducing their bargaining power, taking away unionizing rights, and making it increasingly easier for employers to hire and fire. Even before the pandemic, India had the highest unemployment rate in forty-five years. Even before the pandemic, the purchasing power of the people, reflected in per capita consumption expenditure, was declining.

The BJP has ruled for the big bourgeoisie in general, but its rule has been particularly beneficial to a set of favored capitalists, like the billionaire Ambanis and the Adanis. Mukesh Ambani is the richest Indian; he heads an empire of industries, called Reliance Industries Limited. And then there is Gautam Adani who heads Adani Group, another corporate conglomerate. These groups have benefited disproportionately under Modi's rule. While many other companies are facing great difficulties, especially since the pandemic, Reliance is raising massive amounts of money and is claiming to have gone net-debt free. The Adani Group has just gobbled up six airports. Adani did not have any experience running airports, but it has been awarded the rights [by the Modi government] to run six airports. These are just two examples. Reliance Industries was originally into polyester, textiles, petrochemicals and petroleum, and they have diversified into telecom, Internet, retail, and so on. Adani was into commodity trading and ports, then diversified into power, airports, shipping, etc. They are solidly behind BJP. Privatization of public sector enterprises have accelerated under BJP rule, which has provided massive tax cuts to corporations. The overall support of the corporate executives to BJP is such that 79 percent of corporate donations in India have gone to the BJP in 2018–2019. In 2017–2018 it was 95 percent.

It's not the case that the corporate elites in India hate the Congress, the political party which has ruled India for the longest time. The Congress organization has been weakened considerably, over many years, and it doesn't have any ideology to rally people behind it. BJP has Hindutva. They can talk about Hindu unity; they can preach hatred against Muslims. They offer people something to rally around, even though it is something hideous. The Congress has no ideology to speak of. Other than the prospect of making money by becoming a Congress leader, there is nothing that can attract people to the Congress. It is unable to offer a viable opposition these days. The corporations have not found any need to support the Congress, and the BJP has been successful in keeping them on its side.

The BJP is also aware that to get to power you need mass support. Fascism is propped up by finance capital, but it is also a mass movement. BJP claims that they are the biggest political party in the world, with a membership of 180 million. It's not the case that they're all active members, but it is an indication of the number of people who want to be overtly associated with the BJP. Survey data on the general elections of 2019 shows support for the BJP among the poor has increased to 36 percent compared to 24 percent in 2014. India is a country with steep inequalities. The rich are a tiny minority, and the middle class is also quite small. Any political party would need the support of the lower middle classes and the poor to win. Through various means, the BJP has managed to win the necessary mass support.

From its birth in 1925, the RSS has engaged in a politics centered around communal violence. All incidents of communal violence don't get the same kind of coverage in the media. The Gujarat massacre of 2002 was of course, big news. It got a lot of coverage in the international media as well. But much smaller communal clashes take place in numerous places which don't get that kind of coverage. Such clashes are enough to create polarization in various regions, even if they don't lead to deaths. For example, there might be some procession of Muslims on some festive occasion, somebody throws a stone into their midst and a clash starts. Then, there is the propaganda that Muslims started the clash. So, in that region, people get polarized on religious lines, and thus a "Hindu vote bank" is created. This is a method that has been replicated in numerous places. Communal violence is a key element of the RSS' attempts to reshape India into an increasingly Hindu state.

Propaganda is crucial in order to win mass support, and that is something the RSS-BJP has been extraordinarily efficient at. It controls the media landscape, because the media is dominated by corporate media, and the corporations are lined up behind BJP. They have done solid organizational work for nearly a century, and they have perfected the art of propaganda.

Let me give you an example from the left-ruled state of Kerala. In the entire history of Kerala, the BJP has had only one member in the state's legislative assembly. But even in this state, the BJP is able to mislead people into believing all sorts of things. For example, there is a big housing project known as LIFE Mission, which the left government of Kerala is implementing. Almost 240,000 houses have been built as part of this project. But RSS-BJP activists have been campaigning that this is a scheme of the Modi government, and as a result of sustained propaganda, there are many people who actually believe this claim. Because of its hold over the media, and because of its sheer financial power, flush with corporate money, the RSS-BJP has been able to greatly expand its campaign networks, including on social media: WhatsApp, Facebook, Twitter, all of that. There is a huge apparatus that is often termed the BJP IT cell, which churns out propaganda and pushes it through social media. All these are part of the mechanisms through which the BJP wins mass support, even as its policies favor big capital.

And, of course, there is the network of schools I mentioned earlier. RSS runs numerous schools across India. RSS affiliate Vidya Bharati runs 13,000 schools, with 3.2 million students, and 146,000 teachers. It is the largest private school network in India. There is another RSS organization which runs 54,000 single-teacher schools, mainly in areas where tribal, or Indigenous people, live. These schools have more than 1.5 million students.

In states where the BJP is in power, the syllabus in state-run schools is also changed to enable the teaching of unscientific beliefs, the mixing of myths with history, the peddling of caste prejudices and gender stereotypes, and the propagation of religious hatred. Once children move through this system for decades, you have entire generations trained to hate the religious minorities and well-adjusted to the Hindutva worldview.

MK: The RSS seeks to exploit communalism as the organizing principle of Indian society. In doing so, how does Hindutva engage the other major cleavages, such as caste, that have shaped Indian life and society for so long?

SD: How has the RSS-BJP navigated the issue of caste? That is a complex question. As I said earlier, RSS's theory is not a coherent one. What is this Hindu nation that it seeks to build? In Hinduism, there is the caste system, embedded in traditional Hindu theology. In a Hindu nation, will this be retained?

If you look at earlier Hindutva ideologues, some spoke of caste as an impediment in their efforts to create a unified Hindu unity. On the other hand, there are others such as the current head of the RSS, Mohan Bhagwat who often quotes from the ancient text *Manusmriti*, in which caste divisions are very clearly delineated. Almost eighteen years after the demolition of the Babri Masjid, on August 5, 2020, the foundation stone for a new Ram temple was laid at the spot where the Babri Masjid once stood. Prime Minister Narendra Modi himself attended the ceremony. Mohan Bhagwat recited lines from the *Manusmriti* saying that people should accept Brahmin domination. Recently, BJP activists in Tamil Nadu led a demonstration against remarks made by another political leader against the *Manusmriti*. This may be the first time the BJP has publicly demonstrated in favor of *Manusmriti*.

With the RSS-BJP in power, enjoying so much corporate support, winning elections by a big majority, able to muzzle dissent and imprison political opponents, they feel that they can act with impunity. In this context, despite all talk about Hindu unity, the central cabinet is dominated by dominant castes. Uttar Pradesh, the most populous state in India, has the BJP's Yogi Adityanath, a rabidly communal man, as its chief minister. He and his cabinet ministers are mostly from dominant castes. In July 2017, the BJP government of Uttar Pradesh appointed 312 government lawyers out of which 90 percent were from the dominant castes, with Brahmins alone accounting for almost half the total number. When BJP governments make appointments to powerful positions, dominant castes, who form a minority of the population, are disproportionately favored. The BJP government has slashed budget funds for the welfare of Dalits and Indigenous communities. RSS leaders often speak out against affirmative action for the oppressed castes. Despite all talk of Hindu unity, it seems that the RSS envisions a subordinate position for oppressed castes. Now, in spite of that, how did they win mass support?

If you look at Bajrang Dal, the paramilitary wing of the VHP, a large section of them are unemployed youth and many are from oppressed castes.[7] How does the RSS manage this?

Prabhat Patnaik points out that classical fascism was able to eliminate unemployment through military spending, while contemporary fascism, which is beholden to finance capital, is unable to eliminate unemployment.[8] What do the fascists in India do then? They tell the unemployed youth, "The degeneration caused by the Muslims, Christians, and so on is the reason for your misery. Come and join us. Let us regain the glory of ancient Hindu India." They give a sense of identity to these unemployed youth who have been oppressed their whole lives but who now feel that they are powerful. The RSS and its front organizations also make the effort to invent or reinterpret myths, to provide a "pride of place" for many oppressed castes within Hindu mythology. Instead of substantive rights or redistribution of resources, the RSS offers oppressed castes avenues for their resentment towards the system to be diverted towards violence

---

7 Aijaz Ahmad (in conversation with Vijay Prashad), *Nothing Human is Alien to Me* (New Delhi: LeftWord Books, 2020), 126.

8 Prabhat Patnaik, "The Modi Years," *NewsClick*, April 3, 2019, https://www.newsclick.in/Modi-Years-Attack-Civil-Liberties-Emergency-Indira-Gandhi.

against religious minorities, and to feel good about themselves.

The RSS has no commitment to reform as far as the caste system is concerned. But if they find that opposing a progressive movement or court order on caste is not politically useful, they may not oppose it. For example, there are temples in some parts of India where women are not allowed to enter. One such temple was the Shani Shingnapur temple, in the state of Maharashtra. The BJP was in power there in 2016, when a court order allowed women entry into the temple. The BJP permitted it because they saw no political advantage in opposing it.

Now contrast this with what happened in 2018, when the Supreme Court of India pronounced a verdict that allowed women's entry into the Sabarimala temple in Kerala. The left government of Kerala supported the verdict and said it would implement the verdict. The RSS decided this was a "golden opportunity." Those were the exact words used by the BJP's Kerala State President. The RSS and its affiliated organizations opposed women's entry into the Sabarimala temple and embarked on a violent campaign. Kerala has a long history of struggles demanding that oppressed castes be allowed entry into temples, particularly during the first half of the twentieth century. These constituted an important part of the anticaste struggles in the state. During the Sabarimala turmoil, many in contemporary Kerala connected the legacy of struggles against caste oppression, struggles which produced the fertile ground for the left in Kerala to grow, to the struggle against gender oppression, around the question of temple entry for women.

The RSS is adept at talking in multiple tongues on many issues, including the issue of caste. Going by the pronouncements of the leaders of the Hindutva forces, and going by their actions, we can be certain that the RSS has no interest in reforming the caste system. When there is no commitment, the trend will favor the status quo, to propagate the rule of the dominant castes. This has been reflected, for instance, in violent attacks against Dalits (the most oppressed group of castes) going up under BJP rule. Therefore, under the RSS-BJP's Hindu Rashtra, the lot of the oppressed castes can only worsen.

MK: You're suggesting that the RSS is extremely effective with its propaganda and its mass of front organizations in offering a politics of hatred in place of people's genuine need for dignity. The RSS offers hatred as a container to fill that vacuum, that hole, in so many people. What programs has the left put forward to oppose this—the feeding of hatred—and to fulfill the need for dignity?

SD: It might be useful to look at Kerala, as an example where the left is still the most powerful organizational force, and where the struggle against caste can be seen in somewhat clearer terms. We often say that the communist movement in Kerala grew on soil tilled by social reform movements. These were mostly anticaste movements that tried to eradicate the most horrible forms of caste oppression. Many of the early communist leaders were active participants of these struggles. Some communist leaders, like AK Gopalan, were prominent leaders of such struggles. These movements flourished in the first half of the twentieth century, and by the 1940s, some of the major anticaste struggles were being led by communists. Later on, the struggle against untouchability was bolstered by the work of the agricultural workers' union, which was led by communists. The work of the communist-led All-India Peasants' Union (the All-India *Kisan Sabha*) was crucial in the anti-caste struggle. For peasants to unite and fight their immediate oppressors, the landlords, they had to engage in a struggle over dignity. It was not just a struggle against economic exploitation. They were being humiliated and violently repressed. Through struggle, they began to stand tall before the landlord, address the landlord by his name, to stop using self-denigrating terms, stop speaking of themselves as servants or slaves. They gained the confidence to assert, "if the lord beats us, we'll beat back." This was a militant struggle. In Kerala, the work of the peasants' union, the agricultural workers' union, the Communist Party: all of these have been instrumental in weakening caste oppression. The caste system is still there, but the worst excesses of the caste system, still visible in many parts of India, are not as visible in Kerala. Land reforms, spearheaded by communist-led state governments, broke the dominance of the upper-caste feudal landlords. Land reform allowed the tenant farmers to stand up. They now had their own land. Likewise, the agriculture workers also got some land, their bargaining power increased, and they were organized into trade unions. They built organized strength to fight social oppression and economic exploitation.

This is the story in Kerala, where there has been some success. In the last one and a half decades or so, communists in India have set up various platforms for anticaste struggle in different parts of India. There is the Tamil Nadu Untouchability Eradication Front (TNUEF), a coalition of more than one hundred organizations, led by the CPI(M).[9] There are similar organizations in Andhra Pradesh, Telangana, Karnataka, Maharashtra, and Kerala. At the all-India level, there is the *Dalit Shoshan Mukti Manch* [Forum for the Liberation of Dalits from Oppression]. These are communist-led platforms that coordinate action on the anticaste front.

The TNUEF has led temple-entry struggles and struggles against other practices related to untouchability. Among these is the two-tumbler system. This is a practice whereby people of oppressed castes are not allowed to enter tea shops and instead must stand outside and have tea from glasses kept by the window. There are places where Dalits could not get a haircut in a barber's salon. So, there were struggles demanding the right for Dalits to get their hair cut inside salons. In some temples in Karnataka, for example, devotees belonging to oppressed castes are expected to roll their bodies over leftovers of food that has been eaten by Brahmins. Communists have led struggles against that. These are struggles against inhuman practices. These struggles for basic dignity point the way forward, along with the organization of peasants and workers, to build organized strength against the oppression and exploitation that they face.

MK: You have given us a snapshot of profoundly courageous, painstaking work in different localities around India, organizing some of the most oppressed people to fight their humiliation and degradation, building new social unities through struggle, against Hindutva's politics of hate, which has resulted in such devastating consequences for the vast majority of Indians and incredible returns for the ultrawealthy minority.

---

9   With over 10 million members, the CPI(M), Communist Party of India (Marxist), is the largest left political party in India. It was formed in 1964, from a split in the then-undivided Communist Party of India. See Tricontinental: Institute for Social Research, *One Hundred Years of The Communist Movement in India*, Dossier No. 32, September 2020, https://www.thetricontinental.org/wp-content/uploads/2020/08/20200828_Dossier-32_EN_Web.pdf.

CHAPTER FIFTEEN

Antifascist Organizing and If You Don't They Will's "no. *NOT EVER.*" Project

Cristien Storm and Kate Boyd

Kate Boyd and Cristien Storm are members of If You Don't They Will, a Seattle-based collective working to counter white nationalist organizing in the Pacific Northwest. A key component to their repertoire of organizing is the travelling multimedia exhibition, "no. NOT EVER." which archives legacies of grassroots organizing against the white supremacist "Northwest Territorial Imperative," a late 1970s and 1980s call to (re)create a white homeland in the Pacific Northwest of the United States.

"no. NOT EVER." presents a selection of interviews that Boyd and Storm have undertaken with activists and organizers who disrupted this and many other attempts at white nationalist mobilization. By centering research and cultural work, "no. NOT EVER." operates as a type of mobile resource center and intergenerational bridge for antifascist work.

Our interview with Boyd and Storm explores the history of white nationalism in the Pacific Northwest, strategies for antifascist organizing, and the contradictory intersections of race and gender in white nationalist ascendance. Our discussion is also punctuated by photos of the exhibition space, cards of the text that accompanied the interactive elements, and links to clips of interviews with activists that Boyd and Storm showcase in their exhibit. Together, they highlight the participatory, imaginative, and collaborative possibilities of antifascist organizing in our contemporary moment.

Simón Ventura Trujillo and Alyosha Goldstein: What brought you to your organizing work? In what ways do you conceive of collaborative and coalitional work in the process of organizing?

Cristien Storm and Kate Boyd: In the early 2000s, we were introduced to, mentored by, and supporting a network of rural and suburban organizers who were fighting white nationalism in the six Northwest states. During our visits, we would drive for hours between states, our turquoise Ford Escort racking up miles as we reflected on the scope, shape, and style of coalitional organizing these activists were a part of, which was, for both of us, educational, inspiring, and politically foundational. We thought about one day documenting and celebrating this network of activists, so often invisible, underrecognized, or minimized in the PNW (Pacific Northwest) as well as in antifascist histories more broadly. Their organizing strategies and political imaginaries powerfully shaped our antifascist sensibilities as well as our commitments to building broad-based coalitions that we believe are fundamental to countering the white nationalist movement and fascism, more generally speaking. Fundamental and difficult as all hell.

In 2015, we circled back to collecting the histories of this 1980–1990s coalition of PNW activists as the white nationalist movement continued to gain power in all levels of government, a range of institutions, and mainstream political culture. In our workshops and organizing work, we witnessed a great deal of folks in urban PNW spaces (particularly in some white liberal antiracist groups) either ignore and/or dismiss white nationalism or organize against it using strategies that indicated they didn't fully understand who they were organizing against (dedicated, networked activists). They did not yet recognize white nationalism as a well-organized and well-funded social movement that had been building its base for decades.

For instance, many groups wanted to heal or dedicate time, resources, and energy into saving white nationalist activists. Some wanted to invite white nationalists to join them, convinced that they could talk them through why they should be antiracist instead. Other groups assumed they could out-debate white nationalists, and that the "truth" would rise to the surface in the free marketplace of ideas, à la free speech. Despite so many instances of violence and terror, at times, many folks struggled to connect the organizing and movement links between various white nationalist attacks on synagogues, mosques, Black churches, Native sovereignty, queer bars, immigrant communities, and abortion providers (just to name a few), escalating all over the country.

The more we grappled with how to get workshop participants to understand white nationalism as a social movement—a broad-based coalition of activists—and also key into the urgent need to grow and strengthen antifascist coalitions, the more imperative it became for us to share and transmit the stories, histories, and sensibilities of these activists. Our hope was to underscore current antifascist and antiracist organizing, support those already engaged in antifascist work, and cultivate robust and disparate coalitional networks.

We mused on ways to pass along these coalitional histories without flattening them or unifying them in a singular linear progressive narrative or "hero" story. We wanted to hold the various tensions and contradictions in their coalitional work, which all clearly and proactively said "*no*" to white nationalism, but also had very different strategies, styles, and aesthetics that weren't always in agreement.

We started reaching out to and interviewing the generation of activists we had learned from (and coalesced with) back in 2000. We also began collaborating with video artist and art educator Molly Mac, whose aesthetic practices, political sensibilities, and curating skills created the bones for "no. *NOT EVER.*"

Molly helped us think about how to record and represent activist histories in ways that activate the bodies of viewers, invite participation in current antifascist organizing, and grow antifascist imaginaries. We wanted to shape an immersive space that would help people *feel* that they could join the movement to say "no. *NOT EVER.*" to white nationalism in their own way, in their own contexts. We wanted people to *feel* there are SO MANY ways to fight fascism and we desperately need all of them.

For six months, the three of us spent our weekends talking with folks (now) living in Bellingham, Spokane, Coeur D'Alene, Sandpoint, Portland, Bainbridge Island, Everett, Whidbey Island, and Seattle. These interviews are the foundation for our travelling interactive, immersive living archive and art exhibition "no. *NOT EVER.*"

"no. *NOT EVER.*" is our attempt to represent the coalitional histories of this network of activists, in their complexities, their productive tensions, inherent contradictions, and diverse commitments. "no. *NOT EVER.*" is an installation that combines video footage from archival interviews, interactive research stations, and a community resource guide. This dynamic 'living archive' functions as a participatory teaching tool and as an intergenerational bridge to support ongoing efforts to say no. *NOT EVER.* to white nationalism in a wide range of communities and contexts. We call it a "living archive" because we created an ongoing, evolving coalitional antifascist entity. As it travels it will accumulate more interviews, activities, and stories, and every time a different community or institution hosts the show, its shape transforms to respond to the needs and political contexts of the host community. The forty-plus hours of video footage are edited in a nonlinear fashion and constellate around "organizing nodes" such as "free speech," "cultural organizing," and "research."

SVT and AG: Do you find fascism a useful framework for analysis and action? What might fascism as an activist analytic bring to the table of antiracist politics? Are there things that you think this analytic might obscure in this regard?

CS and KB: For us, an antifascist framework offers a critical "both-and" approach to movement work, encouraging antiracist activists to continue to always fight white supremacy and structural racism *and also* develop the capacity to identify and interrupt white nationalists seeking to create white ethnostate(s).

It makes the case that we are not just talking about individual fascists, but individuals who understand themselves as part of a social movement comprised of various and, at times, disparate groups who are all connected by the goal of creating a white nation-state. As a social movement, white nationalists have many strategies for actualizing their genocidal vision including (but not limited to) electoral organizing, cultural organizing, policy development, research think-tanks, taking over local and national institutions, and a range of youth recruitment efforts.

Further, as Soya Jung, Senior Partner of ChangeLab, recently argued in Highlander Research and Education Center's "Elephant in the Room" series on whiteness and white nationalism, "white supremacy has always tried to capture some portion of the population that will work in service to its project. White nationalism is a different beast. White nationalism is about elimination." White nationalism is one of many rising authoritarian and fascist movements ascending around the globe, and it is mostly but not exclusively white (think Proud Boys). White nationalism, with deep roots in antisemitic conspiracy theories, believes (and argues) that the existing government systems and structures do not represent them or their interests, and that they are unfairly targeted and disempowered. They understand themselves as superior victims.

Antifascism helps us fight white nationalism and white supremacy because we are resisting both historic and systemic systems of oppression

Figure 7. If You Don't They Will presents "no. *NOT EVER.*" Installation view, Henry Art Gallery, University of Washington, Seattle, 2017. Photograph by Mark Woods.

as well as a social movement, and sometimes we need different tools or strategies depending on the particularities and intersections of what we are fighting. Tarso Ramos, Executive Director of Political Research Associates, describes in Highlander's "Elephant in the Room" series the "call and response" relationship between white supremacy and white nationalism: "[w]e live in a white supremacist country and white nationalist movements can change the governing strategies and agenda of structural white supremacy and that's part of what we are experiencing now." We understand antifascism as a commitment to study and counter the "call and response" relationships in our research approaches, organizing strategies, and political sensibilities.

To be clear, an antifascist framework does not suggest we should *only* be fighting white nationalism. It's more like it offers us another lens and a different set of strategies *in addition* to the anti-oppression and structural antiracist work folks are already doing. We draw on the visionary work of Ramos and Scot Nakagawa, Senior Partner at ChangeLab, who articulate three fundamental "both-and" principles/strategies necessary to effectively counter white nationalism: DISRUPT, DEFUSE, COMPETE. The interview footage highlights examples of these principles/strategies and the wall cards included in the show discuss these three fundamentals.

Figure 8. If You Don't They Will presents "no. *NOT EVER.*" Installation detail, Pacific Northwest College of Art Library, Portland, Oregon, 2019. Photograph by If You Don't They Will.

SVT and AG: What are some antifascist strategies or themes that emerged in your interviews?

CS and KB: The show centers several antifascist themes and strategies: cultural organizing; free speech; interviewees' introductions to this particular tradition of organizing; research; relationships with law enforcement; institutionalization as a 501(c)3 nonprofit (or not); rural/urban divides; and gender/sexuality, race and class dynamics within rural and suburban PNW organizing spaces. Viewers are introduced to diverse coalitional strategies, divergent mobilizing approaches, and a cacophony of "Nos" through different modalities including wall cards (with definitions, scenarios, and "quizzes"), interview video footage, and interactive activities.

Many organizers do not know how to say NO to white nationalist claims

Figure 9. If You Don't They Will presents "no. *NOT EVER.*" Installation detail, Henry Art Gallery, University of Washington, Seattle, 2017. Photograph by Dan Paz.

for free speech rights. White nationalists are acutely aware of this and use 'free speech' as an effective strategy to test a space to see how hospitable it is for their recruitment and organizing. Ideally, you and your group will not engage with the 'free speech trap.'

—*If You Don't They Will,* "*no.* NOT EVER." *[wall card, "Don't Fight it With Free Speech"]*

SVT and AG: How have you seen the politics of fascism or white nationalism change over the course of your organizing? What do you think are the most significant differences or continuities evident during the current moment?

CS and KB: Well, to be blunt, back when we were introduced to this work in the late 1990s–early 2000s by our mentors, part of our work was warning people about the impact and implications of white nationalist base-building, grassroots organizing, and mainstreaming strategies. We were worried about the present reality that we have today. We emphasized that this is a social movement we should be taking very seriously with an eye, always, to the frightening future white nationalists were seeking to build.

Also, broad-based coalition work is really hard and we don't think it is

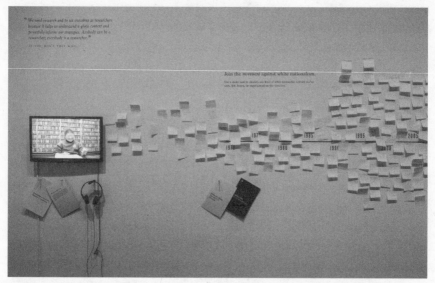

Figure 10. If You Don't They Will presents "no. *NOT EVER.*" Installation detail, Henry Art Gallery, University of Washington, Seattle, 2017. Photograph by Dan Paz.

any easier today. The difficulties of building, nurturing, and maintaining coalitions are a huge reason why we are continually inspired by the activists featured in "no. *NOT EVER.*" We are committed to interviewing (more) people, and to sharing these histories and their badass coalitional responses. Further, the strategies and analysis shared by activists in the interviews are still very helpful for understanding and organizing in the now.

One specific challenge of broad-based coalition work that continues in this moment is sharing and handing off research on white nationalist groups in a manner that is timely, usable for grassroots organizers, and that strengthens relationships. Research is vital to understanding the different shapes and strategies of white nationalists in our various communities and is necessary to make our counterorganizing strategies more powerful and effective. But the information gathered has to be accessible and shareable, and it has to be created and handed off in a way that supports other/multiple modes of organizing.

Research needs to be thought of in terms of cultivating relational power. How might research not only hand off information that is vital to grassroots organizing but also grow relationships and strengthen connections across silos? Research and how we think about and activate research is also

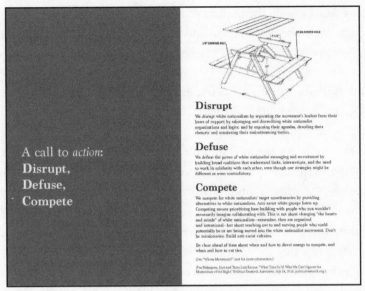

Figure 11. Wall Card. A call to action: Disrupt, Defuse, Compete. If You Don't They Will presents "no. NOT *EVER*." Installation materials, Henry Art Gallery, University of Washington, Seattle, 2017.

key to broad-based coalition and relationship building.

> *We need research and to see ourselves as researchers because it helps us understand a given context and powerfully informs our strategies. Anybody can be a researcher; everybody is a researcher.*
>
> —*If You Don't They Will,* "*no. NOT EVER.*" *[wall text]*

In addition to connecting with histories of antifascist activism, there are so many inspiring (new and long-term) antifascist and antiracist mobilizations working tirelessly to respond to, refuse, and extinguish various waves of white nationalist organizing in the present moment. Part of what is cool about our "living" and traveling archive is that we get to learn from, support, and amplify other people's work. We always track what we learn from our interviews and reflect on how the project should be shifted or transformed based on what we've learned or what has changed in the contemporary moment—we coalesce with the interviewees. The show is designed with the hope of breaking down silos and isolation, encouraging broad-based coalition building, and animating an embodied and felt sense of *being part of* antifascist movements.

SVT and AG: How do the politics of whiteness matter for coalitional organizing against white nationalism and white supremacist movements in the Pacific Northwest and beyond?

CS and KB: As white antiracist, antifascist cultural organizers we are always, to the best of our abilities, tracking and interrupting white supremacy culture as well as reflecting on our own complicity. Our whiteness is always there, always a problem, and there is no escaping it or pretending otherwise. In "no. *NOT EVER.*" we attempt to do the ongoing work of de-centering the white-women savior narrative so often intrinsic in representations of white antiracist and antifascist activism. We know we will fail at this, and we also know we have to keep fighting; this is an inherent tension in everything we do.

There is nothing purporting to be neutral or unbiased about this project or the archive of interviews and immersive activities we created. From who we prioritize in our interviews (and the amount of "air time" they differentially receive), to the politics of the curation and the editing process itself, our organizing intentions are to amplify and center the leadership of people of color. Antifascist activists of color, especially women of color, are often invisibilized in antifascist organizing (as in so many organizing spaces) and in the work of this network of activists in the PNW too. While we most certainly want to celebrate and share the important work being done by these groups and activists, we are not in any way celebrating organizers equally or obscuring the social significance of race and gender.

That said, there are a lot of white people in the PNW and many of the groups were predominantly white and/or working in very white communities. We interviewed around eighteen rural and suburban activists, mostly women identified, mostly over fifty years old, and around 75 percent of whom were white. We don't have consistent demographic information about class, sexuality, (dis)ability, and religion/faith/spirituality. Of the activists we interviewed, some were previously (and currently) involved in antiwar and anti-imperialist organizing; some were involved in countering domestic violence, queer, and gender-based violence in schools; and some were also fighting anti-immigrant groups or attacks on Native sovereignty. There were also some who were not making connections between fighting the Aryan Nations (for instance) and other kinds of movements and struggles. We observed that groups from the 1980s and 1990s that did not link

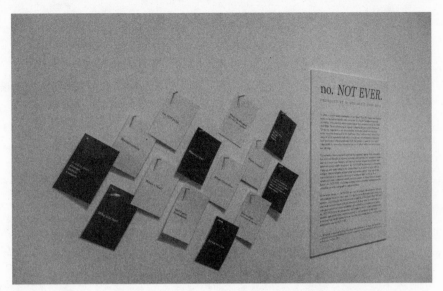

Figure 12. If You Don't They Will presents "no. *NOT EVER.*" Installation detail, Henry Art Gallery, University of Washington, Seattle, 2017. Photograph by Dan Paz.

their organizing against white nationalism to other movement struggles were more likely to dissolve after the urgency of white nationalists' publicly organizing in their community was abated. Some of the groups that did make these connections and commitments, cultivating the "both/and" approach to the "call and response" relationships between white supremacy and white nationalism, are still active today.

We think these activist histories are important for people who are organizing to counter white nationalism today, and especially for white people to connect to and hopefully realize they can/should/must say NO to white nationalism and white supremacy every day and in every way; they do not need to (and do not have to) "reinvent the wheel" and should not believe (as white people often do), that they invented the wheel in the first place; people of color have always been resisting and refusing white supremacy and white nationalism. We try to hold these tensions, and also (critically) celebrate these important organizing histories. We do this while continually attempting to decenter whiteness in both how we historicize and in the show itself, while also knowing that as white people we will repeatedly fail at this (even as we must continue to do this work).

SVT and AG: How has your collective addressed the intersections of gender and sexuality with white dominance? How do you see questions of gender and sexuality as part of, or perhaps even central to, antiracist and antifascist organizing?

CS and KB: Since we started collaborating about two decades ago, we have been working to thread the intersections of gender and sexuality into our analysis and strategy. We are always thinking about how sexism, heteropatriarchy, capitalism, and racist/white feminism inform both our understandings of white nationalism as well as our counterstrategies.

To be clear: white women are, and have always been, actively engaged in white nationalist organizing. In so many ways, the history of white feminism is also a history of white nationalism. Generally white women's presence, power, and agency is ignored in studies of far-right or fascist movements and this goes for the white nationalist movement too. Their participation is minimized through tropes of innocence: they are weak, victimized, or manipulated wives and daughters. Sometimes they are assumed to be survivors of domestic violence who then enter the movement by following men, and/or are unable to leave because of exploitation or economic dependence.

Some of these things are absolutely true. The white nationalist movement is unabashedly sexist and the women who are part of it most certainly experience sexism and misogynistic violence. We have to fight white nationalism and white supremacy in a way that also fights sexism, antisemitism, classism, xenophobia, ableism, homophobia, transphobia, and Islamophobia at the same time.

But also, all of these assumptions position white women as somehow less implicated (because of a perceived victim status) and this obscures the ways white women have (always) participated and accessed power in the white nationalist movement. We need nuanced analysis and practice that understands that the white nationalist movement can be sexist to the core but is also a site in which white women organize to get more proximate to the power white nationalism offers white men.

Moreover, while it is certainly true that domestic violence and economic vulnerability knows no political bounds, these tropes not only invisibilize women themselves, they invisibilize their critical contributions to a violent movement in the past and present. Women's participation in white

Figure 13. If You Don't They Will presents "no. *NOT EVER.*" Installation detail, Henry Art Gallery, University of Washington, Seattle, 2017. Photograph by Dan Paz.

nationalist and fascist movements expands well beyond these limited imaginations of women's roles as wife, mother, and occasional activist. When our analysis minimizes or ignores white nationalist women's activism, our counterresponses are less robust and effective. We need an intersectional lens, of course, when fighting white nationalism too!

SVT and AG: As organizers, you both are also invested in the transformative potential of culture and cultural work. How do you frame and mobilize cultural production in your work? What does a project such as this exhibition offer differently as a political intervention than other forms of organizing, action, and communication?

CS and KB: From video listening stations, to various activities and interactive scenarios, "no. *NOT EVER.*" offers participants multiple ways to cultivate antiracist and antifascist imaginations, cultures, and modes of belonging. It is designed to generate in viewers a sense of participation. We want people to feel like they can join (or are a part of) a broad-based coalition of "no. *NOT EVER.*" The show is framed for a multiracial audience *and* it offers explicit direction to white viewers in some of the cards, activities, scenarios, and interview footage. White nationalists are terrifyingly effective at mobilizing in white and (majority white) communities and white people need to up our game (big time!) in engaging in antifascist struggles. As Alicia Garza, cofounder of Black Lives Matter, stated: "Sit with that for a second . . . we are totally being outorganized by the other side."[1] Yet, we consistently notice hesitancy on the white left to take white nationalism seriously. Eric Ward, Executive Director of Western States Center, says in Highlander's "Elephant in the Room" series, "Why would you leave an entire constituency open to the white nationalist movement?"

The aesthetics of the show, like the activists featured, intentionally work against romanticizing or sensationalizing antifascist organizing. We challenge how it is often portrayed in mainstream media today as more dangerous or more urgent than other forms of antiracist organizing. The materials are 1990s' classroom-esque (yellow "post-it" sticky notes, pencils, plastic chairs, red push-pins, laminated red and white hanging cards); the font references 1990s' community newspapers; and the video is not overly produced. The interviews were filmed in casual settings such as in the activists' homes, on the couch, with their dogs. There is intentionally nothing "flashy"; instead the aesthetics produce a felt-sense of everyday (and every way) modes of fighting white supremacy and white nationalism. In the words of video artist Molly Mac, "In terms of the editing process itself and in terms of how the stories will come together to tell a larger story, [we didn't want to] follow traditional narrative arcs that hold stories to a hero narrative or replicate a charismatic figure leading the antifascism movement, but really looking at what makes the everyday antifascism work, and what that starts to look like if it is just built in to every little part of life."[2]

We thought a lot about how to provoke interactions in viewers that are simultaneously internal, embodied, and external/coalitional. We want viewers to *feel* because feelings are political and key to smashing white nationalism *and* to creating alternatives to the modes of belonging that they are peddling. It matters little if viewers understand the white nationalist social movement on an intellectual level, if they are not moved to *FEEL* part of a resistance

---

1   Interview with Alicia Garza, *United Shades of America with W. Kamau Bell*, Episode 2 Season 4, "Not All White People" on CNN (May 5, 2019), https://www.cnn.com/shows/united-shades-of-america.

2   Video archive of "no. NOT *EVER*." If You Don't They Will in collaboration with Interference Archive, Brooklyn, NY, 2018.

movement or if they are not moved to join resistance efforts. It matters little if viewers have access to facts and statistics about white nationalism if that research does not also mobilize bodies to *FEEL* like they can be, or are part of, an antifascist movement that says hell "no. *NOT EVER.*" to white nationalism.

SVT and AG: What makes you hopeful and excited to keep fighting white nationalism and white supremacy in our contemporary moment?

CS and KB: To keep imagining *What Will Our Antifascist Futures Look Like*, every day and in every way. To keep learning from, interviewing, amplifying, and sharing the amazing work activists all over the country are doing. If you or anyone you know is interested in being interviewed, please contact us through our website, ifyoudonttheywill.com.

Figure 14. If You Don't They Will presents "no. *NOT EVER*." Installation view, Henry Art Gallery, University of Washington, Seattle, 2017. Photograph by Dan Paz.

CHAPTER SIXTEEN

The Returns of Racial Fascism[1]

Alberto Toscano

Like the plague's capacity for mutations, the reappearance of fascism will not be an exact replica of what existed in the past but a significant difference reflecting the particular moment. Owing to its axiomatic relationship to capitalism, the form of fascism, its destruction of subjective autonomy, remains unchanged, but with every new reappearance it brings new content in different, historical presents, as Primo Levi observed in the 1970s, when he declared that every age could expect the return of fascism in new and different materializations. —Harry Harootunian, "A Fascism for Our Time"[2]

Fascism was a monster born of capitalist parents. Fascism came as the end-product of centuries of capitalist bestiality, exploitation, domination and racism—mainly exercised outside of Europe. It is highly significant that many settlers and colonial officials displayed a leaning towards fascism. —Walter Rodney, *How Europe Underdeveloped Africa*[3]

Nothing is more important than stopping fascism, because fascism will stop us all. —Fred Hampton, Chairman of the Illinois chapter of the Black Panther Party, speech delivered April 27, 1969

Just as the aftermath of the 2016 election witnessed the mainstreaming of scholarly or activist discussions of fascism, the frantic quickening of the news cycle on the eve of the 2020 election was again accompanied by multiple efforts to check the authoritarian pulse of the United States of

---

1 'A version of this essay was published as "The Long Shadow of Racial Fascism," *Boston Review*, October 28, 2020, http://bostonreview.net/race-politics/alberto-toscano-long-shadow-racial-fascism. A longer version of the argument explored in these pages can be found in "Incipient Fascism: Black Radical Perspectives," *CLC Web: Comparative Literature and Culture*, Vol. 23, No. 1 (2021), http://docs.lib.purdue.edu/clcweb/vol23/iss1/6.

2 Harry Harootunian, "A Fascism for Our Time," *The Massachusetts Review*, January 6, 2021, https://www.massreview.org/node/9428.

3 Walter Rodney, *How Europe Underdeveloped Africa* (London and New York: Verso, 2018), 243.

America. Despite the deadly farce of the January 6 white riot (America's own beer bong putsch), the departure of the 45th US President has made way for a rushed remaindering in some quarters of the debate on native (or, better, nativist) fascism. The Black radical perspectives on the fascist problematic surveyed in the following pages—with their commonly neglected insistence on the structuring role of fascist potentials to the US body politic—would suggest that we instead stay with the trouble that briefly forced even some liberal partisans of US exceptionalism to consider that fascism was not some dreadful anachronism imported from the Old World but, to paraphrase H. Rap Brown, "as American as cherry pie," deeply enmeshed in histories of enslavement and extermination, dispossession and domination, that continue to shape the American present both materially and ideologically.

Where five years ago attention gravitated towards the incoming administration's organic and ideological links with the alt- and far right (Bannon, Miller, Spencer & Co.), the context of a mass civic insurgency against police murder and racial terror shifted the tenor and relevance of invocations of fascism in ways that should be allowed to resonate irrespective of changed occupancy in the Oval Office. In the months leading up to the 2020 contest, the systemic challenge of the BLM movement was displaced by the US government onto to the familiar figure of the (white) anarchist (or communist) agitator, as *antifa* became a target for William Barr's Department of Justice (still undecided whether this was a "foreign terrorist organization" or an internal "seditious" group). In the interim, the fauna of right-wing agitation grew weirder and more sinister still, care of QAnon, the Boogaloo movement, and the Proud Boys—who clearly took the presidential guidance to "stand down and *stand by*" all too literally. The state's exceptional powers—that dependable matrix of historical fascisms—were flexed in scenes of unidentified federal agents bundling pro-BLM protesters into unmarked rental vans and the shooting of Michael Reinoehl by a US Marshals task force,[4] even if further escalations did not eventuate. Meanwhile, on the ideological stage, critical race theory (along with *The New York Times*' 1619 Project) was loudly declaimed to be an "ideological poison" that must be "quickly extinguished"; the Executive Branch's Office of Management and

---

4   Mike Baker and Evan Hill, "Police Say an Antifa Activist Likely Shot at Officers. His Gun Suggests Otherwise," *The New York Times*, April 10, 2021, https://www.nytimes.com/2021/04/10/us/michael-reinoehl-killing-investigation.html?searchResultPosition=1.

Budget dispatched a memo to all agencies to "cease and desist from using taxpayer dollars to fund ... divisive, un-American propaganda training sessions"; and an Executive Order condemned antiracist critics for advancing a "vision of America that is grounded in hierarchies based on collective social and political identities," a grotesque case of projection if there ever was. This very recent history should not be treated as a freakish blip but, as the persistence of the politics and personnel that made it possible (not least at the level of state legislatures that have ramped up their projects of racial disenfranchisement, dispossession, and ecocide), it demands acknowledgment as the index of an entrenched political potential.

Notwithstanding the changing terrain, talk of fascism has generally stuck to a familiar groove, namely, asking whether present phenomena are analogous to those of interwar European fascisms (the recent *New York Review of Books* debate featuring Peter E. Gordon, Samuel Moyn, and Sarah Churchwell provides an informative panorama of positions on this question).[5] Skeptics of comparison will underscore the way in which the analogy of fascism can either treat the present moment as exceptional, papering over American histories of authoritarianism, or alternatively, be so broad as to fail to define what is unique about our current predicament. Analogy's advocates will instead point to the need to detect family resemblances with past despotisms before it's too late, often making their case by advancing some ideal-typical check list, whether in terms of the *elements* of or the *steps towards* fascism. But what if our talk of fascism were not dominated by the question of analogy?

Attending to the long history of Black radical thought about fascism and antifascist resistance—what Cedric Robinson called a "Black construction of fascism" alternative to the "the historical manufacture of fascism as a negation of Western *Geist*"[6]—could serve to dislodge the debate about fascism from the deadlock of analogical thinking, providing the resources to confront our volatile interregnum. Long before Nazi violence came to

---

5   Peter E. Gordon, "Why Historical Analogy Matters," *The New York Review of Books*, January 7, 2020; Samuel Moyn, "The Trouble with Comparisons," *The New York Review of Books*, May 19, 2020, https://www.nybooks.com/daily/2020/05/19/the-trouble-with-comparisons/; Sarah Churchwell, "American Fascism: It Has Happened Here," *The New York Review of Books*, June 22, 2020, https://www.nybooks.com/daily/2020/06/22/american-fascism-it-has-happened-here/.

6   Cedric J. Robinson, "Fascism and the Response of Black Radical Theorists," in *Racial Capitalism, Black Internationalism and Cultures of Resistance*, ed. H.L.T. Quan (London: Pluto Press, 2019), 149.

be conceived as beyond analogy, Black radical thinkers sought to expand the historical and political imagination of an antifascist left by detailing how what from a European or white vantage point could be perceived as a radically new form of ideology and violence was in effect continuous with the history of colonial dispossession and racial slavery. The pan-Africanist intellectual and activist George Padmore, breaking with the Communist International over its failure to think the nexus between "democratic" imperialism and fascism, would write in *How Britain Rules Africa* (1936) of settler-colonial racism as "the breeding-ground for the type of fascist mentality which is being let loose in Europe today." He would go on to see in South Africa "the world's classic Fascist state" grounded on the "unity of race as against class."[7] Padmore's anatomy of what he termed "colonial fascism" thus anticipated the memorable depiction of fascism as the boomerang effect of European imperialist violence in Césaire's *Discourse on Colonialism*. It was also echoed by the Guyanese historian and activist Walter Rodney when he wrote of the "fascist potential of colonialism" with specific reference to the Vichy regime in colonized Algeria.[8] The anticolonial conviction whereby the standpoint of the targets of racial violence gives the lie to the exceptionality of intra-European fascism was also echoed by African American antifascists. Speaking in Paris at the antifascist International Writer's Congress in 1937, the poet Langston Hughes declared: "In America, Negroes do not have to be told what fascism is in action. We know. Its theories of Nordic supremacy and economic suppression have long been realities to us."[9] This was a lesson that could also be drawn from the monumental historical reckoning with US racial capitalism that is W.E.B. Du Bois' 1935 *Black Reconstruction in America*. As Amiri Baraka suggested, building on Du Bois' own passing mentions of fascism, the overthrow of Reconstruction enacted a "racial fascism" that long predated Hitlerism in its use of racial terror, co-optation of poor whites, and passionate investments in white supremacy among ample sectors of the

---

7 Quoted in Bill Schwarz, "George Padmore," in *West Indian Intellectuals in Britain*, ed. Bill Schwartz (Manchester: Manchester University Press, 2003), 141–142.

8 "The French fascists collaborated with Hitler to establish what was called the Vichy regime in France, and the French white settlers in Africa supported the Vichy regime. A more striking instance to the same effect was the fascist ideology developed by the white settlers in Algeria, who not only opposed independence for Algeria under Algerian rule, but they also strove to bring down the more progressive or liberal governments of metropolitan France." See Rodney, *How Europe Underdeveloped Africa*, 243.

9 Langston Hughes, "Too Much of Race," *Crisis*, Vol. 44, No. 9 (September 1937): 272.

capitalist class, financial as well as industrial.[10] Reading the present via this lens can make palpable "how institutionally the historical furniture filling America's political space has already been arranged in such a way that it would always leave open the prospect of evolving even greater authoritarian forms like fascism."[11]

In this view, an American racial fascism could go unremarked because it operated on the other side of the color line, just as colonial fascism took place at a spatial and epistemic remove from the imperial metropole. As Bill V. Mullen and Christopher Vials have suggested in their vital *U.S. Antifascism Reader*:

> for people of color at various historical moments, the experience of racialization within a liberal democracy could have the valence of fascism. That is to say, while a fascist state and a white supremacist democracy have very different mechanisms of power, the experience of racialized rightlessness within a liberal democracy can make the distinction between it and fascism murky at the level of lived experience. For those racially cast aside outside of liberal democracy's system of rights, the word 'fascism' does not always conjure up a distant and alien social order.[12]

---

10 "The overthrow of the Reconstruction actually united fronts of workers and small farmers, heaved Afro America into fascism. There is no other term for it. The overthrow of democratically elected governments and the rule by direct terror, by the most reactionary sector of finance capital, as Dimitrov termed it. Carried out with murder, intimidation and robbery, by the first storm troopers, again the Hitlerian prototype, the Ku Klux Klan, directly financed by northern capital. What the masses of racially twisted white southerners did not understand was that the overthrow of Reconstruction was necessary not just for pitching Black people into American fascism, but for the complete triumph of imperialism." [Amiri Baraka, "Black Reconstruction: Du Bois & the U.S. Struggle For Democracy & Socialism," *Conjunctions* 29 (1997): 77.] I borrow the term "racial fascism" from Baraka, who crucially posits a violent dialectic between the dynamics of racial domination in the US and imperialism, a theme that Du Bois himself had powerfully underscored as early as "The African Roots of War" (1915): "Andrew Johnson's point position in overthrowing Reconstruction and imposing a racial fascism on Afro America and the Afro-American people readied the whole of the U.S. nation for imperialist rule, which today has moved to complete control of the entire nation" (78).

11 Harootunian, "A Fascism for Our Time." Importantly, Harootunian details the "founding oligarchical intentions" and constitutional constructions that, in conjunction with the material histories of racial capitalism, have seeded *sui generis* fascist potentials into the US body politic and its institutions of rule.

12 Bill V. Mullen and Christopher Vials (eds.), *The U.S. Anti-fascism Reader* (London and New York: Verso, 2020), 271.

Or as Jean Genet observed on May 1, 1970, at a rally in New Haven for the liberation of Black Panther Party (BPP) Chairman Bobby Seale: "Another thing worries me: fascism. We often hear the Black Panther Party speak of fascism, and whites have difficulty accepting the word. That's because whites have to make a great effort of imagination to understand that blacks live under an oppressive fascist regime."[13]

It was largely due to the Panthers, or at least in their orbit, that 'fascism' returned to the forefront of radical discourse and activism in the late 1960s and early 1970s—the United Front Against Fascism conference held in Oakland in 1969 brought together a wide swathe of the old and new lefts, as well as Asian American, Chicano, and Puerto Rican activists who had developed their own perspectives on American fascism (for instance, by foregrounding the experience of Japanese internment during World War II). In a striking testament to the peculiarities and continuities of US antifascist traditions, among the chief planks of the conference was the notionally reformist demand for community or decentralized policing— to remove racist white officers from Black neighborhoods and exert local checks on law enforcement. It is not, however, to leading members of the BPP but to political prisoners close to the Panthers, that we must turn for theories about the specificity of what we could call 'late fascism' (by analogy with 'late capitalism') in the US. While debates about 'new fascisms' were polarizing radical debate across Europe, the writing and correspondence of Angela Y. Davis and George Jackson outlined a theory of fascism forged from the lived experience of the violent nexus between the carceral state and racial capitalism.

In one of his prison letters, collected in *Blood in My Eye*, Jackson offers the following reflection:

> When I am being interviewed by a member of the old guard and point to the concrete and steel, the tiny electronic listening device concealed in the vent, the phalanx of goons peeping in at us, his barely functional plastic tape-recorder that cost him a week's labor, and point out that these are all manifestations of fascism, he will invariably attempt to refute me by defining fascism simply as an economic geo-political affair

13 Jean Genet, "May Day Speech," in *The Declared Enemy: Texts and Interviews*, trans. Jeff Fort, ed. Albert Dichy, (Stanford: Stanford University Press, 2004), 38.

where only one party is allowed to exist aboveground and no opposition political activity is allowed.[14]

We could ask: what happens to our conceptions of fascism and authoritarianism if we take our bearings not from putative analogies with the European interwar scene, but, for instance, from the materiality of the prison-industrial complex, from the "concrete and steel," from the devices and personnel of surveillance and repression?

In their writing and correspondence, marked by interpretive differences alongside abiding comradeship, Davis and Jackson identified the US state as the site for a recombinant or even (in the latter's case) perfected fascism. Much of their writing is threaded through Marxist debates on the nature of monopoly capitalism, imperialism and capitalist crises, as well as, in Jackson's case, by an effort to revisit the classical historiography on fascism. On these grounds, both stress the disanalogies between present forms of domination and European exemplars, while asserting the privileged vantage point provided by the view *from within* a prison-judicial system that could accurately be described as a racial state of terror. This both echoes and departs from Black radical theories of fascism, such as those of Padmore or Césaire, which emerged from the experience of the colonized. The new US fascism that Jackson and Davis strive to delineate is not an unwanted return from the "other scene" of colonial violence, it originates from liberal democracy itself, with its roots in racial domination and settler-colonial dispossession. Indeed, it was a sense of the disavowed bonds between liberal and fascist forms of the state that for Davis was one of the vital lessons passed on by Herbert Marcuse, whose grasp of this nexus in 1930s Germany allowed him to discern the fascist tendencies in the America of his exile.

Both Davis and Jackson also stressed the necessity to grasp fascism not as a static form but as a *process*, profoundly inflected by its political and economic contexts and conjunctures. Checklists, analogies, or ideal types could not do justice to the concrete history of fascism. Jackson spoke of "the defects of trying to analyze a movement outside of its process and

---

14 George Jackson, *Blood in My Eye* (London: Penguin, 1975 [1972]), 121–122. For a contemporary theoretical discussion of Jackson's theses, see ARM (Association for the Realization of Marxism), "George Jackson, monopoly capitalism and the fascist type of state," *The Black Liberator*, Vol. 2, No. 3 (1974/5).

its sequential relationships. You gain only a discolored glimpse of a dead past"[15]; he remarked how fascism "developed from nation to nation out of *differing* levels of traditionalist capitalism's dilapidation."[16]

Where Jackson and Davis did echo their contemporary European counterparts was in the idea that "new" fascisms could not be understood without grasping them as responses to the insurgencies of the 1960s and early 1970s. For Jackson, fascism was a fundamentally counterrevolutionary form, as evidenced by the violence with which it repressed any consequential threat to capital and its state. But fascism does not react immediately against an ascendant revolutionary force; it is a kind of *delayed counterrevolution*, parasitic on the weakness or defeat of the anticapitalist left, "the result of a revolutionary thrust that was weak and miscarried—a consciousness that was compromised."[17] Jackson's provocation was to argue that US-style fascism was a kind of perfected form—all the more insidiously hegemonic because of the marriage of monopoly capital with the (racialized) matrix of liberal democracy. As he declared: "Fascism has established itself in a most disguised and efficient manner in this country. It feels so secure that the leaders allow us the luxury of faint protest. Take protest too far, however, and they will show their other face. Doors will be kicked down in the night and machine-gun fire and buckshot will become the medium of exchange."[18]

In Angela Davis' concurrent thinking, the carceral, liberationist perspective on fascism took on a different inflection. For Davis, fascism in the US was best defined as a *preventive* and *incipient* form. The terminology was adapted from Marcuse, who remarked in a 1970 interview: "In the last ten to twenty years we've experienced a preventative counterrevolution to defend us against a feared revolution, which, however, has not taken place and doesn't stand on the agenda at the moment."[19] Only the horizon of a preventive fascism could really speak to the specificity of the United States, outside of any static analogies with the rise of European fascisms that Marcuse had witnessed firsthand.

---

15 Jackson, *Blood*, 124.

16 Jackson, *Blood*, 125.

17 Jackson, *Blood*, 126.

18 Jackson, *Blood*, 158.

19 Herbert Marcuse, "USA: Questions of Organization and the Revolutionary Subject," in *The New Left and the 1960s: Collected Papers of Herbert Marcuse*, Vol. 3, ed. Douglas Kellner (London: Routledge, 2005), 138.

Some of the elements of his analysis still resonate painfully with our present:

> The question is whether fascism is taking over in the United States. If by that we understand the gradual or rapid abolition of the remnants of the constitutional state, the organization of paramilitary troops such as the Minutemen, and granting the police extraordinary legal powers such as the notorious no-knock law which does away with the inviolability of the home; if one looks at the court decisions of recent years; if one knows that special troops—so-called counterinsurgency corps—are being trained in the United States for possible civil war; if one looks at the almost direct censorship of the press, television and radio: then, as far as I'm concerned, one can speak with complete justification of an incipient fascism. . . . American fascism will probably be the first which comes to power by democratic means and with democratic support.[20]

Davis developed the Marcusean thesis that "fascism is the preventive counter-revolution to the socialist transformation of society,"[21] to specify that transformation from the vantage point of the lived experience of racialized communities in the US—where the most threatening feature of Black revolutionary politics for the state takes the guise not so much of the armed struggle imagined by Jackson but of the "survival programs," the enclaves of autonomous social reproduction practiced by the Panthers and more broadly within Black and racialized communities. What can be gleaned from Davis' account is the differential visibility and experience of both fascism and democracy. In this regard, it can help to attune us to the ways in which race and gender, alongside and through class, can also determine the modality in which fascism is lived. There is a kind of everyday fascism, so to speak, that can shape the interaction of people of color with the state, and which, while acting as the repressive infrastructure of a liberal democracy still steeped in the legacies of white supremacy, also signals the possibility or tendency to generalize this incipient fascism to the population at large.

As Davis put it at the time, fascism is "primarily restricted to the use of the law-enforcement-judicial-penal apparatus to arrest the overt and

---

20 Marcuse, "USA," 137–138.

21 Angela Y. Davis and Bettina Aptheker, Preface, in *If They Come in the Morning: Voices of Resistance*, new ed., ed. Angela Y. Davis (London: Verso, 2016 [1971]), xiv.

latent-revolutionary trends among nationally oppressed people, tomorrow it may attack the working class en masse and eventually even moderate democrats."[22] But the latter are, alas, unlikely fully to perceive this phenomenon, both because of the manufactured invisibility of its *site*—carceral space with its "totalitarian aspirations"—and the dilated character of its unfolding, its *time*. The kind of fascism diagnosed by Davis is a "protracted social process,"[23] whose "growth and development are cancerous in nature."[24] We thus have the correlation in Davis' analysis between, on the one hand, the prison as a racialized enclave or laboratory and, on the other, the fascistic strategy and tactics of counterrevolution, which also flow through the society at large. Both spatially and temporally, the perception of fascist realities and potentialities is occluded by the frame of the prison. As Davis has written more recently:

> The dangerous and indeed fascistic trend toward progressively greater numbers of hidden, incarcerated human populations is itself rendered invisible. All that matters is the elimination of crime—and you get rid of crime by getting rid of people who, according to the prevailing racial common sense, are the most likely people to whom criminal acts will be attributed.[25]

Dylan Rodriguez has powerfully captured the originality and challenge of the "fascism problematic" that Davis and Jackson forged out of the political violence of confinement, pointedly asking: "how might our political understanding of the United States be altered or dismantled if we were to conceptualize fascism as the *restoration* of a liberal hegemony, a *way out* of

---

22 Angela Y. Davis, "Political Prisoners, Prisons and Black Liberation," in *If They Come in the Morning*, 44.

23 Davis and Aptheker, *If They Come in the Morning*, xv.

24 Davis, "Political Prisoners," 41. The same nosological metaphor crops up in Gilles Deleuze and Félix Guattari's "schizoanalysis" of fascism. As Harootunian observes, quoting from *A Thousand Plateaus*: "In this regard, fascism's greatest danger stems from its molecular or micropolitical power, secreting from its grassroots, which aggregate into mass movements—'a cancerous body rather than a totalitarian organism.'" [Harootunian, "A Fascism for Our Time."]

25 Angela Y. Davis, "Race and Criminalization: Black Americans and the Punishment Industry," in *The Angela Y. Davis Reader*, ed. Joy James (Oxford: Blackwell Publishers, 1998), 63.

crisis, rather than as the *symptom* of crisis or the *breakdown* of 'democracy' and 'civil society'?"[26]

The lived experience of state violence of Black political prisoners like Davis and Jackson grounded a theory of US fascism and racial capitalism that interrupted what Robinson called the "euphonious recital of fascism" in mainstream political thought. It can still serve as an antidote to the lures and limits of the analogies that increasingly circulate in mainstream debate. As the BLM movement has made patent, it is not the threat of a "return of the 1930s" but the realities of racialized state terror that animate mass antifascist energies—which cannot be reduced to the necessary but insufficient task of confronting the ideologies and actions of more-or-less self-designated fascists. This does not mean flattening fascism onto the capitalist state and ignoring the autonomous threat that self-styled fascist and far right movements pose in their shifts from system-loyalty to system-opposition and back.[27] But it is worth reflecting further on why theoretical perspectives on fascist potentials articulated by people of color, drawing on lived experiences of racialized rightlessness, have often placed by far the greatest theoretical and strategic emphasis on organized state and capitalist violence rather than on the movements of the far right— sometimes leading to critical differences with an antifascist left that saw the latter as the primary reservoir for the possibility of fascism (which is by no means to gainsay the long-history of militant self-defense of racialized and immigrant communities against far-right non-state violence—to the contrary).[28]

---

26 Dylan Rodriguez, *Forced Passages: Imprisoned Radical Intellectuals and the U.S. Prison Regime* (Minneapolis: University of Minnesota Press, 2006), 137.

27 I take this terminology from Devin Zane Shaw's spirited criticism of the earlier version of this article in *Boston Review*, "On Toscano's Critique of "Racial Fascism,"" *threewayfight*, December 30, 2020, http://threewayfight.blogspot.com/2020/12/on-toscanos-critique-of-racial-fascism.html.

28 For critical remarks on the limits of the antifascist left as well as an account of mass antifascist resistance by Black and Asian youth in the British context, see Darcus Howe, "Enter Mrs. Thatcher" (February 1978) and "The Bradford 12: Reflecting on the Trial of the Decade" (August 1982), in *Here to Stay, Here to Fight: A 'Race Today' Anthology*, ed. Paul Field, Robin Bunce, Leila Hassan, and Margaret Peacock (London: Pluto Press, 2019), 23, 159. In 1978, in the context of a militant criticism of the confusion on the British left between antifascism and antiracism, Colin Prescod observed: "Fascism is a big word. Europeans have it in their history, their civilisation and it frightens them. They tell us that it is terrible, and that in a "fascist state" the law works adversely against the masses, and that people are humiliated, persecuted, brutalised and murdered, with no protection except self defence. We've got something to tell Europeans—their fascism is still alive and kicking in their civilisation. The Black masses have been seeing the "fascist" face of the state in

Stuart Hall once castigated the British left for its passionate attachment to the frame of antifascism, for gravitating to the seemingly transparent battle against organized fascism while ignoring new modalities of authoritarianism. There were indeed fascists (the National Front in the 1970s), but Thatcherism was not a fascism. Yet this made it no less threatening. Conversely, Davis and Jackson glimpsed a fascist process that didn't need fascists. Fascists without fascism, or fascism without fascists? Must we choose? Perhaps to bridge this antinomy we need to reflect on the connection between the features of "incipient fascism"—in the specific case of the US, the normalization of forms of terror and extreme repression against racialized and subaltern populations—and the emergence of explicitly fascistic movements and ideologies. We need to think about the links between the often extreme levels of classed and racialized violence that accompany actually-existing liberal democracies (think, for instance, of the antimigrant militarization of the US and European borders) and the emergence of movements and ideologies paradoxically arguing that state and culture have been occupied by the "radical left" (by "cultural Marxism," by "critical race theory"), that racism is now meted out against formerly dominant ethnonational majorities, and that deracinated elites have conspired with the wretched of the Earth to destroy properly "national" populations that can only be rescued by a revanchist politics of security and protectionism.

Our "late fascism" is an ideology of crisis and decline. It depends—in the words of Ruth Wilson Gilmore, writing in the wake of the 1992 LA uprising—on enlisting supporters on the basis of "the idea and enactment of winning, of explicit domination set against the local reality of decreasing family wealth, fear of unemployment, threat of homelessness, and increased likelihood of early, painful death from capitalism's many toxicities."[29] Its psychological wages and racial dividends, steeped in the longue

---

Britain since the 1950s. Perhaps those Europeans who fear and abhor fascism, and who look back to the 1930s for their fascism, were they to look closely at the Black experience in Britain, would find that they have been looking the wrong way for the resurgence of fascism." See Colin Prescod, "Black People Against State Harassment (BASH) campaign—a report," *Race & Class*, Vol. 58, No. 1 (2016): 96. The article was originally published in *The Black Liberator*.

29 Ruth Wilson Gilmore, "Terror Austerity Race Gender Excess Theater," in *Reading Rodney King/Reading Urban Uprising*, ed. Robert Gooding-Williams (London: Routledge, 1993), 27. Reprinted in Ruth Wilson Gilmore, *Abolition Geography: Essays Towards Liberation*, ed. Brenna Bhandar and Alberto Toscano (London and New York: Verso, 2022).

durée of *Herrenvolk* liberal democracy,[30] do considerable political economic work, perpetuating a brutally unequal regime of accumulation by enlisting bodies and psyches into endless culture wars. The Trump Tax Cuts, and the recent campaigns against critical race theory, or for "law and order" were in that regard intimately connected.

But what is this late fascism trying to prevent? Here is where the superstructure sometimes seems to overwhelm the base, as though forces and fantasies once functional to the reproduction of a dominant class and racial order had now attained a kind of autonomy. No imminent threat to the reproduction of capitalism is on the horizon (at least no *external* one), so contemporary fascist trends manifest the strange spectacle of what, in a variation on Davis and Marcuse, we could call a *preventive counterreform*— one that is parasitic, among other things, on resuscitating the racialized anticommunism of a previous era, now weaponizing it against improbable targets like Kamala Harris, while treating any mildly progressive policy as the harbinger of the imminent abolition of all things American. But, drawing on the rich archive of Black radical theories of fascism, we can also start to see the present in a much longer historical arc, one marked by the periodic recurrence of racial fascism as the mode of reaction to any instance of what Du Bois once called "abolition democracy," whether against the First Reconstruction, the Second Reconstruction, or what some have begun, hopefully, to identify as the Third.[31]

30 Domenico Losurdo, *Liberalism: A Counter-History* (London: Verso, 2014), 150.

31 Jeremy Scahill, "Scholar Robin D.G. Kelley on How Today's Abolitionist Movement Can Fundamentally Change the Country," *The Intercept*, June 27, 2020, https://theintercept. com/2020/06/27/robin-dg-kelley-intercepted/.

V. Solidarity in Struggle

CHAPTER SEVENTEEN

Militant Mangrove School

Sónia Vaz Borges and Filipa César

The resurgence of far-right racist violence in Portugal[1] serves as a stark reminder of the living legacies of the historical convergence of the Estado Novo fascist regime in Portugal (1933–1974) and the brutal denouement of Portuguese colonialism.[2] The anticolonial and antifascist struggle against Portugal by Angola, Mozambique, Guinea-Bissau, Cape Verde, and São Tomé and Príncipe offer crucial lessons for today.

For this edited collection, we asked Sónia Vaz Borges and Filipa César to share some of their collaborative work on the political education initiatives and films of the PAIGC (Partido Africano para a Independência da Guiné e Cabo Verde / African Party for the Independence of Guinea and Cape Verde). The PAIGC was founded in the mid-1950s and engaged in armed struggle for national liberation against Portuguese colonial rule and counterinsurgency from 1963 until 1974. The PAIGC, and PAIGC leader Amílcar Cabral, were vital not only for achieving independence from Portugal but as influential examples in the movement for global decolonization more broadly.[3]

An indispensable yet still relatively under-appreciated feature of PAIGC organizing was its political education initiatives, including the documentary films

---

1 For an account of recent racist right-wing violence and attacks against the antiracist activist Mamadou Ba in Portugal, see: "Urgent Solidarity Call to Support Portuguese Anti-racist Activists," September 3, 2020, https://www.enar-eu.org/Urgent-solidarity-call-to-support-Portuguese-antiracist-activists; Mia Alberti, "Portugal Records Surge in Racist Violence as Far Right Rises," *The Guardian*, September 28, 2020, https://www.theguardian.com/world/2020/sep/28/portugal-sees-surge-in-racist-violence-as-far-right-rises.

2 Rui Lopes and Víctor Barros, "Amílcar Cabral and the Liberation of Guinea-Bissau and Cape Verde: International, Transnational, and Global Dimensions," *International History Review* 42, no. 6 (2020); Branwen Gruffydd Jones, "Race, Culture and Liberation: African Anticolonial Thought and Practice in the Time of Decolonisation," *International History Review* 42, no. 6 (2020): 1238–1256; Luís Nuno Rodrigues, "The International Dimensions of the Portuguese Colonial Crisis," in *The Ends of European Colonial Empires: Cases and Comparisons*, ed. Miguel Bandeira Jerónimo and António Costa Pinto (New York: Palgrave Macmillan, 2015).

3 Aurora Almada e Santos and Víctor Barros, "Introduction: Amílcar Cabral and the Idea of Anticolonial Revolution," *Lusotopie* 19 (2020): 9–35; Firoze Manji and Bill Fletcher Jr. (eds.), *Claim No Easy Victories: The Legacy of Amilcar Cabral* (Dakar, Senegal: Council for the Development of Social Science Research in Africa, 2013).

and mobile screening programs of Guinean filmmakers, such as Sana na N'Hada and Flora Gomes. In 1967, Cabral sent N'Hada, Gomes, José Bolama Cubumba, and Josefina Lopes Crato to study revolutionary filmmaking with Santiago Álvarez at the Instituto Cubano del Arte e Industria Cinematográficos *in Havana, as part of a larger training program Cuba launched in support of the PAIGC liberation struggle.*[4] *In 2011, N'Hada first met Filipa César and showed her the remnants of the PAIGC cinematic archive—canisters of film, much of it unedited or unfinished, in various states of erosion—that survived the 1998–1999 civil war in Guinea-Bissau.*[5]

César and Vaz Borges have been instrumental in bringing attention to the political education endeavors, film production, and everyday politics of the liberation struggle in Guinea-Bissau. In addition to César's remarkable work as a filmmaker, artist, and writer, she began collaborating with the National Film and Audiovisual Institute in Bissau and the Arsenal Institute for Film and Video Art in Berlin to transfer and digitize the PAIGC archive. During this process, César notes, "We stopped calling it an archive and instead a 'collective milieu, an assemblage of shrapnel.' To deal with the shrapnel of colonialism means to deal with all the violence that comes through it; it means embracing the conflicts related with a permanent 'decolonization of thinking' as a condition and as a never-accomplishable task."[6] *At the end of 2014, in part reenacting the*

---

4   On the crucial role that Cuba played in supporting the PAIGC and other liberation struggles on the African continent, see: Catarina Laranjeiro, "The Cuban Revolution and the Liberation Struggle in Guinea-Bissau: Images, Imaginings, Expectations, and Experiences," *International History Review* 42, no. 6 (2020); and Kali Argyriadis, Giulia Bonacci, and Adrien Delmas (eds.), *Cuba and Africa, 1959–1994: Writing an Alternative Atlantic History* (Johannesburg: Wits University Press, 2020). Audiences not familiar with the PAIGC films may nonetheless recall sequences shot by Sana na N'Hada included in Chris Marker's acclaimed experimental documentary *San Soleil* (1983). N'Hada and Flora Gomes became leading figures in Guinean cinema. N'Hada and Gomes subsequently codirected the films *O Regresso de Amílcar Cabral* (1976) and *Anos no Oça Luta* (1978). N'Hada also directed the documentaries *Les Jours d'Ancono* (1978), *Fanado* (1984), and *Os Escultores de Espíritos* (2015), and the fiction films *Xime* (1994) [selected for the Cannes Film Festival], *Bissau d'Isabel* (2005), and *Kadjike* (2013). Flora Gomes directed the first feature film produced in Guinea *Mortu Nega* (1988), the feature films *Udju Azul di Yonta* (1992) and *Po di Sangui* (1996), and codirected the 2007 documentary *As duas faces da Guerra* with Diana Andringa.

5   Filipa César, "A Grin Without Marker," *L'Internationale Online*, February 16, 2016, https://www.internationaleonline.org/research/decolonising_practices/59_a_grin_without_marker/. In subsequent writing, César has also analyzed the significance and radical materialism of Cabral's anticolonial agronomy and its connection to political education. See the brilliant essay by Filipa César, "Meteorisations: Reading Amílcar Cabral's Agronomy of Liberation," *Third Text* 32, nos. 2–3 (2018): 254–272.

6   César, "A Grin Without Marker," 68.

PAIGC mobile political education programs of the early 1970s, César, N'Hada, the radio broadcaster Aissatu Seidi, and a small crew toured Guinea-Bissau for four weeks with a portable screening unit, publicly exhibiting selections of images and sound from the PAIGC collection and inviting the audience to collectively discuss this history and its ongoing relevance in their lives. Sónia Vaz Borges' important 2019 book Militant Education, Liberation Struggle, Consciousness: The PAIGC Education in Guinea Bissau, 1963–1978 *brings long-overdue critical attention to the PAIGC political education programs.*[7] *Vaz Borges' scholarship has been key for moving analysis of the PAIGC from the usual focus on Cabral to thinking with the everyday people who collectively waged the struggle for liberation and for developing a more substantive understanding of what she calls "militant education."*

> *Films by César and Vaz Borges assemble recovered archival fragments from the work of N'Hada and Gomes for the PAIGC but also serve as their own critical practice and pedagogic reflection on the history and ongoing significance of the PAIGC liberation struggle. The following conversation between César and Vaz Borges was originally commissioned and published in German, in conjunction with the exhibition "Education Shock," curated by Tom Holert at HWK [Haus der Kulturen der Welt] in Berlin in 2021.*[8]
> *—Alyosha Goldstein*

Filipa César: We begin here because there is no one point of departure to start connecting with the intricate lived conditions of students and teachers at the schools in the liberated zones. This pendular conversation departs from in-depth research into the militant educational system that the African Party for the Independence of Guinea-Bissau and Cape Verde (PAIGC) developed during the liberation process, the eleven-year armed struggle (1963–1974) against Portuguese colonial occupation and a recurring interest in the imaginary of the *tarafe*—the Creole word for mangrove.[9]

---

7   Sónia Vaz Borges, *Militant Education, Liberation Struggle, Consciousness: The PAIGC education in Guinea Bissau 1963–1978* (Berlin: Peter Lang, 2019).

8   Haus der Kulturen der Welt, "Education Shock: Learning, Politics and Architecture in the 1960s and 1970s," May 2021, https://www.hkw.de/en/programm/projekte/2021/bildungsschock/bildungsschock_start.php.

9   Dicionário do Guineense, Luigi Scantamburlo, Lisboa: Edições Colibri; Bubaque, Guiné Bissau: FASPEDI, DL, 1999.

Figure 15. PAIGC school in the liberated area of Guinea-Bissau, 1974. Photograph by Roel Coutinho.

Sónia Vaz Borges: Marcelino Mutna shared with me: *We studied in the mud. When the water came up to here (gesturing to a bit above the ankle), we would stay there, until we finished the lesson. Then we would all go down and walk through the water to go home. We lived and studied in the mangrove for four years (1966–1969); it was our refuge against the bombings.*[10]

FC: Guinea-Bissau's geography describes an "alluvium ecology," with most of its land under sea level and its tidal coast hosting one of the densest chains of Rhizophora mangle (red mangrove) known around the globe. In one of his speeches to the militants, Amílcar Cabral, agronomist, poet, and revolutionary leader, said: *In Guinea, land is cut by the arms of the sea that we call rivers. But in terms of depth they are not rivers.* River was a Portuguese concept—and Cabral wanted to address the importance of knowledge coming from the specificity of land itself and not one imposed by colonial order.

SVB: In the second year of the war that burst out in 1963, the movement led by Cabral had already started militant educational hubs in villages and on guerrilla bases. In the following years, this grew to 164 schools throughout

10 Vaz Borges, *Militant* Education, 77.

Figure 16. Screening of images and sound curated from the INCA archive by Sana na N'Hada, November–December 2014, Guinea-Bissau. Photography by Jenny Lou Ziegel, 2014, courtesy of Filipa César.

all of the liberated zones. In the last years of war, between 1971–1972, according to PAIGC statistics, there were 14,531 students and 258 teachers distributed in the liberated areas of Guinea-Bissau and its neighboring countries, the Republic of Senegal and the Republic of Guinea.

FC: The mangrove ecosystem encompasses a natural tidal technology of connectivity, protection, and resistance to any kind of monolithic culture. Natasha Ginwala and Vivian Ziherl wrote: *The mangrove is itself just such a place where the earth seems unearthly. It is here that human traces cannot survive as a lasting form, for this tropical coastal ecology is a site of continual refiguration: neither sea nor land, neither river nor sea, bearing neither salty nor fresh water, in neither daylight nor darkness.*[11] Under the most hostile conditions for flora, the mangrove grows on Atlantic shores, between land and sea, between fresh and salty waters, in a permanent amphibian life condition.

SVB: One of the main challenges of the jungle schools was to solve the architectural demands—how to protect students and staff from aerial attacks and ambushes by the Portuguese. The schools had to be accessible by foot

---

11 Natasha Ginwala and Vivian Ziherl, "Sensing Grounds: Mangroves, Unauthentic Belonging, Extra-territoriality," *e-flux Journal* 45 (2013), https://www.e-flux.com/journal/45/60128/sensing-grounds-mangroves-unauthentic-belonging-extra-territoriality/.

Figure 17. Still from *Skola di Tarafe* (dir. Sónia Vaz Borges and Filipa César, et al., 2021). Photograph by Jenny Lou Ziegel.

for ten-year-old children and simultaneously be hidden and inaccessible enough to avoid becoming targets for attacks by *Tugas*, as the Portuguese soldiers were called. Some jungle schools, such as that of Mutna, were built on and within mangroves, rendering the impassable connective, part of the intricate nature that Édouard Glissant described as "roots that intertwine, mix, and mutually assist each other."

FC: The *Rhizophora* mangle surrounding Guinea-Bissau's shores develops stilt roots arising from the trunk or branches that grow towards the soil where the stilt root will develop an underground root system. Once the stilt root hits water instead of soil, the stilt root will grow underwater towards the soil in the ocean.

SVB: Mangroves often do grow in mud which supply almost no oxygen at all. The stilt roots have the ability to allow the exchange of gas in oxygen-poor sediments. The arcuate stilt roots have countless lenticels which provide the gas exchange. The mangroves themselves are prepared for hostile environments, protecting themselves and creating shelter for other beings, including the students threatened by the colonial forces.

FC: The seedlings of mangrove plants can float and bob along for more than a year before taking root. A buoyant seedling lies flat on the seawater, floats, and drifts; when it approaches fresher water, the seedling turns in a vertical position, so its roots point downward. After lodging in the mud, the seedling quickly sends additional roots into the soil. Mangroves store fresh water in thick, succulent leaves. The coating on the leaves' surface, called "suberin," is an inert, impermeable waxy substance present in the cell walls of the mangrove, sealing in water and minimizing evaporation. From the journey of a single seed, a rich ecosystem may flourish.

SVB: Mangroves arch high over the water and their aerial roots take several shapes—some branch and loop off the trunk and lower branches, others are wide, wavy plank roots that extend away from the trunk. Aerial roots broaden the base of the tree and stabilize the shallow root system in the soft, loose soil. A branch can take root or bifurcate in another branch; one grows downwards, another upwards. How does the algorithm defining the growth of the mangrove decide when the next sapling will evolve as root or branch?

FC: Some mangroves grow pencil-like roots that stick up out of the dense, wet ground like snorkels. These breathing tubes, called "pneumatophores," allow the mangroves to cope with the daily tidal floods by inhaling oxygen. This won't happen if they're submerged for too long.

SVB: This reminds me of what Lassana Seidi said: *In that time, there were no tables. We were in the forest. You would search for trees, cut the branches and some palm trees, and we would make tables out of them on the open spaces in the forest. The blackboard would be hung in a tree, and in this way, the teacher would give the classes. In the beginning, there was no school material. When we were learning the A-B-Cs, a normal pencil was cut in two, sometimes even three, according to the number of students. During that time, we would search for paper, or even ... pasteboard. On these pasteboards, the teacher would write the alphabet, and you would repeat and copy.*[12]

FC: Mangroves thrive despite being flooded twice a day by the ocean tides. Growing where land and water meet, mangroves bear the brunt of ocean-borne storms and hurricanes. Resilient, when a tropical storm comes along and with all of its force, hits the mangroves first, before all

---

12 Vaz Borges, *Militant Education*, 79.

the others—plants, animals, and humans. Mangroves protect the shore in many ways, also from colonial ships.

SVB: The constant struggle of the mangrove, with its rhizomatic condition of resilience, echoes Cabral's words: *Repressed, persecuted, betrayed by some social groups who were in league with colonialist, African culture survived all storms. Taking refuge in the villages, in the forests and in the spirit of the generations who were victims of colonialism.... The universal values of African culture are now an incontestable fact; nevertheless, it should not be forgotten that Africans, whose hands, as the poet said, 'placed the stones of the foundations of the world,' have developed their culture frequently, if not constantly, in adverse conditions: from deserts to equatorial forest, from coastal marshes to the banks of great rivers subject to frequent flooding, in spite of all sorts of difficulties.*[13]

FC: Mangroves on the shore also teach us how borders are an artificial construct, and they give us the material proof that borders are, ontologically, floating signifiers. Mud collects around the tangled mangrove roots and shallow mudflats build up. Mangroves grow and change, producing new soils, always on the move, territorializing, deterritorializing, redefining topographies—their root systems create the architectures that sustain constants shifts of land, challenging concepts of territory and ownership.

SVB: In their essay "Rhizome," Félix Guattari and Gilles Deleuze oppose the tree root with the rhizome and propose a critique of Western epistemology by imagining the root-book as the tree of knowledge, departing from a one that gives rise to a two—implying an always traceable origin.[14] For Frantz Fanon, this logic is that of colonialism, a white versus Black perspective that is rooted in fantasies of origin, where the one naturally dominates the two—with the one always the point of reference for as it is and as it should be. The book tells this narrative. The epic narrative, an

---

13 Amílcar Cabral, *Unity and Struggle: Speeches and Writings of Amílcar Cabral* (London: Monthly Review Press, 1979), 49–50. For further reading, see Filipa César, "Meteorisations: Reading Amílcar Cabral's Agronomy of Liberation" *Third Text* 32, nos. 2–3 (2018): 254–272.

14 Gilles Deleuze and Félix Guattari, *A Thousand Plateaus: Capitalism and Schizophrenia*, trans. Brian Massumi (Minneapolis: University of Minnesota Press, London, 1987), 4–25.

origin story. A story that always returns to a homeland. The book makes a tale of violence.

FC: The rhizome sets the term "root" under a certain kind of crisis. We could think about a mangrove book, against this figure of the tree-book, a book that doesn't relate to an origin, but one that is made of the knowledge gained by a constant seeding or a recurring attempt to reach out to surrounding neighbors, projecting new roots that attach or not, and knowledge that evolves from established relations and not from some kind of claim to from whence it comes.

SVB: The learning within an intertidal environment teaches alternatives to the "single-root," and that fixity in place and land is the origin of both violent identitarian and terrifying nationalist myths. For Édouard Glissant, its historical experience, mapped perfectly by its chaotic archipelagic geography, is rhizomatic and nomadic. How could movements of deterritorialization and processes of reterritorialization not be relative, always connected, caught up in one another? Creolized, archipelagic space is defined by its creative chaos and fractal character, rather than by fixity and continuity.

FC: Under the condition of war, the fugitive Guinean students in the liberated zones found shelter in the mangrove schools, a relation student/magrove/school forming a rhizome itself. Mangrove survivance is naturally resistant to external offshore occupations.[15] The learning environment of the *tarafe* is a creolized and archipelagic space—everything is set adrift, yet everything still connects, everywhere a place, a nomad condition.

SVB: The nomad thoughts of Maria da Luz Boal, told that *[s]ome [students] were orphans. Others, the parents were in the war front.... And constantly we received the news that the comrade went and stayed [died]. And so, there was this environment of living the struggle, and the will to be free. It was so strong that those kids would draw the airplanes, rifles, bombings. That was their world. ... You had to explain why the people decided to fight to be free from colonial oppression.... Politics was so evident, that they had to know and understand.*[16]

---

15 On the concept of "survivance," see Gerald Vizenor, *Manifest Manners: Narratives on Postindian Survivance* (Lincoln: University of Nebraska Press, 1999).

16 Vaz Borges, *Militant Education*, 155.

Figure 18. Still from *Skola di Tarafe* (dir. Sónia Vaz Borges and Filipa César, et al., 2021). Photograph by Jenny Lou Ziegel.

FC: As a nomad seed, propagules can survive desiccation and remain dormant for over a year before reaching a suitable environment. Once a propagule is ready to root, its density changes so that the elongated shape now floats vertically rather than horizontally. In this position, it is more likely to lodge in the mud and root, otherwise, it can alter its density and drift again in search of more favorable conditions.

SVB: Like these rhizomes, Marcelino Mutna and other students are carriers of nomad archives. For more than forty years, PAIGC-related stories and experiences of "militant education" had only been remembered in small private groups, as a reminder and shared nostalgic process between those who were part of it.[17] During this time, they rebuilt their lives in Guinea-Bissau, Cape Verde or various other countries, they traveled and worked in different fields, they rebuilt their ideals and memories about the liberation struggle, they forgot major details around the struggle. In this life process, they became "walking archives," meaning an archive that is not housed in one place and whose information is not constant or fixed in time, and whose memories need to be constantly brought to life by the questions and curiosity of the ones who are interested.

---

17 PAIGC, *Educação, Tarefa de Toda a Sociedade* (Comissariado de Estado da Educação Nacional, República da Guiné-Bissau, 1978).

FC: The fragmentary practice of this re-membering, bringing back to the members past experiences challenged from voice to the body, announces the fluid and fictile construction of histories. Glissant wrote, *[t]he notion of the rhizome maintains, therefore, the idea of rootedness but challenges that of a totalitarian root. Rhizomatic thought is the principle behind what I call the Poetics of Relation* [Poetique de la Relation], *in which each and every identity is extended through a relationship with the Other.*[18]

SVB: Located near the villages, schools were to be constructed in a relatively safe place due to the war situation and not too far from a water source. The school structure was not permanent due to the circumstances of war that forced them to have a sort of an itinerant life and structure. They were built with materials easy to transport, in order to be rebuilt in another region: tree leaves, tree trunks, and branches. The forest environment provided a natural protection for school reconnaissance from aircraft, while the conditions of the liberation struggle informed the architecture of the schools.

FC: In this field of suspension and kinship, an affected zone of impasse coexists with the technology of passage. The mangrove is also a natural site of protection for many species, nurturing reproduction. Within this fluctuating architecture, militant knowledge was being produced and transmitted against all odds in the measure of tidal cycles. These strategies were supported by a permanent pedagogical effort towards self-emancipation, employing what radical pedagogue Paulo Freire coined as the coding of language through a situated process of consciencialization [*consciencialização*].[19]

SVB: "Militant education" is a term that I define as an engaged and conscious education process, committed to anticolonial and decolonizing principles focused on an ample concept of liberation. It is rooted in and supported by the realities and necessities of the community and whose pedagogical role combines three aspects: political learning, technical training, and the shaping of individual and collective behaviors. As pupils/students, militants were guided toward the development of his/herself as a liberated

---

18 Édouard Glissant, *Poetics of Relation* (Ann Arbor: University of Michigan Press, 1997), 11.

19 Paulo Freire, *Pedagogy in Process: The Letters to Guinea-Bissau* (New York: Bloomsbury, 1978).

African citizen whose task was to give his/her conscious contribution to the sustainable development of the newly independent liberated country, integrated into an internationalist world understanding.

FC: Under the condition of colonial oppression, particularly of this liberation war, survivance follows up catastrophe then another beginning, another becoming; reterritorialization after deterritorialization. Education in these circumstances is a corollary of this very intrinsic survival mode of the mangrove.

SVB: Marcelino Mutna studied in a school constructed on a mangrove in which the soil was flooded twice a day. When he says "to go down" it refers to how the school was constructed—seats and tables were built with higher legs, in order to avoid their feet being submerged in the water; another structure was constructed so that students could rest their feet during the classes. Mutna describes how the tides were intricate in the process of learning.

FC: Water in, water out: inhalation of knowledge and exhalation of life in the pace of a militant nature. The tidal breath oxygenating a knowledge of resistance in a condition of resistance for knowledge.

SVB: Like the mangroves, militant education is a life condition on the edge. With one foot on land and one in the sea, these botanical amphibians occupy a zone of desiccating heat, choking mud, and salt levels that would kill an ordinary plant within hours.

FC: The mangrove as aerial natural architecture, where, although humans apparently can leave no traces, memory still fluctuates through its tidal root networks. Here, encounter an imaginary from entangling various converging dimensions: the epistemology of the rhizome as situated by Édouard Glissant, concepts of militant and political education developed by the PAIGC and later systematized by Paulo Freire, and botanical notions of the engineering of mangroves with the nomad archives. This cinematic journey will speculate about the telling nature of the rhizome and its resilience.

SVB: The mangroves' schools are not a metaphor for a theory of resistance but rather the very material sharing and producing of knowledge that evolved from an anticolonial struggle, and that takes the rhizomatic ecosystem as a place of permanent struggle: attaching roots/detaching roots, learning/unlearning, the militant condition is a latent becoming.

Special thanks to Diana McCarty for the cosmic advice.

CHAPTER EIGHTEEN

The Resurgent Far Right and the Black Feminist Struggle for Social Democracy in Brazil[1]

Keisha-Khan Y. Perry

> The most potent weapon in the hands of the oppressor is the mind of the oppressed. —Steve Biko

Racial hatred: the long(er) history

Each morning, journalist Eliane Brum and activist Monica Benicio remind us on Twitter of the number of days that have passed since the assassination of Marielle Franco. A Black queer Rio de Janeiro activist and councilwoman from the Maré neighborhood, Franco was killed along with her driver, Anderson Silva, on March 14, 2018, minutes after leaving an event for the empowerment of Black women and girls that was livestreamed on Facebook. Almost two hundred (mostly left-leaning) politicians and activists (Black and Indigenous, fighting against territorial loss) have been killed in the last five years in Brazil, and many of these cases remain unsolved. On March 12, 2019, almost one year after the killing of Marielle Franco, two former police officers with direct ties to Brazilian president Jair Bolsonaro were arrested in connection with her death. The question of who killed Franco may seem to be resolved, but uncertainty remains around who ordered her murder.

In the days leading up to the Brazilian presidential elections of October 2018, Brum published an essay in *El País* titled "*O odio deitou no meu divã*," loosely translated as "Hate Sat on My Couch."[2] She begins her essay

---

1   This chapter was previously published in *American Anthropologist* 122, no. 1 (March 2020): 157–162.

2   Eliane Brum, "O ódio deitou no meu divã [Hate Sat on My Couch]," *El País*, October 11, 2018, https://brasil.elpais.com/brasil/2018/10/10/politica/1539207771_563062.html.

by narrating the resurgence of hate-based threats in Brazil. She presents Silvia Bellintani, a psychoanalyst who describes threats made against his nineteen-year-old gay male client by white fascists:

> He enters without saying a word and starts to cry right away. I ask him what happened and he says, 'I'm frightened,' and that he was approached by a guy at the university with these words: 'Hey there, faggot, have you seen the research? Take advantage of the days until the 28th [election day] to walk holding hands, because when Mito [nickname for Bolsonaro] assumes power, he'll end this nonsense and you'll be beaten until you turn into a man.'[3]

Bellintani tells the story of another client, a seventeen-year-old feminist, who was also threatened just before the elections. Someone left a note in her school textbook that read, "You thought it was all about going out there screaming '#nothim' to stop Bolsomito, feminazi!!! You lost, sad old sack!!!" Brazilian women used the hashtag #nothim to register their opposition to then-candidate Bolsonaro, affectionately nicknamed "Bolsomito" by his supporters.

Brum's article describes the explosion of similar stories recounted on social media by psychologists who have revealed these private conversations (without revealing the identity of their clients) that they say point to the infiltration of hate into Brazilian society. These stories focus primarily on the loathed figure of Bolsonaro, a former army captain who is popularly described, as Brum writes, as a "homophobic, misogynist, racist 'thing.'"[4] For many, Bolsonaro has created an embodied fear and a collective neurosis that have dominated conversations between psychologists and their patients. In another essay, published in *The Guardian*, Brum reminds us that this is not simply paranoia. Bolsonaro has indeed articulated hatred, violence, racism, sexism, and homophobia.[5] He has stated that he is pro-torture and that he would rather his son die than be gay. His platform was won on being explicitly racist and xenophobic, and he is quoted as saying

---

3 All translations are my own.

4 Eliane Brum, "How a Homophobic, Misogynist, Racist 'Thing' Could Be Brazil's Next President," *The Guardian*, October 6, 2018, https://www.theguardian.com/commentisfree/2018/oct/06/homophobic-mismogynist-racist-brazil-jair-bolsonaro.

5 Eliane Brum, "He's Been President a Week—and Already Bolsonaro Is Damaging Brazil," *The Guardian*, January 10, 2019, https://www.theguardian.com/commentisfree/2019/jan/10/jair-bolsonaro-brazil-minorities-rainforest.

that under his leadership, "There'll be no money for NGOs. If it's up to me, every citizen will have a gun at home. Not one centimeter will be demarcated for Indigenous reserves or *quilombolas* [the descendant communities of runaway enslaved peoples]."[6]

Many also point to his sexism in his vehement support for the impeachment of former president Dilma Rousseff, the country's first female leader. (Indeed, I have argued elsewhere that misogynistic ideas about women's leadership were the root cause of her demise.)[7] And he has been unapologetic about his support for the incarceration of former president Luiz Ignácio Lula da Silva, popularly known as "Lula," who was a founding member of the Workers' Party and served for two terms prior to Rousseff. Brum and others point to Bolsonaro's defense of the military regime and his investment in increased militarization of police forces in the country as manifestations of his fascism. What is most striking about Brum's analysis of the fascist hatred on full display in Brazilian society is how she situates it historically. She asserts that this president is "the monstrous product of the country's silence about the crimes committed by its former dictatorship," limiting the scope of Bolsonaro's historical precedent to the last fifty years.

While there has indeed been silence about the country's violent past and present, Black activists in Brazil have consistently reminded us that the violence of the military dictatorship (1964–1980) represented only one moment in the long history of white supremacist colonial violence and the legacy of slavery in the country. As Afro-Brazilian sociologist Vera Benedito has publicly asked, "How is it that Brazil was the last country to abolish slavery in 1888, but it is still known as a racial paradise where everyone is partying and having sex with each other?"[8] Christen Smith, Ana Luiza Pinheiro Flauzina, Maud Chirio, Rebecca Atencio, and numerous other scholars have documented that Black/Brown and poor people— from the *barracoons* [stockades for the confinement of enslaved peoples in West Africa awaiting transport across the Atlantic] to the plantations,

---

6   Benjamin Butterworth, "Jair Bolsonaro: 17 Quotes that Explain the Views of Brazil's Fascist President-Elect," *The I*, October 29, 2018, https://inews.co.uk/news/world/ jair-bolsonaro-quotes-brazil-election-2018-result-president-elect/.

7   Keisha-Khan Y. Perry, "Ask Dilma Why Hillary Lost: Why They Both Lost," *Garnet News*, April 3, 2017, https://garnetnews.com/2017/04/03/ask-dilma-hillary.

8   Vera Benedito, opening remarks at Afro-Brazil and the Brazilian Polity seminar at Brown University, Providence, Rhode Island, April 4, 2011.

quilombos, *favelas*, and *bairros*—have borne the brunt of militarized polic-ing, techniques of surveillance and torture, and state sponsorship of mass killings.[9] It is impossible to maintain slavery for four centuries without rampant sexual violence and a subsequent system of racial apartheid that is always gendered and classed. The resurgence of far-right violence and politics in Brazil—specifically, the concerted attempt to repeal social gains for Blacks, women, and poor people—must be understood through this broad historical context of the ongoing enactment of white supremacy and read through an intersectional approach. As Kimberlé Crenshaw and Black feminist activists globally have shown, an intersectional approach reveals the vulnerabilities and exclusions that have further marginalized racialized and gendered populations, particularly Black women, from equal protec-tion under laws and in policies.[10]

What Brazilian psychologists have only recently been calling the "embod-iment of hate" has thus been entrenched in the everyday and institutional lived experiences of Afro-Brazilians and Indigenous peoples. We must acknowledge that these communities have long dealt with the pervasive anti-Blackness, homophobia and misogyny, massive cuts to public universi-ties, and military violence that some see as only recent phenomena. Critical scholar Denise Ferreira da Silva has referred to this long history of everyday violence as part of the material consequences of gendered racial subjection that has been built into the environment.[11] For example, neighborhood segregation and separate elevators for the public and mostly Black service workers in offices and residential buildings reproduce sociospatial hierar-chies and conflicts that seem unrelated to the political context,[12] but in fact stem directly from centuries-old racist ideas and exclusionary practices.

---

9 Christen Smith, *Afro-Paradise: Blackness, Violence, and Performance in Brazil* (Urbana-Champaign: University of Illinois Press, 2016); Ana Luiza Pinheiro Flauzina, *Corpo Negro Caído No Chão: O Sistema Penal e o Projeto Genocida Do Estado Brasileiro* [*Black Body Fallen on the Floor: The Penal System and the Genocidal Project of the Brazilian State*] (Rio de Janeiro: Contraponto, 2008); Maud Chirio, *Politics in Uniform: Military Officers and Dictatorship in Brazil, 1960–80* (Pittsburgh: University of Pittsburgh Press, 2018); Rebecca J. Atencio, *Memory's Turn: Reckoning with Dictatorship in Brazil* (Madison: University of Wisconsin Press, 2014).

10 Kimberlé Crenshaw, "Mapping the Margins: Intersectionality, Identity Politics, and Violence Against Women of Color," *Stanford Law Review* 43, no. 1 (1990): 1241–1299.

11 Denise Ferreira da Silva, *Toward a Global Idea of Race* (Minneapolis: University of Minnesota Press, 2007).

12 Michael Hanchard, "Black Cinderella?: Race and the Public Sphere in Brazil," *Public Culture* 7, no. 1 (1994): 165–185.

Thus, the right-wing desire for a return to a recent (racialist) past must be understood within longer histories of racialization and white supremacy. When Bolsonaro praises 1960s dictatorship torture chief Carlos Alberto Brilhante Ustra, stating, "We want a Brazil that is similar to the one we had 40, 50 years ago,"[13] this references a longer and ongoing history of anti-Black repression and violence in the country. Indeed, the torture techniques of the military regime in Brazil and Chile during the 1960s that the president refers to had been perfected on the bodies of Black and Brown people long before the (white) leftist activists. These techniques can be traced back to the violent repression of enslaved Africans kidnapped and forced into labor in Brazil.[14] Jurema Werneck, a cofounder of the Black women's NGO Criola and head of Human Rights Watch Brazil, affirms that while most young people have no memory of the military dictatorship, they are very familiar with its aftermath, and many are still living in the *senzalas* [slave quarters] that have always existed adjacent to mansions since the slavery period.[15]

---

13 "*Bolsonaro diz que objetivo é fazer o Brasil semelhante 'ao que tínhamos há 40, 50 anos'* [Bolsonaro said that an objective is to make Brazil similar to 'what we had 40, 50 years ago']," *O Globo*, October 15, 2018, https://oglobo.globo.com/brasil/bolsonaro-diz-que-obje-tivo-fazer-brasil-semelhante-ao-que-tinhamos-ha-40-50-anos-23158680.

14 However, practices of violent repression can also be seen more recently, under the guise of humanitarian aid efforts. An example from a hemispheric perspective can be seen in Brazil's leading role in the United Nations Stabilization Mission in Haiti, which consisted of a militarized humanitarianism that Frank Müller and Andrea Steinke argue was directly related to Brazil's domestic expertise with militarized urban policing. They describe how Brazil's "aid" was actually police training for use against Brazilian citizens at home: "By means of the transnational entanglements of militarisation of humanitarian work between Haiti and Rio de Janeiro and as an effect of the alleged spatial and cultural similarity between the two places, Brazil could learn from the mission to improve its operational-logis-tic knowledge for missions 'at home'" (229). These hemispheric connections are crucial for our understanding of the entanglement of global racisms and how the language of humani-tarianism, pacification, and peacekeeping operate to mask these networks and produce the very violence they claim to suppress. [Frank Müller and Andrea Steinke, "Criminalising Encounters: MINUSTAH as a Laboratory for Armed Humanitarian Pacification," *Global Crime* 19, nos. 3–4 (2018): 228–249, https://www.tandfonline.com/doi/full/10.1080/17440 572.2018.1498336?af=R].

15 Human Rights Watch, *World Report 2018: Events of 2017* (New York: Human Rights Watch, 2017), https://www.hrw.org/sites/default/files/world_report_down-load/201801world_report_web.pdf. Cited in Sidney Chalhoub, Mariana Llanos, Keisha-Khan Y. Perry, Cath Collins, and Mónica Pachón, *Report of the LASA Fact-Finding Delegation on the Impeachment of Brazilian President Dilma Rousseff* (Pittsburgh: Latin American Studies Association, 2017), https://www.lasaweb.org/uploads/reports/brazildele-gationreport-2017.pdf.

Eighty shots: a country at war

On April 7, 2019, beloved Afro-Brazilian musician Evaldo dos Santos Rosa was driving with his family to a baptism in the Guadalupe neighborhood of Rio de Janeiro when the Brazilian military fired more than eighty rounds at his car, killing him and injuring his family, including two children. The army reported that the soldiers mistook the musician for a drug trafficker.[16] Bolsonaro was criticized by journalists, activists, and politicians for his silence on this murder. If Bolsonaro's supporters believe that every Brazilian should own guns (although almost 70 percent of Brazilians polled in the week after the killing of dos Santos Rosa were against the right to bear arms),[17] then Black and Brown people, poor people, and women know precisely who and where the targets of civilian vigilantism will be. The brutal killing of capoeira *mestre* Moa do Katende in Salvador on October 17, 2018, in the hours after declaring that he had voted for Workers' Party candidate Fernando Haddad, provided an example of what was already the social reality for most Black people and what was to come. Following Evaldo dos Santos Rosa's murder, his twenty-nine-year-old son, Daniel Rosa, said, "President Jair Bolsonaro said the Army was here to protect us, not take lives."[18] In mid-February 2019, the Supreme Court denied the transfer of the case of nine military police officers on trial for a massacre in the Cabula neighborhood from Bahia to the federal court. These officers are on trial for killing twelve and seriously injuring another six young men and women between the ages of fifteen and twenty-eight, shot execution-style on February 7, 2015.[19] Despite evidence of a massacre and cover-up, eight of the nine officers continue to work on the streets.

July 2018 also marked twenty-five years since the 1993 Candelaria massacre of eight homeless people, including six children, in front of the Candelária Church in Rio de Janeiro. This massacre occurred within the broader context of 1988 to 1991, during which, according to the Federal

---

16 Brum, "How a Homophobic, Misogynist, Racist 'Thing' Could Be Brazil's Next President."

17 Geraldo Ribeiro and Anna Carolina Torres, "'*Cadê meu pai?,' repete filho de músico que o viu morrer após carro levar mais de 80 tiros de militares* ['Where is my father?' Repeats son of musician who saw him die after a car got hit by military police more than 80 times]," *O Globo Rio*, April 8, 2019, https://oglobo.globo.com/rio/cade-meu-pai-repete-filho-de-musico-que-viu-morrer-apos-carro-levar-mais-de-80-tiros-de-militares-23581550?utm_source=Facebook&utm_medium=Social& utm_campaign=compartilhar.

18 Ribeiro and Torres, "'Cadê meu pai?'"

19 Smith, *Afro-Paradise.*

Police of Brazil, almost 6,000 street children were killed, mostly in Rio de Janeiro and São Paulo.[20]

Although these events have drawn international attention, the violent political discourses and state actions, incarceration of political opponents, and truculent military killings that have occurred in the first six months of Bolsonaro's presidency are not new. Every twenty-three minutes in Brazil, a young Black person between the ages of fifteen and twenty-nine is killed. That is, seventy-five young black people per day, three every hour. On the night before her death, Marielle Franco tweeted about the police murder of twenty-three-year-old Matheus Melo de Castro in Rio, "How many more must die for this war to end?"[21] Activist and founder of the anti-police-violence organization *Reaja ou Será Morta* [React or Die], Hamilton Borges, has stated that the statistics on police violence in Brazil are equivalent to those of "a country at war."[22]

In 2018, the killings totaled 27,000. Between 1980 and 2014, a record one million Black people were killed (approximately 29,000 per year). Between 2009 and 2013, the Brazilian police gave the reason for killing 11,197 people as "resisting arrest." Black men and women, who make up 51 percent of the population, comprised 71 percent of the 318,000 homicide victims in Brazil between 2005 and 2015, and in 2015 police operations accounted for 3,320 murders of Blacks nationwide.[23] Although Black women represent only 24.5 percent of the Brazilian population, 61 percent of the women murdered by the police are Black, and 144 transgender people were murdered in 2016, the majority of whom are also Black and women.[24]

20 M.M.L. Silva, "Killing of 6,000 Street Kids and the Candelaria Massacre," *CJ the Americas* 7, no. 4 (1994): 1–8.

21 @mariellefranco, "Mais um homicídio de um jovem que pode estar entrando para a conta da PM. Matheus Melo estava saindo da igreja. Quantos mais vão morrer para essa Guerra acabe?" March 12, 2018, 10:38 a.m., https://twitter.com/mariellefranco/status/973568966403731456.

22 Jihan Hafiz, "The Cabula 12: Brazil's Police War against the Black Community," *Aljazeera America*, February 25, 2016, http://america.aljazeera.com/watch/shows/america-tonight/articles/2016/2/25/the-cabula-12-brazil-police-war-blacks.html.

23 Instituto de Pesquisa Econômica Aplicada, *Atlas de Violência* [*Atlas of Violence*], http://www.ipea.gov.br/portal/images/stories/PDFs/relatorio_institucional/180604_atlas_da_violencia_2018.pdf.

24 Sayonara Nogueira and Rede Trans Brasil, "*Dossiê: A Geografia Dos Corpos Das Pessoas Trans* [Dossier: The Geography of the Bodies of Trans People]," Rede Trans Brasil, Rede Nacional de Pessoas Trans-Brazil, 2017, http://redetransbrasil.org.br/wp-content/uploads/2019/01/A-Geografia-dos-Corpos-Trans.pdf.

Residents living on the sociospatial margins of Brazilian cities—such as Rodrigo Serrano in the Chapeu Mangueira neighborhood of Rio de Janeiro, killed when police mistook his umbrella for a gun, or as previously cited, dos Santos Rosa, mistaken for "*bandidos*," killed in front of his family on their way to a baby shower —tend to bear the brunt of militarized police violence. But as recent reports show, scholars and activists, both men and women, are not immune to violence sponsored by the state or carried out by local *milicias*, supporters of the new president.

It should not be read as a coincidence that the desire to arm the population, militarize urban neighborhoods, and implement the death penalty (legally or extrajudicially, as the case of Evaldo dos Santos Rosa shows) have appeared in the same political discourses as the urgent need to end affirmative action, eliminate the demarcation of *quilombo* and Indigenous lands, ban the teaching of gender politics in schools, and eliminate all LGBTQ+ rights. Even before Bolsonaro's presidency began, four thousand Cuban doctors were removed from Brazil. To reinvigorate Paul Gilroy's early ideas in *There Ain't No Black in the Union Jack*, class becomes the lexicon through which race and gender are lived.[25] Anti-Blackness and the sponsorship of racial violence (this also includes austerity measures in the form of cuts to public health care, education, housing, and cash benefits) are ever-present without ever needing to utter any explicit ideas around race, gender, and Blackness. The majority of poor people in Brazil are Black, and the majority being criminalized and incarcerated are also Black. The people described as needing the social order and control that the new government promises to implement are Black and female. This is especially clear when we consider the politicization of conservative Catholic and evangelical Christian movements, whose members continue to demonize Afro-Brazilian religions and burn down and demolish *terreiros* [houses of worship] that have strong female, lesbian, and homosexual participation and leadership as well as having more expansive practices of racial and sexual inclusion. The long-delayed extension of democratic rights to Black people, women, gays and lesbians, and poor people over the last fifteen years represents a threat to the gendered racial sociospatial order that the architects of "*ordem e progresso*" [order and progress] have in mind.

---

25 Paul Gilroy, *There Ain't No Black in the Union Jack* (Chicago: University of Chicago Press, 1991).

Gender trouble

Even before the January 1, 2019 inauguration of Jair Bolsonaro, the most important political project on the agenda to be implemented as law was one that conservative evangelicals and Catholics have been pushing in recent years: *Escola sem Partido* [Schools without Politics], inspired by the US organization NoIndoctrincation.org. The proposed law prohibits the teaching of any sort of political ideology or doctrine in schools and universities, a kind of censorship unimaginable in any democratic society. In addition to banning so-called Marxist indoctrination, the most important dimension of this law is a proposed ban on teaching about gender and sexuality. Judith Butler, author of the classic text *Gender Trouble*,[26] widely available in Portuguese, was aggressively verbally attacked during her November 2017 visit to Brazil. This attack was part of the political momentum of the anti-gender-discourse movement and the development of the Escola sem Partido movement. Since the 1994 United Nations Development Program conference in Cairo and the 1995 UN World Conference on Women in Beijing, the emergence of a new discourse of gender as a social construct and calls for gender-specific rights and public policies have sparked an antigender movement in education in Brazil. Schools and universities have been seen as a battleground for maintaining heteropatriarchy and Christian dominance.

Some feminist activists in Brazil have asserted that former president Rousseff ceded to pressure and refused to launch the *Escola sem Homofobia* [Schools without Homophobia] pedagogical materials, and her successor, Michel Temer, removed all references to "gender identity," "sexual orientation," and "teaching without prejudice" from the national, common core curriculum that had been taught since the 1990s.[27] The antigender movement has been pushing the idea of "moral education" and "Brazil for Brazilians" to resemble "America for Americans,"[28] which also has implications for the current required teaching of Afro-Brazilian and Indigenous history. In general, this represents a return to the romantic ideal of a white, heteropatriarchal Brazilian society in which women, Black, and Indigenous

26 Judith Butler, *Gender Trouble: Feminism and the Subversion of Identity* (New York: Routledge, 1990).

27 Chalhoub et al., *Report of the LASA Fact-Finding Delegation*.

28 Erika Lee, *America for Americans: A History of Xenophobia in the United States* (New York: Basic Books, 2019).

people "know their place." Hence, for Black activists like Jurema Werneck, this political shift toward authoritarian rule is a "coup against [Black people], a coup against social rights."[29] The election of Jair Bolsonaro is about "'putting order back in the big house,' rescuing old hegemonies, and 'keeping the poor people in their rightful place.'"[30]

In 2016, anthropologist Joanne Rappaport, then president of the Latin American Studies Association, put together a delegation to Brazil in which I participated to investigate the legitimacy of the impeachment of Dilma Rousseff. As we documented in our fact-finding report, "[s]ocial movement activists were perhaps less interested in the legal technicalities that legitimated this war against social equality."[31] For them, the impeachment was about a white elite reclaiming power and keeping racial and class privilege intact. The impeached were, they felt, "the poor people, black people, and gays and lesbians who have been at the center of small victories gained in the last thirteen years."[32] The delegation report provides rich documentation of the long historical view of how we got to this political point. Several of the people we interviewed, including prominent white politicians and lawyers, asserted that affirmative action in higher education was perhaps the most impactful social transformation in recent Brazilian history. Prior to the implementation of affirmative action in 2012, Black people comprised less than 10 percent of university students, although they represented 50 percent of the Brazilian population—and up to 80 percent in some regions of the country.[33] This is a social gain that led to a local community activist like Marielle Franco attending university and to a rise in the number of college-educated Black people and, subsequently, the shaping of a new political class.

The debates around affirmative action were an early sign leading up to the current crisis, revealing that race structured a class society in Brazil. Few whites on the left were attuned to this racial question, and as Sueli Carneiro stated, "the reaction to affirmative action, the resistance, came from the presupposition that if you open these opportunities, you would

---

29 Chalhoub et al., *Report of the LASA Fact-Finding Delegation*, 45.

30 Chalhoub et al., *Report of the LASA Fact-Finding Delegation*, 45.

31 Chalhoub et al., *Report of the LASA Fact-Finding Delegation*, 45.

32 Chalhoub et al., *Report of the LASA Fact-Finding Delegation*, 46.

33 Sales Augusto dos Santos, *Educação: Um pensamento negro contemporâneo* [*Education: Black Contemporary Thought*] (São Paulo: Paco Editorial, 2014).

have an increase in racism in the society, of racial conflicts. And the subtext, in fact at times an explicit text, is that it was because [white elites] expected activism, violence from Blacks in defense of quotas."[34]

However, as former president and political prisoner Lula affirmed, access to unprecedented social mobility and the public sphere by Black people, women, and poor people made the white elite uncomfortable. This is especially the case for domestic workers and their children who pursued higher education precisely at the moment when labor rights were expanded. It became increasingly difficult for the middle classes to access and afford household and childcare labor, labor often provided by poor Black women.

This emphasis on the gendered racial and class dimensions of Rousseff's impeachment—specifically, the attempts to repeal social gains for Black people, women, and poor people—could be read through an intersectional lens to understand the ongoing enactment of white supremacy. An intersectional approach allows us to analyze the structural gendered racism and state violence against which vibrant social movements in Brazilian cities have been mobilizing. For activists, the lack of abortion rights, the rise in maternal mortality stemming from inadequate public health care, and the lack of basic infrastructure, such as sewers and clean running water in neighborhoods, on the one hand, and deadly local police encounters, on the other, are two sides of the same forces of state violence. For example, it is impossible to understand the history of the militarization of policing in Brazil's northeastern city of Salvador without an understanding of the policing of Black-women-led *terreiros*, street vendors, sex workers, and activists, especially housing and land-rights activists. This approach to understanding state violence and the modern construction of the Bahian city calls for examining multiple forms of exclusion that Black and Indigenous people experience simultaneously, while being attentive to the "urgency of intersectionality," as Kimberlé Crenshaw expresses it.[35] Importantly, this approach also reminds us to not exceptionalize this moment with Bolsonaro as Brazil's elected racist and sexist president.

34 Quoted in Chalhoub et al., *Report of the LASA Fact-Finding Delegation*, 47.

35 Kimberlé Crenshaw, "The Urgency of Intersectionality," TedWomen 2016, October 2016, www.ted.com/talks/kimberle_crenshaw_the_urgency_of_intersectionality?language=en.

The future struggle

In October 2018, Joênia Wapichana became the first Indigenous woman elected to the national congress, and Erica Malunguinho, artist, educator, and creator of the urban *quilombo* and cultural space Aparelha Luzia, was the first trans woman elected to the São Paulo state congress. Numerous other Black women were elected to city councils and state congresses around the country, including those who had worked alongside Marielle Franco.

At an April 2018 conference on Brazil at Harvard's Afro-Latin American Research Institute, Franco was set to speak on a panel with Malunguinho that I chaired. We honored her memory, and at the moment of her scheduled speech, Erica looked into the camera that was transmitting a livestream to the world, with mostly Brazilians watching, and announced her candidacy for political office in the same party as Marielle. She expressed four key points that she considered necessary for the democratic transformation of Brazil: (1) the need to recognize Black people, Black women, and transgender people as hypervisible all over Brazilian cities (as domestic workers in apartment and office buildings, and in large numbers as prostitutes in red-light zones); (2) the hate and violence that targets these Black cis- and transgender women is in stark contrast to the demand for their labor, including sexual labor; (3) the right to education and work is key to the LGBTQ+ fight against anti-Black genocide, as Black transgender people are also killed every day; and (4) the antiracism and antisexism struggle has to be diasporic. Malunguinho recently reminded us in a Facebook post of the brutal murder of Evaldo dos Santos Rosa: "Who is mistaken 80 times? The name of this project is extermination, culture of death, genocide, necropolitics. This is the government and the legislature's public security proposal."[36]

As we reflect on the past year (more than a year since Franco's assassination and eight months since the election of Jair Bolsonaro), the Afro-futures that politicians like Erica Malunguinho envision will have to be a global project as espoused by her predecessors, such as Black left feminist activists Luiza Bairros, Lélia Gonzalez, Thereza Santos, and Franco, and will have to take seriously the global anti-Black genocide taking place in communities across the Americas.

---

36 Erica Malunguinho, "Erica Malunguinho Facebook post '*O que eu vou dizer ao meu filho?*'" Facebook, April 9, 2018, https://www.facebook.com/ericamalunguinho 50888/videos/289849225246509/.

This movement against anti-Black genocide—which is also a clear movement against resurgent white supremacy—has gained momentum in Brazil, especially in the days following the violent murder of nineteen-year-old Pedro Gonzaga in a Rio supermarket on February 15, 2019, by a security guard who held him in a chokehold. Despite the centuries-old plan to eliminate the "enemies within" (abolitionists, Black and Indigenous activists, and students, for example) in Brazil and throughout Latin America,[37] I understand the role of scholars and professors to be even more urgent. I understand the classroom as being ground zero for training new generations of thinkers and doers who envision a democratic society that includes all of us. A global Black liberation project is incomplete if we do not include, in a substantive way, the specific realities of the vast majority of Black men and women living in the Americas.

---

37 Lesley Gill, *The School of the Americas: Military Training and Political Violence in the Americas* (Durham: Duke University Press, 2004).

CHAPTER NINETEEN

The Anti-Imperialist Horizon

Alyosha Goldstein

Figure 19. International African Service Bureau's journal *International African Opinion*. Maitland-Sara Hallinan Collection, Modern Records Centre, University of Warwick.

Confronted with the predations of empire and global capitalism, peoples historically subjected to colonial occupation, racialized oppression, and imperial dominion have by necessity worked to build transnational alliances and to struggle in solidarity. During the 1920s and the 1930s, when what was named fascism first became a mass movement, a number of prominent anticolonial activists and scholars insisted that any condemnation of fascism that did not likewise denounce all forms of imperialism was both incomplete and inadequate. Writing in 1936, George Padmore noted the hypocrisy of England's rebuke of Nazi Germany "when fascism and racial terrorism are flourishing within their own Colonial Empire," maintaining that "[t]he fight against fascism cannot be separated from the right of all colonial peoples and subject races to Self-Determination."[1] The Indian National Congress, closely paraphrasing Jawaharlal Nehru, likewise declared in 1937 that "imperialism and fascism march hand in hand; they are blood brothers."[2] Earlier campaigns of outright genocide, such as by the United States against Native peoples in the process of continental colonization, by Germany against the Herero and Nama in South-West Africa (1904–1908), and by Belgium in what at the time was called the Congo Free State (1880–1908), were manifestations of this vicious confluence and at times understood as antecedents to the systematic mass slaughter perpetrated by Nazism.[3] But as Padmore, Nehru, and others pointed out, these horrors were not aberrations but rather fully within the continuum of conquest and colonial rule.

---

1   George Padmore, *How Britain Rules Africa* (New York: Negro Universities Press, 1969 [1936]), 4. Padmore also linked fascism and colonialism in his writing for the International Trade Union Committee of Negro Workers' publication, the *Negro Worker*, during the late 1920s and early 1930s, as well as in his book *The Life and Struggles of Negro Toilers* (London: R.I.L.U. Magazine, 1931), and subsequently in his articles for the Independent Labour Party periodicals *Controversy* and *New Leader* and in the International African Service Bureau's *International African Opinion*.

2   Quoted in Michele Louro, "Anti-Imperialism and Anti-Fascism Between the World Wars: The Perspective from India," in *Anti-Fascism in a Global Perspective: Transnational Networks, Exile Communities, and Radical Internationalism*, ed. Kasper Braskén, Nigel Copsey, and David J. Featherstone (New York: Routledge, 2020), 115.

3   Jeffrey Ostler, *Surviving Genocide: Native Nations and the United States from the American Revolution to Bleeding Kansas* (New Haven: Yale University Press, 2019); Zoé Samudzi, "Reparative Futurities: Postcolonial Materialities and the Ovaherero and Nama Genocide," in this volume; Adam Hochschild, *King Leopold's Ghost: A Story of Greed, Terror, and Heroism in Colonial Africa* (Boston: Houghton Mifflin, 1998); Jürgen Zimmerer and Joachim Zeller (eds.), *Genocide in German South-West Africa: The Colonial War of 1904–1908 and Its Aftermath* (London: Merlin Press, 2008).

Following the Second World War, with the struggle for decolonization escalating worldwide, writers of the Black and colonial diaspora reasserted the non-exceptionality of Nazism, and the fact that colonized and racially subjected peoples had long experienced the forms of genocide, forced labor, and rule by segregation, terror, and violence that engulfed Europe from the 1920s to the 1940s. In an often-quoted passage from *The World and Africa* (1946), W.E.B. Du Bois observed that "there was no Nazi atrocity—concentration camps, wholesale maiming and murder, defilement of women or ghastly blasphemy of children—which the Christian civilization of Europe had not long been practicing against colored folk in all parts of the world in the name of and for the defense of a Superior Race born to rule the world."[4] In *Discourse on Colonialism* (1950/1955), Aimé Césaire famously described Nazism as a colonial "boomerang effect" that provoked international outrage only because Hitler "applied to Europe colonialist procedures which until then had been reserved exclusively for the Arabs of Algeria, the 'coolies' of India, and the '[n*ggers]' of Africa."[5] Writing in 1957, Albert Memmi observed: "What is fascism, if not a regime of oppression for the benefit of a few? The entire administrative and political machinery of a colony has no other goal. . . . There is no doubt in the minds of those who have lived through it that colonialism is one variety of fascism."[6] In 1958, Claudia Jones argued: "Imperialism is the root cause of racialism. It is the ideology which upholds colonial rule and exploitation. It preaches the 'superiority' of the white race whose 'destiny' it is to rule over those with coloured skins, and to treat them with contempt. It is the ideology which breeds Fascism."[7] Grace Lee Boggs recalled an exchange of letters between James Boggs and Bertrand Russell in the early 1960s, where Boggs "patiently explain[ed] to Russell that what has historically been considered democracy in the United States has actually been fascism for millions of

4   W.E.B. Du Bois, *The World and Africa: An Inquiry into the Part which Africa has Played in World History* (New York: International Publishers, 1965 [1946]), 23.

5   Aimé Césaire, *Discourse on Colonialism*, trans. Joan Pinkham (New York: Monthly Review Press, 2000 [1950]), 36.

6   Albert Memmi, *The Colonizer and the Colonized* (New York: Orion Press, 1965 [1957]), 62–63. Thanks to Vaughn Rasberry, whose course syllabus is included in this edited collection, for bringing this passage to my attention.

7   Quoted in Carole Boyce Davies, *Left of Karl Marx: The Political Life of Black Communist Claudia Jones* (Durham: Duke University Press, 2007), 87. See also Charisse Burden-Stelly, ed., "Claudia Jones: Foremother of World Revolution," a special issue of *Journal of Intersectionality* 3, no. 1 (2019).

Negroes."[8]

Now, when in the United States the racist despotism of Donald Trump provides a lurid foil against which the Biden administration declares its benign governance and enlightened multiculturalism, the constitutive link between imperialism and fascism is crucial for parsing the historical continuities and disjunctures of the present moment. With such a framing in mind, this chapter sketches the relationship between anti-imperialism and antifascism as they have been articulated toward internationalist approaches to revolution, decolonization, and other global justice movements since the First World War. This partial outline is intended to suggest how an anti-imperialist internationalist project fully engaged in the specificities of anticolonial and antiracist struggle might be conceived as the horizon for struggles against fascism or variations on authoritarianism.[9] I situate this history of anti-imperialism in relation to the liberation struggles of Indigenous peoples in what George Manuel called the "Fourth World."[10] Native liberation is indispensable to collective struggle against and beyond the imperialist crisis of which fascism and its associated constellation of reactionary far-right movements are symptomatic and that neoliberal multiculturalism only further compounds.

This has at least partially to do with, but is not limited to, the specific ways in which variations on fascism and white supremacy continue to shape settler colonial nations and imperial nation-states. Thus, how might fascism—or forms of racist authoritarian revanchism akin to fascism—and imperialism be interconnected in especially acute and volatile ways in twenty-first-century colonial, settler colonial, and postcolonial contexts? The counterpart to the liberal and popular naming of fascism today is an

---

8   Grace Lee Boggs, *Living for Change: An Autobiography* (Minneapolis: University of Minnesota Press, 1998), 115.

9   From the location of what is presently the US, such a project would in part be to explicitly reactivate what Cynthia Young calls the "US third world left" further informed by Indigenous anticolonialism to include settler colonial contexts subjected to what Manu Karuka terms "continental imperialism." [Cynthia A. Young, *Soul Power: Culture, Radicalism, and the Making of a U.S. Third World Left* (Durham: Duke University Press, 2006); Manu Karuka, *Empire's Tracks: Indigenous Nations, Chinese Workers, and the Transcontinental Railroad* (Berkeley: University of California Press, 2019).] For a hemispheric perspective see, for instance, Juliet Hooker (ed.), *Black and Indigenous Resistance in the Americas: From Multiculturalism to Racist Backlash* (Lanham, MD: Lexington Books, 2020).

10 George Manuel and Michael Posluns, *The Fourth World: An Indian Reality* (Minneapolis: University of Minnesota Press, 2019 [1974]).

obstinate silence as to how the question of fascism is entangled with settler colonial occupation, imperial predation, and perpetual war. In a place such as what is presently the United States, where the electoral defeat of Trump appears to have diminished or narrowed concerns over contemporary fascism, a reinvigorated imperialism, militarism, and neoliberal multiculturalism has accompanied the reductive framing of far-right violence and white supremacy as a decidedly national predicament of political division and polarization. This framing fundamentally misdirects attention away from the far-reaching imperial entanglements of racial capitalism as a horizon of struggle.

Each of the contemporary regimes most frequently indicted as fascist or as harbingers of fascism to come—Donald Trump, Jair Bolsonaro, Narendra Modi, Benjamin Netanyahu, Recep Tayyip Erdoğan, Rodrigo Duterte, among others—have typically been treated as examples of discrete national trends associated primarily by authoritarian affinities but without more systemic or material reciprocities. After all, taken on their own terms, each regime insistently speaks its own version of the language of nationalist exceptionalism. Yet, the particular nationalism evoked in each case nonetheless remains inextricably entwined with the accelerated crisis of global capitalism, militarism, border imperialism, and racialized and anti-Muslim violence at once catalyzed by, and in excess of, nation-states. It is worth recalling that, even apart from those making an explicitly anti-colonial critique, during the 1920s and 1930s observers on the left emphasized fascism's international context as key for understanding its reactionary formation. For instance, building on Lenin's analysis of imperialism, Clara Zetkin argued in 1923 to the 3rd Enlarged Plenum of the Executive Committee of the Communist International that fascism emerged as a reaction to two specific historical conditions: (1) it was shaped by the inter-imperial conflicts that sought to resolve the world economic contraction of the 1870s–1890s through accelerated European and United States imperialism, negotiated through the frenzy of colonization and plunder sanctioned by maneuvers such as the 1884–1885 Berlin conference but ultimately erupting into the carnage of the First World War; and (2) it was a counterrevolutionary response to the successes of the insurrectionary international movements of communism and anarchism in the context of the Russian and Mexican Revolutions, as well the failed revolutions in

Germany, Hungary, Spain, and Egypt.[11]

During this time, the United States, as a settler colony and aspiring global empire, expanded its campaigns of overseas conquest and consolidated its continental colonial control through military force and then assimilationist efforts such as allotment and boarding schools for Native peoples. This was likewise the era of what Du Bois called the "counter-revolution of property" against the emancipation of enslaved people of African descent and the promise of radical Reconstruction.[12] United States imperialism gained rapacious momentum with—as only a partial list—the 1893 military takeover of the Hawaiian Kingdom, the 1898 wars for overseas colonization, protracted warfare in the Philippines, seizure of territory for the Panama Canal zone, occupation of Haiti (1915–1934), and the 1926 invasion of Nicaragua.[13] The surge of racist, anticommunist, and xenophobic retrenchment during and after the First World War included large-scale white terrorism (e.g., the massacres in East St. Louis in 1917; Elaine, Arkansas and Chicago in 1919; and Tulsa in 1921), the 1919–1920 Red Scare, the 1921 trial of Nicola Sacco and Bartolomeo Vanzetti, and the 1921 and 1924 legislation severely limiting immigration by racially targeted national quotas. State-sanctioned and extralegal racial violence in the US further proliferated with Jim Crow laws, lynching, and the revival of the Ku Klux Klan during the 1920s.[14] Following the decisive turning point of the First World War, the US as an ascendant world hegemon reproduced and expanded its capacities for racial terror, settler colonialism, global capitalism, and imperial militarism.

Starkly divergent internationalist projects emerged from the Russian

11 Clara Zetkin, *Fighting Fascism: How to Struggle and How to Win*, ed. Mike Taber and John Riddell (Chicago: Haymarket Books, 2017).

12 W.E.B. Du Bois, *Black Reconstruction in America, 1860–1880* (New York: Free Press, 1993 [1935]), 580–636.

13 Raphael Dalleo, *American Imperialism's Undead: The Occupation of Haiti and the Rise of Caribbean Anticolonialism* (Charlottesville: University of Virginia Press, 2016); Margaret Stevens, *Red International and Black Caribbean: Communists in New York City, Mexico and the West Indies, 1919–1939* (London: Pluto Press, 2017), 49–66; Peter James Hudson, *Bankers and Empire: How Wall Street Colonized the Caribbean* (Chicago: University of Chicago Press, 2017); Brandon R. Byrd, *The Black Republic: African Americans and the Fate of Haiti* (Philadelphia: University of Pennsylvania Press, 2020).

14 Megan Ming Francis, *Civil Rights and the Making of the Modern American State* (Cambridge: Cambridge University Press, 2014); David F. Krugler, *1919, The Year of Racial Violence: How African Americans Fought Back* (Cambridge: Cambridge University Press, 2015); Jeff Woods, *Black Struggle, Red Scare: Segregation and Anti-Communism in the South, 1948-1968* (Baton Rouge: Louisiana State University Press, 2004).

Revolution and the devastation of the so-called Great War. For the liberal internationalism of Woodrow Wilson and Jan Smuts, given institutional form in the League of Nations, this moment was a recalibration of the methods of world order intended to shore up capitalism and global white supremacy under the auspices of an ostensibly kinder, gentler tutelary disposition. Compelled by the threat of anticolonial insurgency to offer some form of symbolic value for colonized peoples as a counterpoint to the Communist International, the League of Nations promised, if did not fully deliver, a platform for those seeking to gain international leverage against colonial rule. Wilson's infamous snub of Nguyễn Ái Quốc (later known as Ho Chi Minh) at Versailles in 1919 seems to be retrospectively more indicative of the new order than any of the US president's public proclamations or the grand declarations of the League.

Nevertheless, the creation of a multilateral forum by colonial powers acknowledging the right of self-determination provided a new space for Indigenous[15] and colonized and racially subjected peoples to petition for redress at an international scale. This was, of course, not a unique moment for Indigenous peoples, whose political alliances and confederacies were already in effect international relations that long preceded colonization as well as subsequently serving directly anticolonial objectives. (As was the case with, for example, the Pueblo Revolt of 1680, the Andean insurrection of the early 1780s, and Tecumseh's confederacy during the early nineteenth century.) Zitkála-Šá, Charles Eastman, Carlos Montezuma, Laura Cornelius Kellogg, and others affiliated with the Society of American Indians were among those who sought to make use of the promise of the League.[16] The Cayuga leader Deskaheh (Levi General), the Australian Aboriginal activist Anthony Martin Fernando, the Māori emissary Tahupotiki Wiremu Ratana, and Ta'isi Olaf Nelson on behalf of Samoa were among a number of petitioners who traveled to Geneva in pursuit of redress for colonial dispossession.[17] In Peru, by contrast, José Carlos Mariátegui's conception of

---

15 My use of the term Indigenous here is of course anachronistic—this was not yet the global category it became during the 1970s—but is intended to indicate the range of peoples at the time who might now identify as Indigenous.

16 Nick Estes, *Our History Is the Future: Standing Rock Versus the Dakota Access Pipeline, and the Long Tradition of Indigenous Resistance* (London and New York: Verso, 2019), 214–422; David Myer Temin, "Our Democracy: Laura Cornelius Kellogg's Decolonial-Democracy," *Perspectives on Politics* (2020).

17 Joëlle Rostkowski, "The Redman's Appeal for Justice: Deskaheh and the League of Nations," in *Indians and Europe: An Interdisciplinary Collection of Essays*, ed. Christian F.

revolution during the 1920s was predicated on alliances with Indigenous peoples rather than an appeal to liberal internationalism. "Fascism," he wrote, "collaborates with the League of Nations."[18] Mariátegui argued that since the masses "are four-fifths Indian . . . our socialism would not be Peruvian—nor would it be socialism—if it did not establish its solidarity principally with the Indian" with this solidarity in turn serving as the basis of anti-imperialist politics in Peru.[19]

The Communist International (the Third International or Comintern), from its prefiguration at the 1915 Zimmerwald conference until the Stalinist purges of the mid to late 1930s, was animated in part by the failures of the Second International to either oppose imperialist nationalisms or to substantively include colonized peoples. The Comintern thus sought in various ways to build anti-imperialist alliances with colonized peoples on behalf of the project of world revolution.[20] During its meeting in 1920, at sessions devoted to the "National and Colonial Questions," M. N. Roy and V. I. Lenin famously debated how best to bring together a global communist movement and anticolonial liberation.[21] Korean Communist Party leader Pak Chin-Sun argued that "the whole history of the ignominious collapse of the Second International has shown that the Western European proletariat cannot win the fight against its bourgeoisie as long as the

Feest (Lincoln: University of Nebraska Press, 1999); Fiona Paisley, *The Lone Protestor: A. M. Fernando in Australia and Europe* (Canberra: Aboriginal Studies Press, 2012); Robbie Shilliam, *The Black Pacific: Anti-Colonial Struggles and Oceanic Connections* (New York, NY: Bloomsbury, 2015); Tracey Banivanua Mar, *Decolonisation and the Pacific: Indigenous Globalisation and the Ends of Empire* (Cambridge: Cambridge University Press, 2016), 82–113.

18 José Carlos Mariátegui, "Nationalism and Internationalism" (1924), in *José Carlos Mariátegui: An Anthology*, ed. and trans. Harry E. Vanden and Marc Becker (New York: Monthly Review Press, 2011), 259.

19 Quoted in Eric Helleiner and Antulio Rosales, "Toward Global IPE: The Overlooked Significance of the Haya-Mariátegui Debate," *International Studies Review* 19, no. 4 (2017): 683.

20 R. Craig Nation, *War on War: Lenin, the Zimmerwald Left, and the Origins of Communist Internationalism* (Chicago: Haymarket Books, 2009 [1989]); Oleksa Drachewych, *The Communist International, Anti-Imperialism and Racial Equality in British Dominions* (New York: Routledge, 2018); Stevens, *Red International and Black Caribbean*; Ali Raza, *Revolutionary Pasts: Communist Internationalism in Colonial India* (Cambridge: Cambridge University Press, 2020); Fredrik Petersson, "Imperialism and the Communist International," *Journal of Labor and Society* 20 (March 2017); Tom Buchanan, "'The Dark Millions in the Colonies are Unavenged': Anti-Fascism and Anti-Imperialism in the 1930s," *Contemporary European History* 25, no. 4 (2016).

21 John Riddell (ed.), *Workers of the World and Oppressed Peoples, Unite!: Proceedings and Documents of the Second Congress, 1920* (New York: Pathfinder, 1991), 271–368.

bourgeoisie has a source of strength in the colonies."[22] Ahmed Sultanzadeh of the Communist Party of Iran commented that while the Second International "drew up elegant resolutions," these were deliberated and "adopted without the participation of representatives" from the colonies and "were never put into effect." According to Sultanzadeh, the 1920 meeting "marked the first time that this question is being dealt with thoroughly, with the participation of representatives of almost all of the colonized and semicolonized countries."[23] The Comintern's position on the "Negro Question" emerged in tandem with this new orientation, with Claude McKay and Otto Huiswoud invited to address the Fourth Congress in 1922 and subsequent debates leading to the resolutions of 1928 and 1930 on African Americans in the US South as an oppressed nation with a rightful claim to self-determination. The League Against Imperialism established in 1927, and the founding of the International Trade Union Committee of Negro Workers in 1928, were significant if nonetheless fraught organizational initiatives that followed from this expanded alignment.[24]

The so-called interwar period was in fact a time of intensifying anticolonial insurgency and imperial counterrevolution. The militant internationalism of the 1920s and 1930s emerged in conjunction with widespread anticolonial insurrection.[25] The ongoing Irish uprising, the Iraqi Revolt of 1920, the Rif War of 1921–1926 in North Africa, the Turkish War of Independence, the Palestinian uprisings of the 1920s and 1930s, the Syrian Revolt of 1925, the communist rebellions of 1926–1927 in Indonesia, and Samoa's Mau movement each belied the self-serving platitudes of imperial prerogative. In the Philippines, despite his public criticism of US colonial rule, Commonwealth president Manuel Quezon viciously suppressed the independence movement and outlawed the Communist Party of the

---

22 Pak Chin-Sun, "Session 5, July 28," in *Workers of the World and Oppressed Peoples, Unite!*, 313.

23 Ahmed Sultanzadeh, "Session 5, July 28," 303.

24 Michele Louro, Carolien Stolte, Heather Streets-Salter, and Sana Tannoury-Karam (eds.), *The League against Imperialism: Lives and Afterlives* (Dordrecht: Leiden University Press, 2020); Michael Goebel, *Anti-Imperial Metropolis: Interwar Paris and the Seeds of Third World Nationalism* (Cambridge: Cambridge University Press, 2015); Holger Weiss, *Framing a Radical African Atlantic: African American Agency, West African Intellectuals and the International Trade Union Committee of Negro Workers* (Leiden: Brill, 2014); Stevens, *Red International and Black Caribbean*.

25 Ali Raza, Franziska Roy, and Benjamin Zachariah (eds.), *The Internationalist Moment: South Asia, Worlds, and World Views, 1917–1939* (Los Angeles: Sage, 2015).

Philippines.[26] Pedro Albizu Campos led the National Party seeking Puerto Rican independence, while the US responded with brutal repression, including the 1937 Ponce massacre, during the heyday of its "good neighbor" policy.[27]

Yet, by the mid-1930s, sectarian conflicts within the Communist International had fractured a key political forum for connecting antifascism and anti-imperialism. John Munro describes the decade between 1935 and 1945 as the "antifascist interregnum," during which the Popular Front-era Comintern largely withdrew support for anticolonial and anti-imperial movements in favor of prioritizing alliances with imperialist powers against the threat of fascist expansionism.[28] Despite the loss of the Comintern's infrastructure, African diasporic and colonized peoples continued to link antifascism and anti-imperialist solidarity further driven by the exigencies of the Italian invasion of Ethiopia (Abyssinia), the Spanish Civil War (1936–1939), and subsequent rule of Francisco Franco in Spain (1939–1975) and the Estado Novo in Portugal (1933–1974). This was in a context where the United States was increasingly hostile to supposedly misdirected antifascism. US propagandists, policymakers, and federal agencies sought to redirect campaigns against fascism toward virulent anticommunism and Cold War bipolar opposition to left internationalism. The FBI infamously targeted Abraham Lincoln Brigade volunteers who fought against Franco in the Spanish Civil War as "premature antifascists." Such reactionary efforts in the US to preempt movements for solidarity and antiracist internationalism intensified in reaction to the high-profile campaign to raise global awareness against the false charges in the Scottsboro trial and became pervasive by the early Cold War.[29]

---

26 Allan E. S. Lumba, "Left Alone with the Colony," in this volume.

27 Mónica A. Jiménez, "Puerto Rico under the Colonial Gaze: Oppression, Resistance and the Myth of the Nationalist Enemy," *Latino Studies* 18, no. 1 (March 2020); José M. Atiles-Osoria, "The Criminalization of Anti-colonial Struggle in Puerto Rico," in *Counter-Terrorism and State Political Violence: The "War on Terror" as Terror*, ed. Scott Poynting and David Whyte (New York: Routledge, 2012).

28 John Munro, *The Anticolonial Front: The African American Freedom Struggle and Global Decolonisation, 1945–1960* (Cambridge: Cambridge University Press, 2017).

29 Susan D. Pennybacker, *From Scottsboro to Munich: Race and Political Culture in 1930s Britain* (Princeton: Princeton University Press, 2009); Dayo F. Gore, *Radicalism at the Crossroads: African American Women Activists in the Cold War* (New York: NYU Press, 2011).

Mussolini's war of conquest in Ethiopia in 1935 was a pivotal moment in the overt confluence and blatant assertion of colonialism and fascism. The invasion sparked widespread mobilization throughout the African diaspora.[30] The International African Friends of Ethiopia formed in London in 1935, serving as the basis for the International African Service Bureau (IASB) founded in 1937 by George Padmore, C.L.R. James, Amy Ashwood Garvey, T. Ras Makonnen, Jomo Kenyatta, and I.T.A. Wallace-Johnson. As Minkah Makalani argues, a significant aspect of the Bureau was its refusal of "the role of the diasporic vanguard that would direct colonial struggles," describing its purpose instead as supporting "the demands of Africans and other colonial peoples for democratic rights, civil liberties, and self-determination." In order to build a "link between Africans at home (in Africa) and the Africans abroad," the IASB combined analysis of imperialism and colonialism with "facilitating intercolonial exchanges and engagements" through its monthly journal, the *International African Opinion*, and other venues.[31] The IASB was indicative of a Pan-Africanist break with the Comintern during the late 1930s that sought to promote a left anticapitalist, anticolonial internationalism attentive to race and racism.[32]

---

30 Imaobong D. Umoren, *Race Women Internationalists: Activist-Intellectuals and Global Freedom Struggles* (Berkeley: University of California Press, 2018); Cheryl Higashida, *Black Internationalist Feminism: Women Writers of the Black Left, 1945–1995* (Urbana: University of Illinois Press, 2011); Brenda Gayle Plummer, *Rising Wind: Black Americans and U.S. Foreign Affairs, 1935–1960* (Chapel Hill: University of North Carolina Press, 1996); Penny M. Von Eschen, *Race against Empire: Black Americans and Anticolonialism, 1937–1957* (Ithaca: Cornell University Press, 1997). For accounts focused specifically on the Italian invasion of Ethiopia and the Spanish Civil War, see: Joseph Fronczak, "Local People's Global Politics: A Transnational History of the Hands Off Ethiopia Movement of 1935," *Diplomatic History* 39, no. 2 (2015); Mark Falcoff and Fredrick B. Pike (eds.), *The Spanish Civil War, 1936–39: American Hemispheric Perspectives* (Lincoln: University of Nebraska Press, 1982); Ariel Mae Lambe, *No Barrier Can Contain It: Cuban Antifascism and the Spanish Civil War* (Chapel Hill: University of North Carolina Press, 2019).

31 Minkah Makalani, "An International African Opinion: Amy Ashwood Garvey and C.L.R. James in Black Radical London," in *Escape from New York: The New Negro Renaissance beyond Harlem,* ed. Davarian L. Baldwin and Minkah Makalani (Minneapolis: University of Minnesota Press, 2013), 90. International African Service Bureau Press Release, n.d., and "The International African Service Bureau for the Defense of Africans and Peoples of African Descent," pamphlet, quoted in Makalani, 90. Also see Anthony Bogues, "Radical Anti-colonial Thought, Anti-colonial Internationalism and the Politics of Human Solidarities," in *International Relations and Non-Western Thought: Imperialism, Colonialism, and Investigations of Global Modernity,* ed. Robbie Shilliam (New York: Routledge, 2011).

32 Umoren, *Race Women*; Annette K. Joseph-Gabriel, *Reimagining Liberation: How Black Women Transformed Citizenship in the French Empire* (Urbana: University of Illinois Press, 2019); Hakim Adi, *Pan-Africanism and Communism: The Communist International, Africa and the Diaspora, 1919–1939* (Trenton: Africa World Press, 2013); Keisha N. Blain, *Set the World on Fire: Black Nationalist Women and the Global Struggle for Freedom* (Philadelphia:

Black diasporic internationalism and anticolonial coalition-building gained momentum following the Second World War. The World Trade Union Conference, held in London in February 1945, set the stage for the All Colonial Peoples' Conference (also called the Subject Peoples' Conference) four months later, with its manifesto declaring that "for peoples in the colonies, Allied Victory would have no real meaning 'if it does not lead to their own liberation from the tentacles of imperialism.'"[33] Following the conference, a committee was created and charged with drafting a program and constitution with the goal of establishing a "Colonial International."[34] Although this aim did not materialize, the Fifth Pan-African Congress, held in October 1945 in Manchester, expanded on these themes. The Congress issued a "Challenge to the Colonial Powers," asserting that "we are unwilling to starve any longer while doing the world's drudgery" to prop up "a discredited imperialism. We condemn the monopoly of capital and the rule of private wealth."[35] The Congress' "Declaration to the Colonial Workers, Farmers, and Intellectuals" affirmed "all Colonies must be free from foreign imperialist control, whether political or economic . . . Colonial and Subject Peoples of the World—Unite!"[36]

Regardless of the ostentatious proclamations of the 1941 Atlantic Charter and the 1945 United Nations Conference in San Francisco, the imperial powers had little initial interest in substantively addressing the issue of colonialism or the full inclusion of colonized peoples in their new multilateral forum. The UN largely rebooted the League of Nations mandate system in the form of international trusteeship. In *Discourse on Colonialism*, Aimé Césaire references Truman's pronouncement that "the time of the old colonialism has passed" in order to note that, contrary

University of Pennsylvania Press, 2019); Erik S. McDuffie, *Sojourning for Freedom: Black Women, American Communism, and the Making of Black Left Feminism* (Durham: Duke University Press, 2011); Minkah Makalani, *In the Cause of Freedom: Radical Black Internationalism from Harlem to London, 1917–1939* (Chapel Hill: University of North Carolina Press, 2011); Carole Boyce Davies, *Left of Karl Marx: The Political Life of Black Communist Claudia Jones* (Durham: Duke University Press, 2008); Robin D. G. Kelley, *Freedom Dreams: The Black Radical Imagination* (Boston: Beacon, 2002).

33 Quoted in Hakim Adi, "Pan-Africanism in Britain: Background to the 1945 Manchester Conference," in *The 1945 Manchester Pan-African Congress Revisited*, ed. Hakim Adi and Marika Sherwood (London: New Beacon Books, 1995), 20.

34 Von Eschen, *Race against Empire*, 44–68.

35 "Colonial and . . . Coloured Unity: A Programme of Action—History of the Pan-African Congress," ed. George Padmore, in *The 1945 Manchester Pan-African Congress Revisited*, 55.

36 "Colonial and . . . Coloured Unity," 56.

to US posturing, "this means that American high finance considers the time has come to raid every colony in the world." Césaire wryly observes: "American domination—the only domination from which . . . one never recovers unscarred."[37] Partially carrying forward and expanding on the agendas of the anticolonial and Pan-Africanist meetings in 1945, while also contending with the new alignments of Cold War, the 1955 Bandung Conference, the 1957 Afro-Asian People's Solidarity Conference in Cairo, and the 1966 Tricontinental Conference of African, Asian, and Latin American Peoples in Havana further developed the means for an anti-imperialist internationalism.[38]

Still largely left out of such oppositional solidarity, however, were Indigenous peoples under settler colonial rule.[39] This disconnection was buttressed by the United States' successful maneuver in 1960 to exclude peoples under settler colonial occupation—who were not separated by "saltwater" or otherwise territorially noncontiguous with respect to the colonizing country—from qualifying for recognition as a "non-self-governing territory" under Chapter XI of the UN Charter and hence ineligible for

---

37 Césaire, *Discourse on Colonialism*, 76, 77.

38 See Adom Getachew, *Worldmaking after Empire: The Rise and Fall of Self-Determination* (Princeton: Princeton University Press, 2019); Jini Kim Watson, *Cold War Reckonings: Authoritarianism and the Genres of Decolonization* (New York: Fordham University Press, 2021); Luis Eslava, Michael Fakhri, and Vasuki Nesiah (eds.), *Bandung, Global History, and International Law: Critical Pasts and Pending Futures* (Cambridge: Cambridge University Press, 2017); Quỳnh N. Phạm and Robbie Shilliam (eds.), *Meanings of Bandung: Postcolonial Orders and Decolonial Visions* (New York: Rowman & Littlefield, 2016); Christopher J. Lee (ed.), *Making a World after Empire: The Bandung Moment and Its Political Afterlives* (Athens: Ohio University Press, 2010); Su Lin Lewis and Carolien Stolte, "Other Bandungs: Afro-Asian Internationalisms in the Early Cold War," *Journal of World History* 30, nos. 1–2 (June 2019): 1–19; Reem Abou-El-Fadl, "Building Egypt's Afro-Asian Hub: Infrastructures of Solidarity and the 1957 Cairo Conference," *Journal of World History* 30, nos. 1–2 (June 2019): 157–192; Anne Garland Mahler, *From the Tricontinental to the Global South: Race, Radicalism, and Transnational Solidarity* (Durham: Duke University Press, 2018); Quito J. Swan, *Pauulu's Diaspora: Black Internationalism and Environmental Justice* (Gainesville: University Press of Florida, 2020); Vijay Prashad, *The Darker Nations: A People's History of the Third World* (New York: The New Press, 2007). For an especially illuminating account of the Tricontinental Conference from the perspective of US counterinsurgency, see United States Senate, Committee on the Judiciary, Subcommittee to Investigate the Administration of the Internal Security Act and Other Internal Security Laws, *The Tricontinental Conference of African, Asian, and Latin American Peoples: A Staff Study* (Washington, DC: Government Printing Office, 1966).

39 Ronald Niezen, *The Origins of Indigenism: Human Rights and the Politics of Identity* (Berkeley: University of California Press, 2003); S. James Anaya, *Indigenous Peoples in International Law* (New York: Oxford University Press, 2004).

decolonization according the UN framework.[40] Native peoples under US colonial occupation were forced to devote their energy to fighting against "termination"—policy implemented by US Congress in the 1950s that aimed at ending US recognition of Indigenous peoples' political authority, established treaty rights, and collective existence. But by the early 1970s, Red Power activists began to reassert this shared anti-imperial horizon for action and militant redress.

Fascism was again an important referent at this time. During the 1960s and 1970s, the Black Panther Party (BPP) consistently denounced the United States as fascist for its unremitting racist police violence, imperial war in Vietnam, and ubiquitous capitalist predation. The BPP's 1969 United Front Against Fascism conference assembled a broad coalition of activists with the intention of developing a "common revolutionary ideology and political program which answers the basic desires and needs of all people in fascist, capitalist, racist America." Party cofounder and chairman Bobby Seale opened the conference, insisting that "we will not be free until Brown, Red, Yellow, Black, and all other peoples of color are unchained."[41] Penny Nakatsu of the Asian American Political Alliance spoke at the conference as someone from "a generation of children born in [US] concentration camps," noting the continuity from Executive Order 9066 in 1942 to the McCarran Internal Security Act of 1950 to then pending legislative domestic security updates as indicative of "American fascism today" and a threat to "all people . . . who will work for liberation, who will work for the defeat of fascism and imperialism."[42] Attributions of fascism in this sense were not limited to the US context. Describing her experience in Canada, Lee Maracle wrote in 1975: "Toronto is really quite a fascist town; a lot of reactionary politics tied with Nazi-type racism against East Indians, Blacks, Native Americans, and so on. . . . [The fascists are] anti-Indian,

---

40 Alyosha Goldstein, "Toward a Genealogy of the U.S. Colonial Present," in *Formations of United States Colonialism*, ed. Alyosha Goldstein (Durham: Duke University Press, 2014); Banivanua Mar, *Decolonisation and the Pacific*, 114–146.

41 Quoted in Robyn C. Spencer, "The Black Panther Party and Black Anti-Fascism in the United States," January 26, 2017, https://dukeupress.wordpress.com/2017/01/26/the-black-panther-party-and-black-anti-fascism-in-the-united-states/.

42 Penny Nakatsu, "Speech at the United Front Against Fascism Conference, July 1969," in *The U.S. Anti-fascism Reader*, ed. Bill V. Mullen and Christopher Vials (London and New York: Verso, 2020), 271, 272.

anticommunist, anti-everything that wasn't white and patriotic."[43] To invoke fascism at this time was both to identify the racist, militaristic, and colonialist authoritarianism that underwrote liberal settler capitalist nation-states (on behalf of freedom for the white and privileged and oppression for everyone else) and to name an overarching framework against which to assert anticapitalist, antiracist, and anti-imperial solidarities and movement building.

Among the many groups inspired by the Panthers' combination of community survival programs, self-defense, and revolutionary intercommunalism (a version of internationalism focusing on translocal solidarities against racial capitalism) were Indigenous organizations such as the Polynesian Panther Party in Aotearoa/New Zealand, the Australian Black Panther Party, the Native Alliance for Red Power in Canada, and the American Indian Movement (AIM) in the United States.[44] Protest initiatives like the Aboriginal Tent Embassy, established in Canberra, Australia in 1972, mobilized through the framework of Black Power and underscored the international setting of colonial occupation. Gary Foley recalls that the organizers of the Embassy sardonically concluded that "the government had declared us aliens in our own land and so we need an Embassy."[45] A speaker at an Embassy event mused, "I don't know whether we should be trying to establish diplomatic relations with [the Australian government]. I believe they should be trying to establish diplomatic relations with us," but he doubted they would "due to their fascist right attitude."[46] In the aftermath of a violent police offensive against the Embassy, Roberta "Bobbi" Sykes observed that "escalating oppression has forced the people to realize the government's policy of assimilation is false and that the real policy is

---

43 Lee Maracle, *Bobbi Lee: Indian Rebel*, 2nd edition (Toronto: Women's Press, 2017 [1975]), 60, 62.

44 Glen Sean Coulthard, "Once were Maoists: Third World Currents in Fourth World Anticolonialism, Vancouver, 1967–1975," in *Routledge Handbook of Critical Indigenous Studies*, ed. Brendan Hokowhitu, Aileen Moreton-Robinson, Linda Tuhiwai-Smith, Chris Andersen, and Steve Larkin (New York: Routledge, 2021); Gary Foley, Andrew Schaap, and Edwina Howell (eds.), *The Aboriginal Tent Embassy: Sovereignty, Black Power, Land Rights, and the State* (New York: Routledge, 2014); Melani Anae, with Lautofa Iuli and Leilani Burgoyne (eds.), *Polynesian Panthers: Pacific Protest and Affirmative Action in Aotearoa New Zealand, 1971–1981* (Wellington: HUIA Publishers, 2015).

45 Quoted in Edwina Howell, "Black Protest—By Any Means Necessary," in *The Aboriginal Tent Embassy*, 76.

46 "Speeches at the Aboriginal Tent Embassy," in *The Aboriginal Tent Embassy*, 178.

genocide."[47] Other initiatives during this period were conceived as mechanisms for publicizing and pursuing Indigenous demands for self-determination multilaterally. Toward this goal, AIM founded the International Indian Treaty Council in 1974 and the World Council of Indigenous Peoples was established in 1975.[48]

The Secwépemc (Shuswap) Nation leader and founding member of the World Council of Indigenous Peoples George Manuel's idea of the "Fourth World" generatively linked disparate anticolonial struggles. After spending time in Tanzania during the early 1970s, Manuel drew on this experience in his theorization of the "Fourth World" as a political project of building alliances between Indigenous peoples worldwide and a critical revisioning of Third World liberation. In his introduction to the republication of Manuel's book, Glen Coulthard argues that the conception of the "Fourth World" is a "crucial Indigenous intervention into the ideological influence that the decolonization struggles for the 'Third World' had on the North American left's critique of racial capitalism and imperialism in the 1960s and early 1970s." According to Coulthard, "the inherited conceptual apparatus associated with this 'turn to the Third World' provided Indigenous organizers with an appealing international language of political contestation structured around the concept of *self-determination*—economically, politically, and culturally—that they not only inherited but also fundamentally adapted and transformed through a critical engagement with their own local, land-informed situations."[49] If some elements of this radical international Indigenous movement were subsequently rerouted toward juridical arenas and building the momentum to achieve the 2007 UN Declaration on the Rights of Indigenous Peoples, others remained committed to militant direct action and frontline community organizing for land and water defense as the basis for international solidarity and global decolonization.

---

47 Bobbi Sykes, "'Hope's Ragged Symbol,' *Nation Review*, July 29–August 4, 1972," in *The Aboriginal Tent Embassy*, 168.

48 Alyosha Goldstein, *Poverty in Common: The Politics of Community Action during the American Century* (Durham: Duke University Press, 2012), 233–243; Roxanne Dunbar Ortiz, *The Great Sioux Nation: Sitting in Judgment on America* (Lincoln: University of Nebraska Press, 2013 [1977]); Estes, *Our History Is the Future*, 201–245; Glen Sean Coulthard, "A Fourth World Resurgent," in *The Fourth World*; Jonathan Crossen, *Decolonization, Indigenous Internationalism, and the World Council of Indigenous Peoples* (PhD thesis, History, University of Waterloo, Ontario, Canada, 2014).

49 Coulthard, "A Fourth World Resurgent," in *The Fourth World*, x.

The solidarities of the Fourth World that comprise Indigenous internationalism are key to the unfinished global project of dismantling colonialism and imperialism. This radical worldmaking project was in certain respects historically neutralized and redirected through official UN protocols for decolonization, with its nation-state-based framework, and the neocolonial instruments of debt entrapment and fiscal oversight deployed by multilateral financial institutions such as the World Bank and the International Monetary Fund. Today, settler colonial counterinsurgency labels and tyrannizes Native activists as terrorists, capitalist extractivism pursues its catastrophic assault on the human and more-than-human world, Indigenous land defenders and organizers throughout the Americas—such as Berta Cáceres or the Awá People in Colombia—are assassinated with impunity, vigilante and police violence target unsheltered and otherwise vulnerable Native peoples, and the escalation of missing and murdered Indigenous women and girls continues.[50] Fully linking settler colonial contexts and the overarching parasitism and avarice of empires is work that remains to be done, although Native-led coalitional challenges to the global infrastructure of fossil fuel extraction and the platform of organizations such as the Red Nation offer important ways forward with a focus on anti-imperialist internationalism and the militant politics of solidarity.[51]

In the United States, mainstream denunciations of Donald Trump as a fascist menace—ranging from former secretary of state Madeleine Albright to the cofounder of the Federalist Society Steven Calabresi—have sought to recuperate US exceptionalism and disavow the constitutive global economies of dispossession and violence that are the US imperial nation-state.[52] In fact, both Trump's revivification of "America First" and the Democratic Party's neoliberal multiculturalism and "one indispensable nation" rely on exceptionalism and disavowal in different ways to politically cohere

50 Joanne Barker, *Red Scare: The State's Indigenous Terrorist* (Berkeley: University of California Press, 2021); Nick Estes, Melanie K. Yazzie, Jennifer Nez Denetdale, and David Correia, *Red Nation Rising: From Bordertown Violence to Native Liberation* (Oakland: PM Press, 2021); Heather Dorries, Robert Henry, David Hugill, Tyler McCreary, and Julie Tomiak (eds.), *Settler City Limits: Indigenous Resurgence and Colonial Violence in the Urban Prairie West* (Winnipeg: University of Manitoba Press, 2019).

51 The Red Nation, *The Red Deal: Indigenous Action to Save Our Earth* (Brooklyn: Common Notions, 2021).

52 Madeleine Albright, *Fascism: A Warning* (New York: HarperCollins, 2018); Caleb Ecarma, "Conservatives Are Finally Using the F-Word for Trump's 'Delay the Election' Tweet," *Vanity Fair*, July 31, 2020, https://www.vanityfair.com/news/2020/07/conservatives-finally-using-fascist-donald-trumps-delay-election-tweet.

and give credence to the premise of US "democracy." To understand fascism or similar authoritarianisms and white supremacy as constitutively linked to imperialism and colonialism is to refuse the framing of such recent mainstream debates. Fascism as a heuristic can be useful in this moment for addressing the crises and contradictions of imperialism (as an organizing imperative for capitalism rather than one sequential stage) and settler colonial occupation. Ultimately, it is the collective work toward the anti-imperial horizon that matters most of all.

Colonial Fascism
A Syllabus

Vaughn Rasberry

Introduction

The worldwide ascendency of white nationalism and ultra-right-wing move-ments has prompted a renewed interest in fascism and led many observers to connect present developments with past events. In the twentieth cen-tury, fascism at the state level was characterized by racism, xenophobia, ultranationalism, dictatorial governance, and hostility to liberalism and communism—elements all on display among contemporary movements and governments worldwide.

Yet, as historian Priya Satya has asked, how well served is political anal-ysis by drawing analogies between developments today and the fascist formations of the 1930s? Do such analogies obscure deeper genealogies of racism and fascist governmentality in the US or elsewhere? How do we take measure of today's reactionary climate by referencing dark chapters of the past? In contrast to conventional narratives that situate fascism chiefly within Europe's internal historical development, this syllabus addresses these questions by organizing fascism around a constellation of global themes pertaining to racism and colonialism.

From its inception in Mussolini's Italy in the late 1920s, as the stan-dard historiography goes, the fascist progenitors of the *sistema totalitaria*, rejecting what they perceived as the political weakness, materialism, indi-vidualism, and spiritual degeneracy of liberal democracy, envisioned a *total state* defined by dictatorial control, ideological unity, ultranationalism, belligerent expansionism, and obliteration of the division between public and private spheres. One of Mussolini's earliest opponents invented the term, which referred to a foundational repressive act: Mussolini's successful effort to alter Italy's constitution and extant election laws in order to con-solidate power. Only a few months later, the socialist Giovanni Amendola was able to speak expansively of a "totalitarian spirit" animating the fascist movement, one that eventually swept continental politics. The "totalitarian spirit" exalted ideological commitment and collective valor again the stereotypically bourgeois traits of moral flabbiness, spiritual emptiness, political quiescence, and fear of violent death.

Yet fascists in Italy, as elsewhere, aimed not only to transform the nation-state but to expand it with the tools of empire—and in this respect they sought to emulate the liberal empires of the early twentieth century, especially Great Britain. After the Second World War, anticolonial writers articulated sophisticated connections between fascism, colonialism, and liberal empire. "Every colonial nation," writes Albert Memmi in *The Colonizer and the Colonized* (1957), "carries the seeds of fascist temptation in its bosom."[1] Echoing Hannah Arendt's and Aimé Césaire's conceptions of the "boomerang effect" or "*choc en retour*" (reverse shock or backlash, as Michael Rothberg renders the term), Memmi elaborates the dialectical concept of "colonial fascism," a process in which an imperial regime imports repressive governance into a colony, expands this governance into a totalitarian system, and exports it back into the "mother country" as a renewable source of political and social conflict. Expanding the realm of fascism to include not only the movements of Mussolini and Hitler but also liberal colonial regimes, Memmi asks:

> What is fascism, if not a regime of oppression for the benefit of a few? The entire administrative and political machinery of a colony has no other goal. The human relationships have arisen from the severest exploitation, founded on inequality and contempt, guaranteed by police authoritarianism. There is no doubt in the minds of those who have lived through it that colonialism is one variety of fascism. . . . This totalitarian aspect which even democratic regimes take on in their colonies is contradictory in appearance only. Being represented among the colonized by colonialists, they can have no other.[2]

For the Tunisian Jewish writer, this aspect appears contradictory only to subjects whose proximity to democracy's self-mythology has shielded them from racial exclusion and persecution.

Readers will note that this syllabus does not capture all or most of the

---

1   Albert Memmi, *The Colonizer and the Colonized* (Boston: Beacon Press, 1965 [1957]), 62.

2   Memmi, *The Colonizer and the Colonized*, 62–63.

national varieties of fascism and many of the historical manifestations of fascist initiative are necessarily excluded. Instead, it seeks to capture the connections among fascist regimes and ideologies as they intersect with colonialism, from the fin-de-siècle age of imperialism to the present.

Key words

totalitarianism and total war
imperialism
counterfactual history
memory (e.g., queer memory, multidirectional memory)
racial capitalism
enlightenment
antifascist left
historical analogy

Reading list (by topic)

Definitions: Fascism, Neofascism, Post-fascism

What is fascism and what are fascisms? What is the relationship between the fascist movements of the 1930s and today's ultranationalist and white supremacist movements? How does fascism relate to terms such as populism and totalitarianism? What are the historical origins of fascism? How have origin stories of fascism changed over the last half century and why? Are concepts derived from the history of fascism useful for analyzing contemporary political developments?

Robert Paxton, *The Anatomy of Fascism* (New York: Vintage Books, 2005).

Enzo Traverso, *The New Faces of Fascism: Populism and the Far Right*, trans. David Broder (London and New York: Verso, 2019).

Susan Sontag, "Fascinating Fascism," *The New York Review of Books* (February 6, 1975), https://www.nybooks.com/articles/1975/02/06/fascinating-fascism/.

Umberto Eco, "Ur-Fascism," *The New York Review of Books* (June 22, 1995), https://www.nybooks.com/articles/1995/06/22/ur-fascism/.

Nikhil Pal Singh, "The Afterlife of Fascism," *South Atlantic Quarterly*, Vol. 105, No. 1 (Winter 2006): 71–93.

Leni Riefenstahl (director), *Triumph of the Will* (Universum Film AG, 1935).

Fascism's Imperial Heart of Darkness

Each of these thinkers saw the barbarism of colonialism in Africa as a catalyst for the World Wars in Europe. What is the relationship between Europe's "heart of darkness" in Africa and the rise of fascism, totalitarian movements, and total war in Europe? If Arendt identifies imperialism as a harbinger of totalitarianism, her work also formulates an equivalence between communism and fascism that fit Cold War imperatives—but how do colonized writers alternately affirm or challenge this proposition? How does the legacy of colonialism echo in today's European societies, where multiculturalism has been deemed a failure (by Angela Merkel), and Europeans across the political spectrum decry the growth of non-European communities in their midst?

Joseph Conrad, *Heart of Darkness* (New York: W. W. Norton & Company, 2016 [1899]).

Aimé Césaire, *Discourse on Colonialism* (New York: Monthly Review Press, 2000 [1955]).

Hannah Arendt, *The Origins of Totalitarianism* (New York: Harcourt, Brace and Company, 1973 [1955]).

W.E.B. Du Bois, "The African Roots of War," *The Atlantic* (May 1915), https://www.theatlantic.com/magazine/archive/1915/05/the-african-roots-of-war/528897/.

Raoul Peck (director), *Exterminate All the Brutes* (HBO documentary mini-series, 2021).

Colonial Fascism

From varied locales within the European colonial order, writers such as Frantz Fanon, Albert Memmi, W.E.B. Du Bois, and Aimé Césaire translated racial and colonial experience into fascist imaginaries as total war reverberated outside Europe and beckoned the darker races to continental battlefields. Building on the idea of colonialism in Africa—the so-called "Scramble for Africa"—as a catalyst for fascism and total war, this unit explores historical research and literary works that reimagine fascism from the vantage point of the colonized.

George Padmore, *How Britain Rules Africa* (London: Wishart Books, 1936).

Eric T. Jennings, *Vichy in the Tropics: Pétain's National Revolution in Madagascar, Guadeloupe, and Indochina, 1940–1944* (Stanford: Stanford University Press, 2002).

Albert Memmi, *The Colonizer and the Colonized* (Boston: Beacon Press, 1965 [1957]).

Michael Rothberg, *Multidirectional Memory: Remembering the Holocaust in the Age of Decolonization* (Stanford: Stanford University Press, 2009).

Alessandro Spina, *The Colonial Conquest: The Confines of the Shadow* (London: Darf Publishers, 2015).

Vaughn Rasberry, *Race and the Totalitarian Century* (Cambridge: Harvard University Press, 2016).

Maaza Mengiste, *The Shadow King* (New York: W. W. Norton & Company, Inc., 2019).

Queer Lives under Nazism

How did gay and queer people survive and remember the homophobic policies and genocidal practices of fascist regimes? In what ways have Black queer women in Germany sought to recalibrate Europe's public sphere around race, war, identity, and fascism—and why, as Tiffany Florvil argues, have their contributions been largely obscured in scholarly and public discourse? In *Clifford's Blues*, John A. Williams' marvelous but forgotten novel, a gay Black American jazz musician is imprisoned in Germany's Dachau concentration camp for twelve years. Williams's novel is one of many texts by Black authors that imagines how race, sexuality, queerness, and nationality intersect in the era of fascism. Yet in an ironic twist in Europe, today's radical right movements simultaneously uphold the homophobic politics of the past while also gesturing toward tolerance of same-sex liaisons—to avoid marginalization but also as a means to promote Islamophobia and xenophobia in Europe. How does the radical right manage these contradictions along the axes of race, religion, gender, and sexuality?

Audre Lorde, "East Berlin 1989," in *The Marvelous Arithmetics of Distance: Poems: 1987–1992* (New York: W. W. Norton & Company, 1993).

John A. Williams, *Clifford's Blues* (Minneapolis: Coffee House Press, 1999).

Dagmar Shultz (director), *Audre Lorde: The Berlin Years 1984–1992* (Germany, 2012).

Tiffany Florvil, "Queer Memory and Black Germans," *The New Fascism Syllabus: Exploring the New Right Through Scholarship and Civic Engagement*, June 8, 2021, http://newfascismsyllabus.com/opinions/queer-memory-and-black-germans/.

United States Holocaust Memorial Museum, "Persecution of Homosexuals in the Third Reich," https://encyclopedia.ushmm.org/content/en/article/persecution-of-homosexuals-in-the-third-reich.

Samuel Clowes Huneke, "The Duplicity of Tolerance: Lesbian Experiences in Nazi Berlin," *Journal of Contemporary History*, Vol. 54, No. 1 (2019): 30–59.

Frankfurt School Critiques of Fascism

For certain theorists associated with the Frankfurt School (Critical Theory), fascist totalitarianism consummated all of the ills, dissatisfactions, and ruptures of European modernity since the Age of Enlightenment—from the terror of the French Revolution and the rise of nationalism and inter-imperial rivalry to the expanding iron cage of rationalization and secularization; to the emergence of mass media technologies and the science of propaganda; and to the onset of industrialization and the crescendos of mechanized warfare. The confluence of these processes in European modernity prompted Max Horkheimer and Theodor Adorno to famously proclaim (too pessimistically, in the view of some commentators, including Jürgen Habermas): "Enlightenment is totalitarian." This formulation introduces another paradox: any "intellectual resistance [Enlightenment] encounters merely increases its strength." In whatever sense *die Aufklärung* (the Enlightenment) can be understood as totalitarian, this fragmentary text raises a key and still relevant question: how do the array of progressive forces originating in the Enlightenment turn into barbarism?

Max Horkheimer and Theodor Adorno, *Dialectic of Enlightenment*
(Stanford: Stanford University Press, 2007 [originally published in 1947
as *Dialektic die Aufklärung*]).

Walter Benjamin, "Critique of Violence (1921)" in *Reflections: Essays,
Aphorisms, Autobiographical Writings* (New York: Schocken Books Inc.,
1978), 277–300.

Theodor Adorno, Else Frenkel-Brunswick, Daniel J. Levinson, and Nevitt
Sanford, *The Authoritarian Personality* (London: Verso, 2019 [1950]).

Herbert Marcuse, *Counterrevolution and Revolt* (Boston: Beacon Press, 1972).

Anson Rabinbach, "Why Were the Jews Sacrificed? The Place of Anti-
Semitism in *Dialectic of Enlightenment*," *New German Critique* 81
(Autumn 2000): 49–64.

Racial Capitalism and Fascism

Explicating Cedric Robinson's theory of racial capitalism, Robin D. G.
Kelley insists that the roots of (internecine) European racialism run deeper
than the period designated as modernity, and well into the feudal order
and its racialization of the early European proletariat (comprised of Roma,
Gypsies, Slavs, Jews, Irish, and other ethnic groups). Racialization "within
Europe was very much a colonial process," writes Kelley in a commentary
on Robinson cited below, "involving invasion, settlement, expropriation,
and racial hierarchy." To take this thesis seriously is to question the conventional periodization and historical understanding of fascism, as well as to
consider the Black radical tradition's analysis of fascism as a manifestation
of—and not an aberration from—(racial) capitalism. "Although the most
unbridled expressions of the fascist menace are still tied to the racist domination of Blacks, Chicanos, Puerto Ricans, Indians," writes Angela Davis
in "Political Prisoners, Prisons, and Black Liberations," "it lurks under the
surface where there is potential resistance to the power of monopoly capital, the parasitic interests which control this society."

Angela Davis, "Political Prisoners, Prisons, and Black Liberation," in *If
They Come in the Morning* (New York: The Third Press, 1971).

Cedric Robinson, "Fascism and the Intersections of Capitalism,

Racialism, and Historical Consciousness," in *Cedric J. Robinson: On Racial Capitalism, Black Internationalism, and Cultures of Resistance* (London: Pluto Press, 2019), 87–109.

Cedric Robinson, "Fascism and the Response of Black Radical Theorists," in *Cedric J. Robinson: On Racial Capitalism, Black Internationalism, and Cultures of Resistance* (London: Pluto Press, 2019), 149–159.

Singh, "The Afterlife of Fascism."

Robin D. G. Kelley, "What Did Cedric Robinson Mean by Racial Capitalism?," *Boston Review*, June 12, 2017, https://bostonreview.net/race/robin-d-g-kelley-what-did-cedric-robinson-mean-racial-capitalism.

Aaron B. Retish, "'Black radicals not only anticipated the rise of fascism; they resisted it before it was considered a crisis.' An interview with Robin D. G. Kelley," *The Volunteer*, November 14, 2020, https://albavolunteer.org/2020/11/robin-d-g-kelley-on-fascism-then-and-now/.

Alberto Toscano, "The Long Shadow of Racial Fascism," *Boston Review*, October 28, 2020, https://bostonreview.net/race-politics/alberto-toscano-long-shadow-racial-fascism.

The Antifascist Left in the United States

In the 1930s, the antifascist left in the United States adopted a formidable stance on—and in opposition to—Nazism and its imitators in the United States and globally. As literary historian Alan Wald shows, questions of race, gender, and masculinity permeate these movements in the wake of World War II. How did the antifascist front enable a self-conscious rearticulation of Jewish masculinity after the Holocaust? How did Black Americans—constrained by the federal government in their ability to join the fight against Italy's colonial fascist occupation in Ethiopia—nonetheless participate in antifascist struggles in the international realm? What solidarities and tensions flowed from Black and Jewish cooperation in antifascist struggles?

Ann Petry, *The Street* (Boston: Mariner Books, 2020 [1940]).

Richard Wright, *Pagan Spain* (New York: HarperCollins, 2010 [1957]).

Alan Wald, *Trinity of Passion: The Literary Left and the Antifascist Crusade* (Chapel Hill: University of North Carolina Press, 2007).

Bill V. Mullen and Christopher Vials (eds.), *The U.S. Anti-fascism Reader* (London and New York: Verso, 2020).

Robin D. G. Kelley, "This Ain't Ethiopia, But It'll Do: African Americans and the Spanish Civil War," in *Race Rebels: Culture, Politics, and the Black Working Class* (New York: The Free Press, 1994), 123–160.

Fredric Jameson, *Fables of Aggression: Wyndham Lewis, the Modernist as Fascist* (London and New York: Verso, 2008).

It Happened Here: Trumpism and Global White Nationalism

Novelists such as Philip K. Dick and Philip Roth have brilliantly created counterfactual scenarios in which fascism prevails in the United States: Nazi Germany conquers the United States in World War II (Dick) or the Nazi sympathizer Charles Lindbergh defeats Franklin Roosevelt in the US presidential election of 1932 (Roth). In *Nazi Literature in the Americas*, Roberto Bolaño constructs a mock-scholarly tableau of vignettes that link fascist writers and artists in the Americas, both north and south of the Equator. But how do we understand these fictional works—which imagine fascism in the Americas as counterfactual history—in relation to critical histories that identify elements of US history as secret sharers of the fascist ethos?

Philip K. Dick, *The Man in the High Castle* (New York: Mariner Books/ Houghton Mifflin Harcourt, 2011 [1962]).

Philip Roth, *The Plot Against America* (New York: Vintage, 2005).

Roberto Bolaño, *Nazi Literature in the Americas* (New York: New Directions Publishing, 2009).

Arundhati Roy, *Azadi: Freedom, Fascism, Fiction* (Chicago: Haymarket Books, 2020).

Rich Benjamin, "Democrats Need to Wake Up: The Trump Movement Is Shot Through with Fascism," *The Intercept*, September 27, 2020, https://theintercept.com/2020/09/27/trump-supporters-fascism-election/.

Jonathan M. Katz, "It Happened Here," *Foreign Policy*, January 9, 2021, https://foreignpolicy.com/2021/01/09/it-happened-here-live/.

Priya Satya, "Fascism and Analogies—British and American, Past and Present," *The Los Angeles Review of Books*, March 16, 2021, https://www.lareviewofbooks.org/article/fascism-analogies-british-american-past-present/.

Index

253, 291, 301–302, 307, 311

Césaire, Aimé, 4, 57, 72, 102–103, 246, 249, 289, 298–299, 306

Chauvin, Derek, 43

Cherniavsky, Eva, 86–87

civil rights, 15, 47, 49, 126, 132, 137–138, 140, 162–164, 168, 180, 183, 189

civil war, 48–50, 113, 135, 251, 260, 296

Colectivo Las Tesis, 100, 112

colonial continuum, 145–147, 149–151, 155

colonialism, 1–5, 7, 12, 14–15, 33–42, 57, 64, 67, 72–74, 85, 97, 102–103, 109, 115, 126, 128, 145, 147, 149–151, 155–156, 160, 172, 206, 208, 211, 213, 246, 259–260, 266, 297–298, 303–304, 305–308, colonial fascism, 3, 246–247, 306 ; settler colonialism, 1, 5, 14, 55, 67, 85, 97, 103, 208, 213, 292

communalism (India), 216, 222–224

Communism, 3, 6, 73, 76–83, 159–183, 225–226, 244, 291, 293–297, Communist International, 3, 160, 161, 246, 291, 293, 294, 296; Communist Party of India (Marxist), 225–226

community organizing, 203n1, 302

Confederacy, the, 50–51

Coronavirus (COVID-19), 26, 31–32, 43–46, 82, 99, 135, 184, 188, 215

counterrevolution, 8, 15, 49–50, 74, 77, 83, 148, 250, 252, 291, 295

crisis, 1–2, 7–8, 11, 19, 32, 43–47, 49, 52, 66, 75, 86, 93–94, 108, 135, 138, 161, 185, 195, 215, 219, 252, 254, 267, 282, 290–291

Cuarón, Alfonso, 85, 92

D

Daughters of the Confederacy, 50

Davis, Angela Y., 72, 143, 248–255

Davis, Ben, 172–173, 176–178

de Gaulle, Charles, 147

Deferred Action for Childhood Arrivals (DACA), 94, 135

Du Bois, W.E.B., 4, 163, 246, 247n10, 255, 289, 292

Dunbar-Ortiz, Roxanne, 51

Duterte, Rodrigo, 1, 71–72, 78–83, 105, 106, 291

F

fascism, 1–20, 24–57, 72–97, 101–110, 131–195, 204–255, 275–304 (*passim*) across the globe, 45, 105, 110; capitalism and, 41n14, 44; civil society and, 44; economic crisis and, 44, 49; fascist devotion, 20, 88, 90–91, 94, 96; fascist leader, 44, 52, 142; incipient fascism, 251, 254; racial fascism, 246–247, 255

feminism, 6n17, 110, 116, 118, 123, 212, 237

Floyd, George, 13, 32, 43, 135, 196

Franco, Marielle, 273, 279, 282, 284

G

Genet, Jean, 248

genocide, 2, 15, 19, 34n3, 52–57, 59–63, 65–67, 72, 74, 107, 116, 284–285, 289, 302, anti-Black genocide, 284–285

German South-West Africa, 2, 53–54, 56, 59, 65, 288

Gilmore, Ruth Wilson, 101, 208, 211, 213, 254

Gomes, Flora, 260

surveillance, 8–9, 18, 20, 38, 41, 74, 79, 104, 107, 138–140, 159, 171, 179, 213, 249, 276

278, 283–284, 288, 290, 294–295

World War II, 4, 52, 54, 56, 76, 114, 159, 162, 168, 173, 175, 181, 248

T

Tamil Nadu Untouchability Eradication Front (India), 225–226

tarafe, 262, 264, 267, 270

The Infiltrators, 85, 88, 94–97

Tjibaou, Jean-Marie, 153, 156

trans*, 6, 15, 20, 100, 102, 105n12, 108, 110, 112, 284, trans, 15

Tricontinental conference, 1966, 4, 299

Trump, Donald, 1, 23, 26, 43, 48, 50, 88, 96, 110, 131–135, 137, 139, 142–144, 184–189, 191–196, 255, 290–291, 303

Z

Zetkin, Clara, 3, 291–292

U

United Front Against Fascism, 5, 248, 300

US-Mexico Border, 88

Vials, Christopher, 247

W

wages, 46–47, 49–50, 111

walking archives, 268

washerwomen, 49

Werneck, Jurema, 277, 282

Wet'suwet'en, 34–39

White House, the, 23, 88

white supremacy, 1, 7, 41, 50, 74, 88, 104, 139–140, 143, 160, 177, 179, 182–183, 188, 230–232, 236, 238, 240, 247, 251, 276–277, 283, 285, 290–291, 293, 304

workers, 2–3, 14–15, 46–47, 85–86, 99, 111, 127, 160, 168, 171–172, 174–175, 180, 182–183, 188, 215, 217, 219, 225–226, 247, 275–276,

About the Editors

Alyosha Goldstein is a professor of American Studies at the University of New Mexico. He is the author of *Poverty in Common: The Politics of Community Action during the American Century*, the editor of *Formations of United States Colonialism*, and has coedited special issues of *Social Text*, *Theory & Event*, and *South Atlantic Quarterly*. Goldstein is completing a book manuscript on colonialism, racial capitalism, and histories of Native and Black dispossession in what is presently called the United States.

Simón Ventura Trujillo is an assistant professor in the English Department at New York University. He is the author of *Land Uprising: Native Story Power and the Insurgent Horizons of Latinx Indigeneity.*

About the Contributors

Nadia Abu El-Haj is Ann Whitney Olin Professor of Anthropology, codirector of the Center for Palestine Studies, and chairperson of the Governing Board of the Society of Fellows/Heyman Center for the Humanities at Columbia University. She is the author of *Facts on the Ground: Archaeological Practice and Territorial Self-Fashioning in Israeli Society* and *The Genealogical Science: The Search for Jewish Origins and the Politics of Epistemology*. Her third book, *Combat Trauma: Imaginaries of War and Citizenship in Post 9/11 America* (forthcoming from Verso in 2022), is a study of the figure of the traumatized soldier in the American social imaginary and its central role in reproducing contemporary American militarism.

Kate Boyd is an antifascist and antiracist cultural organizer, educator, and public humanities scholar. In 2006, Kate and Cristien Storm cofounded If You Don't They Will, a Seattle-based collaboration that provides concrete and creative tools for countering white nationalism through a cultural lens. This includes creating spaces to generate visions, desires, incantations, actions, memes, and dreams for the kinds of worlds we want to live in.

Charisse Burden-Stelly is assistant professor of Africana Studies and Political Science at Carleton College, and a critical Black Studies scholar of political theory, political economy, intellectual history, and historical sociology. She is the coauthor, with Gerald Horne, of *W.E.B. Du Bois: A Life in American History* and is currently working on a book manuscript tentatively titled *Black Scare/Red Scare: Anti-Blackness, Anticommunism, and the Rise of Capitalism in the United States*, which examines the rise of the United States to global hegemony between World War I and the early Cold War at the intersection of racial capitalism, Wall Street imperialism, anticommunism, and anti-Blackness. Burden-Stelly is also the coeditor, with Jodi Dean, of the forthcoming volume *Organize, Fight, Win: Three Decades of Black Communist Women's Political Writings* (Verso, 2022) and the coeditor, with Aaron Kamugisha, of the forthcoming collection of Percy C. Hintzen's writings titled *Reproducing Domination: On the Caribbean and the Postcolonial State* (University of Mississippi, 2022). She guest edited the "Claudia Jones: Foremother of World Revolution" special issue of *The Journal of Intersectionality*. Her published work appears in journals including *Small Axe, Monthly Review, Souls, Du Bois Review, Socialism & Democracy, International Journal of Africana Studies*, and the *CLR James Journal*.

Filipa César is an artist and filmmaker interested in the fictional aspects of documentary, the porous borders between cinema and its reception, and the politics and poetics inherent to imaging technologies. Since 2011, she has been researching the origins of the cinema of the African Liberation Movement in Guinea-Bissau as a collective laboratory of anticolonial epistemologies. The resulting body of work comprises films, archival practices, seminars, screenings, publications, and ongoing collaborations with artists, theorists, and activists—in particular, with Diana McCarty, Sónia Vaz Borges, and Sana na N'Hada, with whom she initiated the collective project *"Luta ca caba inda* [The Struggle is Not Over Yet]" and the Mediateca Onshore project.

Subin Dennis is a researcher with Tricontinental Research, New Dehli, and a former journalist with the news portal *NewsClick*. He was a research scholar at Jawaharlal Nehru University, New Delhi and was active with the student movement before he joined *NewsClick*, where he wrote analytical articles on economy and politics.

Daniel Denvir is the author of *All-American Nativism: How the Bipartisan War on Immigrants Explains Politics as We Know It* (Verso, 2020), a Visiting Fellow in International and Public Affairs at Brown University's Watson Institute, a writer in residence at *The Appeal*, and the host of *The Dig* podcast on Jacobin Radio. He is a former staff writer at *Salon* and the *Philadelphia City Paper*, and former contributing writer at *The Atlantic*'s CityLab. His work has appeared in *The New York Times, The Washington Post, The Nation, Vox, Jacobin, The Guardian's Comment Is Free, Al Jazeera America, VICE*, and *The New Republic*.

Johanna Fernández is associate professor of History at Baruch College (CUNY) and author of *The Young Lords: A Radical History*, recipient of the New York Society Library's New York City Book award and three Organization of American Historians (OAH) awards: the prestigious Frederick Jackson Turner Award for best first book in history, the Liberty Legacy Foundation Award for best book on civil rights, and the Merle Curti Award for best Social History. Dr. Fernández's 2014 Freedom of Information Law (FOIL) lawsuit against the NYPD led to the recovery of the "lost" Handschu files, the largest repository of police surveillance records in the country—namely, over one million surveillance files of New Yorkers compiled by the NYPD between 1954–1972, including those of Malcolm X. She is editor of *Writing on the Wall: Selected Prison Writings of Mumia Abu-Jamal* and writer and producer of the film *Justice on Trial: The Case of Mumia Abu-Jamal*. Her awards include the Fulbright Scholars grant to the Middle East and North Africa, which took her to Jordan, and a National Endowment for the Humanities Fellowship in the Scholars-in-Residence program at the Schomburg Center in Harlem. She directed and cocurated *¡Presente! The Young Lords in New York*, an exhibition in three NYC museums. She's the host of *A New Day*, WBAI's morning show, from 7:00–8:00 a.m., M–F, at 99.5 FM in New York.

Macarena Gómez-Barris is a writer and author who works at the intersections of authoritarianism, the visual arts, extractivism, and the environmental and decolonial humanities. Her books include *Where Memory Dwells: Culture and State Violence in Chile*, *Beyond the Pink Tide: Artistic and Political Undercurrents* and *The Extractive Zone: Social Ecologies and Decolonial Perspectives*. Her in-progress book is *At the Sea's Edge: Liquidity Beyond Colonial Extinction*. She is founding director of the Global South Center (globalsouthcenter.org) and chairperson of the Department of Social Science and Cultural Studies at Pratt Institute, Brooklyn. She has published in *Social Text*, *GLQ*, and numerous other journals and art catalogs, and is coeditor with Diana Taylor of the Duke University Press series, Dissident Acts.

Elspeth Iralu (Angami Naga) is a doctoral candidate in American studies at the University of New Mexico. Her research centers Indigenous geopolitics and examines how everyday militarism, enacted transnationally, shapes global colonial relations. Her writing has appeared in *American Quarterly*, *The New Americanist*, and *Antipode: A Journal of Radical Geography*. Her current work examines the aerial perspective as a technology of colonial territoriality.

Manu Karuka is an assistant professor of American Studies at Barnard College. He is the author of *Empire's Tracks: Indigenous Nations, Chinese Workers, and the Transcontinental Railroad*. With Juliana Hu Pegues and Alyosha Goldstein, he coedited a special issue of *Theory & Event*, "On Colonial Unknowing," and with Vivek Bald, Miabi Chatterji, and Sujani Reddy, he coedited *The Sun Never Sets: South Asian Migrants in an Age of U.S. Power*. He is a coeditor of 1804 Books.

Dolly Kikon is a senior lecturer in the Anthropology and Development Studies Program at the University of Melbourne. Her research focuses on resource extraction, militarization, development, human rights, migration, gender, and political economy. Kikon's books include *Living with Oil and Coal: Resource Politics and Militarization in Northeast India, Ceasefire City: Militarism, Capitalism and Urbanism in Dimapur* (with Duncan McDuie-Ra), *Leaving the Land: Indigenous Migration and Affective Labour in India* (with Bengt Karlsson), and *Life and Dignity: Women's Testimonies of Sexual Violence in Dimapur (Nagaland).*

Léopold Lambert is a trained architect living in Paris. He is the editor-in-chief of *The Funambulist*, a bimestrial print and online magazine dedicated to the politics of space and bodies. He is also the author of: *Weaponized Architecture: The Impossibility of Innocence*; *Topie Impitoyable: The Corporeal Politics of the Cloth, the Wall, and the Street*; *La politique du bulldozer: La ruine palestinienne comme projet israélien* [*Politics of the Bulldozer: The Palestinian Ruin as an Israeli Project*]; and in 2021, *États d'urgence: Une histoire spatiale du continuum colonial français* [*States of Emergency: A Spatial History of the French Colonial Continuum*].

Joe Lowndes is a professor of political science at the University of Oregon and a scholar of race, populism, and right-wing politics. He coauthored *Producers, Parasites, Patriots: Race and the New Right-Wing Politics of Precarity* with Daniel Martinez HoSang, is the author of *From the New Deal to the New Right: Race and the Southern Origins of Modern Conservatism*, and coedited *Race and American Political Development* with Julie Novkov and Dorian Warren. He has published extensively on populism, presidential politics, political culture, and social movements, and writes frequently for public venues including *The Washington Post, The New Republic*, and *Dissent*. His current project seeks to explain the growing authoritarian trend in US politics and its implications for democracy in the United States.

Allan E. S. Lumba is an assistant professor of history at Virginia Tech. His research explores the historical entanglements between racial capitalism and US colonialisms in the Philippines, and more broadly the Pacific, from the late-nineteenth century to the present. His first book, *Monetary Authorities: Capitalism and Decolonization in the American Colonial Philippines*, is forthcoming (Duke University Press, April 2022).

Dian Million (Tanana Athabascan) is an associate professor in the Department of American Indian Studies at the University of Washington, Seattle. She is the author of *Therapeutic Nations: Healing in an Age of Indigenous Human Rights*, along with several enduring poems and articles: "There is a River in Me: Theory from Life"; "Intense Dreaming: Theories, Narratives and Our Search for Home"; and "Felt Theory: An Indigenous Feminist Approach to Affect and History." Million centers her work on the effects/affects of racial capitalism/settler colonialism on Indigenous family and community health in North America, informed by two generations of Indigenous feminist scholarship and activism. Million seeks to illuminate the ways

Indigenous life reorganizes and resurges, making life and kin intentional in the face of colonial violence.

Nicole Nguyen is associate professor of educational policy studies at the University of Illinois-Chicago. She is author of *A Curriculum of Fear: Homeland Security in U.S. Public Schools* and *Suspect Communities: Anti-Muslim Racism and the Domestic War on Terror.*

Keisha-Khan Y. Perry is the Presidential Penn Compact Associate Professor of Africana Studies at the University of Pennsylvania. Her research is focused on race, gender, and politics in the Americas, urban geography and questions of citizenship, intellectual history and disciplinary formation, and the interrelationship between scholarship, pedagogy, and political engagement. Her first book, *Black Women against the Land Grab: The Fight for Racial Justice in Brazil*, won the 2014 National Women's Studies Association Gloria Anzaldúa Book Prize. She is currently at work on her second book, which is focused on the ways state violence limits activist research and writing.

Vaughn Rasberry is associate professor of English and Comparative Studies in Race and Ethnicity at Stanford University, where he teaches and researches literature of the African diaspora. He is author *of Race and the Totalitarian Century: Geopolitics in the Black Literary Imagination*, recipient of the Ralph Bunche Award from the American Political Science Association, and an American Book Award from the Before Columbus Foundation.

Zoé Samudzi is a postdoctoral research fellow with the ACTIONS Program at the University of California, San Francisco and a research associate with the Center for the Study of Race, Gender, and Class at the University of Johannesburg. Her research engages German colonialism, the 1904–1908 Ovaherero and Nama genocide and its afterlives, biomedicalization, visuality, and the institutional capture of human remains. She is coauthor of *As Black as Resistance: Finding the Conditions for Liberation* and a writer whose work has appeared in *Art in America*, *The New Republic*, *The New Inquiry*, SFMoMA's *Open Space*, and other outlets. She is also a contributing writer for *Jewish Currents.*

Nikhil Pal Singh is professor of Social and Cultural Analysis and History at New York University and founding faculty director of the NYU Prison Education Program. A historian of race, empire, and culture in the twentieth-century United States, Singh is the author, most recently, of *Race and America's Long War*. He is also author of the award-winning *Black Is a Country: Race and the Unfinished Struggle for Democracy*, and coauthor and coeditor with Jack O'Dell of *Climbin' Jacob's Ladder: The Black Freedom Movement Writing of Jack O'Dell*. A new book, *Exceptional Empire: Race, Colonialism and the Origins of US Globalism*, is forthcoming (Harvard

University Press). Singh's writing and interviews have appeared in a number of venues, including *New York Magazine, TIME, The New Republic,* and on NPRs *Open Source* and *Code Switch.*

Anne Spice (Tlingit) is a member of Kwanlin Dun First Nation, an assistant professor of Geography and Environmental Studies at X University, and an associate fellow with the Yellowhead Institute. They are an anticolonial organizer, land defender, and hand-poked tattoo artist. Their writing has been published in *Environment and Society, Jacobin, The New Inquiry,* and *Asparagus Magazine.*

Cristien Storm is an antifascist and antiracist cultural organizer, writer, and politicized healer. In 2006, Cristien and Kate Boyd cofounded If You Don't They Will, a Seattle-based collaboration that provides concrete and creative tools for countering white nationalism through a cultural lens. This includes creating spaces to generate visions, desires, incantations, actions, memes, and dreams for the kinds of worlds we want to live in.

Alberto Toscano is professor of Critical Theory in the Department of Sociology, codirector of the Centre for Philosophy and Critical Theory at Goldsmiths, University of London, and visiting faculty at the School of Communication, Simon Fraser University, Vancouver, British Columbia. He is the author of *The Theatre of Production: Philosophy and Individuation Between Kant and Deleuze; Fanaticism: On the Uses of an Idea; Cartographies of the Absolute* (with Jeff Kinkle); *Una visión compleja. Hacía una estética de la economía; La abstracción real. Filosofia, estética y capital;* and coeditor of *The Italian Difference: Between Nihilism and Biopolitics* (with Lorenzo Chiesa); the three-volume *Handbook of Marxism* (with Sara R. Farris, Beverley Skeggs, and Svenja Bromberg); and forthcoming with Brenna Bhandar, Ruth Wilson Gilmore's *Abolition Geography: Essays Towards Liberation* (Verso, 2022).

Sónia Vaz Borges is an interdisciplinary militant historian and social-political organizer. She received her PhD in History of Education from the Humboldt University of Berlin. She is author of the book *Militant Education, Liberation Struggle, Consciousness: The PAIGC education in Guinea Bissau 1963–1978.* In September 2021, she was appointed assistant professor of History and Africana Studies in the History Department at Drexel University. Vaz Borges is currently developing a book focused on her concept of the "walking archive."

Yazan Zahzah is a community-based researcher and organizer from Southern California. They hold an MA in Gender Studies from San Diego State University and currently work as a lecturer for the California State University system. Zahzah is a longtime member of the Palestinian Youth Movement, a grassroots organization dedicated to the self-determination of the Palestinian people.

About Common Notions

Common Notions is a publishing house and programming platform that advances new formulations of liberation and living autonomy. Our books provide timely reflections, clear critiques, and inspiring strategies that amplify movements for social justice.

By any media necessary, we seek to nourish the imagination and generalize common notions about the creation of other worlds beyond state and capital. Our publications trace a constellation of critical and visionary meditations on the organization of freedom. Inspired by various traditions of autonomism and liberation—in the United States and internationally, historically and emerging from contemporary movements—our publications provide resources for a collective reading of struggles past, present, and to come.

Common Notions regularly collaborates with editorial houses, political collectives, militant authors, and visionary designers around the world. Our political and aesthetic interventions are dreamt and realized in collaboration with Antumbra Designs.

commonnotions.org / info@commonnotions.org

Become a Monthly Sustainer

These are decisive times, ripe with challenges and possibility, heartache and beautiful inspiration. More than ever, we are in need of timely reflections, clear critiques, and inspiring strategies that can help movements for social justice grow and transform society. Help us amplify those necessary words, deeds, and dreams that our liberation movements and our worlds so need.

Movements are sustained by people like you, whose fugitive words, deeds, and dreams bend against the world of domination and exploitation.

For collective imagination, dedicated practices of love and study, and organized acts of freedom.

By any media necessary. With your love and support.
Monthly sustainers start at $12 and $25.
Join us at commonnotions.org/sustain.

More From Common Notions

On Microfascism: Gender, War, and Death

Jack Z. Bratich

978-1-942173-49-6

$20.00

240 pages

Rooted in an understanding of how the fascist body is constructed, we can develop the collective power to dismember it.

Fascist and reactionary populist forces have undeniably swelled in the US in recent years. To effectively counter fascist movements, we need to understand them beyond their most visible and public expressions. To do this, Jack Bratich asserts, we must dig deeper into the psyche and body that gives rise to fascist formations. There we will find *microfascism*, or the cultural ways in which a fascist understanding of the world is generated from the hatreds that suffuse everyday life.

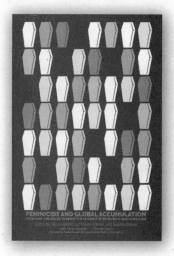

Feminicide and Global Accumulation: Frontline Struggles to Resist the Violence of Patriarchy and Capitalism

Edited by Silvia Federici, Susana Draper, and Liz Mason-Deese with Otras Negras ... y ¡Feministas!

978-1-942173-44-1

$20.00

240 pages

Feminicide and Global Accumulation brings us to the frontlines of an international movement of Black, Indigenous, popular, and mestiza women's organizations fighting against violence—interpersonal, state sanctioned, and economic—that is both endemic to the global economy and the contemporary devalued status of racialized women, trans, and gender non-conforming communities in the Global South.